Rhetorical Mimesis and the Mitigation of Early Christian Conflicts

Rhetorical Mimesis and the Mitigation of Early Christian Conflicts

Examining the Influence that Greco-Roman Mimesis May Have in the Composition of Matthew, Luke, and Acts

Brad McAdon

PICKWICK Publications • Eugene, Oregon

RHETORICAL MIMESIS AND THE MITIGATION OF EARLY CHRISTIAN CONFLICTS
Examining the Influence that Greco-Roman Mimesis May Have in the Composition of Matthew, Luke, and Acts

Copyright © 2018 Brad McAdon. All rights reserved. Except for brief quotations in critical publications or reviews, no part of this book may be reproduced in any manner without prior written permission from the publisher. Write: Permissions, Wipf and Stock Publishers, 199 W. 8th Ave., Suite 3, Eugene, OR 97401.

Pickwick Publications
An Imprint of Wipf and Stock Publishers
199 W. 8th Ave., Suite 3
Eugene, OR 97401

www.wipfandstock.com

PAPERBACK ISBN: 978-1-5326-3772-8
HARDCOVER ISBN: 978-1-5326-3773-5
EBOOK ISBN: 978-1-5326-3774-2

Cataloguing-in-Publication data:

Names: McAdon, Brad.

Title: Rhetorical mimesis and the mitigation of early Christian conflicts : examining the influence that Greco-Roman mimesis may have in the composition of Matthew, Luke, and Acts / Brad McAdon.

Description: Eugene, OR: Pickwick Publications, 2018 | Includes bibliographical references and index.

Identifiers: ISBN 978-1-5326-3772-8 (paperback) | ISBN 978-1-5326-3773-5 (hardcover) | ISBN 978-1-5326-3774-2 (ebook)

Subjects: LCSH: Bible. Matthew—Criticism, interpretation, etc. | Bible. Luke—Criticism, interpretation, etc. | Bible. Acts—Criticism, interpretation, etc. | Mimesis in the Bible.

Classification: BS2555.52 M3 2018 (print) | BS2555.52 (ebook)

Manufactured in the U.S.A. 01/15/18

For Carrie Jean

Contents

List of Tables | ix
Acknowledgments | xi
Abbreviations | xii

1 Introduction | 1

Part 1: Greco-Roman Μίμησις/Imitatio

2 The Prevalence and Practice of Greco-Roman Μίμησις/Imitatio in Greco-Roman Education and Contemporary Applications of Μίμησις/Imitatio to New Testament Texts | 17

Part 2: The Controversy Concerning Jesus's Birth and His Relationship with His Family: Crafting Rhetorical Counter-Narratives

3 A Rhetorical Analysis of Mark 3:20–35 and 6:1–6: Jesus's Family in Mark, and Matthew's and Luke's Mimetic Transformations | 51

4 Matthew's Infancy Narrative (Matt 1–2): Mimetically Transforming Passages from the Septuagint | 74

5 Luke's Mimetic Transformation of Matthew's Birth Narrative: A Rhetorical Analysis of Luke 1–2 | 120

Part 3: The Petrine-Pauline Controversy and Luke's Mimetic Transformation

6   Establishing the Pauline-Petrine Controversy: A Prelude to Luke's Mimetic Transformation of Galatians 1–2 | 163

7   Luke's Mimetic Transformation of Galatians 1–2: A Rhetorical Analysis of Acts 7:58—15: 30 | 181

8   Conclusion | 247

Appendix 1: Ancient Greco-Roman Authors on Μίμησις/Imitatio | 255

Appendix 2: Galatians 2:7–9 as a Later, Post-Pauline Interpolation | 283

Bibliography | 295
Subject Index | 307
Author Index | 310
Ancient Literature Index | 313

List of Tables

Table 1: Synoptic overview of the *Aeneid* and the *Iliad* and the *Odyssey* | 26

Table 2: Verbal similarities in the underworld narratives | 28

Table 3: Verbal similarities in storm narrative | 30

Table 4: MacDonald's and Brodie's criteria for identifying imitated texts | 36

Table 5: Markan "sandwich" (3:20–35) | 52

Table 6: Verbal similarities in Mark's and Matthew's Beezlebul controversy | 59

Table 7: Matthew's and Luke's Beelzebul controversy narratives | 60

Table 8: "Jesus's mother and brothers" narrative | 62

Table 9: Jesus's sermon in Nazareth | 65

Table 10: Matthew's 3 x 14 organizational structure | 78

Table 11: Joseph in the New Testament (my translation) | 92

Table 12: Birth annunciations in the Septuagint | 105

Table 13: Uses of *alma* (עַלְמָה) in the Hebrew Bible | 109

Table 14: Hebrew and Seputagint versions of Isaiah 7:14 | 112

Table 15: Comparison of Isaiah 7:14 LXX and Matthew 1:23 | 114

Table 16: Structural sources for Luke's birth narrative | 125

Table 17: Luke's structural imitation of Matthew 1:18–25 | 129

Table 18: Septuagint Sources for the Magnificat | 133

Table 19: Septuagint sources for the Benedictus | 135

Table 20: Luke's structural imitation of Matthew 2:1–20 | 137

Table 21: Matthew's transformation of Micah 5:1 (LXX) | 140

Table 22: The extent of Luke's structural imitation of Matthew | 142

Table 23: Septuagint sources for the Nunc Dimittis | 147

Table 24: Comparison of the genealogies of Matthew and Luke | 149

Table 25: Synoptic outline of Galatians 1–2 and Acts 7:58—15:30 | 187

Table 26: Paul as persecutor | 188

Table 27: Paul's zealousness | 190

Table 28: Paul's conversion (Galatians 1:15–17 and Acts 9:1–19) | 192

Table 29: Similar narrative themes between Paul's conversion in Galatians 2 and Acts 9 | 194

Table 30: Paul's evangelizing in Damascus and his escape | 197

Table 31: Paul's escape | 200

Table 32: Similarities and differences in the escape narratives | 201

Table 33: Paul's first trip to Jerusalem | 202

Table 34: Similarities and differences in the accounts of Paul's first trip to Jerusalem | 203

Table 35: The "Silent Period" (Acts 9:31—11:24) | 205

Table 36: Parallels between visions | 210

Table 37: Paul's second trip to Jerusalem | 216

Table 38: "This they did" (Galatians 2:6, 10 and Acts 11:29–30) | 219

Table 39: "Taking along" (Galatians 2:1 and Acts 12:25 and 15:37–38 | 220

Table 40: Paul and Barnabas return to Antioch; the so-called "first missionary journey" | 230

Table 41: Similarities between Paul's sermon in Acts 13 and other sermons in Acts | 234

Table 42: Narrative differences between Galatians 2 and Acts 15 | 242

Table 43: Dionysius of Halicarnassus's criteria for judging Herodotus's and Thucydides's mimetic characteristics | 265

Table 44: Lucian's critique of Crepereius's imitation of Thucydides | 281

Acknowledgements

I AM GRATEFUL TO the University of Memphis for granting me a Faculty Research Grant and a Professional Development Assistance grant in 2011, both of which allowed me to begin research on this project in earnest. Mark Goodacre and Karl Olav Sandness both read chapter 5 and provided insightful feedback. Thank you. Much appreciation also goes to Jeff Walker, who read through an earlier version of chapter 7 and then was willing to read a draft of the entire manuscript and offer helpful suggestions. Mike Duncan has read through versions of several chapters over the years, and he and I have discussed and argued about much of the book's content. Thanks Mike. Gene Plunka, colleague and friend, read an early version of chapter 6 and Steve Tabachnick, another colleague and friend, braved reading chapter 7. I am fortunate to have Gene and Steve as colleagues and friends who are always eager to engage in thoughtful and critical discussions about our works in progress. I have learned much from both of you. Some of the material included in this project was also presented, discussed, and argued in graduate seminars at the University of Memphis and undergraduate Bible as Literature courses, and in the Honors seminar "The History of the Bible as a Book as an Artifact." I appreciate students' willingness to engage in what, for many, were new and controversial ideas. Your feedback helped me to articulate more clearly the arguments presented here. Many thanks also to the editors and team at Wipf and Stock for accepting this project and converting it into book form. Lastly, I thank my beloved wife, Carrie Jean, for her never-ending support and willingness both to have a husband who spends so many early mornings, weekends, and holidays upstairs in his office and to carefully read and thoughtfully engage the content herein.

Abbreviations

ABD   *The Anchor Bible Dictionary.* Edited by David Noel Freedman. 6 vols. New York: Doubleday, 1992.

ANF   *The Ante-Nicene Fathers.* Edited by Alexander Roberts. 10 vols. Peabody, MA: Hendrickson, 1994.

BAGD   Bauer, Walter, William F. Arndt, F. Wilbur Gingrich, and Frederick W. Danker. *Greek-English Lexicon of the New Testament and Other Early Christian Literature.* 2nd ed. Chicago: University of Chicago Press, 1979.

BDF   Blass, Friedrich, Albert Debrunner, and Robert W. Funk. *A Greek Grammar of the New Testament and Other Early Christian Literature.* Chicago: University of Chicago Press, 1961.

CBQ   *Catholic Biblical Quarterly*

DDD   *Dictionary of Deities and Demons in the Bible.* Edited by Karel van der Toorn, Bob Becking, and Pieter W. van der Horst. 2nd rev. ed. Grand Rapids: Eerdmans, 1999.

ExpTim   *Expository Times*

GRBS   *Greek, Roman, and Byzantine Studies*

HTR   *Harvard Theological Review*

JNST   *Journal for the Study of the New Testament*

JBL   *Journal of Biblical Literature*

LSJ   Liddell, Henry George, Robert Scott, and Henry Stuart Jones. *A Greek-English Lexicon.* 9th ed. with revised supplement. Oxford: Clarendon, 1996.

LCL	Loeb Classical Library
Neot	*Neoestamentica*
NTS	*New Testament Studies*
NovT	*Novum Testamentum*
OCD	*The Oxford Classical Dictionary*. Edited by Simon Hornblower, Antony Spawforth, and Esther Eidinow. 4th ed. Oxford: Oxford University Press, 2012.
SBL	Society of Biblical Literature
TDNT	*Theological Dictionary of the New Testament*. Edited by Gerhard Kittel and Gerhard Friedrich. Translated by Geoffrey W. Bromiley. 10 vols. Grand Rapids: Eerdmans, 1964–1976.
TLG	*Thesaurus Linguae Graecae*. University of California–Irvine. http://stephanus.tlg.uci.edu.
TynBul	*Tyndale Bulletin*

Chapter 1

Introduction

THIS INTERDISCIPLINARY STUDY SITUATES itself within recent discussions of understanding the composition of New Testament texts within known Greco-Roman rhetorical and compositional practices. More specifically, I examine the role that the Greco-Roman rhetorical practice of μίμησις (*mimesis, imitatio,* imitation) may play in the composition of the canonical gospels of Matthew and Luke and the canonical book of Acts. The broader context of this study is that many, if not most, of the canonical New Testament texts emerged as a result of polemical disputes—that an author would take stylus in hand and craft a document that reflects that author's position within the ideological conflict and that a chronologically later author would then use that earlier document as a source (often his primary source), engage it, and revise or transform it (sometimes radically) in order to reflect his own position in the conflict or to paper over, suppress, or supersede in some way the earlier position(s). This practice of engaging, revising, rivaling, or transforming an earlier text (*mimesis/imitation*) was the primary means by which students were taught writing and literature (and oratory) in Greco-Roman schools and was a widespread and acknowledged practice among the literati. Yet, even though μίμησις/*imitatio* was the primary means by which students were taught composition and literary analysis and was prevalent among the literati, as will be demonstrated in the next chapter, its role in understanding the composition of New Testament texts has not received as much consideration as it warrants by those scholars who approach New Testament texts from rhetorical perspectives.

The apparent dearth of serious interest in *mimesis* within New Testament rhetorical studies is evident in explicit "rhetoric of New Testament" texts. In Duane Watson's *The Rhetoric of the New Testament: A Bibliographic Survey*—which Ben Witherington notes, "lays before us almost every useful article, monograph, or book on the subject published during the first twenty or so years of the discussion"[1]—there are headings under the "Contents" for

---

1. Witherington, *New Testament Rhetoric*, 241.

"New Testament Rhetoric in General" that include invention (ethos, pathos, logos, topoi), arrangement, style, chiasm, chreia, and social-rhetorical analysis, but nothing for *mimesis* or *imitation*. Moreover, under "Matthew," Watson lists 40 references but not one of these includes either *mimesis* or *imitation* in the title. For "Luke-Acts," he lists 29, two of which (written by Thomas Brodie) include *imitation* in the title; for "Luke," he cites 67, three of which include *imitation* (all written by Brodie), and, for "Acts," he lists 72, three of which include *imitation* in the titles (two written by Brodie and the other by Dennis MacDonald).[2] George Kennedy's influential *New Testament Interpretation through Rhetorical Criticism*, likewise, allots only a few sentences to *imitation*, situating it only within the Asianism/Atticism controversy within his discussion of "Style," but does not say anything about one author's mimetic use and revision of an earlier text that was such an important component of the practice of imitation.[3] Similarly, C. Clifton Black's few sentences on *imitation* in his *The Rhetoric of the Gospel* speak only to its stylistic aspects within his discussion of 1 John.[4] Ben Witherington, in his *New Testament Rhetoric*, does not mention it at all, and, perhaps more surprisingly, neither *The New Testament in Its Literary Environment* (David E. Aune), the *Handbook of Classical Rhetoric in the Hellenistic Period 330 B.C.–A.D. 400* (Stanley E. Porter, ed.), nor *The Westminister Dictionary of New Testament and Early Christian Literature and Rhetoric* (David E. Aune, ed.) includes an entry, reference, or discussion for *mimesis, imitatio,* or *imitation*.

The situation is the same with recent discussions that more narrowly attempt to identify the compositional practices of the authors of the synoptic gospels (Mark, Matthew, and Luke) and Acts. In his oft-cited "Compositional Conventions and the Synoptic Problem," F. Gerald Downing examined how Livy, Plutarch, and Diodorus Siculus incorporated their sources into their works in light of what he (Downing) understood to be contemporary composition practices. Yet, even though it is widely recognized that μίμησις/*imitatio* was the primary means by which students were taught composition when these historians were writing, Downing never mentions either. Similarly, because of the "well known fact" of the synoptic gospels' literary relationships, Richard Burridge surmises, "Indeed, it is possible that evidence of rhetorical influence might help with the problem of their literary relationships with each other."[5] However, because he also thinks that "it is unlikely that the [G]ospel writers and their audiences would have had higher rhetorical

---

2. Watson, *Rhetoric of the New Testament*, 6, 97–116.
3. Kennedy, *New Testament Interpretation*, 31–32.
4. Black, *Rhetoric of the Gospel*, 90–93.
5. Burridge, "Gospels and Acts," 510.

training" and because of our deficient understanding of "any firm external evidence about the date, provenance or authorship" of the gospels and Acts, "we cannot form any immediate conclusions about their relationship to rhetoric."[6] These obstacles aside, Burridge considers the possible rhetorical influences of the classical rhetorical canon of invention, arrangement, style, memory, and delivery within the gospels and Acts, without any reference to, or discussion of, μίμησις/imitation. R. A. Derrenbacker recognizes the "general inattention or lack of recognition on the part of Synoptic scholars in dealing seriously with the compositional conventions and specific literary methods of antiquity and their bearing on the literary relationships among the synoptics."[7] To address this deficiency, Derrenbacker discusses "a range of compositional practices attested in antiquity" and then relates "those compositional practices to concrete descriptions and problems associated with the composition of the Synoptic Gospels."[8] Surprisingly, for such a study, he does not discuss, or even mention, the Greco-Roman rhetorical and compositional practices of μίμησις or imitation. A final study to be briefly mentioned here is Alex Damm's *Ancient Rhetoric and the Synoptic Problem*, in which he begins by citing Richard Burridge's sentence cited above, "It is possible that . . . evidence of rhetorical influence might help with the problem of . . . [the gospels'] literary relationship."[9] His "goal is to address this need: to apply rhetorical conventions to the investigation of the synoptic problem" by arguing that "an awareness of rhetorical conventions can help us determine more or less plausible scenarios of adaptation among the synoptic version of a rhetorical form called the *chreia*."[10] Even though Damm restricts his study to the *chreia* (one of the rhetorical tools in the *progymnasmata* tool bag), he, unlike the others, does briefly discuss μίμησις/imitation. After allotting one paragraph of consideration each to the work of Dennis MacDonald and Thomas Brodie, and while acknowledging that "the evangelists likely employed *imitation*," Damm then dismisses μίμησις/imitatio as an appropriate term denoting "composition" because he does "not find the term adequate to describe [the synoptic gospels'] close, sustained use of sources—the use we see for instance through a gospel synopsis."[11]

There are, however, a few scholars who approach the canonical New Testament texts from rhetorical perspectives who have considered *mimesis*'

6. Ibid., 512.
7. Derrenbacker, *Ancient Compositional Practices*, 15.
8. Ibid., 15.
9. Damm, *Ancient Rhetoric*, xv.
10. Ibid., 15.
11. Ibid., 3–4.

role therein. The two most prolific of these representatives are Dennis R. MacDonald and Thomas L. Brodie. MacDonald has argued that the authors of, primarily, Mark and Luke-Acts relied upon and imitated classical Greek and Roman texts, especially the Homeric epics and, most recently, Virgil's *Aeneid*.[12] Brodie, in numerous publications over the past thirty-five years, has argued that an early form of Luke-Acts (his "Proto-Luke") was crafted as an imitation of much of the Elijah-Elisha narrative from the Septuagint (Greek translation of the Hebrew Bible) and that the author of Mark used this "Proto-Luke" in addition to other material from the Elijah-Elisha narratives to craft his gospel.[13] Marianne Palmer Bonz has argued for Virgil's influence on Luke-Acts, contending that the author of Luke-Acts imitated the *Aeneid*'s epic structure and themes in crafting his own (Christian) epic.[14] While I engage MacDonald's, Brodie's, and Bonz's respective methods in chapter 2, my approach is different from theirs in one important respect. Whereas MacDonald argues that the authors of Mark and Luke-Acts imitated themes and (some language) from classical Greek and Latin literature, and whereas Brodie emphasizes, primarily, Luke's imitation of the Elijah-Elisha narratives from the Septuagint, and whereas Bonz contends that Luke imitated the structure and themes of Virgil's *Aeneid*, I propose that while the authors of Matthew and Luke imitated the Septuagint, Matthew also imitated Mark and Luke also imitated Mark, Matthew, and Paul in the Greco-Roman sense of μίμησις/*imitatio*. That is, while there is broad scholarly agreement that there are literary relationships between (especially) the synoptic gospels (i.e., the synoptic problem) and a growing recognition of the relationship between Acts and Galatians, I argue that understanding the Greco-Roman compositional practice of mimesis and the authors of these texts' mimetic compositional practices can help us to understand better than we do now the composition of, and rivalry between, these authors and their texts.

That is, while it is widely recognized that there are literary relationships between Mark, Matthew, and Luke, we rarely read or hear that the author of Matthew *imitated* Mark in the Greco-Roman sense of *mimesis* or that the author of Luke *imitated* Mark or that the author of Luke *imitated* Matthew or that the author of Acts *imitated* Paul. This, however, is the argument that I advance in this study—that there are rhetorical relationships between these texts and that the Greco-Roman rhetorical and compositional practice of

---

12. MacDonald, *Homeric Epics*; idem (ed.), *Mimesis and Intertextuality* and *Luke and Vergil*.

13. Brodie, *Birthing*.

14. Bonz, *Past as Legacy*.

mimesis seems to be the best explanation for these compositional practices and literary relationships.

More specifically, my argument takes the following form: I am going to focus upon two conflicts within early (mid-first through mid-second century) Christianity and demonstrate how these conflicts were radically mitigated or transformed by the Greco-Roman rhetorical and compositional practice of *mimesis*. The first is the controversy surrounding Jesus's relationship with his family (especially his mother) and the closely related issue concerning his (alleged) illegitimate birth that is evident in the gospel of Mark and the author of Matthew's and the author of Luke's recasting of this controversy via mimetic rhetorical and compositional strategies. This study will especially emphasize that the author of Luke knew, used, and mimetically transformed Matthew's infancy narrative (Matt 1–2). The second controversy is the author of Acts' imitative transforming (whitewashing) of the Petrine/Pauline controversy—that the author of Acts mimetically transformed Galatians 1–2, via compositional strategies very similar to how he transformed Matthew's birth narrative, and transformed the intense controversy between the two pillars of earliest Christianity into a unity and harmony that, historically, never existed. The following discussion is divided into three parts.

Part 1: Greco-Roman Mimesis/Imitatio

Chapter 2: The Prevalence and Practice of Μίμησις/Imitatio in Greco-Roman Education

The purpose of this chapter is to establish the prevalence of mimesis/imitation within Greco-Roman culture—especially its importance within educational settings and its prevalence in crafting literary texts. I begin by summarizing references to μίμησις/imitatio in texts from Isocrates (fourth century BCE) to Lucian (second century CE). The authors and/or texts include Isocrates, 'Demetrius' (*On Style*), *Ad Herennium*, Cicero, Dionysius of Halicarnassus, Horace, Seneca the Elder, 'Longinus' (*On the Sublime*), Seneca the Younger, Quintilian, Pliny the Younger, Martial, Theon's *Progymnasmata*, and Lucian's *A Professor of Rhetoric*. The summary is organized under the following headings: Prevalence of the Concept and Practice, Whom to Imitate, What to Imitate, and How to Imitate (reading, writing, paraphrase, and rivalry). After providing brief examples of Virgil's imitation of the Homeric epics and identifying characteristics of his imitative technique (which will serve as a basis for developing my own criteria for recognizing imitated texts), and after discussing and critiquing Brodie's, MacDonald's, and Bonz's approaches of applying mimetic criticism to New Testament texts, I conclude the chapter by establishing the criteria for recognizing imitated texts that will then guide the discussions in the following chapters and by suggesting that it would have been improbable, if not impossible, for the authors of Matthew and Luke and Acts (or Luke-Acts) not to have been exposed to Greco-Roman compositional μίμησις.

Part 2: The Controversy Concerning Jesus's Birth and His Relationship with His Family: Crafting Rhetorical Counter-Narratives

Chapter 3: A Rhetorical Analysis of Mark 3:20–35 and 6:1–6: Jesus's Family in Mark and Matthew's and Luke's Mimetic Transformations

In order to establish the rhetorical context for discussing Luke's revision of Matthew's birth narrative, this chapter concerns itself with two passages in the gospel of Mark that could have been read to suggest both serious tensions between Jesus and his family members, including his mother, and that he was born illegitimately—claims to which Matthew's and Luke's infancy narratives can be read as apologetic responses. The first passage is the "Beelzebul Controversy" (Mark 3:20–35) wherein the author of Mark employs his "sandwiching" rhetorical and compositional device to suggest that Jesus's family (which includes his unnamed mother and his brothers) thought that he was "out of his mind," that they were just as guilty as the scribes who claimed that Jesus was demonically possessed, and that they, including his mother, were not part of his inner circle, not his disciples, but were "outsiders." That Mark depicts Jesus's mother as not being a close follower of Jesus is striking, for if Mary had been visited by the archangel Gabriel and told the things that Luke narrates she was told, she would have probably remembered these things and supported this unique individual. I then demonstrate how the author of Matthew, while retaining much of Mark, dismantled Mark's "sandwiching" structure that aligned Jesus's family with the scribes' criticism in an attempt to distance Jesus's family from any possible wrongdoing, and then how the author of Luke followed Matthew's narrative more than he followed Mark's and, in his extensive transformation of the narrative, even further distanced Jesus's family from the controversy to the extent that any reader who reads only Luke instead of Mark would have no idea of the conflict raised in Mark's narrative. A similar rhetorical transformation is evident in the second passage, Mark 6:1–3, wherein the author of Mark identifies Jesus as "a carpenter" and as the "son of Mary." Both of these identifications suggest possible slurs—that Jesus was of the lower working class and that he was born illegitimately. After discussing these issues in detail, I demonstrate that the author of Matthew read Mark's passage in negative terms and significantly revised it (referring to Jesus as "son of a carpenter" instead of "a carpenter" and rewording his relationship to his mother) to avoid any suggestion of any possible slurs. I argue next that the author of Luke also read Mark in negative terms, was not satisfied with Matthew's revision, and, again relying more upon Matthew than Mark, more radically transformed the passage (referring to Jesus as "son of Joseph" rather than "son of Mary" and completely omitting any mention of a carpenter at all) to eliminate any possible suggestion whatsoever of either possible slur. I conclude the chapter by applying the criteria for dependence/imitation to Matthew's and Luke's revisions and conclude that, according to this criteria, because the author of Matthew and author of Luke demonstrate similar if not exact rhetorical and compositional strategies as demonstrated in Virgil's *Aeneid*, it is reasonable to conclude that Matthew imitated Mark in the Greco-Roman sense of μίμησις and that Luke imitated Mark and Matthew, in the Greco-Roman sense of μίμησις.

Chapter 4: Matthew's Infancy Narrative (Matt 1–2): Mimetically Transforming Passages from the Septuagint

There are two components to this chapter's argument. The first is that the infancy narrative in Matthew, more specifically the foretelling-of-Jesus's-birth narrative (1:18–25), is, at least in (large) part, an apologetic response to issues raised in Mark's gospel and that may have been in wider circulation concerning Mary's pregnancy and Jesus's (alleged) illegitimacy. The second is that, unlike the material considered in chapter 3, Matthew did not have a model of a birth narrative of Jesus to use as his inspiration for his own, so he had to create one, but he did not have to create it *ex nihilo*. Rather, in compositional practices similar to Virgil's use of Homer, Matthew carefully scoured the Septuagint (Greek translation of the Hebrew Bible, abbreviated as LXX throughout) and adapted and transformed a wide variety of passages to create something totally new to shape his argument. After reviewing different scholars' explanations for Matthew's need to craft an infancy narrative, I analyze his genealogy (1:1–17) by considering the rhetorical functions of ancient genealogies, arguing that Matthew adopted the genealogy form from the Septuagint as his model and mimetically transformed genealogies from the Septuagint version of 1 Chronicles and Ruth, and by identifying elements within the genealogy that demonstrate its rhetorical artificiality. A detailed discussion of Matthew's inclusion of four women—Tamar, Rahab, Ruth, and Bathsheba—in his genealogy follows, in which I contend that the only common denominator among these four women and Mary is that each one of them was involved in an inappropriate sexual relationship, and Matthew includes these women in his argument to imply that, even though they were involved in a sexually inappropriate relationship, they were still a part of God's plan—a rhetorical device to assuage the forthcoming narrative fact that Mary was pregnant when she should not have been. Moving on to the annunciation itself (1:18–25), Matthew acknowledges that Mary is pregnant when she should not have been and now offers an *explanation* that is primarily reliant upon the Septuagint version of Isaiah 7:14. Through a detailed philological discussion, I argue that Isaiah 7:14 (LXX) was Matthew's inspiration for his virgin conception narrative and that he altered his Septuagint version of this passage that read "a young woman [νεᾶνις] will be with child" so that it would read "a virgin [παρθένος] will be with child" so as to provide scriptural authority and divine legitimacy to his explanation for Mary's pregnancy when she should not have been. What better way is there to respond to the circulating claim that Jesus was born illegitimately than to argue, instead, that his mother's obvious pregnancy prior to her marriage was part of a divine plan and that she was not an immoral young woman as circulating allegations suggest, but, rather, a pure virgin who conceived by divine providence as foretold by the ancient prophets? Such was one of the author of Matthew's objectives (if not his primary objective) as he set out to craft his infancy narrative.

Chapter 5: Luke's Mimetical Transformation of Matthew's Birth Narrative: A Rhetorical Analysis of Luke 1–2

Several scholars have long acknowledged that, in composing his birth narrative and genealogy (Luke 1–2 and 3:23–38), the author of Luke imitated (in the Greco-Roman sense of μίμησις) a considerable amount of material from the Septuagint, especially material from 1 Samuel (1 Kgs LXX) and the Psalms. However, because of the many and significant differences and contradictions between the birth narratives and genealogies in Matthew and Luke, the vast majority of scholars reject the idea that Luke could have known or used Matthew's narrative in crafting his own. In this chapter, I argue that Luke knew Matthew's birth narrative and genealogy and used them as his models for his own and transformed these by means of rhetorical and compositional strategies very similar to how he mimetically incorporated material from the Septuagint into his narrative. In short, I argue that Luke mimetically and radically transformed Matthew's infancy narrative and genealogy. I begin with a brief consideration of the debate as to whether Luke could have known Matthew and a review of the scholarship that Luke imitated material from the Septuagint. I then provide a table that depicts a structural outline of how Luke interwove material from the Septuagint with material from Matthew (almost) seamlessly into his birth narrative and then use this table as an outline for the ensuing discussion. Then, after comparing the two genealogies and arguing that there are good reasons to think that Luke knew and mimetically transformed Matthew's genealogy, I offer two possible explanations for Luke's mimetic transformation of his sources. First, I contend that Luke vehemently disagreed with much of what Matthew wrote. I argue in the previous chapter 4 that the author of Matthew attempts *to explain* Mary's situation that she is pregnant when she should not be *after the narrative fact of her pregnancy*. Luke, I propose, vehemently disagreed with the implications of Matthew's narrative, has Gabriel appear to Mary *prior to her pregnancy* to explain what *will* come about, and transformed Mary's role in the birth narrative as described by Matthew *to exonerate* her completely from any accusations of wrong doing that Matthew attempted (unsuccessfully in Luke's view) to explain away. A second possible explanation for Luke's transformation of Matthew's birth narrative is offered by Joseph Tyson in his *Marcion and Luke-Acts: A Defining Struggle*, wherein he argues compellingly (in my view) that the birth narrative in Luke was written in response to the views advanced by Marcionites (possibly the most popular form of Christianity in the second century) that Jesus was not a Jew and that he could not have been born of a woman. What Tyson does not consider is that the author of Luke used Matthew as his source for his birth narrative; I argue that he does. But, to counter Marcion, he needed to revise Matthew's account to make Jesus more Jewish than Matthew presents him, which explains, I argue, both why Luke's birth narrative emphasizes Jesus's Jewishness more than Matthew's does and his abundant use of material from the Septuagint, often referred to as "Luke's septuagentisms."

Part 3: The Petrine-Pauline Controversy and Luke's Mimetic Transformation

Chapter 6: Establishing the Pauline-Petrine Controversy:
A Prelude to Luke's Mimetic Transformation
of Galatians 1–2

It was necessary to establish the narrative contexts concerning the problems surrounding Jesus's birth and Mary's pregnancy (chapters 3 and 4) prior to demonstrating Luke's mimetic transformation of Matthew's birth narrative (chapter 5). In this chapter, it is necessary to develop the context of the controversy between Paul and the Jewish leaders of the followers-of-Jesus movement, including Peter, who are thought to have been based in Jerusalem prior to arguing in the next chapter that Luke mimetically transformed and completely whitewashed this controversy and created a unity and harmony among the early Christians that simply never existed. Because scholars recognize that much of the controversy concerning Luke's transformation of this controversy depends upon whether Luke could have known and used Paul's letters (similar to whether Luke could have known and used Matthew's birth narrative), I begin this chapter by presenting a brief review of the arguments against and for Luke's knowledge and use of Paul's letters. I then discuss the evidence from early Christian literature, primarily the New Testament, of the controversy between Paul and the Jerusalem leaders (including Peter) before providing a detailed summary of the controversies in Galatians 1–2, which will set the stage for a discussion in chapter 7 of Luke's mimetic transformation of Galatians 1–2.

Chapter 7: Luke's Mimetic Transformation of Galatians 1–2:
A Rhetorical Analysis of Acts 7:58—15:30

Working from the understanding that the author of Acts is the same author who crafted Luke 1–2, this chapter demonstrates that Luke imitated Galatians 1–2 very similarly to how he imitated Matthew 1–2 and the Septuagint in his birth narrative and genealogy. In this chapter, I argue that the author of Acts knew, used, and mimetically revised Galatians 1–2 so as to paper over the controversy between Paul and the Jerusalem leaders and to depict a unity in earliest Christianity that never existed. After arguing for a late date of composition (ca. 120–130 CE) and dismissing the traditional attribution of composition to "Luke as Paul's companion" in favor of a later anonymous author, I build upon Heikki Leppä's (*Luke's Critical Use of Galatians*, 2002) and Richard Pervo's (*Dating Acts*, 2006) work that identifies verbal and narrative (thematic) similarities between Galatians and Acts. My analysis of Acts as it relates to Galatians demonstrates further that Luke knew and used Paul's letter to the Galatians as his primary source for much of the material in Acts 7:58—15:30. Whereas Leppä and Pervo have demonstrated that there is sufficient evidence that Luke knew and used Galatians, I will build upon their earlier work and "add meat to the bones" that they have established by identifying additional verbal and narrative similarities and demonstrating the extent to which the entire narrative of 7:58—15:30 is mimetically dependent upon Galatians 1–2. Along the way, I demonstrate that the text of Acts 7:58—15:30 reflects such an intimate familiarity with Galatians that Luke must have had it by his side (or on his knee) as he penned this material. I will argue further that Luke's primary objective in this section of Acts is to transform Paul's letter in such a way as to demonstrate that there was, in fact, no controversy between Paul and Peter in Antioch, as is clear from Galatians. Rather, as Luke presents it, the Gentile movement (i.e., Paul's gospel) was already well under way long before Paul is even converted; Peter and the congregation in Jerusalem, Paul's opponents in Galatians, accept and advance Paul's Gentile mission before Paul even begins his so-called "first missionary journey" in Acts 13–14, and Paul is depicted not as "the apostle to the Gentiles" who works independently of the Jerusalem community, as he claims in his letters, but is subservient to the already existing leadership and merely advances their earlier work. Moreover, whereas Galatians 2:11–14 reflects an intense disagreement between Paul and Peter in Antioch, Luke never places Peter in Antioch and never has Peter and Paul speak to one another anywhere within the book of Acts. According to Luke, the controversy in Antioch between Paul and Peter never occurred. Instead, he rhetorically constructs his narrative in such a way that by the time we reach Acts 15, the problem of Galatians 2 had already been resolved by Peter and the Jerusalem leaders' acceptance and advancing of the ideological thrust behind Paul's Gentile mission (Acts 10–11). That Luke has Peter and the Jerusalem leaders engage, accept, and advance Paul's message is, I will argue, the strongest possible evidence as to who Paul's opponents were in Galatians (and 1 Corinthians and 2 Corinthians 10–13). Perhaps more than anything else, this chapter confirms the reality of the controversy between Peter and Paul and demonstrates the extent to which Acts is a carefully and skillfully crafted rhetorical/mimetical fiction.

Presuppositions

Although this study focuses primarily upon Greco-Roman rhetorical and compositional practices in Matthew, Luke, and Acts, the texts under examination herein are biblical, primarily from the New Testament, and those scholars who comment upon these texts are, for the most part, biblical scholars who are trained via a variety of critical and hermeneutical approaches and who bring a variety of presuppositions to these texts. One of these methodological presuppositions is the existence of a hypothetical source of the sayings of Jesus, designated Q, a hypothetical document that, this presupposition maintains, the author of Matthew and the author of Luke hypothetically used along with Mark as their primary sources for composing their respective gospels, i.e., the Two-Source Hypothesis. Representatives of this prevailing methodological position among New Testament scholars contend that the authors of Matthew and Luke did not know each other's texts but wrote their respective gospels independently of the other. As Stephen Carlson's website demonstrates, the Two-Source Hypothesis is just one of many possible approaches to understanding how Matthew, Mark, and Luke developed as written texts—the Synoptic Problem.[15] In chapters 3, 4, and 5, I will not engage in the Q controversy directly for two reasons. First, I do not want to digress from my primary interests of the examination of Greco-Roman mimesis within these texts. Second, the mimetic compositional conventions used by Matthew and Luke in the material that these three chapters discuss not only demonstrate that they are imitated texts, but also offer a satisfactory explanation for the structural and narrative development (or trajectory) of Mark > Matthew > Luke and the verbal similarities and differences in these narratives that are discussed in these chapters, which eliminates the need for a hypothetical source (Q) that might be proposed as a possible explanation for the similarities and differences. Thus, in my view, these narrative-development characteristics (or trajectories) most closely align with the Farrer (or Farrer-Goulder-Goodacre) Hypothesis that dispenses with Q and proposes the priority of Mark, that Matthew used Mark as his primary source, and that Luke used both Mark and Matthew.

---

15. On Carlson's website see "Overview of Proposed Solutions," http://www.hypotyposeis.org/synoptic-problem/2004/09/overview-of-proposed-solutions.html. See also Porter and Dyer, eds., *Synoptic Problem*, which offers discussions of what the editors suggest are the four most widely accepted positions—the Two-Source Hypothesis, the Farrer Hypothesis, the Two-Gospel Hypothesis, and the Orality and Memory Hypothesis, each written by a respected representative of each position, with feedback offered by each representative about the opposing views, and with initial bibliographies for each position.

A second presupposition concerns the relationship between much of the narrative content in chapters 3–7 and this content's relationship with what, historically, may have really occurred. For example, Andrew Lincoln, a recent representative of those addressing the historical reliability of some of the narratives discussed in this study, has recently wrestled with this issue in his *Born of a Virgin?*, wherein he writes:

> For the purposes of the overall argument of this book, historical issues are in an important sense secondary. That overall argument is not dependent on a historical reconstruction of traditions behind the New Testament that attempts to determine what actually happened in the circumstances of Jesus's birth and on the basis of its conclusions about historicity adjudicates whether or not a virginal conception is to be believed and how it is to be appropriated in contemporary theological reflection.[16]

Lincoln is writing as a theologian and (thoughtfully) sorts through the different/conflicting traditions within the canonical texts that speak to Jesus's conception, birth, and parents—a virgin conception, a physical descendant of David through Joseph, or the possibility that Jesus was born illegitimately—in an attempt to offer a meaningful Christology that reflects a critical understanding of the problems that these different traditions and modern biology raise.[17] In sharp contrast to Lincoln's (primarily) theological concerns, this study attempts to understand how the authors of the texts to be considered composed their texts within their respective historical and educational contexts without any concern about contemporary theological reflection. That is, in his "Historical Method in the Study of Religion," Morton Smith contends that the object of historical investigation in the study of religion is to "determine just what did happen at some time in the past."[18] He contends further that a "sound historical method" works from a basic presupposition—an atheism that denies "supernatural intervention in the world's affairs," for the historian requires "a world in which these normal phenomena ["the world's affairs"] are not interfered with by arbitrary and *ad hoc* divine interventions to produce abnormal events with special historical consequences."[19] Three examples of how this "sound historical method" will be applicable to this study are the claims that Paul received a revelation from

---

16. Lincoln, *Born of a Virgin?*, 125.

17. Ibid., 125 and 253–65. Steve Moyise also thoughtfully addresses the historical issues concerning Jesus's birth narratives as they relate to theological concerns in *Was the Birth of Jesus According to Scripture?*

18. Smith, "Historical Method," 9.

19. Ibid., 12.

a resurrected Jesus (Galatians 1), that Jesus was conceived by the Spirit of God and born of a virgin (a young woman who had not had intercourse with a man), and that the texts within the canonical Bible are in some way inspired by God in historical space and time—that they are "God's Word." Because these alleged events or phenomena are "supernatural interventions in the world's affairs," they will not be considered as events that actually occurred in historical space and time. Rather, this study works from the understanding that the texts to be considered were crafted by skilled writers who were engaged in what they considered to be dynamic controversies within their respective historical space in time and who employed a variety of literary and rhetorical techniques and lines of argumentation in attempts to counter opposing positions and/or persuade others to their respective positions. Thus, as this study hopes to demonstrate, before these texts were deemed sacred or holy, they were, first and foremost, rhetorical and polemical narratives. The authors of these texts were engaged in contentious controversies with other early followers of the Jesus movement and these texts were carefully crafted by authors who were trained in rhetorical and compositional conventions that were common to the period in which they lived, and they offered their narratives as contributions to these controversies with which the respective authors were dynamically engaged.

One final presupposition is that scholarship has determined with very high probability, if not certainty, that the authors of our gospels and Acts are not the authors to whom tradition has ascribed authorship. While I recognize and acknowledge that these are anonymous texts, I will retain the traditional names so as to avoid otherwise awkward circumlocutions such as "the author of Mark," "the author of Matthew," "the author of Luke," and "the author of Acts."

Now, on to a consideration of the core of this study—the Greco-Roman rhetorical and compositional practice of μίμησις.

PART I
Greco-Roman Μίμησις/Imitatio

Chapter 2

The Prevalence and Practice of Greco-Roman Μίμησις/Imitatio in Greco-Roman Education and Contemporary Applications of Μίμησις/Imitatio to New Testament Texts

RHETORICAL MIMESIS, AS PRACTICED by Greek and Latin writers in all genres, is here broadly understood as "an author's conscious use of features and characteristics of earlier works."[1] The practice of *mimesis/imitatio* was pervasive and took a wide variety of forms. As a representative statement of its widespread practice, George Fiske has noted that examples of rhetorical imitation "circulate through and animate all literary genres of the ancients: epic, tragedy, comedy, elegy, the pastoral, the philosophic dialogue, the scientific treatise."[2] D.A. Russell's opening remarks in his "De Imitatione" echo the pervasiveness of the practice among Greco-Roman authors:

> One of the inescapable features of Latin literature is that almost every author, in almost everything he writers, acknowledges his antecedents, his predecessors—in a word, the tradition in which he was bred. This phenomenon, for which the technical terms are *imitation* or (in Greek) *mimesis*, is not peculiar to Latin; the statement I have just made about Latin writers would also be true very generally in Greek. In fact, the relationship between the Latin genres and their Greek exemplars may best be seen as

---

1. Fronda, "Imitation (*mimesis, imitatio*)," http://onlinelibrary.wiley.com/doi/10.10 02/9781444338386.wbeaho8087/pdf.

2. Fiske, *Lucilius and Horace*, 26. Brodie cites examples of imitation from epic, lyric, pastoral, and didactic poetry, comedy, satire, and tragic drama before noting, "the list of indebtedness is almost monotonous, but it acts as a corrective to the widespread modern presupposition that literary originality and excellence largely exclude indebtedness" ("Greco-Roman Imitation," 23).

a special case of a general Greco-Roman acceptance of imitation as an essential element in all literary composition.³

The practice of mimesis/imitation was just as widespread in, and the cornerstone of, Greco-Roman education.⁴ Teresa Morgan notes, *mimesis*

> occurs at every stage of *enkyklios paideia* [the student's complete education] and forms one of its most important articulating features. Imitation is a prime means of moving the pupil forward. Hard on the heels of infusion and memory at every stage, it helps the child to learn to speak in infancy, to write, to practice literary criticism, and it is the means by which he practices what he is taught in rhetoric.⁵

Rafaella Cribiore concurs with this assessment and adds, "the principle of imitation inspired ancient education from beginning to end. From the time students learned to wield a pen to when they composed their first declamation, they measured themselves against an exemplar that was either in front of their eyes or inscribed in their memory."⁶

There is no single, extant ancient source that describes or explains the many characteristics of mimesis/imitation. Rather, references to different aspects of imitation are scattered throughout Greco-Roman literature, and, as far as I know, these many references have not been gathered into one document in English that would provide scholars with a convenient reference. While such a source would undoubtedly be useful, its length and diversity would surely be too unwieldy to include in an introductory chapter the purpose of which is to provide readers with an overview of the pervasiveness and characteristics of ancient imitation. In lieu of such a source, Appendix 1 provides many passages (but certainly not exhaustive)

---

3. Russell, "De Imitatione," 1. See also Atkins, *Literary Criticism in Antiquity* (especially 312–13 and 289–90); D'Alton, *Roman Literary Theory* (especially 426–35); Russell and Winterbottom (eds.), *Ancient Literary Criticism*; Ruthven, *Critical Assumptions* (especially 102–18); and, more recently, MacDonald (ed.), *Mimesis and Intertextuality*; idem, *Does the New Testament Imitate Homer?*; Doulamis (ed.), *Echoing Narratives*; Brodie, *Birthing* (especially "The Greco-Roman Tradition: Writing as Rhetorical Imitation," 3–22); and Hunter, *Plato and the Traditions of Ancient Literature*.

4. It is an interesting question to ask whether students were trained via mimesis merely because of its perceived inherent value or because the practice of mimesis/imitation was so prevalent among speakers and writers that students needed to be trained in mimetic techniques so as to be more successful in their future careers, or perhaps a combination of the two.

5. Morgan, *Literate Education*, 251.

6. Cribiore, *Gymnastics of the Mind*, 132. See also Cribiore's *Writing, Teachers, and Students*) and Walker's *Genuine Teachers*. Clark's *Rhetoric in Greco-Roman Education* (especially 144–76) and Bonner's *Education in Ancient Rome* are also still very useful.

in chronological order (as best as this can be determined) that span from Isocrates (fourth century BCE) to Lucian (second century CE) that reflect the prevalence and characteristics of Greco-Roman mimesis/imitation. The following summary of components of mimesis/imitation is derived from the material in Appendix 1.

Prevalence of the Concept and Practice of Μίμησις/Imitatio

"Mimesis is what writers did," so writes Richard Pervo.[7] References to mimesis in respect to the teaching of writing and speaking are evident throughout the ancient Greek and Latin sources that span from the fifth century BCE through the second CE. While we know that literary authors prior to Isocrates (436–338 BCE) were imitating their predecessors' texts, his emphasis that the teacher must "set such an example that the students who have taken form under his instruction are able to imitate [μιμήσασθαί] him" seems to be the first statement (at least among extant texts) that positions imitation and the importance of models to imitate within pedagogical contexts.[8] While Isocrates may have been the first (among extant texts) to emphasize the practice of imitation for pedagogical purposes, 'Longinus' informs us that Herodotus (484–425 BCE) was "Homeric in the highest degree [Ὁμηρικώτατος],"[9] and preceding him were the lyric poet Stesichorus (640–555 BCE) and the elegiac poet Archilochus (680–645 BCE) both of whom 'Longinus' claims were also imitators of Homer,[10] but these pale in comparison to Plato "who drew off for his own use ten thousand runnels from the great Homeric spring."[11] Following Isocrates, almost every author writes as though μίμησις was such a common practice that the respective terms did not require any definition or explanation of what they were (excluding Dionysius of Halicarnassus's theoretical definition, which is considered below). 'Demetrius's' *On the Sublime* demonstrates that the practice of μίμησις is firmly entrenched when he was writing (ca. second century BCE). The author of the *Ad Herennium* (ca. first century BCE) testifies to the widespread practice among the Greek teachers

---

7. Pervo, "Flattery in Its Sincerest Manifestation," 11.

8. Isocrates, *Soph.* 1.17–18.

9. 'Longinus,' *Subl.* 212.

10. Only fragments and quotations survive of Stesichorus's works, but Parsons notes that not only is his diction "Homeric" but that "he seems to know at least individual passages of the *Iliad* and *Odyssey* as we have them" ("Stesichorus").

11. 'Longinus,' *Subl.* 209–15. For Plato's use of Homer, see Hunter's chapter "Homer and Plato" in *Plato and the Traditions of Ancient Literature*.

who preceded him, noting the "prestige of the ancients" and that the rhetorical handbooks in circulation are so full of examples from Greek authors whom students should imitate that, if those examples were removed from the handbooks, there would be nothing left.[12] Cicero translated and borrowed extensively from the Greeks and advocated aspiring orators (and writers) both to study their predecessors and, more specifically, adopt a specific successful orator as their model;[13] Horace encouraged his Roman readers to study the Greeks "by day and by night" and defended his own practice of imitation;[14] Dionysius of Halicarnassus wrote at length on the importance of imitating the strengths and avoiding the weaknesses of a wide variety of Greek models,[15] and Seneca the Elder encouraged his sons to study, learn, and imitate the ancients.[16] Quintilian wrote more on the importance of imitation than on any other single aspect of training for the orator, historian, philosopher, or poet, as each of these would receive the same rhetorical training,[17] and Lucian, the last author considered here, insists that imitation of the ancients is a core component for the training of a historian or rhetor.[18] Based upon this summary, the textual evidence supports the claim that the practice of μίμησις/imitation was probably the most central and fundamental component for preparing students to speak and write in all fields of study in Greco-Roman culture and that its prevalence and importance cannot be overstated.

Whom to Imitate

In *Against the Sophists*, Isocrates states that the teacher must set such an example himself that his students will imitate him, and as a result, clearly distinguish themselves from other students being taught by other teachers.[19] The author of the *Ad Herennium* shares this view and contends that the teacher should not only be an example but should craft his own examples for the students to imitate rather than relying upon examples written by others that are replete in the handbooks. This author also proclaims that the

---

12. *Ad Herennium* 4.3.5.

13. See Quintilian, *Inst.* 10.10.8; and Cicero, *De Inventione* 2.1.4.

14. Horace, *Ars.* 268–69.

15. This is emphasized throughout his works, but see especially *Lys.* 10–13, *Isoc.* 4, *Thuc.* 8–35, and *Pomp.* 3.

16. Seneca the Elder, "Preface," *Controversiae* 6.

17. Quintilian, *Inst.* Book 10. See discussion in Appendix 1.

18. Emphasized throughout Lucian's two works, but see especially *Rhet. praec.* 1–14 and *How to Write History* 7–15.

19. Isocrates, *Soph.* 17–18.

teacher himself should serve as the model, but if he were to choose between a single model or many, he would opt for only one, for teaching students to borrow examples from a variety of orators, poets, and historians would give the students the impression that the totality of rhetorical skills could only be obtained by imitating many and that no individual could master them all.[20] In *De Oratore*, Cicero has Antonius encourage Sulpicius to choose a single model to imitate.[21] The majority of authors—Dionysius of Halicarnassus, Cicero, Horace, Seneca the Elder, 'Longinus', Seneca the Younger, Quintilian, Theon, and Lucian—instruct students to imitate the "greatest and the best" ancient poets, historians, rhetors/orators, and philosophers.

What to Imitate

From Isocrates through Lucian, authors consistently emphasize that every aspect of a speech, poem, or prose work could be imitated, including theme or subject matter, arrangement of material, syntactical structures, and individual phrases and words. Dionysius of Halicarnassus states this explicitly: "In virtually all kinds of discourse two things require study: the ideas and the words. We may regard the first of these as concerned chiefly with subject matter, and the latter with expression; and all those who aim to become good rhetors pay close attention to both these aspects of discourse equally." He then provides specific examples of subject matter, arrangement, and forms of expression from numerous Greek rhetors and historians that the student should (and should not) study and imitate.[22] In his *Panegyricus*, Isocrates exhorts his readers not to weary if one speaks on the same subject as his predecessor and not to shun discoursing (writing and speaking) on a common theme because it is possible to speak/write on the same subject matter in many different ways.[23] Hundreds of years later, Seneca the Younger, in a similar vein, encourages the recipient of his letter not to avoid writing about Mt. Aetna just because Ovid and Virgil had "fully covered it."[24] As will be discussed below, Virgil imitated and inverted the structure of the Homeric epics; 'Demetrius' notes Thucydides's imitation of Homer's words "land" and "wave-surrounded."[25] Seneca the Elder notes Ovid's repetitive use of

20. *Ad Herennium* 4.3.5
21. Cicero, *De or.* 289–90.
22. Dionysius of Halicarnassus, *Comp.* 112–13.
23. Isocrates, *Paneg.* §16.
24. Seneca the Younger, *Epistle 79*.
25. 'Demetrius,' *Eloc.* 112–13.

Virgil's "He's full of the god,"[26] and Lucian criticizes Crepereius Calpurnianus for lifting the whole first line of Thucydides's *History* almost verbatim.[27] In short, any and every component of a discourse could be imitated.

How to Imitate

To avoid overlapping discussions, I have already mentioned above that speaking/writing about a common subject matter or theme was one way that a writer or speaker could imitate an earlier writer or speaker, and examples of this range from a student's paraphrase of the first twenty-one lines of the *Iliad*[28] to Virgil's imitation of the Homeric epics. I have also noted that any aspect of a discourse—subject matter, arrangement of material, syntactic structure, and individual words and phrases—could be imitated. Here, I will summarize how reading and writing, translation, paraphrase, emulation/rivalry were considered within the practice of imitation, and appropriate and inappropriate ways to imitate.

While almost all of the writers considered above recommend reading/studying the best poets, prose writers, philosophers, historians, and rhetors/orators, a few of the writers emphasize the importance of careful and thoughtful reading and re-reading. In his *Dinarchus*, for example, Dionysius of Halicarnassus distinguishes two types of imitation. That form that he describes as "natural" "is acquired by intensive learning and familiarity" (such as Virgil's familiarity with the Homeric epics) whereas the unnatural and contrived is "acquired by following precepts of the art." While Dionysius does not offer any explanation as to what he means by these distinctions, his meaning is clear that the "natural" kind of imitation involves careful study of the source to be imitated.[29] Cicero expresses a similar sentiment when he has Crassus explain his expectations that the aspiring orator will carefully study (cognoscendum) prior to imitating the "most accomplished writers and orators."[30] Similarly, Seneca the Younger, in his metaphor of the bees, suggests that one must "absorb" and "digest" (or internalize) what is read "otherwise it will merely enter the memory and not the reasoning power."[31] Quintilian seems to pick up this digestive metaphor, writing,

26. Seneca the Elder, *Suasoriae, Controversiae* 3.7.
27. Lucian, *How to Write History* §15.
28. See examples in Morgan, *Literate Education*, 198–225.
29. Dionysius of Halicarnassus, *Din.* 266–71.
30. Cicero, *De or.* 2.89–90.
31. Seneca the Younger, *Ep. 84*.

We must return to what we have read and reconsider it with care, while, just as we do not swallow our food till we have chewed it and reduced it almost to a state of liquefaction to assist the process of digestion, so what we read must not be committed to the memory and imitation while it is still in a crude state, but must be softened and, if I may use the phrase, reduced to a pulp by frequent re-perusal.[32]

Reading alone, however, is not enough. Cicero seems to be the first to state explicitly the importance of writing. While acknowledging there is some value in extempore speaking in *De Oratore*, it is "more serviceable" for aspiring and practicing speakers to give more consideration to what it is that they are going to say and the best way to do this is to write: "The pen is the best and most eminent author and teacher of eloquence."[33] Similarly, Theon instructs his readers that eloquent examples from literary works or speeches will not benefit the student unless "each student exercises himself every day in writing" without specifying what kind of writing it was students were to practice.[34] It is Quintilian, though, perhaps influenced by Cicero, who explains that the pen, "which brings the most labor and the most profit," is essential for the rhetorical exercises of translation and paraphrase.[35]

Translation as a form or means of imitation refers primarily to Latin writers translating Greek texts. Cicero, Quintilian, and Pliny testify that translating Greek into Latin expands one's vocabulary, forms of expression, and varieties of figures of speech; Quintilian also notes that translation of Greek is valuable because of the copiousness of their subject matter and Pliny adds that translation "gives one aptitude to invent after their manner."[36] Negatively, Horace and others chastise writers whose slavish translations (still considered to be imitations) are no more than plagiarism.[37] Theon claims that paraphrase, a second means of imitation, was used by all ancient writers, that they rephrased not only their own writing but also the writing of others.[38] Cicero practiced paraphrase orally and did not recommend it,[39] and Theon notes that others oppose it who claim that, once something is said well, it cannot be improved upon. His response, perhaps similar to

---

32. Quintilian, *Inst.* 10.1.15.
33. Cicero, *De or.* 1.151.
34. Kennedy, *Progymnasmata*, 5–6.
35. Quintilian, *Inst.* 10.5.
36. Cicero, *Fin.* 1.3; Quintilian, *Inst.* 10.5; Pliny, *Ep.* 9.
37. Horace, *Ep.* 19, 381–85.
38. Kennedy, *Progymnasmata*, 7.
39. Cicero, *De or.* 1.154–55.

Isocrates's view, is that paraphrasing provides the opportunity for one to improve upon an earlier work.[40] Quintilian also shares this view and adds that a paraphrase is not a bare interpretation but it should *rival or vie* with the original, and, while noting its difficulty, claims that the best way to really understand the greatest of authors is through the close examination of a paraphrase that scrutinizes every phrase of an author's text.[41] Though Dionysius does not discuss paraphrase, his brief description of *natural imitation* acquired by "intensive learning and familiarity" seems to resonate with what Quintilian is describing.[42]

This idea of rivalry (ζῆλος/aemulatio) with a previous text or speech seems to be a primary objective of imitation. Dionysius is the first to define it, as admiring that which is fine, but also uses the term as a synonym for μίμησις.[43] The term seems to take on a second meaning in other writers. It is in 'Longinus' that the terms are first distinguished, as he writes of Plato "contesting the prize" like a "young antagonist" with Homer while citing Hesiod's "Good is this strife for mankind."[44] It is this strife that Quintilian seems to refer to as the objective of paraphrase,[45] and Pliny encourages Fuscus, once he has internalized an author's subject and argument, to "turn his rival."[46] A primary objective of competing with a previous text is to engage it and rewrite it in such a way as "to make it one's own." This concept first occurs in 'Demetrius,' who notes how Thucydides imitated Homer's vocabulary and "made it his own."[47] Horace speaks to the difficulty of making common property one's own but encourages the effort,[48] and the concept of rivalry is especially evident in Seneca the Younger's metaphor of absorbing and digesting material from varied sources prior to creating one's own work.[49]

Such a widespread practice of imitation of "common or traditional property" inevitably leads to the problem of claiming another's work as one's own, which then necessitates the need for distinguishing between appropriate and inappropriate imitation. 'Demetrius' writes that prose writers

40. Kennedy, *Progymnasmata*, 5–6.
41. Quintilian, *Inst.* 10.5.5.
42. Dionysius of Halicarnassus, *Din.* 266–71.
43. Dionysius of Halicarnassus, *Critical Essays*, III, 28, 200.
44. 'Longinus,' *Subl.* 209–15.
45. Quintilian, *Inst.* 10.5.5.
46. Pliny the Younger, *Ep. 9; Letters*, 23.
47. Demetrius, *Eloc.* 112–13.
48. Horace, *Ars.* 128–35.
49. Seneca the Younger, *Ep. 84*.

plagiarized the poets and cites Herodotus as an example, but neither explains what constitutes plagiarism nor provides any examples from Herodotus. He contrasts Thucydides with Herodotus and notes that the former did not plagiarize Homer because he "uses it in his own way and makes it his own property."[50] 'Longinus' notes that Plato's excessive borrowing from Homer was not theft but he does not explain what distinguishes appropriate from inappropriate borrowing.[51] Cicero has Atticus accuse Ennius of stealing from Naevius because the former did not "confess the debt;"[52] Horace censures Celsus for claiming another's work as his own (seemingly without acknowledging the debt),[53] and Martial is more emphatic, calling those who claimed his work as their own respectively, "plagiarist" and "thief."[54] Likewise, Lucian criticizes Crepereius for modeling his work too closely upon Thucydides—copying structure and some of the vocabulary verbatim.[55] Yet, Seneca the Younger contends that one is not stealing another's words or ideas if the one doing the imitating marshals the material in a different way, if the new creation "shows a new face" upon a common or traditional theme.[56] Thus, on the one hand, it seems that acknowledging one's debt (source) and writing upon a traditional topic (common property) and borrowing (imitating) material that could be easily recognized as another's material constitutes appropriate imitation. On the other hand, word-for-word borrowing, slavish translation, and claiming another's work as one's own would constitute inappropriate borrowing (imitation) and was thoroughly denounced.

Example of Ancient Imitation

A brief analysis of a section from book 1 of Virgil's *Aeneid* will serve as an example of one ancient author imitating another in ways very similar, it will be argued in the following chapters, to how the authors of Matthew, Luke, and Acts imitate their sources. The literature on Virgil's use of his sources is vast,[57] so the focus of this brief analysis of Virgil's imitative

50. Demetrius, *Eloc.* 112–13.
51. 'Longinus,' *Subl.* 209–15.
52. Cicero, *Brut.* §6.
53. Horace, *Ep.* 1.3 §14–20.
54. Martial, *Epigrams*, 1:52–53.
55. Lucian, *How to Write History* §15.
56. Seneca the Younger, *Ep.* 84.
57. Knauer, *Die Aeneis und Homer* and "Vergil and Homer"; R. D. Williams, "Virgil and the *Odyssey*"; and Heinze, *Virgil's Epic Technique*.

practices is limited to some of the examples of the compositional conventions evident in the *Aeneid* that pertain to an author's (intentional) use of or borrowing from another writer's organizational structures, narrative concepts and themes, and specific language (whether it be a word, phrase, sentence, or sentences).

First, though, it may be helpful to convey a sense of the overall structural and mimetic relationship of the *Aeneid* to the Homeric epics. It is indisputable that Virgil borrowed material from a wide variety of Greek and Latin authors, but primarily and extensively from the *Iliad* and the *Odyssey*. The ancients referred to this use of earlier writers' texts as μίμησις or imiatio. In his classic study of the literary relationship between the *Aeneid* and the Homeric epics, Knauer identifies about 4,800 passages (60 pages of double-columned citations) in the *Aeneid* that are dependent upon the Homeric epics.[58] In another context, Knauer notes, "The complete structure of the Homeric epics, not simply occasional quotations, was no doubt the basis for Vergil's poem.... Vergil must have intensively studied the structure of the Homeric epics before he drafted in prose his famous first plan for the whole of the *Aeneid*."[59] To invoke Seneca the Younger's metaphor of the bees, Virgil thoroughly studied/digested the Homeric epics.

A more detailed, but still broad and incomplete, representation of the structure of the *Aeneid*'s reliance upon the Homeric epics is depicted synoptically in Table 1:[60]

Table 1: Synoptic overview of the *Aeneid* and the *Iliad* and the *Odyssey*

Aeneid	*Iliad* and *Odyssey*
Books 1–8	*Ody.* books 2–15
Books 1–6	*Ody.* books 5–12
Book 1	*Ody.* books 5, 10, 9, 12
Books 2–3	*Ody.* books 9–12
Book 2	*Ody.* 8.499–520
Book 3	*Ody.* books 9–12
Book 4	*Ody.* 5.1–262

58. Knauer, *Die Aeneis und Homer*, 371–431.
59. Knauer, "Vergil and Homer," 888.
60. This table is derived from G. N. Knauer's *Die Aeneis und Homer* (371–431) and "Vergil and Homer" (870–81).

Aeneid	Iliad and Odyssey
Book 5	*Ody.* 8.96–380; 23.226–897; 10.469–574
Book 6	*Ody.* book 11
Books 7–8	*Ody.* books 13–14; 2–4; 15
Book 7	*Ody.* 12.1–150; 13. 78–119; *Il.* 2.155–168
Book 8	*Ody.* 13.187–440; 2.407–34; 3.1–403 *Il.* 18.369–482; 19.1–39; 18.483–617
Book 9	*Il.* 18.165–202; 8.157–book 12; 10.395–515
Books 10–12	*Il.* books 16–22
Book 10	*Il.* 16, 20, 21
Book 11	*Il.* 7.345–436; 16.783—17.60
Book 12	*Il.* 22; 3–4

The opening words of the *Aeneid*, "Arma virumque cano" ("Arms I sing and the man"), invite an immediate comparison to the *Iliad* and the *Odyssey*. The "arms" or "weapons" (Arma) evoke the battles in the *Iliad*, its greatest hero, Achilles, and the first line of the *Iliad*, "The wrath do you sing, o goddess, of Peleus's son, Achilles" (Μῆνιν ἄειδε, θεά, Πηληιάδεω Ἀχιλῆος οὐλομένην), while "and the man" (virumque) unmistakably refers to Odysseus in the *Odyssey*, the familiar opening line of which is, "Tell me, o muse, of the man of many devices" (Ἄνδρα μοι ἔννεπε, μοῦσα, πολύτροπον).[61] The conclusion of the *Aeneid* invites a similar comparison, for whereas in the *Iliad* Achilles kills Hector, which brings about Troy's doom (book 22), so in the *Aeneid* Aeneas's victory over Turnus inaugurates the future establishment of the city of Rome and its future empire. Another structural similarity is that the first half of both the *Odyssey* and the *Aeneid* concerns the respective hero's wanderings after the Trojan war whereas in the second half of the books the heroes fight for their home—Odysseus for his family and home and Aeneas to establish a new home in a new land.

That both heroes in the *Odyssey* and *Aeneid* make an excursion to the underworld near the middle of each epic (book 11 out of 24 in the *Odyssey*

---

61. Passages from Homer are from *Odyssey* (Murray and Dimock, trans., LCL), and from Virgil's *Eclogues, Georgics, Aeneid 1–6* (Fairclough and Goold, trans., LCL).

and book 6 out of 12 in the *Aeneid*) is another important structural similarity, and these excursions also share many thematic and verbal similarities. In book 10 of the *Odyssey*, Kirke instructs Odysseus to go to Hades to seek the spirit of Teiresias, the legendary seer, "who will tell you of your path, your return, and how you may go over the teeming deep" (10.535–540). After landing in Cumae, Aeneas pleads with the Sibyl to lead him through the underworld to see his father, Anchises (6.103–122), who will reveal to Aeneas his (Aeneas's) fated destiny in establishing the (future) Roman Empire (6.751–885). Both Odysseus (10:518–520) and Aeneas (6.242–260) must offer sacrifices before entering the underworld. Once inside, both heroes meet and converse with many other spirits of the dead. In the *Odyssey*, one of the spirits Odysseus meets is Elpenor, who, we were told toward the end of book 10, was one of Odysseus's men, who, after drinking too much wine, had fallen asleep on a rooftop, was awakened, failed to see the ladder, fell to the ground, broke his neck, and whose spirit then went to Hades (10.550–560 and 11.51–82). Similarly, in the *Aeneid*, Aeneas encounters the spirit of Palinurus, who, in book 5, was Aeneas's helmsman who had fallen asleep, was hurled into the sea, and eventually died. In the *Odyssey*, Odysseus also meets the spirit of his mother, Anticleia, and, in the *Aeneid*, Aeneas, as mentioned above, meets the spirit of his father. Each hero reaches out to grasp and hold his respective parent, but both heroes realized they were grasping only at empty space, a ghostly image. As Table 2 indicates, Virgil merely translated, almost verbatim, the familiar passage from the *Odyssey*.

Table 2: Verbal similarities in the underworld narratives

Odyssey	Aeneid
Three times I sprang towards her, and my heart bade me clasp her and	*Three times, there, he attempted to throw his arms about his neck*;
three times she flitted away from my arms like a shadow or a dream.	*Three times the form vainly collapsed, fled from his hands,*
	even as light winds and most *like a winged dream.*
Τρὶς μὲν ἐφωρμήθην, ἐλεεντί με θυμὸς ἀνώγει,	Ter conatus ibi collo dare brachia circum,
Τρὶς δε μοι ἐκ χειρῶν σκιᾷ εἴκελον ἢ καὶ ὀνείρῳ ἔπατ (11.206-7).	Ter frustra comprensa manus effugit imago,
	Per levibus ventis volucrique simillima somno. (6.700–703)

Even though Virgil's is a translation of Homer, the similarities in language in these two accounts will be very familiar to those who compare verbal similarities between the synoptic gospels. Many more close structural, thematic, and verbal similarities between the *Aeneid* and *Odyssey*, similar to many of the structural, thematic, and verbal similarities within the synoptic gospels, are evident in *Aeneid* 1.60–310.

The *Aeneid* opens with the narrator asking the muse to explain the goddess Juno's wrath against Aeneas, a surviving Trojan soldier who, along with other survivors, departed Troy, after it was sacked by Achilles and the Greeks, in search of a new land where they would establish a new homeland that would eventually become Italy with its new people, the Romans. Juno knew that these Romans would one day destroy Carthage, her favored city, and this fueled her wrath so she used her influence and powers not only to obstruct their travel but to try to totally exterminate them. So, after soliloquizing about Aeneas's ruin, she goes to Aeolia, "the breeding ground of storms," where, in a vast cave, King Aeolus rules the winds and, because of their ferocity, has them "shackled fast." Juno implores Aeolus to release the winds so that they would overwhelm Aeneas's ships near Sicily and "drown them all." Aeolus acquiesces, and, sends winds swooping down upon the sea—"East and South winds together, and the Southwester, thick with tempests—and shoreward roll vast billows" (una Eurusque Notusque runt creberque procellis Africus et vastos volvunt ad litora fluctus, 1.85–86). Virgil's source for this wind narrative is *Odyssey* 5 wherein Odysseus, sailing now for eighteen days since departing from the beautiful Calypso, catches sight of the land of the Phaecians and sails toward it. Poseidon, who raged unceasingly against Odysseus for blinding the Cyclops, caught sight of Odysseus and soliloquizes about preventing this landing lest Odysseus would escape his watery realm, so he stirred up the winds: "the East wind and the South wind dashed, and the fierce blowing West wind and the North wind, born in the bright heaven, rolling before him a mighty wave" (Εὖρός τε Νότος τ' ἔπεσον Ζέφυρός τε δυσαὴς καὶ Βορέης αἰθρηγενέτης, μέγα κῦμα κυλίνδων, 5.295–98). Virgil's account of the storm continues: "in a moment, clouds snatch sky and day from the Trojans' eyes; black night broods over the deep" (eripiunt subito nubes caelumque diemque/Teucrorum ex oculis; ponto nox incubat atra, 1.88-9), which is a close paraphrase of Homer's "hid with clouds the land and sea alike and night rushed down from heaven" (σὺν δὲ νεφέεσσι κάλυψε γαῖαν ὁμοῦ καὶ πόντον; ὀρώρει δ' οὐρανόθεν νύξ, 5:293–4). Virgil merely transposed these two passages of the winds and darkening skies from the *Odyssey* 5.

Following his source, Virgil has the storm take its toll on Aeneas, and Virgil's close dependence upon the *Odyssey* as Table 3 reflects:

Table 3: Verbal similarities in storm narrative

Odyssey	Aeneid
Then were *the knees of Odysseus loosened* and his heart melted, and deeply moved *he spoke to his own mighty spirit*: 'Ah me, wretched that I am! What is to befall me at the last? .... Three time blessed those Danaans [Greeks], aye, four times blessed, who of old perished in the wide land of Troy.... Even so would that I have died and met my fate'	Straightway *Aeneas's limbs weaken* with chilling dread; he groans and, stretching his two upturned hands to heaven, *thus cries aloud*: 'O three and four times blest, whose lot it was to meet death before their fathers' eyes beneath the lofty walls of Troy!... ah! that I could not fall in death on the Ilian plains
Καὶ τότ' Ὀδυσῆος λύτο γούνατα καὶ φίλον ἦτορ, ὀχνήσας δ' ἄρα εἶπε πρὸς ὃν μεγαλήτορα θυμόν; "Ὢ μοι ἐγὼ δειλός, τί νύ μοι μήκιστα γένηται; .... τρὶς μάκαρες Δαναοὶ καὶ τετράκις, οἳ τότ'ὄλοντο τροίῃ (5:297-99)	Extemplo Aenea solvuntur frigore membra; ingemit et duplicis tendens ad sidera palmas talia voce refert: 'O terque quaterque beati, quis ante ora partum Troiae sub moenibus altis / contigit oppetere!.... mene Iliacis occumbere campis non potuisse. (1.93-98a)
Even as thus he spoke, the great wave smote him from on high, rushing upon him with terrible might, and around it whirled his raft. Far from the raft he fell, and let fall the steering-oar from his hand; but his mast was broken in the midst *by the fierce blast of tumultuous winds that came upon it.*	*As he flings forth such words, a gust, shrieking from the North, strikes full on his sail and lifts the waves to heaven. The oars snap, then the prow swings round and gives the broadside to the waves; down in a heap comes a sheer mountain of water.*
Ὣς ἄρα μιν εἰπόντ'ἔλασεν μέγα κῦμα κατ'ἄκρης δεινὸν ἐπεσσύμενον, περὶ δὲ σχεδίην ἐλέλιξε. / τῆλε δ' ἀπὸ σχεδίης αὐτὸς πέσε, πηδάλιον δὲ / ἐκ χειρῶν προέηκε; μέσον δέ οἱ ἱστὸν ἔαξεν / δεινὴ μισγομένων ἀνέμων ἐλθοῦσα θύελλα (5.313-17)	Talia iactanti stridens Aquilone procella Velum adversa ferit, fluctusque ad sidera tollit; / franguntur remi; tum prora avertit et undis / dat latus; insequitur cumulo praeruptus aquae mons. (102-5)

After both heroes struggled in the stormy seas, Virgil has Neptune calm the seas (1.12-42), following Athena's intervention in the *Odyssey* (5.382), and while Odysseus makes landfall in Phaeacia, Aeneas and his crew come ashore in Libya.

Virgil and his remaining seven ships and crew limp into a harbor that had a long, deep bay, huge cliffs on either side, barriers on the sides "on which every wave from the main is broken" (160); no anchor is needed here; neither is there a need for cables to moor a ship. There is a cave with sweet water inside, with seats cut in the native stone, which is home for the nymphs. Whereas Virgil has been following *Odyssey* 5 for his wind and storm narrative, he now shifts his source for this harbor narrative to books 13 and 9 of the *Odyssey*. In book 13, as the Phaecaian ship bearing Odysseus drew near to Ithaca, they steered toward Phorkys's island where the harbor is protected by two projecting headlands at its mouth that, like the "barriers on the sides" in the *Aeneid*, "keep back the great waves." As in the *Aeneid*, there is a "cave sacred to the nymphs" and the ships can lie here unmoored (13:96–110). From the harbor in the land of the Cyclops from book 9 of the *Odyssey*, Virgil imitates Homer's "spring of fresh water flowing from the cave" and that "there is no need for an anchor" (9.136–41). Again, ships can lie unmoored here, and there is a pleasant, shadowy cave nearby that is sacred to the nymphs and that has long looms of stone inside where the nymphs weave webs of purple dye (13.96–110).

After Virgil and his crew make camp near the harbor, they eat, reminisce, and mourn—all imitated from books 10 and 12 of the *Odyssey*. The narrative begins with Aeneas scaling a crag to get a better view of his surroundings (1.180), imitating Odysseus who, after landing on the isle of Aeaea in book 10, "climbed to a rugged height, a place of outlook" (10.147). Upon his return, Aeneid spots a herd of stags along the shore with "branching antlers" (cornibus arboreis, 1.190), following the *Odyssey* wherein, upon his return, Odysseus spots one "great-horned stag" (ὑψίκερων ἔλαφον μέγαν, 10.158) and, transforming the passage in the *Odyssey* wherein Odysseus spots and kills just one stag, Aeneas needed to kill seven, one for each ship and its crew, whereas Odysseus only had one ship. Aeneas returns to camp, divides his kill and wine among his crew, and addresses their "sorrowing hearts," "O comrades—for ere this we have not been ignorant of misfortune" (O socii neque enim ignari sumus ante malorum) and recounting their skirmishes with Scylla and the Cyclops, and encourages them, "Perhaps even this distress will someday be a joy to recall" (forsan et haec olim meminisse iuvabit, 1.198–203). For this narrative, Virgil moves from book 10 to book 12 of the *Odyssey* wherein Odysseus's crew was departing from the island of the Sirens and he encourages them, "Friends, hitherto we have been in no wise ignorant of sorrows" (Ὦ φίλοι, οὐ γάρ πώ τι κακῶν ἀδαήμονές εἰμεν), recounting how the Cyclops penned them in a shallow cave, and encourages them, "these dangers, too, me thinks we shall someday remember" (καί που τῶνδε μνήσεσθαι ὀίω, 12.208–212). Returning to Virgil's narrative, he and his crew "take their fill of old wine and fat venison" (implentur veteris Bacchi pinguisque ferinae, 1:215), which Virgil lifts from book 10 of the *Odyssey*, where all day long Odysseus's crew sat feasting on "abundant flesh and sweet wine" (κρέα τ' ἄσπετα καὶ μέθυ ἡδύ, 10.184). Virgil's crew, after their meal, "in long discourse yearn for their lost comrades, between hope and fear uncertain whether to deem them still alive" (1:216–22), which is imitated from a passage further along in book 12 of the *Odyssey*, after their encounter with the Scylla, wherein "after the meal, they fall to weeping, as they remembered their dear comrades whom Scylla had snatched from the ship and devoured" (12:309–10).

Characteristics of Virgil's Imitative Technique

As noted above, my primary interest in identifying these imitative compositional techniques or practices is to focus upon compositional techniques (structural, thematic, and verbal) evident in the *Aeneid* that were considered above and that, as will be argued in the following chapters, are evident in Matthew, Luke, and Acts. If these compositional techniques or practices in the *Aeneid* are widely recognized as indisputable examples of mimesis/imitation, and if these same techniques are also identified in Matthew, Luke, and Acts, it would seem reasonable to conclude that the authors of Matthew, Luke, and Acts practiced imitative compositional techniques similar to Virgil's imitative compositional techniques—thus, these authors imitated their sources in ways similar to how Virgil imitated his. From the brief consideration of the *Aeneid* 1:60–310 above, we can identify at least seven characteristics of Virgil's imitative technique—(1) his intimate, studied familiarity with the Homeric epics, his dependence upon the Homeric epics for his (2) conceptual and (3) organizational structures, (4) narrative themes and (5) language, (6) his rivalry with these epics, and (7) his acknowledgement of his sources.

The first is Virgil's thorough and intimate familiarity with the Homeric epics. As Gnauer notes, Virgil "did not simply imitate sporadic Homeric verses or scenes. On the contrary, he first analyzed the plan of the *Odyssey*, then transformed it and made it the base of his own poem."[62] Brodie is more succinct: "Virgil did not just allude to Homer; he swallowed him whole,"[63] echoing Seneca the Younger's and Quintilian's metaphor of thoroughly absorbing and digesting one's source material prior to imitating it,[64] and the several other references noted above about the importance of carefully reading/studying the source text to be imitated. Second, Virgil relies upon the Homeric epics for the concepts of the epic form and many of its themes, scenes, characters, voyages, and places. Williams sums it up thusly, "Homer was not an aid to composition, but an originator of Virgil's thought

---

62. Gnauer, "Vergil and Homer," 881.
63. Brodie, *Birthing*, 74.
64. Seneca the Younger, *Ep. 84*; and Quintilian, *Inst.* 10.1.15 and 10.5.8.

and imagination."⁶⁵ It seems reasonable to claim that Virgil's *Aeneid* would not be what it is, or may not even exist at all, if it were not for the existence of the Homeric epics and their profound conceptual influence upon Virgil. A third technique is Virgil's adherence to his primary sources' organizational structure. While Virgil incorporated many Greek and Roman writers into the *Aeneid*, there is no question that the macro-structure (as Table 1 above depicts) and many of the narratives that make up the micro-structure (such as the storm, underworld, and harbor narratives discussed above) are derived from or dependent upon his primary sources, the Homeric epics. That many of Virgil's narratives do not follow the organizational scheme of the Homeric epics does not in any way diminish the fact that Virgil was structurally dependent upon them. Fourth, Virgil imitates parallel narrative themes—a scene, event, character, action, or place—from his source(s) and inserts them into his text in a somewhat similar narrative context or completely different narrative (or conceptual or structural) context than its original narrative (conceptual or structural) contexts. Virgil can adapt these parallel narratives by retaining, adding, or omitting material, without overall structural alteration (as in the "Storm" and "Stag" narratives) while also altering specific details within these narratives (Odysseus's knees grew slack whereas Aeneas's limbs go limp; Odysseus kills one stag whereas Aeneas kills seven; Odysseus meets his mother in the underworld, while Aeneas meets his father).⁶⁶ Fifth, as is evident above, Virgil would freely incorporate words, phrases, a sentence, or sentences from his source(s) into his own narrative. Even though Virgil was translating from Greek into Latin, some of these translations, as noted above, are extremely close to the Greek, if not verbatim. Knauer suggests that Virgil "very often 'translates' or 'quotes' one or several Homeric verses with such a degree of exactitude that his listeners [or readers] would at once recognize the passage in the poet's mind [and that] such *Leitzitate* [citations] were meant to tell the listener that he was now in this or that larger Homeric context,"⁶⁷ a mimetic practice that could also have important implications when similarly close passages are cited in the synoptic gospels. A sixth compositional practice that is clearly evident in the *Aeneid* is rivalry (ζῆλος or aemulatio). Even though Rome had conquered the Greeks militarily and politically, they were not able to conquer or even compete with the literature of the Greeks. Rome had no epic to express its ideals to compete with the *Iliad* and the *Odyssey*, and Virgil's *Aeneid* filled

---

65. Williams, "Virgil and the *Odyssey*," 273.

66. Brodie identifies several forms of adaptations that are common imitation practices: elaboration, compression, fusion, substitution of images, positivization, and internalization (*Birthing*, 9).

67. Knauer, "Vergil and Homer," 876.

this need. From challenging the Greek heroic ideal with the Augustan or the destruction of Troy with the future triumph of Rome to the conceptions of Greek and Roman afterlife, the *Aeneid* rivaled the Homeric epics on so many levels that it is often referred to as "the Roman *Iliad*" or "the Roman *Odyssey*." If ζῆλος/aemulatio, as a characteristic component of μίμησις/imitation, was understood "to rival and vie with the original in the expression of the same thoughts" (Quintilian) while at the same time transforming the original into something new (Seneca the Younger), the *Aeneid* is certainly an exemplar, if not *the* exemplar mimetic compositional technique. The seventh and final compositional technique within the *Aeneid* to be mentioned here is that the imitations or adaptations should be recognizable by the reader (or listener), as it would be difficult, if not impossible, for a reader to know whether a later author "vied with the original expression" or "transformed the original into something new" if the original is not recognized in the imitation of that original. While Virgil's imitative intent may not always be evident, that he was successful to this end is demonstrated by the thousands of structural and narrative similarities that commentators have identified between the *Aeneid* and the Homeric epics over the past two-thousand years.

Contemporary Applications of Mimesis to New Testament Texts

As the preceding discussion of the prevalence of μίμησις/imitatio has attempted to demonstrate, and as Brodie has argued, "it would have been almost impossible to receive a literary and rhetorical training that did not include the practice of imitation" because it "was a basic starting point, often *the* basic starting point, of rhetorical and literary composition."[68] In light of the fact that μίμησις/imitation played such a central role in compositional conventions, in all genres, in ancient Greece and Rome, it is (almost) astonishing that recent studies that concern themselves with compositional conventions within the synoptic gospels have, as discussed in chapter 1, either neglected or outright dismissed its role in the composition of these texts.[69]

In his earlier work, Brodie attributed this neglect to three factors. The first is Neo-orthodox theology's emphasis upon the "transcendence of the Word of God and its discontinuity with the human word." Such transcendence attributed a "uniqueness and apartness" to the Bible and distanced its authors from their historical contexts. The second is the view

68. Brodie, "Greco-Roman Imitation," 33.
69. See "Introduction," 4.

that (hypothetical) oral traditions, rather than contemporary education, literary practices, and contexts, are to be understood as the origins of the composition of the gospels. A third factor has been the rise of redactional criticism, which, while "emphasizing the work of the final author, has done little to deny the formative influence of oral tradition."[70] More recently, Brodie suggests that this neglect of mimesis's role in the composition of many New Testament texts is a deficiency in literary studies as a whole: "Among all the aids for the study of literature, there has been none that summarizes the criteria for judging literary dependence." This deficiency of a general guide, he writes,

> is symptomatic of a greater malaise: modern literary studies, including some biblical studies, are so deeply post-romantic—so imbued with the sense that authorship means originality—that the study of direct literary dependence has never been a clear priority. . . . In some deep way, the discerning of literary dependence is not on the modern mental agenda . . . . At times, literary dependence looks farfetched and complicated and out of control. Therefore the understandable response is to turn away from the phenomenon either by rejecting its possible validity or more simply by ignoring it . . . . It is much easier to invoke something missing (a background or document) or to focus attention on other issues than to wrestle with the evidence in all its weight and detail.[71]

MacDonald's and Brodie's Criteria for Imitation

It is in response to these perceived deficiencies that Brodie articulated his criteria for identifying imitated texts. Because Brodie's and MacDonald's[72] criteria for identifying imitated texts are similar in several respects, I group them together in Table 4.[73] It will be noted that I exclude MacDonald's

---

70. Brodie, "Greco-Roman Imitation," 32.

71. Idem, *Birthing* 43.

72. In his *The Homeric Epics*, MacDonald writes that he developed his criteria "from reading other scholars working on similar problems, including those who investigate allusions to Jewish scriptures in the New Testament and allusions to classical texts in Latin poetry" (8) and in a note refers to Richard B. Hays's *Echoes of Scripture in the Letters of Paul* and Stephen Hinds's *Allusion and Intertext* (207n32). Later, in his *Does the New Testament Imitate Homer?*, he writes only, "I crafted the criteria to reflect descriptions of mimetic practices in Greek and Roman authors, but they apply to all types of direct literary influence" (2).

73. MacDonald's criteria are derived from his *The Homeric Epics* (8–9) and Brodie's

Analogy criterion and Brodie's *Completeness* criterion from this list, but I address these further below.

Table 4: MacDonald's and Brodie's criteria for identifying imitated texts

MacDonald's Criteria	Brodie's Criteria
1) *Accessibility* assesses the likeliness that the author had access to the antetext.	1) *External plausibility* includes chronological concerns similar to MacDonald's.
2) *Density* concerns the volume of [substantive] contacts or similarities between two texts.	2) *Significant similarities* include: similarity of themes, pivotal leads or clues.
3) *Order* is related to density insofar as it assesses the sequence of the parallels. The more often two texts share content in the same order, the stronger the case for literary dependence.	3) *Order* is when random elements occur in two documents in the same order; the similarity requires explanation.
4) *Distinctiveness* is when two texts contain distinguishing characteristics, such as peculiar characterizations or an unusual word or phrase.	4) *Linguistic details* and *complex coherence* (not a complexity that is meaningless or confused but one that is coherent).
5) *Interpretability*, or intelligibility is the capacity of the proposed hypotext to make sense of the hypertext; this may include emulation or transvaluation.	5) *Intelligibility of differences*, Difference is the essence of writing; ... when comparing texts, the issue is not whether there are differences, but whether the differences are intelligible.

After applying MacDonald's and Brodie's criteria to the discussion of the *Aeneid* 1 above, an undeniable example of Greco-Roman imitation, and after addressing MacDonald's *Analogy* and Brodie's *Completeness* criteria, I will fit the mimetic compositional conventions that I identified into their criteria.

The *accessibility/external plausibility* criterion is met as Virgil postdates the *Odyssey* and there is no question about the *Odyssey's* accessibility to Virgil. As for similarities between the *Aeneid* and *Odyssey*, MacDonald's *density* and *distinctive traits* and Brodie's *significant similarities* and *linguistic details* (even though the *Odyssey* is written in Greek and the *Aeneid* in Latin) are met. There are problems with the *Order* criterion, for while Virgil occasionally retained some of the order of the details from some of the narratives that he imitated from the *Odyssey*, more often he radically

The Birthing of the New Testament (44–46), and much of the language in this table is MacDonald's and Brodie's.

altered both the overall structural order and much of the structural order of individual narratives of his source and often conflated passages from different books of the *Odyssey* into his narratives in the *Aeneid*. While it is not clear that this criterion is necessary for identifying imitated texts, it seems reasonable to suggest that the similar occurrences of such order in texts can be a strong indication that one author is imitating or dependent upon another. Finally, MacDonald's *interpretability* and Brodie's *intelligibility of differences* are both met, as Virgil engaged and rivaled Homer's works to transform Homer's Greek epic into his own Roman epic—Virgil "made [the Homeric epics] his own."

MacDonald's criterion of *analogy* states, "The more often ancient authors imitated a particular story, characterization, or plot element, the more likely the case that Mark did too."[74] This criterion works fine for MacDonald's argument that the author of Mark imitated Homer, the latter of which is a text that had been in circulation for hundreds of years prior to the composition of the gospel of Mark. If, however, one were to argue that the author of Luke's infancy narrative imitated the infancy narrative in Matthew, this criterion could be used to weaken that claim because, it could be argued, no one else prior to Luke imitated Matthew's infancy narrative, even though, as will be demonstrated, there is significant evidence of Luke's imitation of Matthew's narrative. Thus, this criterion may not be as useful in some cases as in others. The same could be said of Brodie's criterion of *completeness*, which he explains as, "If only some passages from a possible source appear to be reflected in the finished writing, then a problem arises about the nature of the relationship between the texts. Why should some be missing? And does this absence cast some doubt on the relationship to the rest?"[75] As defined, this criterion is not met in the examples from the *Aeneid* above, for, while Virgil retained much of the Homeric epics, he also omitted more than he retained,[76] and even for more narrow and specific passages that he transformed, he did not always transform the *complete* passage. Moreover, it would be reasonable for one to think that Brodie included this criterion to support his claim that "Luke's use of the Elijah-Elisha text is systematic, *complete*. Each Old Testament episode is used in some form,"[77] and within his explanation of the *completeness* criterion, he writes that his Proto-Luke "not only uses the Elijah-Elisha narrative and Judges; in his own

---

74. MacDonald, *Homeric Epics*, 6.

75. Brodie, *Birthing*, 45.

76. As Knauer notes, "There are 27,803 verses in the *Iliad* and *Odyssey*; in the *Aeneid*, as it has come down to us, only 9,896, i.e., little more than one third of Homer's poems. Such compression can be achieved by cutting down the extensive Homeric battle-scenes, *aristeiai* [prowess], assemblies of gods and men etc., that is, the so-called typical scenes" ("Vergil and Homer," 874–75).

77. Brodie, *Birthing*, 86. My emphasis.

way, he uses *all* of these texts. Such *completeness* is no accident. It indicates systematic dependence."[78] Thus, I think that neither MacDonald's criterion of *analogy* nor Brodie's criterion of *completeness* is a necessary criterion for identifying imitated texts.

MacDonald's *density, order,* and *distinctiveness* and Brodie's *significant similarities, order,* and *linguistic details* are the criteria that deal specifically with similarities between texts. While mimetic compositional conventions of narrative themes (4) and language (5) would fit snugly within these criteria, neither MacDonald nor Brodie explicitly include conceptual structure (2) or organizational structure (3), that Gnauer and Williams identified in Virgil's imitation of the Homeric epics, within their criteria that deal specifically with narrative similarities. Moreover, while the impression that the imitating author must have had an intimate familiarity with the text he is imitating is implied in MacDonald's and Brodie's criteria, neither one states this explicitly. Yet, because of the importance that Dionysius of Halicarnassus, Horace, Quintilian, Seneca the Younger, Theon, and others granted to thoroughly reading, internalizing, and digesting one's source prior to imitating it and, again, Brodie's "Vergil swallowed [Homer] whole," it would seem that a criterion that speaks to such intimate familiarity with the source text would be reasonable.

Concerning MacDonald's *accessibility* and Brodie's *external plausibility,* while it is obvious that an imitating text must post-date its source text, on many occasions, we are not as certain about the dating of some texts that reflect dependency/imitation of one to the other as we are about the Homeric epics and the *Aeneid*. This is especially the case with Luke and Matthew. While most scholars agree that these two texts post-date Mark, there is continuing debate about the chronological order of Matthew and Luke and the possible bi-directionality between them. In cases such as these that, where dependence of one text upon another can be determined, there are other literary clues or trajectories within the imitation that can possibly suggest directionality. Such clues and trajectories will be considered in the chapters that follow.

A final consideration concerning a criterion that is not explicitly stated in either MacDonald's or Brodie's criteria is Adam Winn's "the weight of the combined criteria":

> It is certainly possible that one particular criterion could be strong enough to demonstrate literary dependence, i.e., complex or numerous similarities in narrative structure or a large number of specific details common to both stories. Yet, the case

---

78. Ibid., 45. Brodie's emphasis.

is always more certain when there is a combination of criteria. If two narratives share a number of specific details and also share similar narrative structures, literary dependence is highly probable and perhaps undeniable. The weight of the combined criteria, therefore, is the most convincing evidence of literary dependence, and it cannot be ignored.[79]

It seems reasonable that the weight of the combined criteria be included within a consideration of criteria for identifying imitated texts.

Criticism of MacDonald's and Brodie's Criteria and Method

Perhaps the most common criticism of Brodie's and MacDonald's criteria, and thus methodologies, is aimed at MacDonald's *interpretability* and Brodie's *intelligibility of differences*. As Margaret M. Mitchell states in her review article of MacDonald's *The Homeric Epics and Gospel of Mark*, MacDonald's is a 'have your cake and eat it too' methodology, "since in his argument 'parallels' between the two narratives support direct influence, but divergences do also, since they demonstrate that Mark was not just imitating, but emulating and transforming Homer. This means, in essence, that MacDonald's thesis, once propounded, is theoretically incapable of invalidation."[80] But as was evident with the examples of Virgil's imitation of the *Odyssey* observed above, there are significant divergences in every undeniable parallel, so this criticism does not seem to be warranted. Mitchell also cites several of MacDonald's interpretations that she deems "forced or contorted" and "far-fetched," and these are more reasonable criticisms. One that she mentions is that MacDonald suggests that James and John (whom Jesus renamed 'Boanerges,' "Sons of Thunder") "are meant to remind the reader of Castor and Pollux-Polydeuces, but he does not tell his reader that almost none of the details he assembles about the Diosuri is found in either the *Iliad* or the *Odyssey*." Another "far-fetched" example that she cites is MacDonald's rendering of the stilling of the storm narrative in Mark 4:35–41, which he understands as "an apparent imitation of Homer's story of Aeolus's bag of winds," while only mentioning the similarities between the Markan narrative and the Septuagint version of Jonah—"similarities that actually go far

---

79. Winn, *Mark and the Elijah-Elisha Narrative*, 32–33. Brodie also speaks to the combined strength of the argument: "The overall strength of the chain of literary lineage depends not on the weakest link, but on a whole series of chains. That some are weak does not matter as long as there are enough that are strong . . . Again, the issue is not whether there are mistakes but whether there is enough strong evidence to make the overall connection credible, or at least to make it worthy of further study" (*Birthing*, 47).

80. Mitchell, "Homer in the New Testament?," 252.

beyond any of the parallels with Homeric texts written in this book"—in a footnote."[81] For Mitchell, this is just one example of how MacDonald "repeatedly tries to deny the obvious influence of the Septuagint on the final form of the earlier traditions of Mark."[82]

Margaret Daly-Denton levels similar criticism against Brodie, in that he "always offers an explanation for what does not fit. If, for example, the relationship between a pre-text and a later work can include both continuity and reversal (85), any apparent contradiction can be accommodated within the scheme."[83] Daly-Denton is here referring to Brodie's outline of his "central thesis" wherein he claims that the Elijah-Elisha narrative of 1 Kgs 16:29—2 Kgs 13:25 [3 and 4 Kgs LXX] and Luke contain a continuity of themes: healing; raising the dead; widows, army officers, exotic foreign government ministers in chariots, and rich and poor. Yet, in addition to this *continuity* between the two narratives, Brodie transforms the notorious Ahab and Jezebel (1 Kgs 16:29–34) into the more positive figures of Zechariah and Elizabeth (Luke 1:5–25). For Brodie, these kinds of transformations reflect a "thought-provoking blend of continuity and reversal,"[84] but for Daly-Denton they indicate that "any apparent contradiction can be accommodated within the scheme."[85] Similarly, Tony Chartrand-Burke, while recognizing that intertextual relationships between the Septuagint and New Testament are "impossible to deny," rightly contends that such parallels to this degree "stretch credibility."[86] Again, while divergences are apparent in the *Aeneid/Odyssey* examples above, Brodie and MacDonald may be over zealous in some, if not many, of their alleged parallels.

Bonz and Luke's Imitation of Virgil

Before summarizing the criteria to be adopted for the ensuing discussion, Marianne Bonz's understanding of Luke-Acts' mimetic relationship to Virgil's *Aeneid* will be briefly considered. In *The Past as Legacy: Luke-Acts and Ancient Epic*, Bonz argues, "Just as Virgil had created his foundational epic for the Roman people by appropriating and transforming Homer, so also

---

81. Ibid., 253.

82. Ibid., 255. See also Sandnes, "Imitatio Homeri?"; and MacDonald's response to both Mitchell and Sandnes in his "My Turn" (published on his personal website at http://iac.cgu.edu/drm/My_Turn.pdf).

83. Daly-Denton, Review of *The Birthing of the New Testament*.

84. Brodie, *Birthing*, 85.

85. Daly-Denton, Review of *The Birthing of the New Testament*.

86. Tony Chartrand-Burke, Review of *The Birthing of the New Testament*, 757.

did Luke create his foundational epic for the early Christian community primarily by appropriating and transforming the sacred traditions of Israel's past as narrated in the Bible of the diasporan Jewish communities, the Septuagint."[87] Bonz argues that Virgil's *Aeneid* was the inspiration and model for Luke's epic, citing what she deems to be striking similarities in organizational structure, literary motifs, and stylistic and dramatic techniques.

For example, Bonz contends that just as there is a bipartite structure to the *Aeneid*, as books 1–6 align with the *Odyssey* whereas 7–12 rely upon the *Iliad*, so too does Luke-Acts have a bipartite structure: the gospel of Luke and the Acts of the Apostles. Within the bipartite structure of the *Aeneid*, Bonz cites the widely recognized tripartite structure wherein books 5–7 are considered the center of the *Aeneid* flanked on either side by 1–4 and 5–12 (the Dido and Turnus narratives respectively). Similarly, she argues, Luke-Acts also has a tripartite structure wherein Acts 2 serves as "the narrative center."[88] In addition to these alleged structural similarities, Bonz contends that there is a similar overall narrative theme in both: the "theme of divine mission in the form of a journey that will lead to the formation of a new people," as in both works this theme is "the central narrative thread around which the entire composition is organized."[89] In addition to similar narrative structures and theme, she identifies several similar literary devices. One is that both the *Aeneid* and Luke-Acts include an "opening scene that serves as a harbinger of the major obstacles of the narrative plot that the hero must meet and overcome,"[90] suggesting that, "[j]ust as Virgil places Aeneas within an imaginary continuation of the story line of Homer's *Iliad*, so also does Luke introduce both John the Baptist and Jesus within the imaginary continuation of the story line of Israel's scriptural past."[91] "Strategic placement of divine guidance in the forms of prophecy, visions, and oracles" and "ubiquitous use of divine messengers to aid or impede the progress of the human characters" are other similar literary devices that Bonz recognizes between the two works. It is these similar structures, themes, and narrative devices that, for Bonz, qualify the *Aeneid* "as a paradigm for Luke-Acts."[92]

Bonz suggests that Luke would have known and had access to the *Aeneid* by means of Polybius's Greek prose translation or "paraphrase" (as

---

87. Bonz, *Past as Legacy*, 26.
88. Ibid., 95.
89. Ibid., 56.
90. Ibid., 56.
91. Ibid., 132.
92. Ibid., 56.

she refers to it) of the *Aeneid*, citing a passage from Seneca the Younger's *Consolatio ad Polybium* (ca. 43–44 CE),

> Consider now those poems of both authors [Homer and Virgil], which have become famous by your brilliant effort, and which you have set loose with such skill that, even though their [poetic] form has disappeared, their charm still remains—for you have translated them from one language to another so that all their merits have followed them into a foreign mode of speech, which was most difficult.[93]

In addition to this citation of 11.5 from the *Consolatio ad Polybium*, Bonz also refers the reader, in a footnote, to 8.2, in which Seneca encourages Polybius, ". . . at such times let Homer and Virgil be much in your company, those poets to whom the human race owes as much as everyone owes to you, and they especially, because you have made them known to a wider circle than that for which they wrote."[94]

If Seneca can be trusted, this would indicate that a Greek prose translation or paraphrase of the *Aeneid* would have been in (at least somewhat) wide circulation by about the middle of the first century CE (ca. 43–44). According to Suetonius, Q. Caecilius Epirota (who taught grammar under Augustus) was the first to incorporate Virgil into his curriculum,[95] presumably shortly after it was published after Virgil's death in 19 BCE, and surely in Latin. Bonner notes that immediately after its publication, the *Aeneid*

> began to attract the attention of the *grammatici*, who examined it in the closest detail both in their published works and in their lectures. . . . Virgil became the Latin school-text *par excellence*, and remained so through the centuries. Already in the first century C.E., the assessment of the degree of Virgil's success in 'borrowing' or echoing lines and passages from Homer, the Greek tragedians, and earlier Latin poets, such as Ennius and Lucretius, was a favorite occupation of the *grammatici*, and was still a major interest of the *savants* whose discussions Macrobius reports in late antiquity.[96]

---

93. Ibid., 25; Bonz's translation of *Conolatio ad Polybium* 11.5.

94. Ibid., 25n97.

95. "He is said to have been the first to hold extempore discussions in Latin, and the first to begin the practice of reading Vergil and other recent poets, a fact also alluded to by Domitus Marsus in the verse, 'Epirota, Fond nurse of fledgling bards'" (Suetonius, *De Grammaticis* 16).

96. Bonner, *Education in Ancient Rome*, 213–14. Books 4–6 of Macrobius's *Saturnalia* concern themselves with appreciation and discussion of Virgil's use of, especially, Homer. See Macrobius, *Saturnalia*.

Quintilian corroborates such investigation of the poets in the schools, writing "the interpretation of the poets we demand from the *grammatici* (quem ad modum a grammaticism exigitur poetarum enarratio),"[97] and in his required reading lists, while granting first place to Homer, writes that Virgil "most nearly approaches Homer," and he repeats Domitius Afer's response to his (Quintilian's) question, "Who came nearest to Homer?." "Virgil comes second, but is nearer first than third" (Secundus, inquit, est Vergilius propior tamen primo quam tertio).[98]

So, if Luke was writing toward the end of the first century, which is the date with which Bonz is working,[99] Virgil's *Aeneid*, at least in Latin, was accessible and widely used in the Latin schools, at least in the western portion of the Empire. However, while Seneca's references to a Greek prose paraphrase suggest that it, too, was widely received, we do not have any specific evidence that it was used in the Greek schools, probably in the eastern portion of the Empire. We also do not know what this paraphrase may have included or what Polybius may have omitted from the Latin text. We also do not know whether the author of Luke-Acts read Latin, and, thus, whether he could have had access to a Latin version of the *Aeneid*, or where he resided and wrote—eastern or western portion of the Empire. Bonz suggests that he did not know Latin, asserting that "although most educated Romans read Greek, far fewer educated Greeks knew Latin,"[100] citing a familiar passage in Plutarch's *Life of Demosthenes* (ca. 75 CE) in which he writes, ". . . during the time when I was in Rome and various part of Italy, I had no leisure to practice myself in the Roman language, owing to my public duties and the number of my students in philosophy. It was therefore late when I was well on in years that I began to study Roman literature."[101] Clifford Moore supports this position, claiming the, "Greeks rarely knew Latin" and "Latin was little spoken whenever the Greek tongue was established whether in Greece proper, Asia Minor, Syria, or Egypt."[102] MacDonald, on the other hand, seems to be more optimistic, asserting that "many educated Greek speakers, like Luke, could read Latin, and even if he were not among them, he could have collaborated with someone who could."[103] Bruno Rochette's discussion of Greek

97. Quintilian, *Institutes* 2.5.1.
98. Ibid., 10.1.85–86.
99. Bonz, *Past as Legacy*, 92.
100. Ibid., 64.
101. Plutarch, *Life of Demosthenes* 2.2–3.
102. Moore, "Latin Exercises," 319.
103. MacDonald, *Luke and Vergil*, 4.

and Latin bilingualism leans toward supporting MacDonald's optimism. Rochettte contends that Greek and Latin "coexist" under the Empire "on a basis of complete equality." He cites three lines of evidence. First, he cites Emperor Claudius's (41–54 CE) response to a foreigner who demonstrated knowledge of both languages, "Since you are ready with both of our tongues" (cum uterque sermo noster);[104] the second is Plutarch's observation that "all men now use the Roman language" (Ῥωμαίων νῦν ὁμοῦ τι πάντες ἄνθρωποι χρῶνται),[105] which he recognizes as a probable rhetorical exaggeration, but it still (at least) suggests wide-spread use of Latin, and Rochette's third line of evidence is the fact that many authors wrote in both Greek and Latin, noting Tertullian, Apuleius of Madaura, and Emperor Marcus Aurelius among others. Cribiore adds that the Latin schoolroom texts in Greco-Roman Egypt—"alphabets, writing exercises, glossaries, fables, maxims, [and] passages of authors"—were "all written by experienced hands and show that students at an advanced level studied Latin as a second or third language."[106]

So, the evidence is mixed as to whether someone like the author of Luke-Acts (assuming, for the sake of argument, single authorship and that the author's native language was Greek) would have known Latin, and, thus, could have known the *Aeneid* in Latin rather than in Polybius's Greek prose paraphrase version, concerning which we have no idea what would have been included or omitted from the Latin version. It would seem that, because we do not know which version of the *Aeneid* the author of Luke-Acts may have known and used as his source and inspiration for his own work(s), if he used it at all, that authoritative claims that he did, in fact, know and use the *Aeneid* must be qualified.

Other criticisms with Bonz's argument concern the genre issue, alleged parallels, and the absence of any verbal similarities between the *Aeneid* and Luke-Acts. The *OCD* states that the "narrower, and now usual, acceptance 'epic' refers to hexameter narrative poems on the deeds of gods, heroes, and men, a kind of poetry at the summit of the ancient hierarchy of genres."[107] Virgil's *Aeneid* is a poem written in dactylic hexameter; Luke-Acts is written in Koine Greek prose much influenced by the Greek of the Septuagint. Moreover, Bonz seems to want her readers to understand "epic" in its much broader sense—of "an idealized and extended saga of a people's

---

104. Rochette, "Greek and Latin Bilingualism," 288–89, citing Suetonius's *Claudius* 42.1.

105. Ibid., citing Plutarch, *Moralia* 1010D.

106. Cribiore, *Writing*, 29–30.

107. Hardie, "Epic," *OCD*, 530.

past, through or against which the present may be interpreted and understood"—similar to *Gilgamesh* and narrative within the Hebrew Bible,[108] but as Darryl Palmer points out, "the fundamental issue of [Bonz's] book is the *comparative* treatment of genre,"[109] and whereas there is no question that the *Aeneid* is an epic in the *OED* sense, the prevailing understanding of the gospel of Luke and Acts is, respectively, biography (without debate) and a form of historiography. Just as troubling is that Bonz insists upon a generic unity of Luke-Acts, even though, as George Young notes, "there is a definitive ending to Luke's gospel and a definitive beginning to Acts."[110]

There are also problems with her claim that there is "extensive use of parallelism"[111] between the *Aeneid* and Luke-Acts. She claims that both the *Aeneid* and Luke-Acts share a bipartite structure. The bipartite structure of the *Aeneid* is not in dispute, but Bonz claims that the bipartite structure of Luke and Acts parallels that of the *Aeneid*, while, at the same time, maintaining the generic unity of Luke-Acts. Moreover, whereas the bipartite structure of the *Aeneid* is dependent upon the Homeric epics (*Aeneid* 1-6 is derived from the *Odyssey*, and 7-12 from the *Iliad*) with specific parallel passages and themes that can be identified with precision, such is not the case with the Luke-Acts/*Aeneid* (alleged) parallels. And, Bonz's alleged tripartite parallel between the two works has been described as "ill-defined"[112] and "inappropriate."[113] She also suggests that the theme or "central action" of Luke-Acts—"a divinely willed mission to proclaim the kingdom of God and to establish the composition of its chosen people"—parallels the primary theme of the *Aeneid*,[114] but this "central action" seems to be much more parallel to the Exodus-2 Kings narrative, and, in addition, Palmer notes that the *Aeneid* is clearly not an account "of a divinely willed mission to proclaim the kingdom of God."[115] Another parallel that Bonz considers are the "catalogue[s] of names" in Acts 2:9-11 and *Aeneid* 6.792-96 and 8.722-28, the former of which (*Aeneid* 6) she acknowledges "bears little resemblance to the catalogue of nations in Acts 2:9-11, either in scale or in content," and

---

108. Bonz, *Past as Legacy*, 20.
109. Palmer, Review of *The Past as Legacy*.
110. Young, Review of *The Past as Legacy*, 181.
111. Bonz, *Past as Legacy*, 190.
112. Young, Review of *The Past as Legacy*, 179.
113. Palmer notes, "The alternative 'bipartite or tripartite' division of the twelve books of the *Aeneid* is a commonplace of Vergilian scholarship. But an alternative tripartite division of Luke-Acts (Luke 1-19A, Luke 19B—Acts 7, Acts 8-28) is inappropriate" (Review of *The Past as Legacy*).
114. Bonz, *Past as Legacy*, 190.
115. Palmer, Review of *The Past as Legacy*.

names in the latter "bear no discernible correlation with those listed in Acts 2, so there is no question of Luke's having actually used the *Aeneid's* list as his source."[116] Finally, while it is not absolutely essential that verbal parallels or similarities exist between a pretext and its imitator, one could reasonably expect that in a narrative the length of Luke-Acts, there would be at least one recognizable verbal similarity or parallel between Luke-Acts and its (alleged) model and source of inspiration even somewhat similar to those discussed above between the *Aeneid* and *Odyssey*, but there is not even one.

Thus, because we know so little about the author of Luke-Acts, so little about whether he would have known Latin, or so little about what a Greek prose paraphrase of the *Aeneid*, if it in fact existed, may have included because the structural and narrative parallels between Luke-Acts are not as similar as Bonz asserts they are, and because of the apparent absence of any verbal similarities, her evidence to support her claim that the *Aeneid* is the "inspiration and paradigm" for Luke-Acts is not convincing. That said, as this study proceeds, it will become evident that Matthew and the author of Luke-Acts used mimetic compositional conventions that are similar, if not identical, to those identified in the *Aeneid*, an observation that at least suggests that imitative techniques or practices commonly identified in the *Aeneid* were taught in Greco-Roman educational settings.

Criteria for Identifying Imitated Passages

After considering MacDonald's, Brodie's, and Bonz's methodologies and criteria and criticisms of their methods, I adopt the following for identifying imitated texts for my ensuing discussion:

1. *External plausibility* (recognizing the difficulty of dating some texts);
2. *Significant similarities* in compositional conventions with those identified in Virgil's *Aeneid* (in organizational and conceptual structures, action, theme, plot, order, and linguistic or verbal details);
3. *Evidence of intimate familiarity with source* (evidence of careful scrutiny or "digesting" of the source);
4. *Intelligibility of differences* (understanding the importance of rivalry and transformation of previous texts); and
5. *Weight of the combined criteria.*

---

116. Bonz, *Past as Legacy*, 107–8.

In addition to these criteria, every effort will be made to avoid the criticisms to which MacDonald's, Brodie's, and Bonz's are vulnerable—parallels that are forced, contorted, far-fetched, non-existent, or that stretch credibility. After carefully analyzing the texts under consideration in each respective chapter, I will conclude each chapter with consideration as to how well the discussion of the material aligns with these criteria.

PART 2

The Controversy Concerning Jesus's Birth and His Relationship with His Family

Crafting Rhetorical Counter-Narratives

Chapter 3

A Rhetorical Analysis of Mark 3:20–35 and 6:1–6

Jesus's Family in Mark, and Matthew's and Luke's Mimetic Transformations

Mark 3:20–35 and Matthew's and Luke's Mimetic Transformations

Two passages in Mark concerning Jesus's relationship with his family have troubled scholars. The first is 3:20–35, which is understood to be an example of Markan "sandwiching" in which the author interrupts the coherence of one narrative or tradition by sliding another seemingly unrelated narrative into the middle of the first one, which suggests an A1 > B > A2 organizational scheme. This inserted middle narrative typically serves as the interpretive key to the first passage in that the interpretation of the first passage must be understood through the second, inserted passage, and, combined, the intent of the sandwiching technique is to achieve a greater rhetorical effect.[1] Perhaps the most obvious example of the Markan sandwiching technique is the Jairus's daughter narrative in 5:21–43, where, in the first narrative (vv. 21–24), Jairus comes to Jesus and begs him to heal his daughter. As Jesus begins to make his way toward Jairus's home, a second and seemingly unrelated narrative is inserted (vv.

---

1. Edwards ("Markan Sandwiches") identifies eight other passages in Mark as "sandwiches" or intercalations: The Parable of the Sower (4:1–20), Jairus and the Woman with a Hemorrhage (5:21–43), The Mission of the Twelve (6:7–30), The Cursing of the Fig Tree (11:12–21), The Plot to Kill Jesus and His Anointing (14:1–11), Predictions of Jesus's Betrayal and the Institution of the Lord's Supper (14:17–31), Peter's Denial (14:53–72), and The Women at the Cross and the Empty Tomb (15:40–16:8). See also "Intercalation" in Aune (ed.), *Westminster Dictionary*, 230–32, which identifies six sandwiches in Mark. For consideration of possible precursors who may have influenced Mark's sandwiching technique, see Edwards, "Markan Sandwiches" and, more recently, Downing, "Markan Intercalation."

25–34) wherein the woman with a hemorrhage believes she will be healed by merely touching Jesus's cloak. After she is healed, the narrative returns to Jairus's daughter (vv. 35–43) where we learn from those coming to Jairus from his home that his daughter has died, to which Jesus responds, "Do not fear, only believe," before he arrives there, takes her by the hand, and returns her to life. Here, the middle narrative of the woman *believing* that she would be healed by merely touching Jesus is the interpretive key to the Jairus narrative—only *believe*. Table 5 depicts Mark 3:20–35 in its Markan "sandwich" (A1 > B > A2) form.

Table 5: Markan "sandwich" (3:20–35)

Then he went home; ²⁰and the crowd came together again, so that they could not even eat.

A¹ ²¹When his family heard it, they went out to restrain him, for people were saying, 'He has gone out of his mind.'

B ²²And the scribes who came down from Jerusalem said, 'He has Beelzebul, and by the ruler of the demons he casts out demons.' ²³And he called them to him, and spoke to them in parables, 'How can Satan cast out Satan? ²⁴If a kingdom is divided against itself, that kingdom cannot stand. ²⁵And if a house is divided against itself, that house will not be able to stand. ²⁶And if Satan has risen up against himself and is divided, he cannot stand, but his end has come. ²⁷But no one can enter a strong man's house and plunder his property without first tying up the strong man; then indeed the house can be plundered.

²⁸'Truly I tell you, people will be forgiven for their sins and whatever blasphemies they utter; ²⁹but whoever blasphemes against the Holy Spirit can never have forgiveness, but is guilty of an eternal sin'— ³⁰for they had said, 'He has an unclean spirit.'

A² ³¹Then his mother and his brothers came; and standing outside, they sent to him and called him. ³²A crowd was sitting around him; and they said to him, 'Your mother and your brothers and sisters are outside, asking for you.' ³³And he replied, 'Who are my mother and my brothers?' ³⁴And looking at those who sat around him, he said, 'Here are my mother and my brothers! ³⁵Whoever does the will of God is my brother and sister and mother.'

This "sandwich" reading of 3:20–35 understands v. 20 as an introduction to the whole (vv. 21 and 31–35) as a related narrative into which Jesus's controversy with the scribes (vv. 22–30) is inserted. Thus, the passage can be arranged, as above, in an A¹ (the first narrative), B (seemingly unrelated narrative), A² (returning to the first narrative) format, and it will be argued here that the middle narrative, the Beelzebul narrative, is the interpretive key to sandwich.[2]

2. In addition to Edwards, see "Intercalation" in Aune (ed.), *Westminister Dictionary*;

Mark sets the narrative scene in v. 20 by having Jesus, even though he is not mentioned by name, enter a house, followed by a crowd large enough to prevent anyone from being able to eat.³ Our sandwich begins with v. 21 wherein we are told that either his family or intimate associates (οἱ παρ'αὐτοῦ) heard something (ἀκούσαντες) that prompted them to go out and seize him, for, they (οἱ παρ'αὐτοῦ) said, "He is out of his mind [ἐξέστη]." The vast majority of scholars concur that οἱ παρ'αὐτοῦ refers to Jesus's family, including his mother and brothers referenced in vv. 31–35. The exact construction οἱ παρ'αὐτοῦ is not very common in ancient Greek texts; its earliest occurrence is in the Maccabean literature (ca. third to second century BCE), and this is the only occurrence in the texts that comprise our New Testament. The construction can refer to close associates such as one's fellow soldiers and to "others who are intimately connected with someone," especially family or relatives.⁴ The latter is adopted here. We are not told what the family members heard that prompted them to seize Jesus and that led them to claim, "He is out of his mind." The nearest possible passage for the narrative's context could be 3:10–11 where Jesus, by the lakeside, was healing and casting out demons.⁵ It is possible that, from a narrative perspective, it was Jesus's actions here that led to his family's actions. To claim that someone is "out of his mind" is a rare expression in ancient Greek literature.⁶ Xenophon recounts one of Socrates's conversations in which Socrates reproves Xenophon for expressing the temptation of kissing the handsome son of Alcibiades because doing so would enslave him (Xenophon) to spending money on harmful pleasures in pursuit of this youth—"ends that not even *a lunatic* [ἐξίστησιν] would bother about"—rather than pursuing the truly

---

see Crossan, "Mark and the Relatives of Jesus"; Lambrecht, "Relatives of Mark"; Best, "Mark III.20, 21, 31–35"; Goulder, "Those Outside"; Lüdemann, *Jesus after Two Thousand Years*, 23–25; and Yarbro-Collins, *Mark*, 226–37.

3. Because v. 20 does not follow coherently from vv. 13–19, there was considerable uncertainty among early copyists as to how this sentence should read, as the fewer number of manuscripts read the singular "he came [ἔρχεται] into a house," while a large majority read the plural "they came [ἔρχονται]," which, as Bruce Metzger notes, "is the easier reading" following upon verses 13–19, wherein Jesus chooses his twelve disciples (*Textual Commentary*, 81).

4. BAGD, 610. See also BDF (124), who understand the construction here to denote "his own people, family"; similarly, Moule renders the construction in Mark 3:21 "his relatives" (*Idiom Book*, 52). Two unambiguous references to family members are *Susanna* (LXX) 33.1 and Josephus's *Antiq.* 1.193.5.

5. So, Yarbro-Collins, *Mark*, 226.

6. See Oepke, "ἐξίστημι" in *TDNT* 2. 459–60; "ἐξίστημι" in LSJ, 595; and "ἐξίστημι" in BDF, 276; all of which discuss the term's denotation of "to lose one's mind" or "to be out of one's senses."

good.[7] In the *Antiquities of the Jews,* Josephus recounts that when Jeremiah claimed that those in Babylonian captivity would return to rebuild the temple, "the greater part believed him, but the rulers and those who were wicked despised him, as *one disordered in his senses* [ἐξεστήκοτα]."[8] Mark's use of ἐξέστη here is the only occurrence of this term in this form in Greek literature prior to two occurrences in the fourth century.[9] If this is the case, Mark's coining of this expression in this way—claiming that Jesus's family members sought to "seize" him because "He is out of his mind"—seems an exceptional compositional means of conveying a tension between Jesus and his family in the opening line of this intercalation.

In vv. 22–30, the author inserts an exchange between Jesus and the scribes from Jerusalem, our B narrative, which is the meat and interpretive key to the sandwich. The transition from v. 21 to v. 22 is awkward. That scribes from Jerusalem would "come down" to a house where Jesus might have been to engage him seems historically implausible, but the author is not concerned here with a historical account. The scribes make two related charges. The first is that Beelzebul possesses Jesus, and the second is that because of this possession by the ruler of demons he is able to cast out other, lesser demons. Beelzebul is an enigmatic demonic figure, probably of Semitic origin,[10] but for Mark's rhetorical purposes here it suffices to note that he is the "prince of the demons" and in the following verses identified synonymously with Satan. Mark has Jesus respond to the second charge first with syntactically complex conditional sentences. Jesus's first response about a kingdom divided against itself (v. 24) is a present general condition; the second about a house divided (v. 25) is a future more vivid condition, and the third about Satan standing against himself is a past condition.[11] Combined, Jesus, the Palestinian Jew from the rural community of Nazareth who probably did not know Greek,[12] argues like a trained Greek dialectician and demonstrates the hollowness of his opponents' charges. He then turns to

---

7. Xenophon, *Memorabilia* (trans. Dakyns); the Greek is from *TLG*.

8. Josephus, *Works* Book 10, ch. 7, 114.

9. Based upon a *TLG* search for "ἐξέστη."

10. See Lewis, "Beelzebul"; and Alderink, "Baal Zebub."

11. Following Smyth's (*Greek Grammar*) classification of conditional sentences, §2297 (516) and §2291.2 (51). See also Yarbro-Collins, *Mark*, 232.

12. For arguments as to whether Jesus spoke and/or taught in Greek, see Porter, "Did Jesus Teach in Greek," where he argues in the affirmative. For rebuttal, see Casey, "In Which Language"; and for Porter's response to Casey see Porter, "Jesus and the Use of Greek." Consideration must also be given to the rhetorical training required for one to be able to read and write complex prose in Greek and the availability of such training. For discussion, see Morgan, *Literate Education*; and Cribiore, *Gymnastics of the Mind*. Once literary training is considered, it is difficult to disagree with Vegge's assessment:

respond to the scribes' first charge, that Beelzebul possesses [ἔχει] him,[13] and equates this charge—that the spirit that empowers him is demonic—with blasphemy and condemns those who make it with committing an "eternal sin" (αἰωνίου ἁμαρτήματος), which is a difficult and problematic expression as it occurs only here in all of Greek literature through the fifth century CE.[14] The point that Mark has Jesus make here is clear: "Associate the spirit that moves me with an unclean spirit and you have committed a grievous, unpardonable offense." Jesus's family in v. 21 has called him "mad," "out of his mind;" the scribes from Jerusalem have associated his spirit with Satan; the two are of a piece. Mark now returns to Jesus's family.

In vv. 31–35, the A² narrative in the sandwich, Jesus's mother is mentioned specifically in early Christian literature for the first time, though not by name. It is important to note that Joseph is not mentioned either here or anywhere else in Mark—an important point to be considered in the next chapter. Jesus's mother and his unnamed brothers came and are standing outside (ἔξω), calling to Jesus who is inside. That his mother and brothers "came" (ἔρχεται) creates a problem with the narrative's coherence, as this would suggest that they left the home after v. 21, were not present while the scribes were there, and then returned. Again, the author of Mark is not concerned with narrative coherence but with depicting tension. A crowd (ὄχλος) is with Jesus inside; from a narrative perspective, possibly the same crowd of v. 20. When this crowd informs Jesus that his mother and brothers are seeking him, Jesus responds that it is not his family members outside who are his mother and brothers, but, instead, those seated around him, those "who do the will of God," who are his mother and brothers, which unmistakably implies that Jesus's mother and brothers do not "do the will of God"—an astonishing assertion that Mark has Jesus make.

The literary style of [Jesus's] teaching in the gospels presupposes a literary competence at home in a narrow layer of the population—an elite or no more than 10%—who possessed a corresponding good literary education. To propose such a literary education for the historical Jesus would need further substantiation, as the dominant opinion in NT research is that Jesus most likely possessed no literary education exceeding elementary instruction ("Literacy of Jesus," 31–32).

13. For other examples that where ἔχω denotes possession, see Matt 11:18; Luke 7:33; 8:27; and John 7:20. See also BDAG, "ἔχω" (331–33).

14. That this expression created significant problems for later copyists is evident beginning with Matthew, who alters it to, "there will be no forgiveness either in this age or the age to come" (12:22–32); Luke completely deletes it from his account (11:14–23), and, as Metzger notes, still later copyists added "judgment" and "torment" to the passage "in order to relieve the difficulty of the unusual expression in the text" (*Textual Commentary*, 82).

Commentators have recognized the tension that Mark creates between Jesus and his family members by means of this rhetorical sandwiching. Many, if not most, scholars agree that Mark is "hostile to the family of Jesus," that he "sharpens the sense of the alienation between Jesus and his natural kin," and places "Jesus's relatives in the same category as the hostile scribes."[15] The family mistakenly and blasphemously attempts "to restrain Jesus from his mission or redirect him to another course;"[16] they are not among Jesus's close-knit group of followers, but on the outside (ἔξω), outsiders looking in;[17] they have blasphemed the Spirit that moves him and dishonored[18] and rejected him, his work, and his mission.[19]

While in agreement on these points, there is sharp disagreement as to how this Markan sandwich should be understood, especially whether the narrative reflects a reliable historical account or whether it should be understood more metaphorically or polemically. Lüdemann contends that the narrative's claims that Jesus's family thought he was out of his mind and wanted to seize him is too offensive to be invented by the early Christian community, and, as such, it is "historical bedrock."[20] Dewey, too, concludes that this passage "probably reflects the historical tension of Jesus versus his family."[21] Allegorical interpretations take two forms—homiletical and polemical. E. Best, for example, while recognizing that Mark depicts Jesus "as alienated from his family, who regard him as out of his mind," contends that the author's intent is not polemical, but pastoral, homiletical, encouraging his readers as to how they should react in a similar situation.[22] Similarly, Lambrecht, who, as noted above, recognizes Mark's harsh treatment of Jesus's family, offers the possibility that Mark is instructing "his fellow Christians on what in his view 'true' kinship really means,"[23] which is echoed by

---

15. Barton, *Discipleship*, 67–75. Barton also points out the parallel between Jesus's family being "outside" (ἔξω) the circle of disciples in Mark 3:31–35, with Jesus's explanation to the Twelve within the Parable of the Sower in Mark (4:11–12) that, "To you the secret of the kingdom of God has been given, but to those outside [ἔξω] everything comes by way of parables, so that they may look and look, but see nothing; they may listen and listen, but understand nothing; otherwise, they might turn to God and be forgiven" (76–81). Also see Goulder, "Those Outside."

16. Edwards, "Markan Sandwiches," 210.

17. Lambrecht, "Relatives of Jesus," 256–59.

18. Crossan, "Mark and the Relatives of Jesus," 113.

19. Yarbro-Collins, *Mark*, 226n93 and 227.

20. Lüdemann, *Jesus after*, 24.

21. Dewey, "Family of Jesus," 81.

22. Best, "Short Stories," 317.

23. Lambrecht, "Relatives of Jesus," 258. Yarbro-Collins shares this view: "The Markan scene, then, functions not primarily to record an incident in the life of Jesus but to

Barton—that this new community is not based on "ties of blood heredity but a voluntary association."[24] Edwards, however, senses more of a hostile element: Mark's message, he writes, is a "hard one": the attempt to restrain Jesus from his mission or redirect him to another course, even though it comes from his most intimate associates, nay, even from his mother and brothers, is ultimately as mistaken and blasphemous as confusing Jesus with Satan! To avert Jesus from his mission is satanic. (8:33).[25] And Crossan explicitly links Mark's "hard" line to early Christian polemics between the Markan community (whom Crossan associates with the Paulines) and the leaders of the Jerusalem church (whom he associates with the Petrines) by composing his narrative

> so that there is severe opposition between Jesus and his relatives: they have blasphemed against the Holy Spirit; they have dishonored Jesus and are without faith in him; and they are directly involved in the failure of the Jerusalem community to receive his resurrectional summons to Galilee [as there are no resurrection appearances to the disciples in Mark]. This Markan condemnation reflects the polemics of the Markan community against the Jerusalem mother-church not only as a doctrinal debate (against the disciples) but also as a jurisdictional debate (against the relatives) as well.[26]

Similarly, Goulder suggests that "Mark must have a reason for telling these stories like this; and it could perhaps be that he is a Pauline who is trying to counter constant assertions by Jerusalem followers of Jesus that the leaders of the church were Jesus's family, and Paulines should do what they said. He might be countering this by saying, 'Well, Jesus's family were not much use to him in his lifetime.'"[27]

---

make the point that doing the will of God is more important than one's relationships with mother, brothers, and sisters" (*Mark*, 236).

24. Barton, *Discipleship and Family Ties*, 85.

25. Edwards, "Markan Sandwiches," 210. Yarbro-Collins counters that Edwards "goes too far in arguing that the juxtaposition implies that the activity of the relatives of Jesus is satanic" (*Mark*, 226n93).

26. Crossan, "Mark and the Relatives of Jesus," 113.

27. Goulder, *St. Paul versus St. Peter*, 11. Even the editors of *Mary in the New Testament* acknowledge that "the 'outside' vs. 'inside' framing indicates that the physical family members are not among those whom Jesus currently regards as his eschatological family," but they also add, "the passage itself [vv. 31–35] does not exclude the physical family members from eventual participation in the eschatological family" (Brown et al., *Mary*, 53 and reiterated at 9n102).

The earliest commentators on the passage—Matthew and Luke—were also troubled by Mark's narrative, so they revised Mark's account of Jesus's relationship with his family. Their revisions suggest that they understood Mark's narrative polemically, and there is a trajectory in these narratives from Mark to Matthew to Luke to defuse, tone down, and even eliminate or erase the tension in Mark's narrative that is achieved by means of rhetorical mimesis.

Matthew seems to have recognized Mark's "sandwiching" strategy, as he retains Mark's rhetorical structure almost precisely in his versions of the Parable of the Sower (13:1–23) and Jairus's Daughter (9:18–26) and more or less in three others.[28] Yet, he completely disassembles Mark's sandwich narrative here in 3:2–35. Whereas Mark situates his narrative after his "Multitude by the seaside" (3:7–12) and "The choosing of the Twelve" (3:13–19), Matthew does not use the former anywhere in his gospel and places "The choosing of the Twelve" over two chapters (10:1–4) before his Beelzebul controversy, which he situates at 12:22–32. Whereas Mark has Jesus enter a house with such a crowd that they were not able to eat (3:20), Matthew decided to delete this and begins with a demon possessed, blind, and mute man brought to him (from where we do not know),[29] whom he heals (12:22). Matthew also chose to omit or delete[30] Mark's controversial claim in v. 21 that Jesus's "family went out to seize him for they said, 'He is out of his mind'" (ἐξέστη). Yet, in narrating the crowd's reaction to Jesus healing the demon possessed, blind, and mute man, it seems to be more than a coincidence that Matthew uses the same verb while writing, "They [the crowd] were amazed" (ἐξίσταντο) that Mark uses in 3:21 to have Jesus's family claim "He is out of his mind," strongly suggesting that Matthew was indeed aware of what Mark wrote in 3.21 but, by recasting it as he did, attempts to obfuscate the problematic passage. As for the Beelzebul controversy, Matthew revises Mark's scribes to Pharisees (11:24), adds that Jesus "knows their thoughts" (εἰδὼς δὲ ἐνθυμήσεις αὐτῶν), and concisely retains the substance of Jesus's response. Matthew also adds 1) Jesus's question: "If by Beelzebul I cast out demons, by whom do your sons cast them out?" (12:27); 2) v. 28 about the kingdom of God coming upon them, and 3) "Whoever is not with me is against me" (v. 30), before revising Mark's warning about blaspheming against the Holy Spirit in v. 32.

---

28. Compare Matt 26:1–16 with Mark 14:1–11; Matt 26:20–35 with Mark 14:17–31; and Matt 26:57–75 with Mark 14:53–72.

29. Matthew does not provide a specific location for this pericope. The nearest contextual reference to a place is 12:9, where we are told that he "went to another place and entered their synagogue," from which he later "withdrew" (12:15).

30. Lüdemann opts for "delete" (*Jesus after*, 24).

In addition to these thematic and organizational similarities between Mark's and Matthew's accounts, there are also several verbal similarities that indicate Matthew's dependence upon Mark. First, of the 141 total Greek words within Mark 3:22–30, Matthew copies 56 of them, 40 percent, verbatim or almost verbatim, as Table 6 exemplifies:

Table 6: Verbal similarities in Mark's and Matthew's Beezlebul controversy

Mark	Matthew
How is Satan able to cast out Satan?	If Satan casts out Satan . . .
Πῶς δύναται Σατανᾶς Σατανᾶς ἐκβάλλειν; (v. 23).	εἰ ὁ Σατανᾶς τὸν Σατανᾶν ἐκβάλλει (12:26)
But no *one can enter a strong man's house and plunder his property without first tying up the strong man; then indeed the house can be plundered.*	How *can one enter a strong man's house and plunder his property, without first tying up the strong man? Then indeed the house can be plundered.*
Οὐ δύναται οὐδεὶς εἰς τὴν οἰκίαν τοῦ ἰσχυροῦ εἰσελθὼν τὰ σκεύη αὐτοῦ διαρπάσαι ἐὰν μὴ πρῶτον τὸν ἰσχυρὸν δήσῃ, καὶ τότε τὴν οἰκίαν αὐτοῦ διαρπάσει (v. 27)	Πῶς δύναται τις εἰσελθεῖν εἰς τὴν οἰκίαν τοῦ ἰσχυροῦ καὶ τὰ σκεύη αὐτοῦ ἁρπάσαι ἐὰν μὴ πρῶτον τὸν δήσῃ ἰσχυρόν, καὶ τότε τὴν οἰκίαν αὐτοῦ διαρπάσει; (12:28)

Mark's narrative about Jesus and his mother and brothers follows immediately upon the Beelzebul narrative. Matthew inserts three additional narratives that expand Jesus's controversy with the Pharisees—A tree and its fruits (vv. 33–37), The demand for a sign (vv. 38–42), and The return of the unclean spirit (43–45), fourteen verses (34 lines of the Greek, UBS, text)—significantly distancing his narrative of Jesus's dismissal of his mother and brothers from his Beezebul controversy. By deleting Mark's controversial 3:21 that Mark closely aligned with his Beelzebul controversy and by expanding his Beelzebul controversy and, as a result, distancing his narrative about Jesus and his mother and brothers, the author of Matthew radically revised, radically altered Mark's narrative, stripping it of its harsh depiction of the tension between Jesus and his family members that Mark so carefully crafted.

In crafting his account of the Beelzebul controversy, Luke follows Matthew very closely and perhaps even more closely than Matthew follows Mark.[31] Table 7 indicates the similarities of the narrative order:

31. Goulder's observation that Luke's account of the Beelzebul controversy "is one of the very few Markan pieces which Luke has taken in the Mattaean order, and from

Table 7: Matthew's and Luke's Beelzebul controversy narratives

Matt 12:22–31	Narrative order	Luke 11:14–26
²²Then they brought to him a demoniac who was blind and mute, and he cured him, so that the one who had been mute could speak and see.	The deaf and mute man	¹⁴Now he was casting out a demon that was mute; when the demon had gone out, the one who had been mute spoke.
²³All the crowds were amazed and said, "Can this be the son of David?"	Crowds were amazed	and the crowds were amazed. ("Son of David" not in Luke.)
²⁴But when the Pharisees heard it, they said, "It is only by Beelzebul, the ruler of the demons, that this fellow casts out the demons."	He casts out demons by the ruler of demons	¹⁵But some of them said, "He casts out demons by Beelzebul, the ruler of the demons."
Not in Matthew.	Demanding a sign	¹⁶Others, to test him, kept demanding from him a sign from heaven.
²⁵He knew what they were thinking …	He knew what they were thinking	¹⁷But he knew what they were thinking …
²⁵and said to them, "every kingdom divided against itself is laid waste, and no city or house divided against itself will stand."	Every kingdom divided	¹⁷and said to them, "Every kingdom is divided against itself becomes a desert, and house falls on house."
²⁶"If Satan casts out Satan, he is divided against himself; how then will his kingdom stand? ²⁷If I cast out demons by Beelzebul, by whom do your sons cast them out? Therefore, they will be your judges. ²⁸But if it is by the Spirit of God that I cast out demons, then the kingdom of God has come to you."	Satan divided	¹⁸"If Satan also is divided against himself, how will his kingdom stand? ¹⁹If I cast out the demons by Beelzebul, by whom do your sons cast them out? Therefore, they will be your judges. ²⁰But if it is by the finger of God that I cast out the demons, then the kingdom of God has come to you.

---

the Matthaean version" is spot on (*Luke*, 502).

Matt 12:22–31	Narrative order	Luke 11:14–26
²⁹"Or how can one enter a strong man's house and plunder his property without first tying up the strong man? Then indeed the house can be plundered."	Strong man	²¹"When a strong man, fully armed, guards his castle, his property is safe. ²²But when one stronger than he attacks him and overpowers him, he takes away his armor in which he trusted and divides his plunder.
³⁰"Whoever is not with me is against me, and whoever does not gather with me scatters."	Whoever is not with me	²³"Whoever is not with me is against me, and whoever does not gather with me scatters."
³¹Therefore, I tell you, people will be forgiven for every sin and blasphemy, but blasphemy against the Spirit will not be forgiven. ³²Whoever speaks a word against the Son of Man will be forgiven, but whoever speaks against the Holy Spirit will not be forgiven, either in this age or in the age to come."	Blasphemy against the Spirit	Luke moves this to a completely different context at 12:10.

Like Matthew, but unlike Mark, Luke's account opens with a narrative about a mute and demon-possessed man whom Jesus heals (11:14). Whereas Matthew narrates that the "whole crowd was amazed" (ἐξίσταντο πάντες οἱ ὄχλοι), Luke slightly alters this by changing the verb to read "the crowd was astonished" (ἐθαύμασαν οἱ ὄχλοι), perhaps removing any trace of the ἐξίστημι in Mark. As for the Beelzebul controversy proper, Luke follows Matthew's order very closely, excluding Matthew's "Son of David" (11:14; cf. Matt 12:23) and adding the "demand for a sign" (11:16). In addition to the thematic and organizational similarities, Luke also uses more of Matthew's language than Matthew does of Mark's. Of the 214 Greek words in Matthew's account (12:22–32), Luke uses 98 of them, 45 percent. Almost verbatim similarities are evident at Luke 11:17 (Matt 12:25); 11:18 (Matt 12:26); 11:19 (Matt 12:27); 11:20 (Matt 20:28); and 11:23 (Matt 12:30).

There are, however, two significant differences between the accounts. The first is that Matthew, following Mark, includes the warning against blaspheming against the Spirit within the Beelzebul controversy proper (v. 32). However, Luke separates this warning by 97 lines of the Greek text (UBS), adding four additional narratives wherein Jesus speaks to the crowd/Pharisees (11:24–36), another in which he denounces the Pharisees (11:37–54), two more warnings against hypocrisy and whom to fear (12:1–7), before relocating the warning against blaspheming against the Spirit into a context of confessing Jesus before men wherein the disciples (rather than the crowd or Pharisees) are the audience (12:10!), while closely following Matthew's syntax and adopting/mimicing most of his language.

The second significant difference between (Mark's), Matthew's and Luke's accounts concerns Luke's relocation of the "Jesus's mother and brothers" passage. There are three points to consider: the positioning of the passage, the verbal similarities, and Luke's revisions. Table 8 facilitates with discussing these points.

Table 8: "Jesus's mother and brothers" narrative

Mark 3:31–35	Matt 12:46–50	Luke 8:19–21
[31]Then his mother and his brothers came; and standing outside, they sent to him and called him. [32]A crowd was sitting around him; and they said to him, 'Your mother and your brothers and sisters are outside, asking for you.' [33]And he replied, 'Who are my mother and my brothers?' [34]And looking at those who sat around him, he said, 'Here are my mother and my brothers! [35]Whoever does the will of God is my brother and sister and mother.'	[46]While he was speaking to the crowd, behold his mother and brothers were standing outside seeking to speak to him. [47]['Someone said to him, 'Behold, your mother and your brothers are standing outside seeking to speak to you.'] [48]Answering, he said to one speaking to him, 'Who is my mother and who are my brothers?' [49]And extending his hand to his disciples, he said, 'Behold, my mother and my brothers; [50]for whoever should do the will of my father in the heavens, he is my brother and sister and mother.'	[19]His mother and brothers came to him, and they were not able get near him because of the crowd. [20]It was told to him, 'Your mother and your brothers are standing outside desiring to see you.' [21]Answering he said *to them*, 'These [my mother and brothers] are those hearing and doing the word of God.'

Again, Mark positions the passage immediately following the Beelzebul controversy. Whereas Matthew separates his account of Jesus's dismissal of his mother and brothers by (a mere) 34 lines of the Greek text, Luke distances the passage by a whopping 371 lines of text, relocating it much earlier (8:19–21) so that it follows upon his version and explanation of the Parable of the Sower, so far removed from the Beelzebul controversy that no reader of his text would have any idea whatsoever that this passage was linked to the controversy by Luke's source—the person who initially composed it, the author of Mark. Luke borrows from both Mark and Matthew for his version of the narrative. Luke (v. 19) follows Mark (v. 31) by having Jesus's family come to where Jesus was, but with different language. Matthew omits this. Luke seems to follow Matthew as to who told him his family was outside, for whereas Mark states that it was "the crowd seated around him" (ἐκάθητο περὶ αὐτὸν ὄχλος) who said to him (v. 31), Matthew writes only the indefinite "someone" (τις) said to him, while Luke offers the passive construction, "It was told to him" (ἀπηγγέλη δὲ αὐτῷ). As for what was told to Jesus, Matthew (v. 47) follows Mark almost verbatim, adding only "standing" (εἰστήκεισαν) and "to speak to you" (σοι λαλῆσαι). Luke follows Matthew here, retaining Matthew's "standing" (εἰστήκεισαν) only replacing Matthew's pluperfect with the perfect. Further evidence that Luke is following Matthew is that in narrating Jesus's response, Mark has, "and answering them, he said" (καὶ ἀποκριθεὶς αὐτοῖς λέγει), whereas Luke copies Matthew's, "but answering them, he said" (ὁ δὲ ἀποκριθεὶς εἶπεν). It is also extremely important to notice who the recipients of Jesus's response are. English translations are not as clear on this as the Greek is. In Mark, Jesus responds "to them" (αὐτοῖς), the dative plural pronoun. The nearest plural antecedent to this pronoun is the third person plural "they [the crowd] said" (λέγουσιν), so Jesus's response about who his family is, after pointing to those seated around him, to the crowd. In Matthew, "Someone" (τις), the masculine, singular indefinite pronoun reports to Jesus that his family is outside. Jesus responds "to the one [singular] speaking to him" (τῷ λέγοντι αὐτῷ) after stretching out his hand "to his disciples" (τοὺς μαθητὰς αὐτοῦ) leaving the impression that it is they, the disciples, who, according to Jesus, are doing the will of God.[32] Luke's account is different still. As noted above, Luke uses the passive construction, "It was told to him" (ἀπηγγέλη δὲ αὐτῷ) without any idea who did the telling. His construction of Jesus's response, however, provides evidence of the recipients, as he writes, "Answering, he said to them" (ὁ δὲ ἀποκριθεὶς εἶπεν πρὸς αὐτούς). "To them" is the πρὸς αὐτούς, the masculine plural pronoun. The only plural antecedent in the passage is, "and they [Jesus's family] were not able to reach him" (οὐκ ἠδύναντο συντυχεῖν αὐτῷ) where the verb ἠδύναντο is third person plural. Moreover, whereas both Mark and Matthew use the singular and indefinite pronoun and verb forms in the construction "whoever does the will o . . . " (ὃς γὰρ ἂν ποιήσῃ), Luke uses the masculine, plural demonstrative pronoun οὗτοι. Whereas indefinite pronouns are indefinite— "whoever," demonstrative pronouns are "used to point to someone present"[33]

---

32. It is also interesting to notice here that Mark does not include the disciples here as "those who do the will of God," while Matthew does. It is possible that this could be another example of Mark's harsh treatment of the disciples that Matthew revises.

33. BDF, 151.

or "something near in place, time, or thought."[34] Thus, it is Jesus's mother and brothers who are the recipients of Jesus's statement, "These [my mother and brothers] are those hearing [plural participle] and doing [plural participle] the word of God" (v. 21)—an astounding transformation of both Mark's and Matthew's accounts!

By way of summary, in Mark 3:20–35, by means of a rhetorical device, a Markan sandwich or intercalation, the author creates a tension between Jesus and his (unnamed) mother and brothers (who claim that Jesus is out of his mind) by aligning them with the scribes who are accused of blasphemy because they associate the Spirit that empowers Jesus with Satan. Matthew used Mark as his source, seemingly recognizes the sandwich device, and dismantles it by deleting Mark's 3:21 (that Jesus's family claimed he was "out of his mind") and separating Mark 3:30–35 (Jesus's dismissal of his family) from the Beelzebul controversy by inserting three other narratives between. By doing so, Mark's harsh depiction of tension between Jesus and his family is mitigated if not eliminated. The author of Luke followed Matthew (almost) exclusively and significantly by completely altering the context and expanding the distance between the Beelzebul controversy and the warning of blaspheming the Spirit that empowers Jesus. Luke also relocates the "Jesus's mother and brothers" narrative to a completely different (and earlier) context and radically transforms this passage from one that associated Jesus's family with the scribes in the Beelzebul controversy to one that associates them with "hearing and doing the will of God." Matthew's and Luke's revisions of Mark rendered Mark's harsh depiction of Jesus's relationship with his family unrecognizable. There is a rhetorical trajectory from Mark > Matthew > Luke that reflects engagement with and revision of earlier views and texts that were not acceptable and that needed to be radically revised. This rhetorical trajectory also indicates a mimetic compositional relationship between these texts that will be considered at the end of this chapter.

Mark 6:1–6 and Matthew's and Luke's Mimetic Transformations

A similar trajectory is evident in Matthew's and Luke's respective revisions of Mark 6:1–6, "Jesus's Sermon in Nazareth," the second passage in Mark that refers to Jesus's mother and brothers, which is provided in Table 9.

---

34. Smyth, *Greek Grammar*, 307.

Table 9: Jesus's sermon in Nazareth

Mark 6:1–6	Matt 13:53–58	Luke 4:16–22
¹He left that place and came to his home town, and his disciples followed him. ²On the sabbath he began to teach in the synagogue, and many who heard him were astounded. They said, 'Where did this man get all this? What is this wisdom that has been given to him? What deeds of power are being done by his hands! ³*Is not this the carpenter, the son of Mary* and brother of James and Joses and Judas and Simon, and are not his sisters here with us?' And they took offence at him. ⁴Then Jesus said to them, 'Prophets are not without honour, except in their home town, and among their own kin, and in their own house.' ⁵And he could do no deed of power there, except that he laid his hands on a few sick people and cured them. ⁶And he was amazed at their unbelief.	⁵³He went away from there, ⁵⁴and coming to his own country, he taught them in their synagogue, so that they were astonished, and said, "Where did this man get this wisdom and these mighty works? ⁵⁵*Is not this the carpenter's son? Is not his mother called Mary?* ⁵⁶And are not his brothers James and Joseph and Simon and Judas? And are not all his sisters with us? Where then did this man get all this?" ⁵⁷And they took offense at him. But, Jesus said to them, "A prophet is not without honor except in his own country and in his own house."	¹⁶And he came to Nazareth, where he had been brought up, and he went to the synagogue, as his custom was, on the Sabbath day. And he stood up to read, ¹⁷and there was given to him the book of the prophet Isaiah. He opened the book and found the place where it was written, ¹⁸"the Spirit of the Lord is upon me because he has anointed me to preach good news to the poor. He has sent me to proclaim release to the captives and recovering of sight to the blind, to set at liberty those who are oppressed, ¹⁹to proclaim the acceptable year of the Lord.' ²⁰And he closed the book and gave it back to the attendant and sat down, and the eyes of all in the synagogue were fixed on him. ²¹And he began to say to them, 'Today this scripture has been fulfilled in your hearing.' ²²And all spoke well of him, and wondered at the gracious words which proceeded out of his mouth; and they said, '*Is not this Joseph's son?*'

In 6:1–3, the author of Mark offers a narrative about Jesus returning to his fatherland and teaching in the synagogue on the Sabbath to the astonishment of all in attendance, which leads them to ask about the source of Jesus's wisdom and mighty works before asking, "Is this not the carpenter, the son of Mary [οὐχ οὗτός ἐστιν ὁ τέκτων, ὁ υἱὸς τῆς Μαρίας] and brother of James and Joses and Judas and Simon? Are not his sisters here with us?" (6:3). Something about the narrative fact that the crowd knows Jesus's family members leads them to "take offense" at him, which prompts Jesus's retort,

"A prophet is not without honor, except in his own country, and among his own relatives, and in his own house" (6:4). Two statements in this passage—Jesus as a carpenter and Jesus as the "son of Mary"—could be understood as slurs against Jesus, and Jesus's retort to the crowd is further evidence of Mark's depiction of Jesus's relationship with his family. The author of Matthew recognized these problems and radically revised what Mark wrote, and then Luke further revised Mark's and Matthew's texts.

The first possible slur against Jesus is the reference to him as a carpenter (ὁ τέκτων). Views vary as to whether manual labor was considered degrading in ancient Israel. Gundry, for example, while acknowledging Hellenistic Greeks' views that manual labor was degrading, asserts that was not the case with Palestinian Jews and that "Mark hardly wants to portray Jesus in a poor light."[35] In a similar vein, David Flusser, while acknowledging that scribes could be arrogant because of their social position, cites a scribe from the generation before Jesus as stating, "Love manual work and hate mastery," and notes also that scribes demanded that fathers teach their sons a trade, that many scribes themselves knew a trade, and that "[c]arpenters were regarded as particularly learned. If a difficult problem was under discussion, they would ask, 'Is there a carpenter among us, or the son of a carpenter, who can solve the problem for us?'"[36] On the other hand, others, represented by Yarbro-Collins, recognize that "criticism of social background was a standard mode of invective in antiquity" and, citing this passage from ben Sirach's *Ecclesiasticus*, suggests that the reference to Jesus as a carpenter could be understood as a slur:

> The wisdom of the scribe comes about because of the opportunity for leisure, and the man who has less business will become wise. How will the man who lays hold of the plow become wise, who boasts in the shaft of an ox-goad, drives cattle and who is busy in his work, and whose conversation is about young bulls? He concentrates on producing furrows, and gives his attention to fodder for calves. In this way every carpenter (τέκτων) and master-builder [ἀρχιτέκτων] [does], whoever continues [working] by night and by day.[37]

---

35. Gundry, *Mark*, 290. Gundry begs the question here that Mark would want to present Jesus "in a poor light," as Mark may just be narrating a historical fact or tradition with no intention at all of degrading Jesus.

36. Flusser, *Jesus*, 32–33. See also Vermes, *Jesus the Jew*, 21–22.

37. Yarbro-Collins, *Mark*, 290, citing the apocryphal *Ecclesiasticus* 38:24–27a (LXX).

While contemporary commentators may disagree whether Mark's account is to be understood as a slur, Matthew and Luke, the first two writers to engage Mark's text, significantly, and radically, revised it, suggesting that they understood his statement negatively. Whereas the author of Mark has the crowd ask, "Is this not the carpenter" (οὐχ οὗτός ἐστιν ὁ τέκτων, 6:3), the author of Matthew, in his revision of Mark, has them ask, "Is this not the carpenter's son?" (οὐκ οὗτός ἐστιν ὁ τοῦ τέκτονος υἱός, 13:55).[38] For the author of Matthew, who may have a more reverential view of Jesus than the author of Mark, Jesus is not a carpenter at all, contra Mark, but *the son of* an unnamed carpenter. The author of Luke follows Matthew here in further distancing Jesus from the carpentry trade by simply, but cleverly, deleting the reference to Jesus as a carpenter and having the crowd ask, instead, "Is not this Joseph's son?" (Οὐχὶ υἱός ἐστιν Ἰωσὴφ οὗτος; 4:22), which serves to decisively distance both Jesus and his alleged, and now named, father from the carpentry trade. And, when we recall that Joseph makes no appearance, has no role whatsoever, in the gospel of Mark, Luke's revision is even more striking, as he attributes the fatherhood of Jesus to a person who simply does not exist in the chronologically earlier narrative that he is using as his source. It is important to emphasize here that Mark does not mention a Joseph, and this silence about Joseph has led scholars to read chronologically later texts back into Mark's to explain his silence. Swete, as a representative of this view, cites Luke's birth narrative that Joseph was still alive when Jesus was twelve (2:41–51) and concludes that Mark's silence here "confirm[s] the supposition that he died before" Jesus's ministry began.[39] Such a conclusion surely begs the question that the author of Mark knew anything about a Joseph as the father of Jesus. A better methodological approach is not to read later texts into earlier texts, but to conclude that, based on the evidence in Mark, the author did not know anything about Joseph or the chronologically later birth narratives in Matthew and Luke. And as I will argue in the next chapter, the Joseph tradition grew out of late first or early second century apologetics surrounding Jesus's birth. Thus, to sum up, if both Matthew and Luke used Mark as their primary source, why would they radically

---

38. There are variant readings of Mark 6:3. While the vast majority and most important of manuscripts read "Is this not the carpenter . . ." (οὐχ οὗτός ἐστιν ὁ τέκτων), others read "Is this not the son of the carpenter" (οὐχ οὗτός ἐστιν ὁ τοῦ τέκτονος υἱός), which is the text of Matthew. For the editors of the Greek NT, there is no question that the former is the best and earliest reading for Mark and that these variants result from the objections of later scribes to Mark's text who then adopted or assimilated Matthew's revision back into Mark in attempts to appease their objections. See Metzger, *Textual Commentary*, 88–89 for brief discussion.

39. Swete, *Mark*, 112. Other explanations for Joseph's absence in Mark will be considered in the next chapter.

revise Mark's assertion that Jesus was a carpenter? One would not think that they would have revised or deleted Mark's reference to Jesus as a carpenter if they thought that ὁ τέκτων denoted a "learned man" or "scholar" as Flusser, Vermes, and others suggest.[40] Rather, the better explanation seems to be that Matthew and Luke understood Mark's reference to Jesus as a carpenter in negative terms, to be a slur of some kind, and such a view needed to be erased from the record.

The second possible slur in Mark 6:3 is the reference to Jesus as "the son of Mary" (ὁ υἱὸς τῆς Μαρίας).[41] The primary point of contention is whether or not the expression indicates illegitimacy. Yarbro-Collins represents the majority position that it does, as "it would have been expected in most social circumstances that Jesus would be named as the son of his (legal) or (deceased) father."[42] Donahue and Harrington represent a counter position: "Though some authors say that naming a person in relation to a mother is insulting, with a hint of illegitimacy, other men at the time of Jesus were identified by their mothers" and then offer two contemporary examples from Josephus in support their claim.[43] According to the former line of reasoning, not to be named as the son of one's father suggests or (for some) indicates illegitimacy. Explicit accusations that Jesus was born illegitimately are dated to the second half of the second century with Celsus, who accuses Jesus of being

> born in a certain Jewish village, of a poor woman of the country, who gained her subsistence by spinning, and who was turned out of doors by her husband, a carpenter by trade, because she was convicted of adultery; that after being driven away by her husband, and wandering about for a time, she disgracefully gave birth to Jesus, an illegitimate child.[44]

40. Flusser, *Jesus*, 33; and Vermes, *Jesus the Jew*, 21–22.

41. The literature on these issues is considerable. Yarbro-Collins, *Mark*, 291–92; Brown, *Birth*, especially 534–42; Schaberg, *Illegitimacy*, 141–44; Meier, *Marginal Jew*, 1:222–30; Lüdemann, *Virgin Birth?*, especially 46–59, along with sources cited in the following notes are good introductions to the issues raised in Mark 6:3.

42. Yarbro-Collins, *Mark*, 288. Others who support this view include Stauffer, *Jesus and His Story*, 15–19; Lachs, *Rabbinic Commentary*, 55; Lüdemann, *Virgin Birth*, 51; and Schaberg, *Illegitimacy of Jesus*, 141–44.

43. Donahue and Harrington, *Gospel of Mark*, 184–85. They note "John the son of Dorcas" from Josephus's *J.W.* (4.145) and "Joseph the son of Iatrine" in his *Life* (185). See also McArthur, "Son of Mary"; Ilan, "Man Born"; Brown, *Birth*, 540; and Meier, *Marginal Jew*, 1:226.

44. Origen, *Against Celsus*, book 1, ch. 28 (*ANF*). Celsus's philosophical polemic against the Christians, *The True Doctrine*, was probably written ca. 175 CE. It survives only in Origen's *Against Celsus*, wherein he cites Celsus's text directly and then offers

Celsus continues, claiming that when the mother of Jesus was pregnant "she was turned out of doors by the carpenter to whom she had been betrothed, as having been guilty of adultery, and that she bore a child to a certain soldier named Panthera."[45]

Celsus's claims raise the issue of whether such accusations of illegitimacy are merely an opponent's later polemical responses to the earlier claims of divine conception as recorded in Matthew and Luke or whether the claims of illegitimacy existed prior to the composition of the birth narratives and that the birth narratives were composed, at least in part, as apologetical responses to these circulating claims. Like the question as to whether referring to Jesus as a carpenter is a slur of some kind, this question may best be answered by considering Matthew's and Luke's, the earliest commentators of Mark's text, revisions of Mark's text. Whereas Mark has the crowd ask whether Jesus is "the son of Mary" (ὁ υἱὸς τῆς Μαρίας), a possible slur, Matthew has the crowd restate this as, "Is not his mother called Mary?" (οὐχ ἡ μήτηρ αὐτοῦ λέγεται Μαριάμ . . .). In English, it may not seem like much of a difference between these two expressions. In Greek there is a significant difference. In Greek, the verb for "named" or "called" is λέγεται; the root of this verb, λέγω, is usually translated "say" or "speak," but in the passive form, as it is here in Matthew, it denotes "call by name" or "called." The passive λέγεται occurs only eight times in the New Testament. Examples include: Jesus carrying his cross to the place which is called 'The Skull,' "which in Hebrew is called [λέγεται] Golgotha" (John 19:17); "Jesus said to her, 'Mary.' She turned and said to him, 'Rabbuni,' which is called [λέγεται] teacher" (John 20:16); and in Acts, the narrator introduces the readers to "Tabitha, which translated is called [λέγεται] Dorcas" (9:36). This is the only occurrence of the passive construction of λέγεται in Matthew and his use of it here radically alters his source, Mark 6:3. The expression "son of (the mother)" in Mark allows for the possibility (at the least) of a slur. In Matthew, the author eliminates this possible understanding by replacing the troubling "son of" nomenclature with an innocuous expression that merely refers to Jesus's mother's name. That is, whereas in Mark the syntactical emphasis is on Jesus's pedigree relationship to his mother, in Matthew the emphasis is merely on Mary's name—Is she not called Mary?—lessening, if not removing, any possibility of understanding the passage as a slur against Jesus.

Luke, like his revision of "Jesus as a carpenter," completely eliminates even the slightest possibility of a negative connotation about Mary by

his rebuttal.

45. Ibid., Book 1, ch. 32.

omitting the reference to her altogether and having the crowd ask, "Is this not Joseph's son" (Οὐχὶ υἱός ἐστιν Ἰωσὴφ οὗτος; 4:22)? Moreover, Luke's revision of Jesus's response to the crowd even further distances his "Is this not Joseph's son" from either Mark's or Matthew's narrative. Mark's account of Jesus's response to the crowd is brief (twenty words). According to Mark, the crowd's "taking offense" (ἐσκανδαλίζοντο) against Jesus immediately follows upon the references to Jesus's mother, brothers, and sisters, as though they are "taking offense" that someone with that family background could possess the wisdom and have the ability to perform the deeds attributed to him. Jesus's response to the crowd—that "A prophet is not without honor except in his hometown [πατρίδι], among his family [συγγενεῦσιν], and in his own home [οἰκίᾳ]"—supports the contention that the crowd's offense is aimed more against Jesus's family than anything else. Matthew's account is even briefer (thirteen words), but Matthew adds "Where then [did] this one [get] these things?" between the reference to Jesus's family members and the crowd taking offense against him, at least suggesting that the cause of offense is not Jesus's family as much as it is the origin of his wisdom and power. In addition, in revising Jesus's response to the crowd, Matthew's omission of Mark's "his family" (συγγενεῦσιν) erases Mark's implication that Jesus's family members do not honor or respect him. Luke's account (over 110 Greek words) is about five times longer than Mark's and over eight times longer than Matthew's. After Luke has Jesus read from the Septuagint,[46] Luke writes, "All spoke well of him and were amazed at the gracious words that came from his mouth" (v. 22), which suggests a positive view of Jesus. This is followed by his "Is this not Joseph's son?," which does not seem to be a derogatory question, followed by two cynical retorts by Jesus implying that he, like notable prophets of old, was sent to Gentiles rather than Israel. Of the many differences between Luke's account here and Mark's and Matthew's accounts, two points are relevant to this immediate discussion. First, whereas Mark has his Jesus say that a prophet is not honored in his homeland, by his relatives, or household, and Matthew's Jesus omits the relatives, Luke's Jesus, however, says only, "No prophet is welcome in his hometown [ἐν τῇ πατρίδι αὐτοῦ]" (v. 24), omitting both family (συγγενεῦσιν) and household (οἰκίᾳ) and thus eliminating any possibility whatsoever that Jesus was not accepted by his family members. Second, in Mark, Jesus's response to the crowd followed immediately upon their expressed "offense" concerning his family; there are no words in the Greek text between concern about Jesus's family and Jesus's response. In Matthew, Jesus's response follows the crowd's

---

46. It is highly improbable that Jesus, the Galilean Jew, would read from the Greek translation of the Hebrew Bible. For references to the issue of whether Jesus would be literate enough in Greek to read the Septuagint, see note 12 above.

"offence" about the origins of his abilities by adding five Greek words inserted between the concern about Jesus's family and Jesus's response. Luke radically rearranges and expands Mark's and Matthew's narratives. After the crowd's radically revised question about Jesus's family ("Is this not Joseph's son?") that sidesteps the "son of Mary" problem, Luke significantly expands Jesus's response to this question to about 110 words by adding the two cynical retorts (v. 23 and vv. 25–27). Then, it is these two retorts of Jesus that lead Luke's crowd to become "filled with rage" (ἐπλήσθησαν πάντες θυμοῦ), not "offended" as in Mark and Matthew and charge Jesus (something that does not happen in either Mark or Matthew). It is important to emphasize two final points. Mark's crowd was "offended" at Jesus because of his family, not at anything that Jesus said; Matthew's crowd was "offended" at the origin of Jesus's abilities, not at anything that Jesus said; Luke's crowd became enraged only because of what Jesus said in his two retorts to their question, "Is this not Joseph's son?," not because of what his biological relationship to his family might have been or the origin of his wisdom and abilities. Luke's revision of his sources here demonstrates remarkably impressive rhetorical and compositional—mimetic—skills.

Applying Mimetic Critiera to Matthew and Luke

Did Matthew imitate Mark and did Luke imitate Mark and Matthew? The five criteria for dependency discussed in the previous chapter are *external plausibility, significant similarities, evidence of intimate familiarity with source, are the differences intelligible?*, and *the weight of the combined evidence*. Applying these criteria to Matthew, most all scholars agree that Mark was written prior to Matthew and that Matthew had access to and used Mark, satisfying the first criterion. In both of these passages considered, Mark 3:20–35 and 6:1–3 and the Matthean parallels, there is no question that Matthew's narrative structures are similar to Mark's or that Mark's narratives are the conceptual foundation for Matthew's narratives, as it is very doubtful that Matthew's narratives would exist if it were not for Mark's. There is also no doubt that Matthew and Mark share similar and specific narrative details and much verbatim vocabulary. There is no question that Matthew was intimately familiar with Mark—he "swallowed him whole." The weight of the combined evidence makes for a strong, if not irrefutable, case for Matthew's dependence upon Mark. What about the differences? Are they intelligible? Matthew could not accept Mark's implication or explicit claims that Jesus may be illegitimate and that his family members, especially his mother, were not part of his inner circle of followers but, rather his opponents, outsiders, so he significantly altered his source via compositional strategies similar to how Virgil altered the Homeric epics. If Virgil digested, absorbed, and imitated the *Odyssey* as Greco-Roman writers and educators understood the term *imitate* and in accordance with the above criteria, and if the author of Matthew used similar if not identical compositional strategies in his rewriting of Mark and meets the above criteria, it seems then that a strong case can be made that Matthew digested, absorbed, imitated, and rivaled Mark.

Applying these criteria to Luke, most scholars would agree—whether they think Luke knew Matthew or not—that Matthew is chronologically earlier than Luke. Working from the understanding that Matthew is chronologically prior to Luke and from the understanding that the author of Luke had access to other Greek texts—including but not limited to the Septuagint, Paul's letters, and Josephus[47]—it is *plausible* that he could have also had *access* to Matthew, which was the most popular gospel in the second century.[48] Based on the analysis above, there is no question that Luke shares similar and identical narrative structure, specific narrative details and verbatim vocabulary with both Mark and especially Matthew, and many of the narrative similarities and much of the verbatim vocabulary with Matthew occur in passages that are not in Mark. Based on the analysis above, Luke had just as intimate a familiarity with Matthew as Matthew had with Mark and as he had with Mark. Conceptually, because of Luke's strong dependence upon Matthew, it would seem that Matthew's text influenced Luke's. The differences between Luke and his two sources can be reasonably explained. Like Matthew, Luke disagreed with what Mark wrote about Jesus's relationship with his family members, especially his mother, and he was not at all satisfied with Matthew's revisions and thus distances Jesus further from the controversy than Matthew did, while using Matthew's revi-

---

47. See Pervo, *Dating Acts*, especially 51–258; and chapter 6 below.

48. In his careful study of the text of Matthew in the second century, Bellinzoni writes,

> The evidence also suggests that toward the middle of the second century the Gospel of Matthew was known and used in various regions of the Church: Palestine, Syria, the area east of the Jordan, Phrygia, Egypt, and Rome. This relatively widespread use suggests that the Gospel of Matthew shared a popularity accorded to no other Gospel of that period. What we cannot say, however, is what status the Gospel of Matthew had within these several communities in that period. It apparently did not have the status of scripture. Neither was it cited by name (except by Papias) or with great care or precision. The authors of the writings in this period seem rather to have alluded to Matthew or cited it with considerable freedom, perhaps from memory. ("Gospel of Matthew in the Second Century," 236)

sions as his conceptual and narrative model. As Matthew altered his source, so Luke transformed his sources via Greco-Roman mimetic compositional strategies similar to how Virgil transformed the *Odyssey*. If Virgil digested, absorbed, and imitated the Homeric epics as Greco-Roman writers and educators understood the term *imitate*, and if Luke used similar if not identical compositional strategies in his rewriting of Mark and Matthew, it seems then that a strong case can be made that Luke digested, absorbed, imitated, and seriously rivaled both Mark and Matthew.

Matthew transformed Mark and "made it his own:" Luke transformed Mark and Matthew "making them his own" in ways similar to how students and authors of the period were encouraged to "make it their own" via the rhetorical and compositional practice of μίμησις.

Chapter 4

Matthew's Infancy Narrative (Matt 1–2)

Mimetically Transforming Passages from the Septuagint

EVEN THOUGH THE MAJORITY of scholars acknowledge that the author of Matthew used Mark as his primary source, few of them understand Matthew's birth narrative as a response of any kind to anything that Mark wrote. I have argued and attempted to demonstrate in the previous chapter that, via Greco-Roman mimesis, the author of Matthew engaged, revised/(radically) transformed statements in Mark that concern Jesus's relationship with his family, including his mother. This chapter considers further the issues raised in Mark, and there are two prongs to the following argument. First, the birth narrative in Matthew, more specifically the foretelling-of-Jesus's-birth narrative (1:18–25), is, at least in part, a further response to issues raised in Mark's gospel and that may have been in wider circulation concerning Mary's pregnancy and Jesus's birth. Second, and as I noted in the Introduction, Matthew did not have a model of a birth narrative of Jesus, as he did, for example, of the Beelzebul controversy, to use as his inspiration or model, so he had to create one, but he did not have to create it from scratch. Instead, it will be demonstrated that he carefully studied the Septuagint, as Virgil studied Homer, and adapted and transformed a wide variety of passages, via compositional practices very similar to Virgil's use of Homer, to create something totally new that became his response to the issues raised in Mark and that were probably in wider circulation concerning Mary's pregnancy and Jesus's birth. Such a careful rhetorical analysis of Matthew's birth narrative is a necessary precursor to the next chapter, wherein I will argue that Luke knew and used Matthew's birth narrative as his primary source for his foretelling-of-Jesus's-birth narrative (1:18–25) and Jesus's-birth-and-visitors narrative (2:1–12) and, by means of the Greco-Roman rhetorical and compositional practices of mimesis, radically transformed them.

What exigence existed that prompted Matthew to craft his genealogy and birth narrative (or, perhaps better, conception narrative) of Jesus?

Representing many scholars' responses to this question, Raymond Brown[1] lists as one of the more obvious possibilities that early followers of Jesus were curious about his ancestors, immediate family, and place of birth. Another that he suggests is the possibility that Matthew was responding to Jewish skepticism that their Messiah could be born in Galilee as reflected in John 7:41–42, 52.[2] There is nothing in Paul's letters concerning the birth of Jesus that would necessitate the need for a birth narrative. Mark, Matthew's primary source for his gospel material, did not include a genealogy or birth narrative that he could engage like he engaged other portions of Mark. As noted in the last chapter, Celsus raised issues surrounding Jesus's birth that seemed to warrant a rebuttal, but he was writing within the last quarter of the second century (ca. 180) and the prevailing view is that Matthew was written at least in some form similar to our current critical editions before then. While we cannot ignore the possibility that Celsus was presenting views concerning Jesus's birth that existed as early as the first century and that Matthew, in his genealogy and birth narrative, was responding to these views, we are confident that Matthew did use Mark as his primary source and that there is narrative material in Mark that could be understood to suggest that Jesus was born illegitimately. What better way is there to respond to the circulating claim that Jesus was born illegitimately than to argue, instead, that his mother's obvious pregnancy prior to her marriage was part of a divine plan and that she was not an immoral young woman but, rather, a pure virgin who conceived by the Spirit of God as foretold by the ancient prophets? Such was one of the author of Matthew's objectives as he set out to craft his birth narrative. The author of Matthew is here constructing an argument as a counter-narrative concerning Mary's pregnancy and Jesus's lineage and birth and employs a variety of rhetorical devices—genealogy, grammatical constructions, appeals to divine authority and legitimacy, imitations and transformations of authoritative texts—to achieve his apologetical and rhetorical objectives.

---

1. Brown, *Birth*, 28.

2. Ibid., 28. Within the context of Jesus speaking in Jerusalem, John writes, "On hearing his words, some of the crowd said, 'This must certainly be the Prophet.' Others said, 'This is the Messiah.' But others argued, 'Surely the Messiah is not to come from Galilee? Does not scripture say that the Messiah is to be of the family of David, from David's village of Bethlehem?' Thus he was the cause of a division among the people" (7:41–43). Brown relates the question of Jesus's illegitimacy to this passage and suggests the possibility that the birth narrative was crafted as an apologetical response thereto.

The Genealogy

In the ancient world, genealogies served several functions that range from documenting actual kinship relationships among individuals, to establishing census lists, and especially for grounding "a claim to power, status, rank, office or inheritance in an earlier ancestor." The latter were typically used by rulers, priests, or those in authoritative positions to justify and support their claims to leadership.[3] With the rise of the importance of the priesthood in ancient Israel after their return from Babylonian captivity, it is easy to understand why the genealogies in our Hebrew Bible (especially Ezra–Nehemiah and 1 and 2 Chronicles) were penned by scribal priests, for if someone who claimed to be a priest could not demonstrate his priestly ancestral inheritance, he would not be able to assume this culturally important and powerful position. The apologetical and rhetorical aims of crafting such genealogies are patently obvious, as Johnson's concluding summary of his study of Old Testament genealogies indicates:

> So it becomes clear that in the OT the genealogical form was used in a variety of ways, but above all for apologetic purposes, both national and theological. As such, a kind of midrashic exegesis could be utilized to construct genealogies that communicated the convictions of the author.... [I]n the work of the Chronicler, we have a mass of genealogical material, the purpose of which is to center attention on the institution of the temple cultus by David as well as on the loyalty of all Israel to the Davidic theocracy. For the Chronicler, above all, 'la généalogie était une œuvre e'art' ["the genealogy was a work of art"]. This means, in essence, that the genealogical form could be used as an alternative to narrative or poetic forms of expression, that is, as one of several methods of writing history and of expressing the theological and nationalistic concerns of a people.[4]

Matthew relied upon and borrowed genealogies in the Septuagint, especially 1 Chronicles (1 Para LXX) 1:27—2:15 and Ruth 4:18–22, to craft his genealogy of Jesus, and I hope to demonstrate that his genealogy, like those within the Old Testament, is not only fictional[5] but, more interestingly, apologetically, polemically, and rhetorically motivated.

---

3. Wilson, "Genealogy." See also idem, "Old Testament Genealogies"; Thomas, "Genealogy"; and M. Johnson, *Purpose of the Biblical Genealogies*.

4. Johnson, *Purpose of the Biblical Genealogies*, 81–82.

5. Luz articulates the scholarly consensus: "... scholarship, probably in this case with finality, has recognized that it is a fiction" (*Matthew*, 87).

For convenience of reference during this discussion, Matthew's genealogy is provided, and I translate the text so as to convey the consistency of the Greek text ("A begat B") until we get to Jesus, where the pattern is broken, an important syntactical move that will have important implications when we consider Luke's genealogy in the next chapter.

> ¹The book of [the] genealogy of Jesus Christos, son of David, son of Abraham. ²Abraham begat Isaac, Isaac begat Jacob, Jacob begat Judah and his brothers. ³Judah begat Perez and Zarah, their mother was Tamar, Perez begat Hezron, Hezron begat Ram, ⁴Ram begat Amminadab, Amminadab begat Nahshon, Nahshon begat Salmon, ⁵Salmon begat Boaz, his mother was Rahab, Boaz begat Obed; his mother was Ruth; Obed begat Jesse; ⁶Jesse begat David, the king. David begat Solomon, from the wife of Uriah, ⁷Solomon begat Rheoboam, Rehoboam begat Abijah, Abijah begat Asa, ⁸Asa begat Jehoshsphat, Jehoshaphat begat Joram, Joram begat Uzziah, ⁹Uzziah begat Jotham, Jotham begat Ahaz, Ahaz begat Hezekiah, ¹⁰Hezekiah begat Manasseh begat Amon, Amon begat Josiah; ¹¹Josiah begat Jeconiah and his brothers at the time of the deportation to Babylon. ¹²After the deportation to Babylon, Jeconiah begat Shealtiel, Shealtiel of Zerubbabel, ¹³Zerubbabel begat Abiud, Abiud begat Eliakim, Eliakim begat Azor, ¹⁴Azor begat Zadok, Zadok begat Achim, Achim begat Eliud, ¹⁵Eliud begat Eleazar, Eleazar begat Matthan, Matthan begat Jacob, ¹⁶Jacob begat Joseph, the husband of Mary, who gave birth to Jesus who is called the Christos. ¹⁷There were thus fourteen generations from Abraham to David, fourteen from David until the deportation to Babylon, and fourteen from the deportation until the Christos.

Matthew informs readers that the genealogy is organized into three groups of fourteen generations (v. 17), which, as Davies and Allison note, is "obviously artificial rather than historical,"[6] and scholars have proffered a wide variety of possible explanations for this organizational structure.[7]

---

6. Davies and Allison, *Gospel According to Saint Matthew*, 1:161.

7. Davies and Allison briefly discuss seven possible reasons for this 3 × 14 scheme before settling upon their favorite: the Hebrew practice of gematria, attributing numerical value for letters, words, and phrases. As they explain it, "David's name has three consonants, the numerical value of which amounts to fourteen in Hebrew: $d + w + d = 4 + 6 + 4 = 14$. So the suggestion is this; Matthew's genealogy has 3 × 14 generations because David's name has three consonants whose sum is fourteen" (163). The first problem with this is that Matthew was writing in Greek, not Hebrew, and using the Septuagint, written in Greek, and expecting a Greek reading audience. Brown (*Birth*, 80n38) discusses other problems.

As Table 10 indicates, there are problems with this 3 x 14 organizational scheme.

Table 10: Matthew's 3 x 14 organizational structure

Number of generations	Abraham to David (Matt 1:2–6a)	David to Babylonian Captivity (Matt 1:6b–11)	Deportation to the Χριστός (Matt 1:12–16)
1	Abraham to Isaac	David to Solomon	Jeconiah to Shealtiel
2	Isaac to Jacob	Solomon to Rehoboam	Shealtiel to Zerubbabel
3	Jacob to Judah	Rehoboam to Abijah	Zerubbabel to Abiud
4	Judah to Perez	Abijah to Asa	Abiud to Elakim
5	Perez to Hezron	Asa to Jehoshaphat	Eliakim to Azor
6	Hezron to Ram (Aram)	Jehoshaphat to Joram	Azor to Zadok
7	Ram to Amminadab	Joram to Uzziah	Zadok to Achim
8	Amminadab to Nashon	Uzziah to Jotham	Achim to Eliud
9	Nashon to Salmon	Jotham to Ahaz	Eliud to Eleazar
10	Salmon to Boaz	Ahaz to Hezekiah	Eleazar to Matthan
11	Boaz to Obed	Hezekiah to Manasseh	Matthan to Jacob
12	Obed to Jesse	Manasseh to Amon (Amos)	Jacob to Joseph
13	Jesse to David	Amon (Amos) to Josiah	Joseph to Jesus
14	—	Josiah to Jeconiah	—
Total number of narrative years	From Abraham to David, approximately 750 years	From David to deportation to Babylon, approximately 400 years	From deportation to Jesus's birth, 600 years
Span of generations	Approximately 58 years (750 divided by 13)	Approximately 28.5 years (400 divided by 14)	Approximately 46 years (600 divided by 13)

The two most obvious problems are that only thirteen generations are listed in the first (Abraham to David) and last (Deportation to Jesus's birth) sections of the genealogy and that the span of years comprising a generation varies from 28.5 to 46 to 58.

There are other problems. In 1:3, Matthew has Hezron as the father of *Aram*. In 1 Chronicles 2:9 of the Hebrew Bible, the three sons of Hezron are: Jerahmeel, *Ram*, and Chelubai, and in the genealogy in Ruth 4:19 of the Hebrew Bible, *Ram* is listed as the son of Hezron. However, the Septuagint account of 1 Chronicles 2:9 has *Aram* instead of *Ram*, and the genealogy in Ruth in the Septuagint is different still with Arran as the son of Hezron. Matthew appears to have followed the Septuagint version of 1 Chronicles 2:9. More interestingly, however, is that Hezron is listed as the son of Perez in Genesis 46:12 within the context of Jacob making the trip to Egypt, whereas Amminidab, the son of Aram in Matthew's genealogy, does not appear until the Israelites' wanderings in the desert in Numbers 1:7, approximately 400 narrative years later. As Brown notes, "Matthew allots one name, Aram (never mentioned in the Pentateuch), and only two generations to a period which traditionally (and perhaps factually) lasted some 400 years."[8] Another problem is Matthew's claim that Rahab is the mother of Boaz (1:5). There is simply no other biblical support in either the Hebrew Bible or Septuagint that Rahab is the mother of Boaz. Just as troubling is that Rahab appears in the conquest narratives of Joshua 2 and 6 whereas Boaz's appearance in Ruth is "at the time of the Judges" (Ruth 1:1), a narrative span of approximately 200 years. Davies and Allison suggest, "Maybe we have here the product of Matthean fancy," but I suspect Matthew is more rhetorically motivated than Davies and Allison allow. Why Matthew may have inserted her name here will be discussed below. The next problem is 1:8, "Joram [is the father of] Uzziah." Matthew omits three kings and three generations between Joram and Uzziah—Ahaziah (842 BCE), Jehoash (842–837 BCE), and Amaziah (837–800 BCE)—who are listed in 1 Chronicles 3:11–12. The most likely explanation for the omissions is to retain his 3 x 14 organizational structure.[9] The next problem is 1:11, "Josiah was the father of Jeconiah and his brothers." According to 1 Chronicles, Josiah was not the father of Jeconiah. Rather, Josiah's second son, Jehoiakim, was the father of Jeconiah, so Josiah would be his grandfather (3:15–16). Again, one king and one generation is omitted, probably to retain the fourteen generation organizational structure. The names between Zerubbabel and Joseph create more serious problems. According to 1 Chronicles 3:19–20, Zerubbabel had seven sons and nothing similar to an Abiud is among them. In addition, there is no information in the Hebrew Bible about any of the men inclusively named between Aliud and Jacob, Joseph's alleged father in Matthew. As Allison and

---

8. Brown (*Birth*, 61), allows more possibility of historical "factuality" to the Pentateuch narrative than I think it warrants.

9. Davies and Allison, *Matthew*, 1:176; and Brown, *Birth*, 60.

Davies note, "About five hundred years lie between Zerubbabel (who disappeared from history around 519 B.C.) and Joseph. For this period Matthew has only nine names, excluding Zerubbabel and Joseph.... Nothing could reveal more clearly the incomplete and inexact character of the evangelist's list of Jesus's ancestors."[10] From a rhetorical and compositional perspective, one could conclude that, because there was no textual evidence to draw upon, Matthew, out of necessity to try to maintain his fourteen generation structure, simply filled in the gap with fictitious names in an attempt to keep his structure from crumbling. I will consider how Joseph fits within these fictitious names below.

The Four Women

Another problem within the genealogy are the references to the four women—Tamar, Rahab, Ruth, and "the wife of Uriah" (Bathsheba). Because of the rhetorical/apologetical importance of these women in Matthew's genealogy (and argument), the inclusion of these women warrant brief comments. Scholars often note that the appearance of women in (Hebrew) genealogies is unusual. Yet, no less than twenty-four women are mentioned by name or referred to in the genealogy in 1 Chronicles 2–3, arguably Matthew's primary source for his genealogy.[11] Two of those in Matthew's genealogy are also listed in 1 Chronicles, Tamar and Bathsheba, but not in any way that either aligns them with or distinguishes them from the other women in the genealogy whereas their appearance in Matthew's genealogy along with Rahab and Ruth has attracted considerable scholarly attention,[12] and given rise to a number of different views as to why Matthew included them in his genealogy. First, a consideration of the women.

According to the narrative of Genesis 38, Tamar, a Canaanite, is the wife of Judah's oldest son, Er, who "did wicked in the eyes of the Lord," so

---

10. Davies and Allison, *Matthew*, 1:181.

11. These include Bathshua (2:3), Tamar (2:4), Zeruiah and Abigail (2:16), another Abigail (2:17), Azubah (2:18), Eprath (2:19), Machir (2:21), Ephratah (2:24), Abijah (2:25), Atarah (2:26), Abihail (2:29), Sheshan's unnamed daughter (2:34-35), Ephah (2:46), Maacha (2:48), Achsah's daughter (2:49), Ahinoam (3:1), another Abigail (3:1), Maacah (3:2), Haggith (3:2), one of David's wives, Eglah (3:4), Bathsheba (3:5), Tamar, David's sister (3:9), and Shelomit (3:19).

12. The literature on these women in Matthew's genealogy is extensive: Brown, *Birth*, 71–74; Davies and Allison, *Matthew*, 1:170–74; Schaberg, *Illegitimacy*, 32–43; Nolland, "Four (Five) Women"; Weren, "Five Women"; Freed, *Stories of Jesus' Birth*; Loubser, "Invoking the Ancestors"; Smit, "Something about Mary?"; and Lincoln, *Born of a Virgin?*, 149–59.

he killed him. Judah encouraged Er's brother, Onan, to marry Tamar, which he did, and, in accordance with the levirate marriage custom,[13] raise his brother's offspring, which he did not, as he "spilled his seed on the ground" (38:9), which was wicked in the Lord's sight so he killed him too. Judah then sent Tamar back to her father's home with the promise that he would send his youngest son, Shelah, to her when he was old enough, something Judah, for fear of his son's life, never planned to do. In response, Tamar schemed revenge by donning the dress and veil of a prostitute and situating herself in Judah's path as he returned from shearing his flock. After encountering Tamar and negotiating the terms, Judah "lay with her and she became pregnant" (38:24). Three months later Judah receives word that his daughter-in-law "played the prostitute and got herself pregnant," and in his righteous indignation he demanded her death before it was demonstrated that he was the father.

Rahab's story begins in Joshua 2 when two men sent by Joshua to spy the land of Canaan spend the night at the house of a Canaanite prostitute named Rahab. As the legendary story of the conquest of Jericho is told,[14] word reaches the king of Jericho that these two men are exploring the land and are staying at Rahab's home; in turn, he sends troops to capture the men, but Rahab deceives the troops by telling them that the men had already left, when they were actually hiding in the straw on her roof. Because of her protection of these Hebrew spies, they promise to spare her home and family when they conquer the land, a promise that is kept four chapters later when the Hebrews invade and conquer.

While there is no question that Tamar schemed to have sex with her father-in-law and that Rahab was a prostitute, the question of whether Ruth engaged in any illicit sexual activity with Boaz is more complicated. The

---

13. "When brothers live together and one of them dies without leaving a son, his widow is not to marry outside the family. Her husband's brother is to have intercourse with her; he should take her in marriage and do his duty by her as her husband's brother" (Deut 25:5–6). See also Gen 38:8, 10, 26; and Ruth 4:1–13.

14. Finklestein and Silberman's summary of their study of the Israelites' conquest of Canaan is insightful:

> Jericho was among the most important. As we have noted, the cities of Canaan were unfortified and there were no walls that could have come tumbling down. In the case of Jericho, there was no trace of a settlement of any kind in the thirteenth century BCE, and the earlier Late Bronze settlement, dating to the fourteenth century BCE, was small and poor, almost insignificant, and unfortified. There was also no sign of a destruction. Thus the famous scene of the Israelite forces marching around the walled town with the Ark of the Covenant, causing Jericho's mighty walls to collapse by the blowing of their war trumpets was, to put it simply, a romantic mirage. (*Bible Unearthed*, 81–82)

story of Ruth begins when Elimelech, his wife Naomi, and their two sons resettle from Judah to Moab. There, Elimelech dies; his two sons marry Moabite women, one of whom is Ruth; after ten years the two sons die, and Ruth accompanies Naomi back to her hometown of Bethlehem in Judah, which is also home to one of Elimelech's accomplished relatives, Boaz. As Ruth gleaned wheat in his fields, Boaz took notice of her, learned of her relationship to Naomi, and allowed her privileged access in the fields beside the reapers. Naomi schemed a plan to see Ruth settled and secured (married), so she encourages her to present herself to Boaz one evening while he was at the threshing floor celebrating the harvest:

> Now, here is our kinsman Boaz, with whose young women you have been working. See, he is winnowing barley tonight at the threshing-floor. Now, wash and anoint yourself, and put on your best clothes and go down to the threshing-floor; but do not make yourself known to the man until he has finished eating and drinking. When he lies down, observe the place where he lies; then go and *uncover his feet* and lie down; and he will tell you what to do. (3:2–4)

Ruth obeyed, and

> When Boaz had eaten and drunk, and he was in a contented mood, he went to lie down at the end of the heap of grain. Then she came quietly and *uncovered his feet* and lay down. At midnight, the man was startled and turned over, and there, lying at his feet was a woman! He said, 'Who are you?' And she answered, "I am Ruth, your servant; *spread your wing* over your servant, for you are next of kin [or redeemer]. (3:7–9)

As commentators have acknowledged, the author crafts a scene of sexual allusion with ambiguous language that has led to a variety of interpretations that range from nothing sexual transpired between Boaz and Ruth to Ruth offered herself for marriage and presented a "sexual challenge"[15] to Boaz and the two consummated their marriage on the threshing floor to, because of the ambiguity of the language, we just do not know what happened. The sensuality begins with Naomi's instructions to Ruth to bathe and anoint herself (with perfume)—"to make herself enticing"[16]—before dressing herself in what many understand to be a wedding dress and then making her way down to the threshing floor, a place occupied only by males, in the middle of the night, to quietly lie next to a man who has been celebrating the harvest by eating and

---

15. Sasson, *Ruth*, 70.
16. Campbell, *Ruth*, 120.

drinking. Naomi's instruction for Ruth to "uncover his feet" heightens the sexual possibility because "feet"/"foot" is an acknowledged euphemism for a man's genitals[17] and the expression "uncovered his feet" raises the question of how much of Boaz Ruth may have uncovered. Similarly, "spread your wing" is "a metaphor indicating the protective care of the groom for his bride,"[18] an idiom meaning "to marry," without necessarily referring to sexual intercourse,[19] but could give the reader the impression that the marriage was consummated immediately or shortly after the proposal of marriage.[20] Campbell's observation, "It is simply incomprehensible to me that a Hebrew story-teller could use the words 'uncover,' 'wing' (3:9), and a noun for 'legs' which is cognate with a standard euphemism for the sexual organs, all in the same context, and not suggest to his audience that a provocative set of circumstances confronts them,"[21] is reiterated by Hubbard, "The audience probably squirmed with both fear and excitement."[22]

That ancient readers could have understood that Boaz and Ruth could have engaged in sexual activity in Ruth is further supported by what D.R.G. Beattie terms "something of a systematic bowdlerization in the course of its transmission," as translators were "at pains to remove any hint of indelicacy from the threshing floor scene."[23] He observes that the Septuagint, the first translation of the Hebrew text, omits that Boaz drank ("he drank") and that Ruth laid down ("she lay down") next to Boaz in 3:7 and that the later Syriac translation of the Hebrew Bible, the Peshitta, which was probably the work of Jewish translators, omits that Ruth "uncovered" Boaz's feet and the "lie down" and instead reads simply that Ruth "lie down at his feet,"[24] revisions that significantly alter the earlier text. In addition to translators, later commentators offered embellishments and additions to the text of Ruth 3 in attempts to explain or sidestep some of the problems. In his *Legends of the Jews*, Louis Ginzberg collected an enormous number of "sayings of the fathers" and cast them into a paraphrased form for each book of the Hebrew Bible. For example, whereas, in the biblical account of Ruth, Naomi initiated her scheme to marry Ruth off to Boaz—a bold and culturally unconven-

17. Sasson, *Ruth*, 70; Campbell, *Ruth*, 121; and Korpel, *Structure*, 163.
18. Korpel, *Structure*, 165.
19. Hubbard, *Book of Ruth*, 212 and 212n34.
20. Hubbard notes that the gesture of spreading one's wing "no doubt symbolized the man's protection of her and probably his readiness for sexual consummation as well" (ibid., 212).
21. Campbell, *Ruth*, 131.
22. Hubbard, *Book of Ruth*, 210.
23. Beattie, *Jewish Exegesis*, 167.
24. Ibid.

tional plan, in Ginzberg's *Legends*, the commentator of *Ruth Z* explains that "Boaz showed kindness not only to Ruth and Naomi, but also to their dead. He took upon himself the decent burial of the remains of Elimelech and his two sons." It was this kindness that "begot in Naomi the thought that Boaz [initially] harbored the intention of marrying Ruth;" then, it was only when Naomi was not able to elicit any information about Boaz's plan from Ruth that she (Naomi) "made Ruth a partner in a plan to force Boaz into a decisive step."[25] Ginzberg also explains that the reason that Boaz slept on the threshing floor is because "moral conditions in those days were very reprehensible ... so that his presence might act as a check upon profligacy."[26] Beattie recounts that the author of *Ruth Rammah* wrote that Boaz was "in good spirits" (3:7) "not because he had eaten and drunk, but because he had recited grace after his meal, he had eaten sweet things, he was busy studying the Torah and he was looking for a wife."[27] One last example of later commentators' elaborate revisions or interpretations of the text narrates Boaz's moral resolve:

> All that night his Evil Inclination contended with him saying, 'You are unmarried and seek a wife, and she is unmarried and seeks a husband. Arise and have intercourse with her and make her your wife.' And he took an oath to his Evil Inclination saying, 'As the Lord liveth I will not touch her.'"[28]

The allusions of sexuality and the ambiguity of the language in Ruth allow for an interpretation of the narrative that something sexual took place on the threshing floor and later Jewish commentators' attempts at clarification or explanation further support such a reading. Freed may be correct when he writes, "The legends about Ruth do protest too much. Rabbis overly stress that Boaz did not touch Ruth on the threshing floor, obviously to counteract the euphemisms for sexual relations in the Hebrew text of Ruth."[29] While these Rabbinic texts post-date the composition of Matthew, there is no apparent reason for thinking that such views of the text of Ruth could not also have been in circulation about the time that Matthew was crafting his genealogy.

The fourth woman mentioned in Matthew's genealogy is "the wife of Uriah" (τῆς τοῦ Οὐρίου, v. 6). Schaberg observes that Bathsheba is not

---

25. Ginzberg, *Legends*, 4:33 and 6:192.
26. Beattie, *Jewish Exegesis*, 167.
27. Ibid., 173, citing *Ruth Rammah* V 15.
28. Ibid., 180, citing *Ruth Rammah* VI 4.
29. Freed, *Stories of Jesus' Birth*, 40.

mentioned by name in Matthew and suggests that this is "because identification of her as the wife of Uriah stresses her adultery and not her subsequent marriage to David."[30] It is interesting to note that within the Septuagint account of David and Bathsheba's affair (2 Kgs LXX 11:1—12:19) Bathsheba is mentioned by name only once (11:3), but referred to as the "wife of Uriah" therein three times (γυνὴ Οὐρίου 11:3 and 12:15; γυναῖκα Οὐρίου in 11:10), which may support Schaberg's observation and which may have influenced Matthew's phrasing. The tale is familiar. As David walked on the roof of his palace, he saw a beautiful woman who was identified as Bathsheba, the wife of Uriah. He brought her to his place, had intercourse with her while she was purifying herself from her menstrual cycle, and she conceived. David attempted to get her husband (Uriah), who was on the battlefield, to go home where he would sleep with her (so that he would be responsible for her pregnancy); he refused, as he would rather remain with his troops, so David sent him to the front lines of battle where he was killed, and after a period of mourning, David brought her to his palace where she became his wife; he "went into her and had intercourse with her," and she conceived (2 Kgs 11:1—12:25 LXX).

As noted above, the inclusion of these women in the genealogy has generated a wide variety of possible explanations as to why Matthew included them. The following is not exhaustive, but represents the more prevailing views.[31]

1. The four women were sinners—that they engaged in questionable sexual activities. Two somewhat related reasons are offered as to why Matthew included them: because it was the divine plan that the Davidic line be accomplished "despite human sin and failure"[32] a view first espoused by Jerome (*In Matt* 9), and because "it foreshadowed for readers the role of Jesus as the Savior of sinful men."[33] The first problem with this view is that the Hebrew Bible does not present these women as sinners.[34] Moreover, Johnson and others argue that

---

30. Schaberg, *Illigitimacy*, 39; and Luz, *Matthew 1-7*, 83.

31. Brown, *Birth*, 71–74; M. Johnson, *Purpose of Biblical Genealogies*, 153–59; Schaberg, *Illigitimacy*, 32–33; Davies and Allison, *Matthew*, 1:170–73; Weren, *Stories*, 288–90; and Luz, *Matthew*, 83–85 provide discussion of the different views of Matthew's purpose and critiques of the same. My discussion of these views is derived, in part, from these.

32. Davies and Allison, *Matthew*, 1:170.

33. Brown, *Birth*, 71.

34. Schaberg, *Illigitimacy*, 32.

the four were highly esteemed in later Jewish tradition.³⁵ One problem with Johnson's argument is that the traditional material in which the women were highly esteemed is later than the composition of Matthew; another problem is that it may beg the question that Matthew viewed these women as highly esteemed. A third problem is that if the women and their situations are to prefigure Mary in some way, Mary would not seem to fit the bill, as Mary is not depicted as a sinner in the birth narratives.³⁶

2. The women were foreigners and Matthew included them to indicate that Jesus, the Jewish Messiah, "has foreign blood in his veins"³⁷ and this reflects a "universalistic undertone"³⁸ and an interest in the salvation of Gentiles. This view works for Ruth (a Moabite) and Rahab (a Cannanite), but the Hebrew Bible does not provide information concerning Tamar and Bathsheba. And, again, if these four women and their situations are to prefigure or align with Mary in some way, this view must be rejected.

3. The third possible explanation has two related components: a) There is something extraordinary or irregular in the four women's union with their partners and these irregular unions are related to Mary's irregular relationship with Joseph, and b) the women's initiative or role in the divine plan was by means of the Holy Spirit, as was Mary's conception. But, as Luz notes, the Jewish sources for b) are "either late or non-existent."³⁹ In criticizing a), Luz argues that it is difficult to define "irregular": "It can lie, for example, in the special nature of the relationship of the women to their partners. But are Ruth's marriage, Bathsheba's adultery, and even Mary's betrothal at all comparable?"⁴⁰ Luz rejects that Matthew intends any relationship between the four and Mary and cites 1:16 as his support ("Jacob begat Joseph, the husband of Mary, *from whom Jesus was begotten*"), as therein the formulaic

---

35. See especially Johnson, *Purpose of Biblical Genealogies*, 159–78.

36. Weren rejects this view because "this interpretation is a classical example of an androcentric exegesis which associates the women with sexuality, connects sexuality with sin, and shuts eyes to the far from irreproachable conduct of many of the men in the genealogy" (*Stories of Jesus' Birth*, 288).

37. Ibid., 289.

38. Luz, *Matthew*, 85.

39. Ibid., 84. M. Johnson offers discussion of the evidence (*Purpose of Biblical Genealogies*, 153–76).

40. Luz, *Matthew*, 84.

"begat" that occurs in vv. 3 and 5–6 is replaced with the passive "was begotten," but Luz's argument here is not at all convincing.

The view adopted here is that Matthew included the four women as literary allusions and rhetorical devices as one component of a larger argument. As literary allusions and rhetorical devices, Matthew's references to, and inclusion of, the women suggest that they play an extremely important role in what Matthew, *qua* author, is trying to achieve. Moreover, the only common denominator among the four women and Mary is that each one of them was engaged in some kind of sexual situation outside of marriage. That this is the case with Mary is evident in 1:18 and will be discussed below. In the case of Ruth, this means that Matthew recognized that something sexual took place between Ruth and Boaz, which, as noted above, is a very plausible reading of Ruth 3, a reading that many later Jewish commentators attempted to squelch or explain with elaborate additions to the text. It is also important to note and even emphasize that, in his genealogy, Matthew simply fabricated the relationship between Rahab and Boaz by claiming that she was his mother, an indication of the extent to which the author was willing to go to include Rahab, the prostitute, into Jesus's lineage. While Matthew never makes the relationship between these four women and Mary explicit, the inference is that even though these women have been involved in inappropriate sexual relationships, they were all part of a divine plan.

Joseph

The last problem within the genealogy to be considered here is the person, or character, Joseph. Concluding his genealogy, the author of Matthew writes, "Jacob begat Joseph, the husband of Mary, from whom Jesus, who is called the Christos, was born" (1:16). It is interesting to observe that, while many contemporary scholars acknowledge the fictional nature of the genealogy in Matthew, most still infer (explicitly or implicitly) that Joseph was a historical person and rely upon appeals to tradition and the criterion of multiple attestation to support their position. For example, in their discussion of the birth narrative in Matthew, Davies and Allison, claim that "certain elements of our story," including "at least the names of Jesus, Mary, and Joseph," "must be traditional because they must be historical."[41] Davies and Allison infer that the names must be traditional because they are historical because "they also appear in Luke 1–2,"[42] which, in their view, is an example

---

41. Davies and Allison, *Matthew*, 1:193.
42. Ibid., 1:194n15.

of multiple attestation. As employed in historical scholarship of the gospels, multiple or wide attestation "offers some assurance that sayings and actions of Jesus which are attested by sources independently of one another may be authentic."[43] "Independence" is the key component of multiple attestation, and Davies and Allison are adherents of the prevailing view that Matthew and Luke were written independently from one another.[44] R. E. Brown also represents this position:

> Since it is generally agreed among scholars that Matthew and Luke wrote independently of each other, without knowing the other's work, agreement between the two infancy narratives would suggest the existence of a common infancy tradition earlier than either evangelist's work—a tradition that would have a claim to greater antiquity and thus weigh on the plus side of the historical scale.[45]

According to Brown, this pre-Matthean tradition includes:

- Joseph and Mary are engaged, have not had sex, and are the parents of Jesus (Matt 1:18; Luke 1:27,34);
- Joseph is of Davidic descent (Matt 1:16, 20; Luke 1:27; 2:4);
- An angelic announcement of Jesus's forthcoming birth (Matt 1:20–23; Luke 1:30–35);
- Mary's conception not through Joseph but the Spirit of God (Matt 1:20–25; Luke 1:34);
- An angelic announcement that the child is to be named Jesus (Matt 1:21; Luke 1:31);
- An angelic statement that Jesus is to be a savior (Matt 1:21; Luke 2:11);
- Birth takes place after parents live together (Matt 1:24–25; Luke 2:5–6);
- Birth in Bethlehem (Matt 2:1; Luke 2:4–6);
- Birth chronologically related to reign of Herod the Great (Matt 2:1; Luke 1:5);
- Child reared at Nazareth (Matt 2:23; Luke 2:39).[46]

---

43. Lüdemann, *Jesus after*, 5. For a fuller discussion of the various forms of criteria used in history of Jesus research, see Meier, *Marginal Jew*, 1:166–77.

44. Davies and Allison, *Matthew*, 1:167.

45. Brown, *Birth*, 34. See also Tatum, "Historical Quest," especially 16 and 19; and Fitzmeyer, *Luke*, 307.

46. Brown, *Birth*, 34–35. Fitzmeyer follows Brown's list but adds that Jesus is of Davidic descent ("son of David"), citing Matt 1:1 and Luke 1:32 (*Luke*, 307).

The line of reasoning here is that this material common to both Matthew's and Luke's birth narratives existed and circulated (either orally or in writing) prior to the composition of both Matthew and Luke and that Matthew and Luke reworked or reshaped (redacted) this traditional material into their respective texts to serve their respective narrative or rhetorical ends. But, that these two authors worked independently of one another, according to this line of reasoning, yet included similar or identical material suggests (or indicates) an earlier common core in the tradition and because this material is allegedly earlier, it has a stronger claim of historicity. Fitzmeyer, writing subsequent to Brown (1981), recognizes these similarities as "the historical nucleus of what the evangelists had to work with."[47] Meier, writing ten years later (1991), claims that the agreements between Matthew and Luke, due to multiple attestation, "become historically significant" because "such agreements in two independent and sharply contrasting narratives would, at the very least, go back to earlier tradition and not be the creation of the evangelist." "As a matter of fact," he continues, "some of the points of agreement are generally accepted by scholars as *historical* . . . . Both infancy narratives agree that Jesus's putative father was named Joseph and his mother Mary; facts supported by a few scattered references in different streams of Gospel tradition."[48] Thus, for advocates of this view, the evidence that the birth narratives have historical roots is compelling.

While many who accept the idea of the existence of earlier traditional material are inclined to think that these earlier traditions may have a stronger claim to historicity, others argue that Matthew and Luke used earlier traditions independently in their birth narratives but question or deny these traditions' historical worth. As a representative of this view, Ulrich Luz (2007) posits that the genealogy in Matthew probably "comes from a Greek-speaking Jewish Christianity that was influenced by the LXX" and that Matthew then reworked this genealogy into its present form and included it in his birth narrative, but also concludes, "too much speaks against the historicity of this genealogy for us to take it seriously" because "scholarship, probably in this case with finality, has recognized that it is a fiction."[49] Contra Davies and Allison, Brown, and Meier, Luz concludes concerning Matthew's foretelling-of-Jesus's-birth narrative (1:18–25), which includes the angel's appearance to Joseph and the virginal conception of Mary, that "it is hopeless to ask about the historicity;"[50] concerning the wise men's visit

---

47. Fitzmeyer, *Luke*, 306–7.
48. Meier, *Marginal Jew*, 1:214.
49. Luz, *Matthew*, 87.
50. Ibid., 105.

that it is "a briefly told legend that is not interested in the laws of historical probability"—"the story contains no historical core;"[51] and concerning the "Flight to Egypt" narrative" (2:13–23) that only one point could be taken seriously, and that is Jesus's sojourn into Egypt and this only because of rabbinic and Celsus's testimony that Jesus went to Egypt to work and, while there, learned magic."[52]

Three points in respect to these claims of earlier traditions, the historicity of Joseph, and multiple attestation will guide the subsequent discussion. First, like the hypothetical Q, we have no literary evidence of traditions found in the birth narratives that pre-date the composition of Matthew's gospel. These alleged traditions are based upon hypothetical speculation. Regardless of this fact, scholars who subscribe to this pre-Matthean traditional material, like scholars who subscribe to the existence of Q, often state its existence as fact rather than hypothetical. The authentic Pauline letters are recognized to be the earliest examples of Christian literature and there is not even a hint therein that indicates that he knew anything about such traditions. Nothing. Neither is there any material whatsoever in Mark that suggests that author's awareness of earlier pre-Matthean traditions regarding Jesus's birth. Nothing. Did this earlier tradition arise only between the interval of the completion of Mark's gospel and the composition of Matthew's? To outright deny that the author of Matthew could have created this material in his birth narrative but, instead, merely edited and inserted pre-existing material into his narrative egregiously begs the question of this material's earlier existence and that Matthew could not have composed it himself. It seems, however, that the need for this earlier tradition arises primarily because of the significant differences between the two birth narratives and the assumption that one author could not have known and used the other because, if he did, his birth narrative would not be so drastically different than the earlier one—thus, the apologetical need for an earlier tradition. The second point, the historicity of Joseph, requires a brief discussion.

Concluding his genealogy, the author of Matthew writes, "Jacob begat Joseph, the husband of Mary, from whom, Jesus, who is called the Christos, was born" (Ἰακὼβ δὲ ἐγέννησεν τὸν Ἰωσὴφ τὸν ἄνδρα Μαρίας ἐξ ἧς ἐγεννήθη Ἰησοῦς ὁ λεγόμενος Χριστός, 1:16). This is the chronologically first reference to, or occurrence of, a "Joseph" as Jesus's father in Christian literature. As noted above, neither Paul nor Mark wrote of a Joseph as Jesus's father. Stanley Porter offers the most commonly cited explanation for Mark's

---

51. Ibid., 106.

52. Ibid., 120 and 120n21. See also Ingram, *Was Jesus a Magician?*, http://wasjesusamagician.blogspot.com/.

silence: "The limitation of the Joseph material to Matthew and Luke has led some scholars to speculate that Joseph . . . died sometime after Jesus's 12th year (Luke 2:41–50) and before the beginning of his ministry,"[53] and since Mark begins his gospel when Jesus is much older, there is no need for him to mention Joseph. Brown, too, asserts that Joseph would "almost certainly" "have been dead by that time," and proffers that "the failure to mention him in Mark 6:3, where the list of Jesus's family in Nazareth is being invoked, would otherwise be inexplicable."[54] Borg and Crossan, via their "historical approach" of "ancient text in ancient context,"[55] go so far as to imagine that Joseph was killed while defending the tiny hamlet of Nazareth against the Roman invasion of Sepphoris (about four miles from Nazareth), led by Gaius, in 4 BCE. While acknowledging that we have no account whatsoever of this invasion (much less inhabitants from Nazareth's participation in such a defense), they cite Josephus's description from the *Jewish Wars* of Vespasian's invasion of Gerasa in 67–68 CE when they killed thousands, imprisoned women and children, plundered the homes, and then torched the village. It is within this context that they imagine what Jesus's "actual coming-of-age might have entailed" and it is worth citing here in full:

> One day, when he was old enough, Mary took Jesus up to the top of the Nazareth ridge. It was springtime, the breeze had cleared the air, and the wildflowers were already everywhere. Across the valley, Sepphoris gleamed white on its green hill. "We knew they were coming," Mary said, "but your father had not come home. So we waited after the others were gone. Then we heard the noise, and the earth trembled a little. We did too, but your father had still not come home. Finally, we saw the dust and we had to flee, but your father never came home. I brought you up here today so you will always remember that day we lost him and what little else we had. We lived, yes, but with these questions. Why did God not defend those who defended God? Where was God that day the Romans came?"[56]

Porter's and Borg and Crossan's representative explanations are no more than mere speculation and seem to be apologetically driven in order to grant some semblance of historicity to Joseph and account for his absence from earliest Christian literature. It seems more reasonable to understand that neither Paul nor Mark knew of a Joseph as Jesus's father because a

---

53. Porter, "Joseph, Husband of Mary."
54. Brown, *Birth*, 33 and 33n20.
55. Borg and Crossan, *First Christmas*, 35.
56. Ibid., 76–78.

tradition of Joseph as Jesus's father had not yet existed because the author of Matthew had not yet created a birth narrative in which Joseph is the leading character. But here, in the beginning of what would become the gospel of Matthew, the author crafts an artificial and fictional genealogy that includes fictional characters between Zerubbabel and Joseph—Abiud, Eliakim, Azor, Zadok, Azchim, Eliud, Eleazar, Matthan and Jacob—and, I argue, Matthew's genealogy and birth narrative also introduces the fictional character of Joseph because Jesus's mother needed a husband as part of the plan to explain and counter the charges that Mary was pregnant when she should not have been and that Jesus was born illegitimately.

As for the multiple attestation arguments—that similarities in narrative materials in texts written independently of one another are a strong indicator of the material's historicity—a stronger case can be made that every reference to Joseph in the canonical New Testament texts can be traced back to Matthew. Consider Table 11.

Table 11: Joseph in the New Testament (my translation)

Mark	Matt	Luke	John
Οὐχ οὗτός ἐστιν ὁ τέκτων;	Οὐχ οὗτός ἐστιν ὁ τοῦ τέκτονος υἱός;	Οὐχὶ υἱός ἐστιν Ἰωσὴφ οὗτος;	Οὐχ οὗτός ἐστιν Ἰησοῦς ὁ υἱὸς Ἰωσήφ, οὗ ἡμεῖς οἴδαμεν τὸν πατέρα καὶ τὴν μητέρα;
Is this not the carpenter? (6:3)	Is this not the son of the carpenter? (13:55)	Is this not the son of Joseph? (4:22)	Is this not Jesus, the son of Joseph, whose father and mother we know? (6:42)
			Εὑρίσκει φίλιππος τὸν Ναθαναὴλ καὶ λέγει αὐτῷ, Ὃν ἔγραψεν Μωυσῆς ἐν τῷ νόμῳ καὶ προφῆται εὑρήκαμεν, Ἰησοῦν υἱὸν τοῦ Ἰωσὴφ τὸν ἀπὸ Ναζαρέτ.
			Philip found Nathanel and said to him, "We have found the one whom Moses wrote about in the law and prophets, Jesus, son of Joseph from Nazareth. (1:45)

Other than the references to Joseph in the genealogies and birth narratives in Matthew and Luke, these are the only references to Joseph in the canonical gospels. The similarities in syntax and vocabulary in Mark 6:3, Matt 13:55, Luke 4:22, and John 6:42 are striking, even more striking when it is realized that there are only five occurrences of the verbal arrangement οὐχ οὗτος ἐστιν in (extant) Greek texts prior to its occurrence in Mark 6:3.[57] I argued in the last chapter for a trajectory from Mark > Matt > Luke as the question occurs in the same narrative event (Jesus preaching in his hometown) in all three gospels. Working from the understanding that the gospel of Luke is chronologically later than Matthew, Luke's revision of Matthew's "son of a carpenter" to "Joseph" here can be reasonably explained by Luke's familiarity with Matthew's birth narrative where Joseph is introduced. Combine his knowledge of Matthew's birth narrative (to be demonstrated in the next chapter) with his interest in further distancing Jesus from any possible slur (as argued in the previous chapter), and the appearance of "Joseph" here is understandable. As for the verbal arrangement's occurrence in John, John's wording is more similar to Mark's and Matthew's but his inclusion of "Joseph" as Jesus's father is more similar to Luke's. All that is necessary for John's reference to Joseph as Jesus's father in 6:42 would be his familiarity with the birth narrative in either Matthew or Luke and that 6:42 is very close to Luke. 4:22 is at least suggestive of his knowledge of Luke. In addition, the literary fact that it is only in Luke that it is explicitly stated that Joseph is Jesus's "father" suggests that Luke could be John's source here.[58] Moreover the reference to Jesus as "son of Joseph from Nazareth" in 1:45 also suggests familiarity with either Matthew's or Luke's birth narrative, as these are the only two extant narratives that (probably) predate John that situate Joseph in Nazareth. Of these two, Matthew clearly situates Joseph (and Mary) in a house (εἰς τὴν οἰκίαν) in Bethlehem (2:11) and then redirects them to settle in Galilee rather than returning to Bethlehem (2:22–23). It is only in Luke, however, that Joseph is said to be from Nazareth, as the author of Luke has Gabriel sent "unto the city [of] Galilee, which is named Nazareth" (ἦ ὄνομα Ναζαρέθ)" where Mary is engaged to a man named Joseph (1:26–27), from which "Joseph goes up from Galilee, from the city of Nazareth" (Ἀνέβη δὲ καὶ Ἰωσὴφ ἀπὸ τῆς Γαλιλαίας ἐκ πόλεως Ναζαρέθ) to Bethlehem to register for the census (2:4), and to which he, Mary, and Jesus return after Jesus's presen-

---

57. The verbal arrangement occurs in Plato, *Phaedo* 66a7; Lysias 85.195.10 (fragment); Demosthenes, *In Timocratem* 128.2; 2 Para (LXX) 32:12; and Philo, *De Specialibus Legibus* 1.31.2). Greek text from *TLG*.

58. While Matthew goes out of his way to keep from calling Joseph Jesus's "father," Joseph is explicitly referred to as Jesus's father (ὁ πατὴρ) in Luke 2:33 and 2:48, and he is referred to as Jesus's "parent" (τοὺς γονεῖς) in 2:27 and 2:43.

tation in the temple, "their own city, Nazareth" (εἰς πόλιν ἑαυτῶν Ναζαρὲθ, 2:39). Finally, as far as I am aware, no scholars have argued that the author of John also had access to the (hypothetical) pre-Matthean traditional material to which Brown and Fitzmeyer refer (as cited above). If the author of John did not have access to that same source, then he would have needed another, as yet unidentified, source that identifies a Joseph, whose hometown was Nazareth, and who was also the father of Jesus. It seems much more reasonable to understand that the references to Joseph in John are dependent upon either Matthew or Luke, most likely Luke, which, I will argue in the next chapter, is dependent upon Matthew.

An additional line of reasoning that casts serious doubt upon the historicity of Joseph is the author of Matthew's emphasis that Joseph is not the physical, biological, or historical father of Jesus—"Jacob begat Joseph, the husband of Mary, from whom Jesus, who is called the Christos, was born" (Ἰακὼβ δὲ ἐγέννησεν τὸν Ἰωσὴφ τὸν ἄνδρα Μαρίας ἐξ ἧς ἐγεννήθη Ἰησοῦς ὁ λεγόμενος Χριστός, 1:16). As I noted with the translation at the beginning of this chapter, from 1:2 through 1:16a, the author consistently writes that "A begat [ἐγέννησεν] B" 39 times, employing the aorist active indicative form of the verb γεννάω. Matthew then goes out of his way to break this pattern when he gets to Joseph and Jesus by identifying Joseph, not as the father of Jesus, but as the husband (τὸν ἄνδρα) of Mary, by inserting a relative clause governed by the feminine relative pronoun ἧς the antecedent for which is "Mary," and by switching from the aorist active form of the verb to the aorist passive ἐγεννήθη ("was begotten"). The end result of Matthew's syntactical emphasis is that Joseph had absolutely nothing to do with Jesus's birth, that Jesus was "begat" or "born" "of" or "from" (ἧς) Mary—that "Jesus is the son of Mary" (without a physical father) which is a sentiment very similar to the expression that Mark has the crowd make that Jesus is "the son of Mary" (Mark 6:3) that, I argued in the last chapter, could be understood as a possible slur against Jesus. It cannot be overstated that the author of Matthew here is not denying the claim that Mark has the crowd make that Jesus is the "son of Mary." Rather, he is acknowledging it and will next (vv. 18–25) offer an explanation for it. Thus, Joseph's only role in this genealogy is to serve as Mary's husband; it is a literary role, a narrative role, a rhetorical role.

Matthew's Foretelling-of-Jesus's-Birth-Narrative (1:18–25)

Matthew 1:18–25

[18]The birth of Jesus Christos came about in this way.

After Mary his mother was betrothed to Joseph, before which time they came together, it was found that she was pregnant from a spirit which is holy [ἐκ πνεύματος ἁγίου]. ¹⁹But Joseph, her husband, was a righteous man and not desiring to make an example of her, he decided to set her free secretly. ²⁰While he was contemplating these thoughts, behold an angel of the Lord appeared to him in a dream saying,

"Joseph, son of David, do not be afraid to take Mary as your wife; for that which has been begotten in her is from a spirit that is holy. ²¹She will bear a son and you will call his name Jesus; for he will save his people from their sins."

²²All of this happened in order that that which has been spoken through the prophet might be fulfilled, saying, ²³"Behold, the virgin will become pregnant and she will bear a son, and they will call his name 'Emmanuel,'" which is translated "God with us."

²⁴After Joseph was raised from sleep, he did as the angel of the lord ordered him and took his wife, ²⁵and he did not know her until which time a son was born, and he called his name, Jesus. (My translation.)

The discussion here will be limited to the literary (fictional), apologetical, and rhetorical characteristics of the passage. That the probability that Matthew's account of Jesus's birth (1:18–25) is no more grounded in history than his genealogy is heightened by Michael Satlow's observation that "during the entire Second Temple period [ca. 530 BCE–70 CE] (most?) Jews neither customarily 'betrothed' (in the biblical sense) nor did they even have a firm understanding of what such a betrothal would mean. Instead, they followed Greek practices, and understood the biblical institution of betrothal within their own Hellenistic contexts."[59] In fact, he notes further that "the only contemporary source that does suggest that Jews practiced a constitutive form of betrothal is Matthew 1:18–19."[60] Satlow recognizes that betrothal relationships are evident in rabbinic literature (dated after the destruction of the Jerusalem temple in 70 CE) but also that "Rabbinic

---

59. Satlow, *Jewish Marriage*, 69.

60. Ibid., 72. While stating this, Satlow also seems to accept that the account in Matthew is historical, as he writes that 1:18–19 "testifies that at least some Jews in the first century, probably in the rural Galilee, were practicing a form of inchoate marriage. Moreover, the fact that the author of Matthew does not find it necessary to explain the legal background of this passage indicates an assumption that such an institution was familiar to its intended audience" (82). Because of the overall fictional aspects of the genealogy and (I will argue) birth narrative in Matthew, I cannot grant much, if any, historicity to these accounts, and thus disagree with Satlow.

legislation does not reflect what contemporary [i.e., pre-rabbinic period] Jews were doing."[61] And, if Jesus was born during the reign of Herod the Great (as is the scholarly consensus) and since Herod died in 4 BCE, it is even the more questionable whether betrothals recognized post-70 CE were in practice 75–80 years earlier.

Another observation about 1:18–25 that further heightens the probability that 1:18–25 is a rhetorical fiction is the author's subjective omniscient narrative perspective. That is, how did the author of Matthew know:

1. That Joseph and Mary were betrothed?
2. That Mary was pregnant when she should not have been?
3. That Joseph was a "righteous man"?
4. That Joseph contemplated what to do with Mary once he became aware of her pregnancy?
    a. That Joseph did not desire to make an example of Mary?
    b. That Joseph desired to set her free secretly?
    c. That while he was contemplating these things, an angel appeared to him in a dream?
5. What the angel said to Joseph?
6. That Joseph arose from his sleep and did as the angel commanded him to do?
7. That Joseph did not have sexual intercourse with Mary until the child was born?
8. That Joseph named Jesus?

Scholarly commentary on the possible sources that Matthew might have used to craft 1:18–25 complicate these questions. Brown, for example, speculates that the author of Matthew as we now have it had little to do with the composition of 1:18–25, adding only 1) 1:18 as a transition from the genealogy to the birth narrative; 2) the so-called "formula citation" that includes the "prophecy" from Isaiah (1:22–23); and 3) to provide assurance of Mary's continued virginity, that Joseph did not have sex with Mary until Jesus was born (1:25), to a pre-Matthean narrative (the origin of which is completely unknown and purely hypothetical) while shaping the whole to reflect his Matthean style.[62] Davies and Allison reject the possibility that Matthew composed 1:18—2:23 on his own

61. Ibid., 81.
62. Brown, *Birth*, 96–119.

(freely) primarily because of what they consider to be "internal tensions" or inconsistencies within.[63] They also reject the view, similar to Brown's, that the author served as primarily a final redactor who stitched a variety of previously independent narratives into the whole. Rather, they contend that the author "more or less reproduces a pre-Matthean narrative" and adds only the five so-called "formula-quotations," which means that for 1:18–25 the author's only contribution is 1:22–23.[64] It is important to note that these "pre-Matthean" narratives that Brown and Davies and Allison (and others) rely upon are completely hypothetical constructs of commentators, as we do not have a shred of evidence that such ever existed. But even if they did exist, which I doubt, it would mean that the author of Matthew, according to either model, would have served only a minor role in the creation of the material, primarily, shaping up and passing along historically unfounded tradition while adding the so-called "formula quotations." Such a view of the author of 1:18–25 *qua* primarily editor or redactor not only makes any responses to the questions posed above meaningless but also suggests a very messy and complicated process of redaction based upon hypothetical documents for which there is not a shred of evidence for their existence. On the other hand, even Davies and Allison recognize that the author's use of subjective omniscient narrator in 1:20 is "consistent with his stance as an omniscient narrator" in the rest of Matthew and note several examples. They note that the author

> informs us about the secret meeting between Herod and the magi (2.7) and about the latter's dream (2.12). He narrates an event at which only Jesus and Satan were present (4.1–11). He gives us the thoughts of the Pharisees (9.3) and the feeling of Herod (14.9). He tells us that Peter was afraid (14.30) and that Jesus was hungry (21.18). He recounts the Pharisees' perceptions (21.45–6). He even knows the feelings and convictions that motivated Jesus 99.36; 12.15; 13.58; 14.14).[65]

To these can be added Jesus's prayer in Gethsemane (26:36-46). How did our author know that Jesus, who left his disciples behind, prayed, "My Father, if it is possible, let this cup pass me by; yet not my will but yours?" (v. 39). How did the author know about the conversation within Caiaphas's

---

63. They claim, for example, that the move from Israel to Nazareth is a "very artificial addition" and they are puzzled why, for example, the magi could find Jesus very easily but Herod could not (Davies and Allison, *Matthew*, 1:190–91).

64. Ibid., 1:190–91. The other four formula quotations that Matthew works into his birth narrative are 2:6, 15, 17, and 23.

65. Ibid., 1:205–6.

home and the beating Jesus received therein (26:56–68)? Similarly, how did the author know about the exchange between Jesus and Pilate (27:11–19) and especially the note Pilate received from his wife while sitting in court that he (Pilate) "have nothing to do with that innocent man; I was much troubled on his account in my dreams last night?" These examples of subjective omniscience perspective throughout Matthew are consistent with what we find in 1:18–25 (and the rest of the birth narrative) and are not only indicative of the extent of fictional narrative throughout Matthew but also suggest that the author of the rest of Matthew also crafted 1:18–25 (and the rest of the birth narrative).

So, from a rhetorical and compositional perspective, if 1:18–25 is fictional, why would Matthew make the rhetorical, compositional decision to craft a betrothal scene to describe Jesus's birth? A most likely answer could be that because a betrothal and birth narrative scene would be a conducive literary means to explain why Mary was pregnant when she should not have been—that she was involved in an inappropriate sexual relationship, which is the only historical kernel of the narrative, and is the only reasonable narrative explanation of the four women in the genealogy.

The first observation regarding Matthew's explanation concerning Mary's pregnancy is that the author of Matthew does not deny that Mary is pregnant when she should not be—between the time of the betrothal and when they were to "come together"—when Joseph was to take her into his own home. The fact that Matthew not only acknowledges Mary's pregnancy but begins the foretelling-of-Jesus's-birth narrative with this acknowledgement indicates that it was beyond dispute that Mary was pregnant when she should not be—that it was known widely enough that the author needed to address it. But, Matthew also offered an *explanation* for it. The narrative for this explanation is somewhat awkward as the narrator informs the reader that Mary's pregnancy is "from a spirit which is holy" (v. 18) before Joseph is informed of this by the angel in v. 20.

A second observation is the language the author of Matthew uses to describe the "discovery" of Mary's pregnancy—"it was discovered," εὑρέθη, an aorist passive. This is the same form of the verb used in several passages in Deuteronomy that speak to wrong-doers and their punishments. For example, Septuagint Deuteronomy 17:2–7 instructs the community, "If it is discovered ['Ἐὰν δὲ εὑρεθῇ]" that a man or woman does what is wrong . . . and they are found guilty, they shall be stoned to death;" "if she is not discovered [μὴ εὑρεηθῇ]" not to be a virgin . . . she must be stoned to death" (22:20 LXX); and "if it is discovered ['Ἐὰν δὲ εὑρεθῇ]" that a man was lying with a married woman . . . they must both be put to death (22:22). This is the only occurrence of this verb form in Matthew; it may be mere coincidence, but it is also possible that Matthew is directing the reader of the Septuagint to this context in Deuteronomy.

Our subjective omniscient narrator then informs us that Joseph—"her husband"—was a "righteous" [δίκαιος] man. It is interesting to note that, while Mary is referred to as "his [Jesus's] mother" in 1:18, here Joseph is not referred to as Jesus's father but only to "her husband"—another point of emphasis that Joseph is not to be understood as Jesus's physical father in Matthew. Most commentators agree that by referring to Joseph as "righteous" Matthew is telling his readers that he was a Torah-observant, a law-abiding man, but there are three views as to how Joseph's righteousness could be understood.[66] One view is that by "righteous" Joseph was understood to be kind or merciful and that his kindness or mercy manifests itself in that he was not willing to enforce the law against Mary. A problem with this view is that the necessity for the angel's visit and admonition to Joseph not to fear taking Mary would seem to indicate that Joseph had serious concerns with Mary's pregnancy. A second view is that Joseph was righteous because he knew of the divine plan, was in awe of it, and did not want to interfere. This view, however, does not square with the narrative fact that Joseph was not informed of the supernatural origin of Mary's pregnancy until the next verse. A third view is that Joseph was obedient to the law in the strictest sense of the term, and scholars cite the reference in Luke 1:6 that both Zacharia and Elizabeth were "righteous" (ἦσαν δὲ δίκαιοι ἀμφότεροι) "in observing all of the commandments and ordinances of the Lord." It is this third interpretation—that Joseph was obedient to the law and observing all the commandments—that best fits his contemplation about what to do with Mary, a serious enough contemplation that necessitated an angelic intervention.

We are told next that Joseph "was not desiring to make an example" of Mary but had determined "to set her free secretly" (καὶ μὴ θέλων αὐτὴν δειγματίσαι, ἐβουλήθη λάθρᾳ ἀπολῦσαι αὐτήν, v. 19). According to our narrator, the two options before Joseph were to "make an example of her" or to "set her free," to divorce her, and it was after he had considered (ἐνθυμηθέντος) these two options and opted to "set her free" that an angel was dispatched to appear to him in a dream. These two options will be briefly considered.

The term that I have translated as "make an example of her" (δειγματίσαι) is a rare word in Greek literature meaning "to exhibit," "to make public," or "to bring to public notice," especially, as Schiler notes, "that

---

66. For discussion, see Brown, *Birth*, 125–28; Davies and Allison, *Matthew*, 1:202-4; and Schaberg, *Illigitimacy*, 50–51.

which seeks concealment," so that it almost has the sense of "to expose"[67] and occurs in the Greek New Testament only here and in Colossians 2:15. In the latter passage, the author claims that Jesus "disarmed the cosmic powers and authorities" on the cross and "made a public spectacle [ἐδειγμάτισεν] of them." The term does not occur in the Septuagint, but a consideration of the five possible scenarios from Deuteronomy 22 for dealing with either a wife who was not a virgin when she married or a betrothed or married woman who had intercourse with a man other than her husband while betrothed or married may provide some insight into how the author of Matthew is using the term here.

1. If, after the betrothal and marriage, the man has intercourse with his wife for the first time and there is no evidence of her virginity (no blood on the sheets), then *the woman is brought to the door of her father's house and the men of the town stone her to death*, because "she has committed an outrage in Israel by playing the prostitute in her father's house: you must rid yourselves of this wickedness" (Deut 22:13–21, REV).

2. When it has been discovered/proven that a man had sex with a woman who was another man's wife, both the adulterer and the adulteress are to be put to death; "you must purge Israel of this wickedness" (Deut 22:22, REV).

3. When, within the city, a man has sex with a woman who is betrothed to someone else and that woman does not cry out for help, *both are to be brought out to the gate of that town and stoned to death*; the girl "because she did not cry out for help, and the man because he violated another man's wife: you must rid yourselves of this wickedness" (Deut 22:23–24, REV).

4. If, however, a man rapes a woman in the country, only the man is to be killed; nothing is to be done to the girl, as "no guilt deserving of death attaches to her" (Deut 22:28–29, REV).

5. When a man forces a virgin who is not yet betrothed to another to have intercourse with him and it is found out, he must pay the girl's father 50 pieces of silver, take her as his wife, and he cannot divorce her as long as he lives (Deut 22:28–29, REV).

The situation in option 1 above clearly does not apply to Joseph and Mary, but it is worth noting that the punishment for the adulteress in this scenario is that her adultery would be "exposed," "made public" and that her

67. Schlier, "δειγματίζω." In *TDNT*, 2.31.

execution would be carried out by fellow townspeople and a public event. According to Matthew's narrative, neither 4 nor 5 would apply either. This leaves either 2 or 3 and in both cases both the adulterer and the adulteress are to be put to death. Number 2 does not explain a means of death but 3, like 1, describes a public exposure and public execution: *"both are to be brought out to the gate of that town and stoned to death"*—language very similar to the meaning of the rare word that the author of Matthew uses as one of the options Joseph was considering, δειγματίσαι: "to make public," or "to bring to public notice," especially, "that which seeks concealment, so that it almost has the sense of "to expose." The text also suggests, that it would be the man who initiates the allegation against the wife or betrothed but it would be the townspeople who would carry out the execution at the entrance of her father's home. As Goodfriend notes, it appears as though "the law is prosecuted irrespective of the wishes of the offended party."[68] This seems to be supported by the fact that whereas, in other Near Eastern law collections, men were permitted to waive harsh punishments, this was not the case in ancient Judaism.[69] As the texts above suggest, when a capital crime was brought to the attention of the community, it was the community who carry out the punishment immediately. But, was this also the case several hundred years later when, in Matthew's narrative, Mary is found to be pregnant when she should not have been? Jane Schaberg notes the difficulties of determining the application of these strict laws in the first century CE. She notes on more than one occasion that there is only "slight," or "slim" evidence that the old laws that required execution for adultery were enforced and that the bulk of the evidence that does exist—Mishanic and Talmudic views—post-dates the period of Matthew's birth narrative and are only useful when corroborated by earlier evidence. She notes that "the evidence for its application in the first century CE is slight"[70] and that "Execution for adultery in the Old Testament and intertestamental period, then, appears to have been extremely rare. Not a single case is reported."[71] But while there may not be a single case of execution for adultery reported, there are literary references that the practice was still in effect. In the apocryphal *Susanna* (LXX), for example, probably written around 100 BCE, it is stated on several occasions that the penalty for adultery is death,[72] and Philo

---

68. Goodfriend, "Adultery," 1:83. Goodfriend also notes that later commentators "contend that initiation of proceedings was the exclusive right of the husband."

69. "Adultery." This article cites Pritchard's discussion in his *Texts* of the *Code of Hammurabi*, the *Middle Assyrian Laws*, and the *Hittite Laws*.

70. Schaberg, *Illigitimacy*, 53.

71. Ibid., 57.

72. *Susanna* (LXX) 28, 41, 42, and 44.

of Alexandria, writing at the turn of the eras, seems to indicate that the strict penalty was still in effect when he writes, "If one commits adultery... death is the penalty for such wickedness,"[73] a passage that Schaberg recognizes. Two of her conclusions on the punishment for adultery that are relevant to my understanding of the author of Matthew's use of δειγματίσαι ("to make an example of her") are, "that forgiveness from a Law-observant man would follow the punishment and divorce, if not the death, of his convicted wife"[74] and that a "Torah-observant man would probably not complete the marriage with an adulteress."[75] If this latter conclusion is accurate and if Matthew was familiar with this understanding, this could explain his narrative and polemical need to send the angel to Joseph.

The second option that the author of Matthew has Joseph consider, and the one he settles upon, is "to set her free secretly" [λάθρᾳ ἀπολῦσαι αὐτήν], to divorce her secretly. This option seems to raise a problem because, in a historical context anyway, if Joseph suspected that Mary was pregnant and he knew that she could not have become pregnant by him, then, by Jewish law at the time, his only options (that we know of), as a Torah-observant man, would have been 2 or 3 above, as these pertain exclusively to suspicions of adultery. While Deut 24:1–4 primarily concerns itself with not allowing a man to remarry a woman he has previously divorced or "sent out," it is the primary passage in the Hebrew Bible that speaks to the process of a man divorcing a wife. The Septuagint version, which the author of Matthew was using, reads,

> ¹Now if anyone takes a wife and lives with her, and it shall be, if she does not find favor before him because he found a shameful thing [ἄσχημον πρᾶγμα] in her, then he shall write her a bill of divorce and shall give it into her hands and shall send her out [ἐξαποστελεῖ] of his house, ²and if, having gone out [ἀπελθοῦσα], she becomes another man's ³and the last man hates her, then he will write her a bill of divorce and give it in her hands and send her out [ἐξαποστελεῖ] of his house, of if the last man who took her for himself as wife dies, ⁴the former man, who sent her away, shall not be able, having returned, to take her for himself as his wife after she has been defiled, for it is an abomination before the Lord your God, and you shall not defile the land that the Lord your God is giving you as an allotment.[76]

73. Philo of Alexandria, *Hypothetica* (7.1), http://www.earlychristianwritings.com/yonge/book37.html.

74. Schaberg, *Illigitimacy*, 58.

75. Ibid., 63.

76. From Pietersma and Wright (eds.), *New English Translation of the Septuagint*.

Two brief points from this that seem relevant to the Matthew 1:19 are the "sending out" of the woman and the reason for the sending out. First, this passage refers to the "sending out" of the wife three times—twice with the verb ἐξαποστελεῖ and once with the feminine participle ἀπελθοῦσα ("the woman who was sent out"). The word that the author of Matthew uses to refer to Joseph's second option to "set her free" is ἀπολῦσαι, the primary meaning of which is "set free" or "release from." Different forms of the word occur throughout the Septuagint but not within any context of divorce, but ἀπολῦσαι in Matthew seems to be synonymous with ἐξαποστελεῖ in Deuteronomy. Second, the Septuagint's rendering "shameful thing" is the Greek translation of the Hebrew *erwat dabar*, which the translators of the *Tanach* translate as "a matter of immorality,"[77] which Richard Davidson, who translates the expression as "indecency," explains as "some type of serious, shameful, and disgraceful conduct of indecent exposure probably associated with sexual activity, but less than actual illicit sexual intercourse."[78] Davidson excludes sexual intercourse from the term's meaning because Deut. 22 had previously explained the punishments for women engaging in intercourse with another man when they should not have (death) and divorce, or "sending them out" was not an option.[79] Of course, we do not know if the author of Matthew had Deuteronomy 24 in mind when he penned Joseph's second option, but there are close similarities. In addition to "it was found" mentioned above, the author of Matthew has Joseph decide to "set Mary free," to divorce her, because of his suspicions of her sexual misconduct, which, however, seems to conflict with Joseph's first option of "exposing" her because, if his suspicions are founded (which they seem to be, as it is acknowledged that Mary is pregnant when she should not be), he, as a "righteous" (Torah-observant) man, would be required to expose her. Moreover, there is no evidence in biblical literature to corroborate the idea that Joseph would "send her away secretly" if he thought she committed adultery, and there are also practical problems with this. Among these are that our narrator has already informed us that Mary was pregnant and while we are not informed as to how it was found or discovered that Mary was pregnant, sooner or later it would become obvious to those who encountered her. And, finally, as Brown notes, "According to the practice known from later rabbinic writings, a totally secret divorce was not possible, since the writ of repudiation [letter

---

77. *Tanach*, 483.
78. Davidson, "Divorce and Remarriage," 7.
79. Ibid., 6.

of divorce] had to be delivered before two witnesses"[80] and these witnesses would probably recognize a pregnancy.

Despite these narrative problems, the author of Matthew has Joseph decide to divorce Mary and this decision reverberated in the heavens as an angel was dispatched to Joseph in a dream. It is widely acknowledged that angelic visitations, dreams, visions, and pronouncements made therein served as rhetorical/literary devices that would grant authority and legitimacy to both the messenger and the message.[81] Matthew uses only the expression *angel of the Lord* (ἄγγελος κυρίου), without the definite article[82] and without a name, to refer to this supernatural messenger. Matthew's use of "angel of the Lord" should probably be distinguished from the similar expression in the Old Testament (and Septuagint), which would often refer to the presence of the Hebrew God himself, as the concept of angelic beings as heavenly messengers is a later development in Jewish apocryphal and pseudepigraphic literature. But, then again, if Matthew is seeking to grant the utmost of authority to this message, he may be invoking the Hebrew Bible usage and understanding.

After greeting him by name, the messenger exhorts Joseph, "Do not be afraid [μὴ φοβηθῇς] to take Mary as your wife" (v. 20). The exhortation (or command) not to be afraid is a common component of angelic (or messenger) pronouncements in the Old Testament. These exhortations (or commands) are either in the aorist subjunctive (as here) or the present imperative (μὴ φοβοῦ) as in some of the examples below and often, but not always, are followed with an explanation as to why the recipient should not fear, often introduced with a γάρ ("for") or ὅτι ("because") clause. Some of these (from the Septuagint) include:

- "The Lord's word came to Abraam in a vision: 'Do not fear [Μὴ φοβοῦ]...'" (Gen (15:1 LXX).

- "God's angel called from heaven to Hagar, 'What is it, Hagar? Do not be afraid [Μὴ φοβοῦ], for [γάρ] God has given ear to the voice of your child" (Gen 21:17–18 LXX).

- "On that night, the Lord appeared to [Isaac], 'I am the God of your father Abraam,' he said; 'do not be afraid [Μὴ φοβοῦ], for [γάρ] I am with you'" (Gen 26:24 LXX).

---

80. Brown, *Birth*, 128.

81. See especially, Pagels, *Gnostic Gospels*, 7–14.

82. The absence of the definite article may be, as Davies and Allison suggest, a Septuagintism to reflect the Hebrew construct state—*mal'ak YHWH*, *angel of the Lord* (*Matthew*, 1:206).

- "The Lord said to Moses, 'Do not be afraid [μὴ φοβηθῇς] of [King Og of Bashan] because [ὅτι] I will deliver him to you'" (Num 21:34 LXX).
- "The Lord said to Joshua, 'Do not be afraid [μὴ φοβηθῇς], for [γὰρ] I have delivered these kings unto your hand'" (Josh 10:8 LXX).
- "He went on, 'Do not be afraid [Μὴ φοβοῦ], Daniel, because [ὅτι] from the very first day . . .'" (Dan 10:12 LXX).

Like these and other examples from the Septuagint,[83] the author of Matthew has an unnamed angel of the Lord offer an explanation to Joseph why he should not fear, "for [γὰρ] that which is in her has been begotten from a spirit which is holy" (το γὰρ ἐν αὐτῇ γεννηθὲν ἐκ πνεύματός ἐστιν ἁγίου, v. 20).[84] Whereas in v. 16 above, we were told via emphatic syntactical structure that Jesus was begotten from Mary, here, again via a passive verb, he was begotten from a "spirit which is holy," the narrative again clearly indicating that Joseph was not Jesus's father.

Matthew then has this angelic messenger continue his explanation as to why Joseph should not fear: "She will bear a son, and you will call his name Jesus, for he will save his people from their sins." This birth pronouncement follows a literary format common to birth annunciations in the Septuagint as Table 12 indicates.

Table 12: Birth annunciations in the Septuagint

LXX texts	The annunciation
Gen 16:11	Ἰδοὺ σὺ ἐν γαστρὶ ἔχεις καὶ τέξῃ υἱὸν καὶ καλέσεις τὸ ὄνομα αὐτοῦ Ἰσμαηλ Behold, you will conceive and bear a son and you will call his name Ishmael.
Gen 17:19	Ἰδοὺ Σαρρα ἡ γυνή σου τέξεταί σοι υἱὸν σοι καὶ καλέσεις τὸ ὄνομα αὐτοῦ Ισαακ Behold, Sarra, your wife, will bear a son to you and you will call his name Isaac . . .
Judges 13:5	ἰδοὺ σὺ ἐν γαστρὶ ἔχεις καὶ τέξῃ υἱόν behold, you will conceive and you will bear a son . . .

---

83. Other examples include Gen 28:13; 46:3; Deut 3:2; Josh 8:1; and Judg 6:23.

84. I adopt Brown's rendering of "from a spirit which is holy," as not only is there no definite article, but "spirit" and "holy" are separated by the verb "is" (ἐστιν). For discussion, see Brown, *Birth*, 124–25.

LXX texts	The annunciation
Isa 7:14	ἰδοὺ ἡ παρθένος ἐν γαστρὶ ἕξει καὶ τέξεται υἱόν καὶ καλέσεις τὸ ὄνομα αὐτοῦ Ἐμμανουήλ Behold, the young woman will conceive and bear a son and you will call him Emmanuel.
Matt 1:21	Τέξεται δὲ υἱόν καὶ καλέσουσιν τὸ ὄνομα αὐτοῦ Ἰησοῦν She will bear a son and they will call him Jesus . . .

That Matthew has his angelic messenger strictly follow a well-established literary structure is another example of the extent to which the Matthean birth announcement is artificial, a literary fiction—albeit a rhetorical fiction. Because Matthew cites Isaiah 7:14 in 1:23, it is probably safe to think that he followed the Septuagint version of Isaiah's text (rather than one of the others) here as well, changing only "you will call" (καλέσεις) to "they will call" (καλέσουσιν), a significant revision that will be discussed below.

The angelic annunciation ends with v. 21, followed by the first of his formula quotations: "All this has come about in order that the word by [the] Lord through the prophet might be fulfilled, saying, 'Behold, the virgin [ἡ παρθένος] will conceive and she will bear a son, and they will call his name Emmanuel.'" The scholarly literature on the author of Matthew's formula quotations, his use of Isaiah 7:14 here, and Isaiah 7:14 is immense and intense, which may be a reason for Hans Wildberger's claim that Isaiah 7:14 is "the most controversial passage in the Bible" and that more commentary has been written about this verse than any other verse in the Old Testament.[85] My interest here is to argue that Matthew inserted his revision of Isaiah 7:14 into this birth annunciation in order to offer further support to his explanation as to why Mary was pregnant when she should not have been. Matthew has been making an argument concerning Mary's pregnancy when she should not have been pregnant, and this first formula quotation is another, and final, line of evidence that he provides to support his argumentation. After a relatively brief examination of the key points of interpretation with Isaiah 7:14, I will return to consider Matthew's use/revision of the passage.

Recognizing the many problems with corroborating the historical and narrative contexts of Isaiah 7, Ahaz became king of Judah in the seventeenth year of Pekah's (the king of Israel or Ephraim) reign (ca. 740 BCE). Rezin, the king of Syria (Aram, Damascus) and Pekah besieged Jerusalem, but could not lure Ahaz into battle. Instead, Ahaz sent messengers to Tiglath-pileser III of Assyria asking for assistance, which Tiglath-pileser was happy to lend,

---

85. Wildberger, *Isaiah 1–12*, 306, 307.

after receiving handsome gifts from Ahaz. This is the context underlying Isaiah 7:2: "When it was reported to the house of David that the Arameans [Rezin, Syrians] had made an alliance with the Ephraimites [Pekah, Israelites], king [Ahaz] and people shook like forest trees shaking in the wind." Isaiah is then told to take his son, Shear-jashub ("A remnant will return") and go to Ahaz with the following message: "Remain calm and unafraid;... The Aramaeans with Ephraim have plotted against you to invade Judah.... This will not happen" (7:3–9). He then encouraged Ahaz to ask for a sign that would indicate the truthfulness of Isaiah's claim, but Ahaz refused, "No, I will not put the Lord to the test by asking for a sign." This refusal prompted Isaiah's Immanuel prophecy:

> Hear now, O House of David: Is it not enough for you that you scorn human [prophets], that you scorn even my God? Therefore, my Lord himself will give you a sign: Behold, the maiden will become pregnant and bear a son, and you will name him Immanuel. He will eat cream and honey as soon as he knows to abhor evil and choose good. For before the child will know to abhor evil and choose good, the land of the two kings whom you fear will be abandoned. (*Tanach*, Isa 7:13–16)

Setting aside the issue of whether this is a post-event prophecy, the narrative context of Isaiah's pronouncement was the unsuccessful siege of Jerusalem by Israelite and Syrian armies about 734 BCE. Isaiah of Jerusalem was encouraging Ahaz not to fear this invasion but to trust in God (Immanu'el, God-with-us) because by the time that this child, Immanuel, reached maturity ("knows how to reject bad and choose good"), the two kings and their kingdoms would be desolate. The demise of these two kingdoms is recorded in 2 Kgs 15:30 and 16:9. In the former, "Hoshea, son of Elah, formed a conspiracy against Pekah, son of Remaliah, attacked and killed him, and usurped his throne in the twentieth year of Jotham, son of Uzziah" (ca. 732 BCE), and, as for the latter, 2 Kgs reports that "The king of Assyria advanced on Damascus, captured it, deported its inhabitants to Kir, and put Rezin to death" (16:9).

Having established this historical/narrative context, four points concerning Isaiah's pronouncement, especially as they relate to the author of Matthew's use of the passage, will be considered: the meaning of *almah* (the Hebrew word translated *young woman* above in Isa 7:14); whether the woman "is" or "will be" pregnant, the identity of the person who is naming the Immanuel child; and who the Immanuel child himself is. After these four points are considered, I will return to comment upon Matthew's use of Isaiah 7:14.

Perhaps one of the most effective ways of demonstrating the problems between Isaiah 7:14 and Matthew's version of it in 1:23 is to examine several translations of Isaiah 7:14 from contemporary Bibles. The King James Version (KJV) and The New King James Bible (NKJV), published in 1982, The New American Standard Bible (NASB), revised in 1985, and The New international Version (NIV), revised in 2011, are among the most popular Bibles in the United States, and their respective translations of Isaiah 7:14 are:

- "Behold, *the virgin* [*ha almah*] shall conceive [*harah*] and bear a *Son*, and shall call *His* name Immanuel" (KJV, NKJV).
- "Behold, *a virgin* [*ha almah*] will be with child [*harah*] and bear a *Son*, and she will call *His* name Immanuel" (NASB).
- "*The virgin* [*ha almah*] will conceive [*harah*] and give birth to a son, and will call him Immanuel" (NIV).

In sharp contrast to these translations, the translations in the 1966 New Jerusalem Bible (NJB) and the 1989 New Revised Standard Version (NRSV) Bibles (neither of which is within the top ten purchased Bibles in the United States) read:

- "*The young woman* [*ha almah*] *is with child* [*harah*] and will give birth to a son whom she will call Immanuel" (NJB).
- "Look, *the young woman* [*ha almah*] *is with child* [*harah*] and shall bear a son and shall name him Immanuel" (NRSV).

Notice that the first three translations translate *ha almah* as either "the virgin" (with the definite article) or "a virgin" (without a definite article) whereas the latter two translate *ha alma* as "the young woman" (with the definite article) with no suggestion or indication whatsoever as to the woman's sexual status or experience. Similarly, the first three translations translate *harah* in the future tense, "will conceive" whereas the latter translate it in the present tense "is with child" ("is pregnant"). A correct understanding of the translation of these terms is imperative for understanding the passage in Isaiah and then Matthew's use of Isaiah 7:14 and for understanding the problems with the different translations in contemporary Bibles.

The issue with *almah* is whether the term denotes "virgin." According to *The Brown-Driver-Briggs Hebrew and English Lexicon* (BDB), *almah* (עלמה) denotes "young woman (ripe sexually; maid or newly married)"[86] without any explicit reference to the woman's sexual experience (although, if one were "newly married," it can be assumed that she has engaged in sexual

---

86. BDB, 761.

intercourse, and would then not be a virgin). BDB also lists a corresponding masculine form of the *word, elem*, which denotes "young man".[87] In contrast to *almah*, the Hebrew word for "virgin" is *bethula* (בתולה). The two terms are not synonymous.

Alma is a rare term, occurring only eight other times in the Hebrew Bible. In two of these instances (1 Chr 15:20 and Ps 46:1), it is used to refer to musical instruments and in Ps 68:25 it refers to "timbrel playing young girls" without any suggestion whatsoever about their sexuality, so these three occurrences are irrelevant to our understanding of the term's meaning. Table 13 reflects the remaining uses of the term.[88]

Table 13: Uses of *alma* (עַלְמָה) in the Hebrew Bible

Hebrew term	Transliteration	Meaning	#	Reference	Comments
הָעַלְמָה	h'almah	the young woman	3	Gen 24:43; Exod 2:8; Isa 7:14	The noun *almah* always signified a young woman of marriageable age.
בְּעַלְמָה	bealmah	with a young woman	1	Prov 30:19	
עֲלָמוֹת	alamot	young women	1	Song 1:3	Plural of *almah*.
וַעֲלָמוֹת	va'alamot	and young women	1	Song 6:8	

In Genesis 24:43 Abraham's servant is seeking a wife for Isaac when he refers very specifically to Rebecca as "the young woman" (*ha almah*) who comes to the well. While the context here has nothing whatsoever to do with Rebecca's sexual experience but, instead, has everything to do with her as "a woman of marriageable age," earlier in the narrative the narrator writes, in reference to Rebecca, that "the maiden [*enor*] is very fair to look upon; a virgin [*bethula*] whom no man had known" (24:14).[89] These two passages (Gen 24:43 and 24:14) distinguish the difference in meanings between *alma* and *bethula* very clearly. In Exodus 2:8 we are told that the Pharaoh's daughter instructed "the [specific] girl" (*ha almah*), who was

---

87. Ibid.
88. This table is adapted from Yosef, "Isaiah 7:14—Part 1."
89. *Tanach*, 24:14.

Moses's sister, to summon a wet nurse from the Hebrew women. As in the case with Rebecca, there is no concern whatsoever here with Moses's sister's sexual experiences, but merely that she is a "young woman." Based upon the definition of *almah*, the corresponding masculine form, and the other two uses of the term in Gen 24 and Ex 2:8, along with the vast majority of scholarship, including Clifford Durrousseu's conclusion, "*Almah* as 'young woman' is not a non-Christian or Jewish translation: it is the correct translation,"[90] *ha-almah* in Isaiah 7:14 should be rendered as "the young woman" with no concern as to her sexual experience and, because of the definite article, the term refers to "the [specific] young woman" known to Isaiah, Ahaz, and anyone else who was present.

As for "will conceive" where *harah* is understood as a future tense verb (*will be pregnant*) or as a predicate (*is pregnant*), the Hebrew form is identical (הָרָה) for both. Uri Yosef's and Durrousseu's discussions on *harah* are helpful for assisting non-experts in Hebrew grammar to understand the difference between the verbal and the predicate constructions. Both agree that in Isaiah 7:14 *harah* (הָרָה) is a predicate of the noun "young woman." Yosef explains that there are 12 occurrences of *harah* in the Hebrew Bible, one verb and 11 adjectival forms. If a verb form, it is a third person, masculine, past tense, and the only example is Psalms 7:15: "Behold, he is in labor with iniquity and he has conceived [וְהָרָה, *vehar*] mischief," understanding *harah* here as "to conceive or scheme a thought that spawns in a person's mind."[91] In contrast, "when used in connection with a female, הָרָה is the adjective that describes the noun. In such cases the relevant verb is the present tense of the verb 'to be,' which is implicit,"[92] and in such cases the event is understood either in the present (present tense) or the imminent near future.[93] Examples of this predicate construction include 1 Sam 4:19 where the "wife of Phineas [is] pregnant [*Phineas harah*, פִּינְחָס הָרָה]" and Gen 38:24 where Tamar played the harlot and "behold [she is] pregnant [*hinoh harah* הִנֵּה הָרָה]." Isaiah 7:14 is identical to these examples: "Behold, the young woman [is/will in the imminent future will be, implied] pregnant [*ha almah harah*, הָעַלְמָה הָרָה]." On these grammatical grounds alone, Durousseau's translation, "Look, the young woman is pregnant," understanding "is" as implied because of the adjectival construction, is adopted here[94] (while also recognizing the implied verb can have an imminent future sense).

90. Durousseau, "Isaiah 7:14B," 178.
91. Yosef, "Isaiah 7:14—Part 1," 11 (Table II.E.3-2).
92. Ibid., 10.
93. Ibid., 5.
94. Durousseau, "Isaiah 7:14B," 177.

The next points to consider in Isaiah 7:14 are the identity of the person who will name the Immanuel child and the significance of the child Immanu El, as these will have implications as important as "young woman" and "[is] pregnant" when we return to consider Matthew's use of Isaiah 7:14. As for who will name the Immanuel child, the Hebrew text, which reads from right to left, reads: וְקָרָאת שְׁמוֹ עִמָּנוּ אֵל (veqarat shmu Immanu El), and is translated as "and she will name or call him Immanu El." The Hebrew verb here is a compound of קָרָאת + וְ (ve +qarat) comprised of וְ (a vav consecutive conjunction, "and") and the verb קָרָאת in the second person, singular, feminine form ("you [feminine] will call"). Yosef notes, "The verb is normally taken as an archaic third feminine singular form here, and translated, 'she will call.' However the form (קָרָאת qara't) is more naturally understood as second feminine singular, in which case the words would be addressed to the young woman mentioned just before this."[95] He also emphasizes the importance that the difference between third- and second-person makes when interpreting the passage: "The common translation as a third-person, feminine conjugation introduces ambiguity, whereas the grammatically accurate second-person, feminine conjugation leaves no doubt that these events would occur contemporaneously, i.e., in the second half of the eighth century BCE."[96]

As for the significance of the Immanu El child within the context of Isaiah 7:14–16, the narrative is clear that Isaiah's prophecy to Ahaz was intended to reassure him that the two invading armies would not only not be successful in overthrowing Jerusalem, but they would also be destroyed. The child Immanu El—God-with-us—would be the sign to Ahaz of this divine protection within this immediate crisis.

Thus, to briefly summarize, Isaiah 7:14 within its immediate narrative and historical contexts should be understood as: Behold, the young woman (of marriageable age) is (or imminently will be) pregnant and she will bear a son and she (or "you, the young woman") will name him Immanu ʽEl, (and he will be the sign that will assure you [Ahaz] that those armies besieging Jerusalem will not only not be successful but will be destroyed before Immanu El reaches maturity).

Returning now to the author of Matthew's use of Isaiah 7:14, I will first compare the Hebrew text of Isaiah 7:14 to the Septuagint's, then the Septuagint's to Matthew 1:23, and discuss Matthew's use of Isaiah 7:14 within his birth of Jesus narrative.

---

95. Yosef, "Isaiah 7:14—Part 1," 5.
96. Ibid., 13.

First, in Table 14, I will compare Yoseph's rendering of the Hebrew translation of Isaiah 7:14 with the Septuagint's rendering of the same.

Table 14: Hebrew and Septuagint versions of Isaiah 7:14

Hebrew text	Septuagint
הִנֵּה הָעַלְמָה, הָרָה וְיֹלֶדֶת בֵּן, וְקָרָאת שְׁמוֹ, עִמָּנוּ אֵל	ἰδοὺ ἡ παρθένος ἐν γαστρὶ ἕξει καὶ τέξεται υἱόν, καὶ καλέσεις τὸ ὄνομα αὐτοῦ Ἐμμανουήλ.
The young woman [is/imminently will be] pregnant and she will bear a son and she [or "you" (the young woman)"] will name him Immanu El.	The virgin will be pregnant and she will bear a son, and you (singular) will call his name Emmanouel. (My translation.)

There are four differences between these two passages: 1) the young woman/the virgin, 2) is/imminently will be pregnant/will be pregnant, 3) she/you will name him and you will name him, and 4) the name Immanuel/Emmanouel to be briefly considered.

As for the first difference, according to Liddell and Scott, παρθένος can denote "a maiden, girl" without providing any indication as to the girl's sexual experience or virginity. It can also denote "virgin" as opposed to γυνή, *woman* or *wife*, or it can refer to "unmarried women who are not virgins," the "Virgin Goddess, as a title of Athena," and, in the masculine sense, as an unmarried man," again without any indication of the man's sexual status.[97] Παρθένος occurs in the Septuagint about 50 times (excluding apocryphal texts not in the Hebrew Bible). In 49 of these occurrences, παρθένος translates the Hebrew word for virgin, *bethula*.[98] It is interesting and puzzling to note that παρθένος translates *bethula* four times in Isaiah. In Isaiah 23:4, the Hebrew text reads, "nor have I raised youths or reared virgins (*bethuloth*) and is translated in the Septuagint as παρθένους, the corresponding plural form; in 37:22, the Hebrew text reads "The virgin [*bethula*] daughter of Zion, she scorns you" and is translated παρθένος; in 47:1, the Hebrew text reads "Get down and sit on the dirt, O virgin [*bethula*] daughter of Babylonia," and in the Septuagint it is translated as παρθένος;

---

97. LSJ, 1339.

98. Gen 24:16 (2); Exod 22:15, 16; Lev 21:3, 13, 14; Deut 22:14, 15, 17 (2), 19, 20, 23, 28; 32:25; Judg 11:37, 38; 19:24; 21:12; 2 Sam (2 Kgs LXX) 13:2, 18; 1 Kgs (3 Kgs LXX) 1:2; 2 Kgs (4 Kgs LXX) 19:21; 2 Chr (2 Par LXX) 36:17; Esth 2:3, 17; Ps 44:15; 78:63; 148:12; Amos 5:2; 8:13; Joel 1:8; Zech 9:17; Isa 23:4; 37:22; 47:1; 62:5; Jer 2:32; 18:13; Lam 1:4, 15, 18; 2:10, 13, 21; 5:11; Ezek 9:6; 44:2.

and, in Isaiah 62:5, the Hebrew text reads, "As a young man will take a virgin [*bethula*] in marriage . . .," and in the Septuagint it is translated παρθένος. This is puzzling because the Hebrew word for *virgin* is used in Isaiah at least four times, so if *virgin* was meant in 7:14, it is puzzling why *bethula* is not used there. The other two Hebrew words that παρθένος translates are *enor* ("young woman," four times[99]) and *alma* (young woman, Isa 7:14 and Gen 24:43). As for *enor*, in Genesis 34, we are informed that Shechem "violated" (raped) Dinah in v. 2, but in v. 3, we read, "he loved the maiden [*enor*/παρθένου] and appealed to the maiden's [*enor*/παρθένου] emotions." According to the narrative, Dinah could not have been a virgin in v. 3 after she was raped by Shechem in v. 2, but yet she is referred to as a *parthenos* here, a young woman of marriageable age. Finally, in addition to παρθένος translating the Hebrew *alma* in Isaiah 7:14, it also translates *alma* in Genesis 24:43. Therein, Abraham's servant is seeking a bride for Isaac with the hope that Rebecca, the "young woman [*alma*/παρθένος] who comes to draw water," will be this future bride. There is nothing in this immediate passage that indicates Rebecca's sexual experience or status and there are at least two possible explanations for the translation of *alma* by παρθένος. First, παρθένος could denote "young woman" here as with Dinah in Genesis 34:2 as noted above. Second, in Genesis 24:16, the narrator refers to Rebecca as a "virgin [*bethula*] whom no man had known," which the translator translated as παρθένος. Thus it could be understandable that if the translator of 24:16 is also the translator of 24:43, he could have read *bethula* into *alma* there and translated *alma* as παρθένος. While this explanation seems reasonable for this passage, there is no similar reasonable explanation for παρθένος in Isaiah 7:14. This will be considered further below.

The second difference between the Septuagint version and the Hebrew is that whereas in the Hebrew there is an immediate sense of the pregnancy, in the Septuagint "she will conceive" (ἐν γαστρὶ ἕξει) is clearly in the future tense but also ambiguous in that the future could mean immediately after the future verb is expressed or any other indeterminate time in the future. When we discuss Matthew's use of the passage it will be obvious that he intends the far future (about 750 years) but this use/meaning is based on Matthew's transformation of Isa 7:14 not on the syntax of verb tense. The third difference, "she/you (singular) will name him" in the Hebrew Bible and "you (singular) will name (καλέσεις) him" in the Septuagint could be a direct translation of קָרָאת (*qara't*) from the Hebrew text if the Septuagint translator understood the Hebrew verb form as second feminine singular as explained above. As for the name of the child, it

---

99. Gen 24:14, 55; 34:3 (twice).

appears that the Septuagint translator merely transliterated the Hebrew name, which raises the question of whether a Greek reading audience who did not know Hebrew would have understood the significance of the name within the broader context of Isaiah 7-8.

In returning to the author of Matthew's use of Isaiah 7:14, Matt 1:23 will be compared only to the Septuagint text in Table 15, since that is the text Matthew used and altered.

Table 15: Comparison of Isaiah 7:14 LXX and Matthew 1:23

Isaiah 7:14 LXX	Matthew 1:23
ἰδοὺ ἡ παρθένος ἐν γαστρὶ ἕξει καὶ τέξεται υἱόν, καὶ <u>καλέσεις</u> τὸ ὄνομα αὐτοῦ Εμμανουηλ.	ἰδοὺ ἡ παρθένος ἐν γαστρὶ ἕξει καὶ τέξεται υἱόν, καὶ <u>καλέσουσιν</u> τὸ ὄνομα αὐτοῦ Ἐμμανουήλ.
Behold, the virgin will conceive and she will bear a son and <u>you (second person singular)</u> will call his name Emmanouel.	Behold, the virgin will conceive and she will bear a son and <u>they (third person plural)</u> will call his name Emmanouel.

The only difference between Matthew's text and the Septuagint is that whereas the Septuagint reads "you (singular) will call" (second person, singular, καλέσεις), Matthew writes "they will call" (third person, plural, καλέσουσιν). This is a very important difference that will be discussed below.

In considering the author of Matthew's use of Isaiah 7:14 here in the birth narrative, one of the first questions to ask is: Did Matthew follow an already existing version of the Septuagint of Isaiah that included ἡ παρθένος as a translation for *ha-alma* [הָעַלְמָה]? This question leads to a second: Would a Jewish translator of the Hebrew Bible have translated הָעַלְמָה (*ha-alma,* "the young woman") with ἡ παρθένος (*parthenos,* "the virgin") with the intention of meaning "virgin"—a woman who had not had intercourse with a man—instead of "young woman"?

In an attempt to answer these questions and, thus, try to gain a better understanding of Matthew's rhetorical use of Isaiah 7:14, we have textual evidence that testifies to the existence of Greek versions of the Septuagint that date to about the middle of the first century BCE. Prior to considering these, it is important to note that scholars are still uncertain about when a complete Greek translation of the entire Hebrew Bible first came into existence. While evidence exists that indicates that the Pentateuch existed in a Greek translation by the middle of the third century BCE, scholars do not think that translations of at least most of the rest of the books existed until about the middle of the first century BCE.[100] Moreover, while a few earlier fragments written by Jewish translators have been preserved, the primary manuscripts upon which critical texts of our Septuagint are based date to the middle of the fourth century CE, and these because of the efforts of Christian, not Jewish, scribes. The importance of this fact cannot be overstated—Christian editors/scribes of the first half of the fourth century CE are responsible for the text of the Septuagint that we have today.

Dialogue with Trypho (ca. 150 CE)

The earliest textual reference to earlier versions of the Septuagint is in Justin Martyr's *Dialogue with Trypho* wherein Justin, in engaging his (fictional) Jewish counter-part, Trypho, writes,

> But since you [Trypho] and your teachers dare to claim that in the prophecy of Isaiah it does not say, 'Behold the virgin [ἡ παρθένος] will conceive,' but 'Behold, the young woman [ἡ νεᾶνις] will conceive [λήψεται] and bear a son ...'

Justin continues,

> For you [Trypho] assent to those [claims] that I have brought to your attention, except that you contradict the statement, 'Behold the virgin [ἡ παρθένος] will conceive,' and say it should read, 'Behold, the young woman will conceive [ἡ νεᾶνις ἐν γαστρὶ λήψεται].'"[101]

While Justin does not inform us as to who these teachers (οἱ διδάσκαλοι) might be, Irenaeus, writing ca. 180 CE does:

> God, then, was made man, and the Lord did himself save us, giving us the token of the virgin. But not as some allege, among those now presuming to expound the scripture, "Behold, a young woman [ἡ νεᾶνις] shall conceive, and bring forth a son," as Theodotion the Ephesian has interpreted, and Aquila of Pontus, both Jewish proselytes.[102]

We do not know much about Aquila, but it is thought that, after receiving training from Jewish rabbis, possibly in Jerusalem, he translated the Hebrew

---

100. For discussion, see Jobes and Silva, *Invitation to the Septuagint*, especially ch. 2, "The Transmission of the Septuagint"; Rahlfs, "History of the Septuagint Text," in Rahlfs (ed.), *Septuaginta*; and Law, *When God Spoke Greek*.

101. Justin Martyr, *Dialogue with Trypho* 43 and 71. Greek text from *TLG*.

102. Irenaeus, *Against Heresies* 3.21 (*ANF*). Greek text from *TLG*.

Bible into Greek, basing his translation upon a recently revised Hebrew text seeking "to correct perceived deficiencies in the Septuagint, including those that affected Jewish-Christian disputes."[103] Similarly, little is known of Theodotion. He is thought to have been a convert to Judaism and to have lived in Ephesus about the end of the second century CE, and, like Aquila, his translation of the Hebrew text was literal.

There were other Greek translations of the Hebrew Bible besides these mentioned,[104] but the point I am making here is that other Greek versions of the Hebrew Bible were in existence near, even prior to, the time that the author of Matthew penned his gospel for which we have textual evidence that the Greek text of Isaiah 7:14 read, "Behold, the young woman [ἡ νεᾶνις] will conceive" rather than, "Behold, the virgin [ἡ παρθένος] will conceive." This fact leads to the intriguing possibility that no text of the Greek Old Testament that read "Behold, the virgin [ἡ παρθένος] will conceive" existed until Christians created such a text to advance their claim that Jesus was born of a virgin, and this leads me to Matthew's use of Isaiah 7:14 in his birth narrative, which is cumulative, and takes the following form:

1. A virgin giving birth without having had intercourse with a male was simply not conceivable in the Jewish mindset; thus, to claim, "A virgin will conceive," and mean by this a woman who has not had sexual intercourse with a man will conceive, is not something that a Jewish scribe would conceive, write, or translate.

2. *Bethula* (the Hebrew word for *virgin*) and *alma* (the Hebrew word for *young woman*) are not synonymous, as the former specifically denotes a woman's sexual status/experience whereas the latter does not.

3. *Parthenos* translates *ha-almah* only twice in the Septuagint. One of these (Gen 24:43), as noted above, can be reasonably explained. This leaves only Isaiah 7:14, which cannot be reasonably explained, unless it is to be understood therein as "young woman" without any reference to the woman's sexual state or experience.

4. The translation of *parthenos* for *ha-almah* is an exceptionally unusual translation. The vast majority of times that *parthenos* occurs in the Septuagint it translates *bethula*, the Hebrew word for *virgin*.

5. The major manuscripts upon which the Septuagint text is based date to the middle of the fourth-century CE.

---

103. Jobes and Silva, *Invitation*, 39.

104. See ibid., especially 29–104 ("The History of the Septuagint"); and Rahlfs, *Septuaginta*, xxi–lx.

6. We do not know when Matthew penned his birth narrative, but scholars surmise somewhere between 80–110 CE. The occurrence of *parthenos* in Matthew is the chronologically first occurrence of the *parthenos* translation for *ha-almah* that is extant.

7. The author of Matthew:
   - Is offering an explanation within a polemical context for Mary's pregnancy when she should not have been by someone other than her husband; his explanation is apologetical.
   - Crafted an artificial and fictitious genealogy that included four women, and the only common denominator among them is that they were all involved in some kind of sexual impropriety;
   - Invented names to fill in the genealogy;
   - Created the fictitious character of Joseph to provide Mary with a husband;
   - Created a fictitious birth narrative (1:18–25) that is to serve as a counter-narrative to the claims in circulation;
   - Altered his Greek Old Testament version of Isaiah 7:14 that read νεᾶνις (young woman) to read παρθένος (with the intended meaning of "virgin") and, at the same time, altered "you [singular] will call" (καλέσεις) in his source to "they will call" (καλέσουσιν) because Jesus was already named Jesus when the author of Matthew penned his birth narrative, so he had to have Joseph name the child Jesus instead of Immanuel, so he changed the verb to the third person, plural "they will call him Immanuel," whoever "they" might be, even though Jesus is never referred to again as Immanuel anywhere in the New Testament texts—a deviously clever transformation of his source.

8. From Justin Martyr and Irenaeus (ca. 150–180), we know that translations of Isaiah 7:14 were in circulation that were written by Jewish writers that translated *ha-almah* with *neanis*, the Greek word for "young woman" and that there was controversy between Jewish and Christian writers as to which term was the original (correct) term in the earliest version(s) of the Hebrew scriptures in Greek.

9. The earliest evidence that we have that an earlier version of the Hebrew scriptures in Greek read *parthenos* for *ha-alma* is Matthew's claim made within a clearly polemical context in which he is trying to offer an explanation for Mary's pregnancy when she should not

have been pregnant—a pregnancy that he (somewhat astonishingly) does not deny.

10. We know that it was Christian editors, rather than Jewish editors, who edited the manuscripts upon which our Septuagint is based.

From the above, I conclude that it is highly improbable, if not certain, that Jewish scribes would have translated *parthenos* for *ha-almah* in Isaiah 7:14. Rather, Matthew is directly responsible for the claim that a Greek text of Isaiah 7:14 read, "Behold, a *virgin* will be with child and she will bear a son and *they* will call his name Immanuel." Matthew would also be responsible for altering/transforming the text from *neanis* (young woman) to *parthenos* (virgin). There is no doubt that the author of Matthew 1:23 had to alter the "you [second person singular] will call" to "they [third person plural] will call" because Jesus was already named Jesus when the author of Matthew was writing, so he had to alter his source. It is a short step from that alteration to altering νεᾶνις to παρθένος. Moreover, because of the polemical context to which Matthew is responding in Matthew 1 and because of the argument he is making therein, it seems reasonable to conclude that it was the author of Matthew who altered his source so that the revised version would grant authoritative textual, prophetic, and divine support to his claim that the origin of Mary's pregnancy was due to divine intervention rather than an adulteress affair.

The remainder of the birth narrative in Matthew—the visit of the magi, their flight to Egypt, Herod's slaying of the infants in Bethlehem, and the family's return from Egypt and settling in Nazareth—do not pertain directly to Mary's pregnancy when she should not have been by someone other than her husband and will not be considered here, but the relationship of the magi narrative to Luke's birth narrative will be considered in the next chapter.

Applying Mimetic Criteria to Matthew's Narrative

There is no question that the author of the Matthean birth narrative intimately knew his source, the Septuagint—as especially the genealogies, laws, the four women, and Isa 7:14 were unquestionably the conceptual sources for his narrative. Matthew demonstrates intimate familiarity with and adapts a variety of Old Testament themes: birth annunciations, genealogies, narratives concerning the four women considered here, Deuteronomic law codes, and especially Isa 7:14, satisfying the *intimate familiarity* and *significant similarities* criteria. Matthew's rewriting of the roles of the genealogies and especially Isa 7:14 satisfy the *linguistic details* and *complex coherence* criteria. Matthew's borrowing and recasting of material in Matthew 1 reflects different mimetic strategies than were identified in the last chapter. There, we saw that Matthew followed Mark's narrative structures while altering them. Here, there were no real narrative structures to follow, other than the genealogies. Rather, Matthew borrowed themes, persons, and longer (genealogies) and shorter passages (Isa 7:14)—similar to how Virgil would pluck individual narrative components out from the *Odyssey*—and recast them into narratives of very different contexts that Jewish readers of the Septuagint and Hebrew Bible had never conceived. What readers would have thought that the women mentioned in Matthew's genealogy would have played any role whatsoever in the lineage of the Jewish Messiah? What readers would have thought that a sentence crafted by a Hebrew scribe in the eighth century BCE would foretell of a virgin birth 750 years later? If my argument above of Matthew's revision of Isa 7:14 is correct, he skillfully and deceptively transformed an essentially innocuous passage from the Hebrew Bible into a foundational pillar of Christianity. The historical import of Virgil's mimetic transformation of Homer's epics pales in comparison and posed a challenge to Judaism that has endured for almost 2,000 years. From a rhetorical and compositional perspective, Matthew 1 demonstrates that the author was a skillful writer; he carefully selected material from his source to craft his argument as an apologetical response to claims that must have been in circulation while in the process completely transforming his source. There is little doubt that Matthew borrowed and radically transformed these passages from the Septuagint, but there is considerable doubt that Luke borrowed from, imitated, and transformed Matthew's birth narrative. In the next chapter, I will demonstrate that he did.

Chapter 5

Luke's Mimetic Transformation of Matthew's Birth Narrative

A Rhetorical Analysis of Luke 1–2

I NOTED IN THE previous chapter that the vast majority of New Testament scholars reject the possibility that Luke knew and used any portion of the birth narrative in Matthew's gospel as he crafted his own. Rather, these scholars maintain that Matthew and Luke wrote independently of one another. Because of the importance of this prevailing view to this chapter's discussion, I again cite Brown's representative position on the issue:

> Since it is generally agreed among scholars that Matthew and Luke wrote independently of each other, without knowing the other's work, agreement between the two infancy narratives would suggest the existence of a common infancy tradition earlier than either evangelist's work—a tradition that would have a claim to greater antiquity and thus weigh on the plus side of the historical scale.[1]

Fitzmeyer, writing subsequent to Brown, slightly enhances Brown's list of details of this common tradition found in both birth narratives that, in his view, form the "historical nucleus of what the evangelists worked with."

1. Jesus's birth is related to the reign of Herod (Luke 1:5; Matt 2:1);

2. Mary, his mother to be, is a virgin engaged to Joseph, but they have not yet come to live together (Luke 1:27, 34; 2:5; Matt 1:18);

3. Joseph is of the house of David (Luke 1:27; 2:4; Matt 1:16, 20);

4. An angel from heaven announces the coming birth of Jesus (Luke 1:28–30; Matt 1:20–21);

5. Jesus is recognized himself to be a son of David (Luke 1:32; Matt 1:1);

---

1. Brown, *Birth*, 34.

6. Jesus's conception is to take place through a spirit which is holy (Luke 1:35; Matt 1:18,20);
7. Joseph is not involved in the conception (Luke 1:34; Matt 1:18-25);
8. The name "Jesus" is imposed by heaven prior to his birth (Luke 1:31; Matt 1:21);
9. The angels identify Jesus as "Savior" (Luke 2:11; Matt 1:21);
10. Jesus is born after Mary and Joseph come to live together (Luke 2:4-7; Matt 1:24-25);
11. Jesus is born at Bethlehem (Luke 2:7-7; Matt 2:1); and
12. Jesus settles, with Mary and Joseph, in Nazareth in Galilee (Luke 2:39, 51; Matt 2:22-23).[2]

Those who adhere to this notion of independence maintain that Matthew and Luke would have received or inherited these or similar components of tradition at different times and in different places. Then, each author would have, without any knowledge whatsoever of the other author's work, incorporated these components of tradition into his respective narrative so as to reflect or promote his own understanding of this tradition's relevance in explaining the significance of Jesus's origins. It is important to note that advocates of this common tradition, like advocates of the Q document, speak and write as though these traditions/sources existed *in fact* rather than emphasizing that they are hypothetical constructs their existence of which is necessary to explain difficulties, inconsistencies, and contradictions in the gospel narratives.

On the other hand, a growing number of scholars question this common tradition hypothesis. John Drury, writing in 1976, argued that Luke builds upon Matthew's foundation.[3] H.B. Green, while recognizing that the case for independence is due to the "wide divergence of content," countered that the "close structural correspondence"—that both accounts include "pre-natal" and post-natal" narratives—indicates dependence.[4] In his *Luke: A New Paradigm*, Michael Goulder argued at length that Luke's birth narrative is dependent upon Matthew's, even that Matthew's account is a "fundamental resource" for Luke's.[5] Eric Franklin, writing in 1994, asks: "Is such a 'common tradition' more likely than that which Brown dismisses, namely the dependence of one evangelist upon the other?," and, building

2. Fitzmeyer, *Luke*, 307.
3. Drury, *Tradition and Design*, 143.
4. Green, "Credibility of Luke's Transformation of Matthew," 143.
5. Goulder, *Luke*, 207-8.

upon Goulder, answers his own question by arguing that Luke's account of the virgin conception "can be satisfactorily explained as a development of Matthew."[6] While I will argue below, in contrast to Franklin here, that Luke's account is a counter to Matthew's, we share the underlying understanding that Luke's account is dependent upon Matthew's. In 2002, Mark Goodacre, after briefly reviewing a few of the thematic similarities between Matthew's and Luke's birth narratives, concludes, "The theory that Luke could not have known Matthew because he does not copy wholesale from his Birth Narrative is not, therefore, especially convincing. Indeed like many arguments for Q, reflection on the evidence can lead in quite the opposite direction, in favor of Luke's familiarity with Matthew."[7] David Landry has argued that the author of Luke knew Matthew's birth narrative, was dissatisfied with much of it, and, in his revision of Matthew, removed or omitted the material with which he was dissatisfied.[8] More recently, Francis Watson, finding Goodacre's articulation of the view that Luke knew and used Matthew (The Farrer Hypothesis) "compellingly restated," observes that "Luke's [birth] narrative works so well as the obverse of Matthew's that it is hard not to conclude that it was intended as such—in spite of the scholarly consensus that 'Matthew and Luke wrote independently of each other, without knowing the other's work.'"[9] Andrew Lincoln, writing subsequent to these scholars, is a representative of those not persuaded by the similiarites in the narrative themes and structures that lead these scholars to the conclusion that Luke knew and used Matthew, stating, "The similarities in the birth narratives, however, are simply not remarkable or numerous enough to persuade anyone to abandon the dominant Two Source theory on which they are readily explained by independent use of common traditions."[10]

Here, I am going to argue that Luke intimately knew—even thoroughly digested—the birth narrative in Matthew, that Matthew's narrative was the inspiration for Luke's, and that Luke used it as a (or maybe better *the*) primary source for composing, specifically, the foretelling-of-Jesus's-birth narrative (Luke 1:26–28) and the birth-of-Jesus-and-visitors (shepherds and angels) narrative (Luke 2:2–21).

In addition, I will demonstrate that Luke imitates sections of Matthew's birth narrative in ways that parallel his imitation of passages from the Septuagint, especially 1 Samuel (1 Kgs LXX), within the rest of his

6. Franklin, *Luke*, 358–60.
7. Goodacre, *Case Against Q*, 57.
8. Landry, "Luke's Revsion."
9. Watson, *Gospel Writing*, 135.
10. Lincoln, *Born of a Virgin?*, 132.

birth narrative. Scholars have long recognized Luke's use of the Septuagint in the birth narrative. Alfred Harnack, writing in 1908, after identifying about 40 references or allusions to Septuagint passages in the Magnificat and Benedictus of Luke 1, noted, "it is plain that St. Luke in composing [the Magnificat and Benedictus] has *purposely* kept to the language of Psalms and prophets (LXX). The Hebraisms, whether adopted or inserted from the Old Testament, are intentional; the whole style is artificial, and is intended to produce an infusion of antiquity—a purpose which has been really fulfilled."[11] In his classic *The Making of Luke-Acts* (1927), Henry Cadbury observed that "imitation (μίμησις) of definite authors became a rhetorical practice for young students that finished authors never outgrew," that "in the birth stories [the Greek Old Testament] has affected both the matter and manners, and frequently elsewhere it is quoted, echoed or imitated," and that "the songs and prayers of Luke's nativity stories belong to the same category [as *Psalms of Solomon* and Ecclesiastes] of imitation of earlier Hebrew poetical material and adoption of earlier phrases."[12] Writing in 1940, Eric Burrows's thesis stated "that the author of Luke 1–2 composed a narrative in the style of the Old Testament, using for his principal model the history of the child Samuel."[13] Burrows identified this method as "imitative historiography," by which the author of Luke 1–2 "sought a model and an appropriate style in the infancy-stories of the Old Testament, and found in Samuel a narrative providentially suited to his purpose, and so was able to give his history the atmosphere of sacred scripture."[14] Michael Goulder and Murray Sanderson (1957)[15] recognize numerous themes and verbal similarities between the LXX, especially Genesis, and Luke 1–2, and, in 1965, John Martin Creed builds upon Harnack's identifications of Greek Old Testament passages within Luke 1–2, adds many more, and it is his outline of the relationship between 1 Samuel (1 Kgs LXX) and Luke 1–2 that I adapt below.[16] Brown (1970 and later revisions) and Fitzmeyer (1981) build upon this earlier work and identify additional passages from the Greek Old Testament that the author of Luke relied upon as he crafted his birth narrative. It is interesting to note, though, that Fitzmeyer adopts Burrows's "imitative historiography" but uses it "in a slightly different way," as Fitzmeyer writes, "Calling the in-

11. Harnack, *Luke the Physician*, 217–18. Harnack's emphasis.
12. Cadbury, *Making of Luke-Acts*, 123, 122, and 192.
13. Burrows, *Gospel of the Infancy*, 1.
14. Ibid., 1.
15. Goulder and Sanderson, "St. Luke's Genesis."
16. Creed, *Luke*, 8–46.

fancy narratives 'imitative historiography' means that whatever historical matter has been preserved by the two evangelists has been assimilated by them to other literary accounts, either biblical or extra biblical."[17] When one recalls Fitzmeyer's list of the "historical nucleus of what the evangelists worked with" cited above, it seems that he is much more interested in aligning the author of Luke's literary and, thus, artificial structure and style with his "historical nucleus" so as to grant the birth narratives more historical verisimilitude than Burrows's imitative historiography would have allowed. Bovon, writing in 2002, while recognizing the debt that the author of Luke 1–2 owes to 1 Samuel (1 Kgs LXX) in the Septuagint, notes that there is also substantial contact between the Magnificat and the apocryphal *Psalms of Solomon*.[18] Concluding this brief review, Richard Pervo (2009) acknowledges that the author of Luke's greatest "facility is an ability to 'write like the Bible,' that is, to imitate the language of the LXX, most notably in Luke 1–2. He can suit style to matter,"[19] and, in his brief commentary on Luke (2014) notes,

> The story of Jesus opens [in Luke] like one of the Hebrew Bible's stories of remarkable births; much of Luke 1–2 is written in 'biblical language," i.e., the language of the LXX. Language and content are two forms of imitation. Mimesis, to use the familiar Greek term, was a major component of ancient education. Just as you will see art students copying paintings in museums, students in the Greco-Roman world learned by imitating the masters. Imitation [also] extends to narrative units.[20]

While these scholars all recognize the importance and use of μίμησις in Greco-Roman education and literary practice, and while they recognize that the author of the Lukan birth narrative imitated the Greek Old Testament, not one of them, excluding Goulder and Sanderson, mentions the possibility that Luke also imitated the birth narrative in Matthew in ways very similar to how he imitated the Septuagint in composing his own birth narrative. The following discussion will make just this argument. I will demonstrate that within this larger structure of imitation of passages and style from the Septuagint, Luke relies upon/imitates the narrative themes and structure of Matthew's foretelling-of-Jesus's-birth narrative (1:18–25) and the birth-of-Jesus-and-visitors narrative (2:1–20) while also maintaining his septuagintalizing style within these narratives he borrows from Matthew.

17. Fitzmeyer, *Luke*, 309.
18. Bovon, *Luke*, 56–57.
19. Pervo, *Acts*, 28.
20. Idem, *Gospel of Luke*, 7.

I will proceed in the following way. I will begin working through Luke's birth narrative in its narrative order beginning with 1:5-25 (the foretelling of John the Baptist's birth) and demonstrate, in some detail, its structural, thematic, and verbal reliance upon the Septuagint. Luke then moves on to his foretelling-of-Jesus's-birth narrative (1:26-38), where his dependence shifts from the Septuagint to Matthew 1:18-25. He returns to the Septuagint for his material for the Visitation, Magnificat, birth and naming of John narrative, and the Benedictus (1:39-80), but, when he begins his birth-of-Jesus-and-visitors narrative (2:1-20), he returns to Matthew 2:1-12, after which he returns to the Septuagint as his source for concluding his birth narrative (2:21-52). Graphically, the alternating arrangement described here is depicted in Table 16, using the Seputagint titles of the Old Testament books.

Table 16: Structural sources for Luke's birth narrative

Source (Old Testament from LXX)	Subject	Luke 1–2
Elkanah and Hannah, and Hannah's barrenness (1 Kgs 1:1–2).	Introduce parents, genealogies, female's barrenness	Zechariah and Elizabeth and Elizabeth's barrenness (1:5–7).
Elkanah at the temple in Shiloh; Hanna's vow to give her son as a Nazarite (1 Kgs 1:3–8).	Temple scene, consecration by second of the Nazarite vows	Zechariah performing temple service; the angelic appearance that informed him that Elizabeth would conceive and that the son would be a Nazarite (1:8–22).
Elkanah and Hannah returned home, and she conceived (1 Kgs 1:19).	Return home, divine conception	Zechariah returned home; Elizabeth conceived (1:23–25).
An angel explains why Mary is pregnant (Matt 1:18–25).	Annunciation concerning Mary	Gabriel announces to Mary that she will conceive (1:26–38).
Hannah's song and many other passages from the LXX (1 Kgs 2:1–11).	Visitation, Magnificat	Mary visits Elizabeth and sings her Magnificat (1:39–56).
Samuel's birth and naming (1 Kgs 1:20).	Birth and naming of child	John the Baptist is born and named (1:57–66, 80).
Many passages from the LXX	The Benedictus	1:67–79: Zechariah's praise.

Source (Old Testament from LXX)	Subject	Luke 1–2
Jesus's birth; the magi (Matt 2:1–12).	Jesus's birth	Joseph and Mary's journey to Bethlehem; shepherds; Jesus's birth (2:1–20).
The covenant of circumcision (Gen 17; Lev 12).	Jesus's circumcision	Jesus is circumcised (2:21).
Elkanah, and Hannah at temple scene (1 Kgs 1:22–25).	The Presentation	Joseph and Mary present Jesus at the temple (2:22–24).
Eli blessed them (1 Kgs 2:19–24).	Simeon	Simeon's Nunc Dimittis (2:25–35.
No parallel	Anna	2:36–38
No parallel	Family's return to Galilee; child continues to grow	2:39–40
1 Kgs 2:26	Temple scene	Jesus is left behind during Passover (2:41–52).

After working through Luke's birth narrative, I briefly consider his genealogy, suggesting that there are compelling reasons to think that Luke's idea of a genealogy also stems from Matthew's and that he used it as his model for his own, engaged it, revised it, and via Greco-Roman imitation, made it his own. Finally, I consider two possible reasons as to why Luke would use and so radically transform Matthew's birth narrative and genealogy.

Luke 1:5–25: Foretelling of John's Birth

In 1 Kgs (LXX) 1–20, we are immediately introduced to Elkanah, informed of his family roots ("son of Jeroham son of Elihu son of Tohu") and that he had two wives, one of whom was Hannah, who "had no children." Similarly, in Luke 1:5–7, we are immediately introduced to a priest named Zechariah, "who belonged to the priestly order of Abijah" and to his wife, Elizabeth, who herself was a descendant of Aaron. Like Elkanah and Hannah, Zachariah and Elizabeth "had no children" because, like Hannah, "Elizabeth was barren." In addition to these structural/thematic similarities, there are also close verbal similarities. 1 Samuel 1 (1 Kgs LXX) opens with "There was a [certain] man . . . and the name to him [was] Elkanah" (Ἄνθρωπος ἦν . . . ὄνομα αὐτῷ Ελκανα, 1:1, LXX), which is very similar to "[There was] a certain priest by name Zachariah" (ἱερεύς τις ὀνόματι Ζαχαρίς, 1:5), the latter of which Brown notes is "good LXX style."[21] A second verbal similarity is the expression that "Hannah had no children" (Αννα οὐκ ἦν παιδίον, 1:2) and Luke's "there was no child to them [Zachariah and Elizabeth]" (οὐκ ἦν αὐτοῖς τέκνον, 1:7). Luke's expression that "Elizabeth was barren" (ἦν ἡ Ἐλισάβετ στεῖρα) is the common form of expressing the same idea throughout the Septuagint; examples include "Sara was barren" (ἦν Σαρα στεῖρα, Gen 11:30) and "Rachel was barren" (Ραχηλ δὲ ἦν στεῖρα, Gen 29:31).[22] The expression that Zachariah and Elizabeth were both righteous "before God" (ἐναντίον τοῦ θεοῦ, 1:6) does not occur in Greek literature prior to the Septuagint and occurs therein on five occasions,[23] here, and Acts 8:21, and that Zachariah and Elizabeth were "advanced in age" (προβεβηκότες, 1:6) is a very rare expression in ancient Greek, occurring only once in the Septuagint in reference to Abraham and Sarah who were "very old" (πρεσβύτεροι προβεβηκότες, Gen 18:11).

Thematic and verbal similarities continue between 1 Kgs (LXX) 1:3-19 and Luke 1:8-35. Whereas Elkanah goes to the Temple in Shiloh to sacrifice (1:3), Luke has Zachariah in the Jerusalem temple conducting the incense-offering (1:10). Next, in 1 Kgs, Hannah vows that if she is given a male child, "then I will set him before you as a Nazirite until the day of his death. He shall drink neither wine nor intoxicants [οἶνον καὶ μέθυσμα οὐ πίεται], and no razor shall touch his head" (1:11), citing one of the Nazirite vows recorded in Num. 6.[24] In Luke, the author employs an annunciation scene very similar to other annunciation scenes discussed in the last chapter wherein the angel pronounces to Zachariah: "Do not be afraid, Zachariah, for your prayer has been heard. Your wife Elizabeth will bear you a son, and you will name him John.... He must never drink wine or strong drink [οἶνον καὶ σίκερα οὐ μὴ πίῃ]" (1:13-15), language very similar to that in 1 Kgs. In 1 Kgs 1:19 (LXX), Eklanah and Hannah return to their home, have intercourse, and Hannah conceives (συνέλαβεν) with divine assistance, whereas, in Luke, when Zachariah's term was completed, he returned home and Elizabeth conceives (συνέλαβεν), a common verb for conceiving in the LXX, but its only occurrence in the New Testament is here.

---

21. Brown, *Birth*, 258.
22. See also Gen 25:21 and Judg 13:3.
23. Exod 28:29; Num 10:4; Josh 24:1; 1 Chr (1 Para LXX) 24:1; and Jer 3:25.
24. It is interesting to note that this stipulation that the child must abstain from wine and strong drink is not in the Hebrew text of 1 Samuel, but only the LXX (1 Kgs).

In addition to these structural and verbal similarities between 1 Samuel 1 (1 Kgs LXX) and Luke 1, there are also many verbal similarities between Luke 1:8–35 and the Septuagint. In Luke 1:10, we are told that "the whole multitude of people" (πᾶν πλῆθος) were praying outside the temple; this expression occurs 12 times in the Septuagint and only in Luke and Acts in the New Testament.[25] In Luke 1:11, the angel is standing at the right side of the "alter of incense" (θυσιαστηρίου τοῦ θυμιάματος), a phrase that occurs only one other time in Greek literature in Lev 4:7. In Luke 1:13, the angel, following stereotypical annunciation form, tells Zachariah not to fear because "your petition has been heard" (εἰσηκούσθη ἡ δέηχις). The only other occurrences of this expression in Greek literature are the three in the Septuagint[26] and one in Acts 10:31 where the angel appears to Cornelius informing him that his "prayer had been heard" (εἰσηκούσθη σου ἡ προσευχὴ). In Luke 1:18, Zachariah asks the angel, "How can I know this?" (κατὰ τί γνώσομαι), a form that occurs in Greek literature only in Gen 15:8 where Abram asks, "How can I know [κατὰ τί γνώσομαι] that I will occupy the land?" In Luke 1:25, after Elizabeth conceives, she exclaims, "The Lord has taken away my humiliations [ἀφελεῖν ὄνειδός μου] among men." The only other form of this expression is in Gen 30:23 (LXX) where, after she conceived and bore a son, Rachel exclaimed, "God has taken away my humiliation" (Ἀφεῖλεν ὁ θεός μου τὸ ὄνειδος).

Luke 1:26–38: Annunciation to Mary

It is after Elizabeth's exclamation of the removal of her humiliation at 1:25 that Luke departs from his model/source, for whereas in 1 Samuel 1 (1 Kgs LXX) the announcement that Samuel was born follows immediately after the narrative announcement that Hannah conceived (v. 20), Luke interrupts the announcement of John's birth with the foretelling of Jesus's birth (1:26–38), Mary's visit to Elizabeth during which time Mary recited her Magnificat (vv. 39–55), and Mary's return home (v. 56), before returning to narrate John's birth, his naming, and Zachariah's Benedictus in 1:57–79.[27] Just as Luke has used 1 Samuel 1 (1 Kgs LXX) for much of his birth narrative

---

25. In the LXX, Exod 12:6; 2 Kgs 7:13; 1 Chr (1 Para) 29:16; 2 Chr (2 Para) 31:18; 1 Esd 9:6, 10, 38, 41, 47; 1 Macc 9:63, 3 Macc 13:2; Ezra 32:3; 39:11. It occurs in Luke 8:37; 19:37; 23:1; and in Acts 15:12; 25:24.

26. Εἰσηκούσθη ("has been heard") occurs in Tob 3:16 with προσευχὴ; in *Sirach* with ἡ δέησις, and in Dan 10:12 with τὸ ῥῆμα.

27. Following Burrows's observation (*Gospel of the Infancy*, 2).

discussed thus far, he models his foretelling-of-Jesus's-birth narrative upon the parallel narrative in Matthew, as Table 17 reflects.

Table 17: Luke's structural imitation of Matthew 1:18–25

Matthew	Similar event, concept	Luke
μνηστευθείσης (1:18)	Mary is engaged to Joseph.	ἐμνηστευμένην (1:27)
1:18	Joseph "finds" Mary to be pregnant when she should not be.	Author omits; see below.
ἐν γαστρὶ ἔχουσα (1:18).	Mary is or will be pregnant.	Συλλήμψῃ ἐν γαστρὶ (1:31).
1:19	Joseph contemplates putting Mary away or divorcing her.	Author omits; see below.
An angel of the Lord speaks to Joseph in a dream/vision (1:20–21).	Angelic appearance (annunciation)	Gabriel has a conversation with Mary face-to-face (1:26–38).
To Joseph Μὴ φοβηθῇς (1:20).	"Do not fear"	To Mary Μὴ φοβοῦ (1:30).
Do not fear to take Mary as your wife, for (γὰρ) that which is in her (1:20).	Angel's reassurance/ explanation	Do not fear, Mary, for (γὰρ) you have found favor with God (1:30).
She will bear a son (1:21).	Bear a son	You will bear a son (1:31).
You will call his name, Jesus.	Naming Jesus	You will call his name, Jesus.
ἐκ πνεύματος ἁγίου She was found to be with child from a spirit which is holy (1:18, 20).	Angel explains that Mary's conceiving due to a spirit which is holy.	Πνεῦμα ἅγιον ἐπελεύσεται ἐπὶ σὲ καὶ δύναμις ὑψίστου ἐπισκιάσει σοι. A spirit which is holy will come upon you and a power from [the] highest will overshadow you (1:35).
By citing Isaiah 7:14 (1:23).	Mary a παρθένος	"I have not known a man."
1:22 By citing Isaiah 7:14.	Jesus's birth a fulfillment	1:54–5, 70, 73; 2:29, but no citation of Isaiah 7:14 (1:34).

Matthew	Similar event, concept	Luke
Save (σώσει) his people from their sins (1:21).	Jesus will:	Be great and son of the highest (1:37); rule upon the house of Jacob (1:33); be a savior (σωτὴρ, 2:11, 28–32) (1:32).
Joseph did not know her. (οὐκ ἐγίνωσκεν αὐτήν) (1:25).	"Knowing"	Mary: "I have not known a man" (ἄνδρα οὐ γινώσκω) (1:34).
"You (Joseph) will call his name, Jesus" (καλέσεις τὸ ὄνομα αὐτοῦ Ἰησοῦν) (1:25).	Naming the child	"You (Mary) will call his name, Jesus (καλέσεις τὸ ὄνομα αὐτοῦ Ἰησοῦν) (1:31).
Joseph did what he was told (1:24).	Response to angelic annunciation	Mary: "Let it be to me according to your word" (1:38).

As Table 17 demonstrates, the narrative structure, order, and especially the themes in these two accounts are strikingly similar. While many of the similarities are due to the stereotypical form of biblical annunciations, there are also similarities in these two narratives that are not included in the other annunciations: Mary and Joseph are *betrothed*, using the same verb (μνηστευ-) a verb that occurs only in Deut 22–24 in the Septuagint and only in these passages in the New Testament; Joseph did not have intercourse (οὐκ ἐγίνωσκεν) with Mary (Matt 1:25) and Mary was not having intercourse (οὐ γινώσκω) with a man (Luke 1:34); both Joseph and Mary individually name the child Jesus (Matt 1:25; Luke 1:31); and that Jesus's birth is a fulfillment of (different) prophetic utterances (Matt 1:22–23; Luke 1:54-5, 70, 73; 2:29). Such striking thematic, structural, and verbal similarities indicate dependence.

Yet, while recognizing these structural, thematic, and verbal similarities with the foretelling-of-Jesus's-birth narrative in Matthew, Luke continues mimicking/incorporating language from the Septuagint into his birth narrative. For example, whereas the author of Matthew cites Isaiah 7:14 that the *parthenos* "will conceive" (ἐν γαστρὶ ἕξει), Luke writes "she will conceive" (συλλήμψῃ, 1:31), found only here in the New Testament, but also in Judges 13:5 (B) where the angel of the Lord informs Samuel's mother that "she will conceive" (συλλήμψῃ). In Luke 1:35, in response to Mary's question, "How can this be, for I am not having a sexual relationship with a man?," the author has Gabriel respond that "a spirit which is holy will come upon you and power of the most high will overshadow [ἐπισκιάσει] you."

The verb for "will overshadow" (ἐπισκιάσει) occurs rarely in Greek literature but a few times in the Septuagint. For example, in Exod 40, Moses was instructed to set up the "tent of witness" and once he completed his task, the cloud covered the tent "and the tent was filled with the glory of the Lord. And Moses was unable to enter into the tent of witness, because the cloud was overshadowing [ἐπεσκάζεν] it, and the tent was filled with the glory of the Lord" (vv. 34–35). The imagery and symbolism that Luke is conveying here is lost in the English translations, but clearly recognizable when one realizes that he is here imitating the style and diction of the Septuagint that is used to represent the overshadowing of "the glory of the Lord" in Exod 40.[28] Also in Luke 1:35, it is the "power of the most high" that will be overshadowing Mary, and "the most high" (ὁ ὑψίστος) is an extremely common expression (occurring over 100 times) in the Septuagint in reference to the Hebrew God and, when combined with the verb for "overshadowing," the imagery much more effectively expresses the role of the Spirit in Mary's conception than does Matthew's account—a perfect example of a later author using his source, making it one's own, and improving it. Gabriel then offers one more assurance to Mary that that which he is telling her will come to pass—that her kinswoman, Elizabeth, who was barren, is now in her sixth month, "because nothing that God says is impossible" (ὅτι οὐκ ἀδυνατήσει παρὰ τοῦ θεοῦ πᾶν ῥῆμα, 1:37), which is a minor alteration of God's response to Abraham concerning Sarah's laughing to herself that she could become pregnant: "Can it be that a matter is impossible with God?" (μὴ ἀδυνατεῖ παρὰ τῷ θεῷ ῥῆμα, Gen 18:14).

Concluding the annunciation scene, Luke transitions from Matthew's foretelling-of-Jesus's-birth narrative as his source back to Hannah's song in 1 Kgs (LXX) as his source for Mary's Magnificat by way of Mary's visit to Elizabeth. Here, too, themes and language are dependent upon the Septuagint. When Mary meets Elizabeth, "the child leaps in her [Elizabeth's] womb" (ἐσκίρτησεν τὸ βρέφος ἐν τῇ κοιλίᾳ αὐτῆς), which mimics who would become Esau and Jacob leaping inside Rebecca's womb (ἐσκίρτων δὲ παιδία ἐν αὐτῇ) in Gen 25:22. Upon receiving Mary into her home, Elizabeth cried out with a "great shout" (κραυγῇ μεγάλῃ, 1:42), a rare expression that occurs twice in Exodus as the Egyptians let out a "great cry" (κραυγῇ μεγάλῃ) throughout the land when the Hebrew God slaughtered the first-born from each Egyptian home.[29] In her "great cry," Elizabeth heaps two praises upon Mary, "Blessed are you among women"

---

28. See also Ps 90(91):4 and 139(140):7. It is the same verb in the transfiguration scene in Luke 9:34 and Matt 17:5.

29. Exod 11:6 and 12:30.

(Εὐλογημένη σὺ ἐν γυναιξὶν), a mimicking of Judges 5:24, "May Iael be blessed among women" (εὐλογηθείη ἐκ γυναικῶν), and "Blessed is the fruit of your womb" (εὐλογημένος ὁ καρπὸς τῆς κοιλίας σου), a mimicking of the Deuteronomist's second blessing upon the Israelites if they would obey their God, "Blessed be the children of your womb" (εὐλογημένα τὰ ἔκγονα τῆς κοιλίας σου, 28:4).

The Magnificat

As noted above, scholars are in agreement that Hannah's Song in 1 Samuel (1 Kgs LXX) served as Luke's primary model for the Magnificat while also recognizing that many of the expressions within the Magnificat are scattered throughout the Greek Old Testament. Fitzmeyer may have stated it best that the Magnificat is "a mosaic of OT expressions drawn from the LXX."[30] In Table 18, I align in parallel columns the Magnificat and passages from the Septuagint that reflect the content of the Magnificat's passages, while setting off in *italics* some of the closest parallels.[31] As Creed notes, the first half of the Magnificat "expresses the personal thankfulness of the speaker. In the second half we pass over from the thought of God as σωτὴρ [savior] of the individual to God as savior of Israel from her haughty oppressors. In this general character, as well as in the detail, it closely resembles the song of Hannah."[32]

---

30. Fitzmeyer, *Luke*, 359.

31. The passages from the Septuagint collected here are from my own observations and those of Harnack (*Luke the Physician*, 206–14, includes Greek texts), Creed (*Luke*, 22–26, includes Greek texts), Brown (*Birth*, 346–65), Fitzmeyer (*Luke*, 356–71), and Bovon (*Luke*, 1:60–64).

32. Creed, *Luke*, 23. For comparison of the Greek texts, see Harnack, *Luke the Physician*, 206–14; and Creed, *Luke*, 22–26.

Table 18: Septuagint sources for the Magnificat[33] [34]

Passages from the Magnificat (1:47–55)	Passages from the Septuagint
And [Mary] said, 'My soul magnifies the Lord (46), and my spirit rejoices in God my Savior (47),	And [Hannah] said, 'My heart was made firm in the Lord; my horn was exalted in my God' (1 Kgs (LXX). 2:1).
	But my soul shall rejoice in the Lord: it will delight in his salvation (Ps 34:9).
	Yet I will rejoice in the Lord; I will exult in the Lord; I will rejoice in God my savior (Hab 3:18).
for he has looked with favor on the lowliness of his servant (48). Surely, from now on all generations will call me blessed;	And she vowed a vow to the Lord, saying, O Lord God of Sabaoth, if looking you will look on the humiliation of your slave (1 Kgs 1:11).
	I will rejoice and be glad in thy mercy because you looked upon my humiliation; you saved my soul from dire straits (Ps 30:7 LXX).
	Leah conceived and bore a son to Jakob, and she called his name Rouben, saying, 'In as much as the Lord has seen my humiliation" (Gen 29:32).
	And Leah said, 'Happy am I! For the women will pronounce me happy' (Gen 30:13).
for the Mighty One has done great things for me, and holy is his name (49).	He is your God who did among you these great and glorious things that your eyes have seen (Deut 10:21).
	Holy and fearful is his name (Ps 110:9 LXX).
His mercy is for those who fear him from generation to generation (50).	But the mercy of the Lord is from generation to generation on those who fear him (Ps 102:17 LXX).

---

33. There is debate among scholars as to whether Mary or Elizabeth was the original speaker of the Magnificat. For discussion, see Metzger, *Textual Commentary*, 130–31, who, while sympathetic to the view that neither name was original but that the text simply read "and she said" (καὶ εἶπεν), explains that the United Societies Committee weighed in favor of the external evidence for the reading "Mary." See also Creed, *Luke*, 22–23, who, in my view, provides more compelling argumentation for the view that neither Elizabeth nor Mary was original but that the text read "and she said" (καὶ εἶπεν).

34. The translations from these Old Testament passages are from Pietersma and Wright (eds.), *New English Translation of the Septuagint*. Thus, 1 Sam is 1 Kgs and 2 Sam is 2 Kgs.

Passages from the Magnificat (1:47–55)	Passages from the Septuagint
He has shown strength with his arm; he has scattered the proud in the thoughts of their hearts (51).	The Lord's right hand produced power (Ps 117:15 LXX). It is you who brought low a proud one like one wounded; with the arm of your power you scattered your enemies (Ps 88:10 LXX).
He has brought down the powerful from their thrones, and lifted up the lowly (52);	The Lord makes poor and makes rich; he brings low and raises on high. He raises up the needy from the ground and lifts the poor from the dunghill (1 Kgs 2:7–8). Thrones of rulers the Lord brought down, and he seated the gentle in their place (Sir 10:14). He sends away priests into captivity, and overthrows the mighty ones of the earth (Job 12:19).
he has filled the hungry with good things, and sent the rich away empty (53).	... because he fed an empty soul and a hungry soul he filled with good things (Ps 106:9).
He has helped his servant Israel, in remembrance of his mercy (54),	But you, Israel, my servant, Jakob, whom I have chosen, the offspring of Abraam, whom I have loved, you whom I took hold of from the ends of the earth, and I called you from its mountain peaks (Isa 41:8). He has remembered his mercy to Jakob (Ps 97:3).
according to the promise he made to our ancestors, to Abraham and to his descendants forever' (55).	He will give truth to Jacob, and mercy to Abram, as you swore to our fathers in former days (Mic 7:20). He magnifies acts of deliverance of his king, and doing mercy to his anointed, to David and for his offspring forever (2 Kgs 22:51).

After the Magnificat, Mary returns to her home in Nazareth, and the birth of John and Zachariah's prophecy (Benedictus) are narrated. We are told that "the time for Elizabeth to give birth was completed" (τῇ Ἐλισάβετ ἐπλήσθη ὁ χρόνος τοῦ τεκεῖν αὐτὴν, 1:57), which is a verbal and stylistic imitation of Gen 25:24: "the days for [Rebecca] to give birth were completed" (καὶ ἐπληρώθησαν αἱ ἡμέραι τοῦ τεκεῖν) where the only differences are the plural days and the corresponding plural verb form in the latter. On the eighth day, the child is taken to be circumcised, adhering to the language of Gen 17:12 and Lev 12:3;[35] the child is named John to the astonishment of those in attendance; Zachariah's voice and sight return, and they all pondered "What will this child be?" Luke closes the scene with the observation, "The hand of the Lord [χεὶρ κυρίου] was with him" (1:66). The "hand of the Lord" is a common expression in the Septuagint, occurring over 25 times. Two examples include the Hebrew God's warning to the Egyptian Pharaoh (through Moses) that "the hand of the Lord" (χεὶρ κυρίου) would be against him, his people, and their animals if they did not do what Moses would instruct them to do (Exod 9:3) and Samuel's warning to the men of Israel concerning their desire for a king that if they "should not heed the voice of the Lord and contend with the mouth of the Lord, the hand of the Lord [χεὶρ κυρίου] will also be against [them] and [their] king" (1 Kgs 12:15).

In contrast to the Magnificat that is primarily modeled upon Hannah's song in 1 Samuel (1 Kgs LXX), Zachariah's prophecy, the Benedictus, is not dependent upon a specific text from the Septuagint, but, like the Magnificat, it is also a mosaic of passages from the Septuagint. My interest here, like my interest in the Magnificat, is merely to demonstrate the extent to which Luke imitated themes and language from the Septuagint into his text, as Table 19 indicates.

Table 19: Septuagint sources for the Benedictus

The Benedictus (1:68–79)	Passages from the Septuagint
'Blessed be the Lord God of Israel,	Blessed be the Lord, the God of Israel (Ps 41:14).
	Blessed be the Lord God, the God of Israel (Ps 71:18).
	Blessed be the Lord God of Israel (Ps 105.48).
for he has looked favorably on his people and redeemed them (68).	Redemption he sent to his people (Ps 110:9).
He has raised up a mighty savior [κέρας σωτηρίας] for us in the house of his servant David (69),	He . . . is my mighty savior (κέρας σωτηρίας, Ps 17:3).
	The Lord . . . is my mighty savior (κέρας σωτηρίας, 2 Kgs 22:3).

---

35. Gen 17:12 (LXX) reads, "And a youngster of eight days shall be circumcised among you—every male—throughout your generations"; and Lev 12:3 (LXX), "And on the eighth day she [the mother] shall circumcise the flesh of his foreskin."

The Benedictus (1:68–79)	Passages from the Septuagint
as he spoke through the mouth of his holy prophets from of old (70), that we would be saved from our enemies and from the hand of all who hate us (71).	And he saved them from the hand of people who hate them and redeemed them from an enemy's hand (Ps 105:10). He will rescue me from my powerful enemies and from those who hate me (Ps 17:18).
Thus he has shown the mercy promised to our ancestors, and has remembered his holy covenant (72), the oath that he swore to our ancestor Abraham, to grant us (73) that we, being rescued from the hands of our enemies, might serve him without fear (74), in holiness and righteousness before him all our days (75).	You will give truth to Jakob, mercy to Abraam, as you swore to our fathers in former days (Mic 7:20). He remembered his covenant forever, a word that he commanded for a thousand generations, that he pledged to Abraam (Ps 104:8). And he remembered his covenant and showed regret according to the abundance of his mercy (Ps 105:45).
And you, child, will be called the prophet of the Most High; for you will go before the Lord to prepare his ways (76), to give knowledge of salvation to his people by the forgiveness of their sins (77).	Behold, I am sending my messenger, and he will oversee the way before me (Mal 3:1). A voice of one crying out in the wilderness; 'Prepare the way of the Lord' (Isa 40:3).
By the tender mercy of our God, the dawn from on high will break upon us (78), to give light to those who sit in darkness and in the shadow of death, to guide our feet into the way of peace' (79).	Oh you people who walk in darkness see a great light! Oh you who live in the country and in the shadow of death, light will shine on you! (Isa 9:2). Then your light shall break forth early in the morning, and your healings will rise quickly, and your righteousness shall go before you, and the glory of God will cover you (Isa 58:8).

After Zachariah concludes his prophecy, Luke returns to John the Baptist, informing readers that "the child grew and was strengthened in spirit" (τὸ δὲ παιδίον ηὔξανεν καὶ ἐκραταιοῦτο πνεύματι, 1:80) in language very similar to Judges 13:24, where "the boy (Samson) grew" (ηὐξήθη τὸ παιδάριον), 1 Sam (1 Kgs LXX) 2:26 where we are told that Samuel "grew and became great," and later in Luke 2:40 where the identical language is used to inform the reader that "the child [Jesus] grew and was strengthened while being filled with wisdom" (τὸ δὲ παιδίον ηὔξανεν καὶ ἐκραταιοῦτο πληρούμενον σοφίᾳ).

The Birth-of-Jesus-and-Visitors Narrative in Luke

Luke now returns to narrate the birth-of-Jesus-and-visitors narrative. His source for this narrative is Matthew 2:1–23, which he follows more closely than he follows any of his other sources in his birth narrative. Table 20 reflects the similar narrative themes.

Table 20: Luke's structural imitation of Matthew 2:1–20[36]

	Matthew	Similar narrative themes/events	Luke
1	"In [the] days of Herod the king" (2:1).	When these events occurred	"In the days of Herod the king" (1:5; 2:1).
2	Bethlehem in Judea (2:1–12).	Joseph and Mary's hometown prior to Jesus's birth	Nazareth of Galilee (2:1–7)
3	Bethlehem (2:1).	City where Jesus was born	Bethlehem (2:4).
4	a house (2:11).	Place where Jesus was born	"their accommodation" (ἐν τῷ καταλύματι) (2:7).
5	Magi (2:1–12).	Revelation of Jesus's birth to visitors who were out of the immediate area	Shepherds (2:8–21).
6	2:1–12	These visitors become the center/focus of the narrative	2:8–21
7	By means of a star (2:2).	These visitors journey to Bethlehem via revelatory intervention.	By means of an angel of the Lord (2:9).
8	2:10 χαρὰν μεγάλην.	The visitors are "overjoyed"	2:10 χαρὰν μεγάλην.
9	2:4	Jesus as Messiah within the context of the visitors' narratives	2:11
10	2:11	The visitors find the child with Mary and Joseph.	2:16
11	"King Herod was deeply perturbed and so was all of Jerusalem" (2:3).	The response to what the visitors say about the child.	"And all who heard were astonished at what the shepherds said" (2:18).

36. In item 4 in this table, Stephen Carlson has made a compelling argument that ἐν τῷ καταλύματι in Luke 2:7 should be understood, not as the traditional "inn," but as "their [Joseph and Mary's] apartment," "a marital chamber built for the newly married men of the family" ("Accommodations of Joseph and Mary," 342).

	Matthew	Similar narrative themes/ events	Luke
12	2:12	Visitors return to place of origin.	2:19

These similar, if not identical, narrative themes are striking. The narrative order of these themes is also almost identical. It is also important to note that at the beginning of this chapter, I cited Fitzmeyer's list of details common to the (hypothetical) tradition that he, Brown, and others identify as the "historical nucleus of what the evangelists had to work with."[37] Yet, the only narrative themes from this list immediately above that they include in their lists are that Jesus's birth took place in the time of Herod (1) and that Jesus was born in Bethlehem (3). In light of the striking similarities in narrative themes between Matt 2:2–12 and Luke 2:1–19, Brown's comment that "the whole of Matt 2:2–22 has no parallel in Luke, just as most of Luke 1 (outside 1:26–35) and most of Luke 2 have no parallel in Matthew"[38] is puzzling and difficult to understand. But, about 400 pages (and probably a period of time) later, he acknowledges that "the real parallel for the annunciation to the shepherds [in Luke 2] is . . . the magi story in Matt 2:1–12. In both Matthean and Lucan infancy narratives, after a first chapter that informs one parent of the forthcoming birth of Jesus, there is a similar sequence of events early in chapter 2."[39] Brown does not attribute the parallel to Luke's use of Matthew because he is adamant that the two wrote independently of one another.[40] Rather, he explains that the messengers' narratives in both Matt and Luke are to be understood in view of the "christological moment" of the resurrection—that the proclamation of the resurrection was initially met with either *acceptance and homage* or *rejection and persecution*. Brown explains that in Matt 2, the proclamation was through the star and that the magi *accepted* it and paid *homage*, whereas Herod *rejected* it and *persecution* followed. Similarly, in Luke, the proclamation is through an angel to the shepherds who *accepted* and *praised* and then Brown reaches all the way to the Simeon narrative—which is after the narratives of the shepherds, Jesus's circumcision, and purification—who warns of *rejection and persecution*

---

37. Fitzmeyer, *Luke*, 307.
38. Brown, *Birth*, 35.
39. Ibid., 412.
40. Ibid., 34. Goulder notes that Brown's recognition of the parallels between the visitors in Matt and Luke "seem to defy his conclusion that Luke was unaware of the Matthean form of the story" (*Luke*, 248).

(2:25–32).⁴¹ That this is an unacceptable explanation is suggested from the fact that Fitzmeyer, who regularly engages Brown's commentary whether he agrees with it or not, completely ignores it. Rather, Fitzmeyer says nothing about any possible textual relationship between the magi in Matt and the shepherds in Luke. Instead, he suggests that Luke introduces the shepherds "because of the [hypothetical tradition's] association of Jesus's birth with Bethlehem, the town of David"⁴² and because "there is enough in the OT tradition about Bethlehem and David to explain the relation of the shepherds to the birth of Jesus."⁴³ One of these OT passages that Fitzmeyer has in mind here is Micah 5:1 (5:2 LXX), which, he notes, "speaks of Bethlehem as a place from which shall come forth a 'ruler in Israel' (like David, even though it was among the insignificant clans of Judah)." Fitzmeyer continues that "this OT verse is actually quoted (in a slightly expanded form which makes the ruler into a 'shepherd') in Matt. 2:6. But Luke makes no allusion to this OT passage, even though he undoubtedly knew it; and it may well have figured in his thinking in depicting Jesus as a ruler born in shepherd-country."⁴⁴ While Fitzmeyer observes that Micah 5:1 (LXX) is cited in Matt 2, he fails to consider that Luke could have made the same observation and then used Matthew's revision of Micah 5:1 (LXX) as his inspiration for casting his visitors as shepherds instead of magi.

The suggestion that Luke knew of Matthew's revision of Micah 5:1 (LXX) takes the following form. In Matt 2, the magi arrive in Jerusalem asking where they could find the recently born king of the Jews, which prompted Herod to inquire of the priests and the scribes who responded "in Bethlehem," which sets the narrative stage for Matthew's second so-called "formula or fulfillment citation": "for it has been written through the prophet,

> And you Bethlehem, land of Judea, are in no way least among the leaders of Judea; for from you will come a leader, who will shepherd my people, Israel" (2:6).

Here, Matthew revises Micah 5:1 (LXX) in ways somewhat similar to how he revised the Septuagint account of Isaiah 7:14, as Table 21 demonstrates.

---

41. Brown, *Birth*, 412.
42. Fitzmeyer, *Luke*, 395.
43. Ibid., 396.
44. Ibid., 395.

Table 21: Matthew's transformation of Micah 5:1 (LXX)

Matthew 2:6	Micah 5:1 (LXX)
Καὶ σὺ Βηθλέεμ, γῆ Ἰούδα, οὐδαμῶς ἐλαχίστη εἶ ἐν τοῖς ἡγεμόσιν Ἰούδα. ἐκ σοῦ ἐξελεύσεται ἡγούμενος, ὅστις ποιμανεῖ τὸν λαόν τὸν Ἰσραήλ.	Καὶ σὺ Βηθλέεμ, οἶκος τοῦ Εφραθα, ὀλιγοστὸς εἶ τοῦ εἶναι ἐν χιλιάσιν Ἰουδα. ἐκ συ μοι ἐξελεύσεται τοῦ εἶναι εἰς ἄρχοντα ἐν τῷ Ισραηλ, καὶ αἱ ἔξοδοι αὐτοῦ ἀπ' ἀρχῆς ἐξ ἡμερῶν αἰῶνος.
And you, Bethlehem, land of Judah, are by no means least among the leaders of Judah; for from you will come a leader who will shepherd my people Israel.	And you, Bethlehem, house of Ephrata, are very few in number to be among the thousands of Judah; one from you shall come forth to me to become ruler in Israel, and his goings forth are from old, from ancient days.

While Matthew makes several revisions to his source, the only one to be noted here is that whereas in Micah the leader who is to come forth from Bethlehem is to "become ruler in Israel," Matthew alters this to read that this leader "will shepherd [ποιμανεῖ] my people Israel." That the visitor narrative in Matthew's birth narrative includes this metaphorical phrasing of shepherding and that the visitor narrative in the birth narrative in Luke, not only includes many of the exact same narrative themes in very similar narrative order but also casts its visitors as shepherds seems to be more than a coincidence. It does not take much imagination to conclude that Luke adopted Matthew's reference to shepherding and used it as his inspiration for making his visitors shepherds, and, as will be discussed below, casting his visitors as shepherds aligns very well with Luke's interest in emphasizing the Jewishness of the birth narrative.

In addition to these overall structural similarities (narrative themes and narrative order), there are also two verbal similarities within the visitor narrative worthy of note. Matthew situates the birth of Jesus "in the days of Herod the king" (ἐν ἡμέραις Ἡρῴδου τοῦ βασιλέως, 2:1); Luke, likewise, situates his birth narrative "in the days of Herod the king" (ἐν ταῖς ἡμέραις Ἡρῴδου Βασιλέως τῆς Ἰουδαίας, 1:5). Brown explains, Luke's phrasing is similar to Matt 2:1 "except that Luke uses the article after 'king' and 'before' Judea."[45] Fitzmeyer also notes the similar dating,[46] but neither Brown nor Fitzmeyer explain that these are the only two occurrences of this prepositional phrase in all of Greek literature. Such almost identical verbal simi-

---

45. Brown, *Birth*, 257.
46. Fitzmeyer, *Luke*, 321.

larities within identical narrative contexts (birth narrative of Jesus) strongly suggests dependence. For the second verbal similarity, in Matthew, the magi are "overjoyed" (χαρὰν μεγάλην) in seeing the star that led them to Joseph and Mary's house (2:10), just as the angelic messenger announced to the shepherds, in Luke, news of "great joy" (χαρὰν μεγάλην) that a savior had been born in the city of David (2:10). This expression of χαρὰν μεγάλην is very rare in ancient Greek literature, occurring only twice in the Septuagint (Jonah 4:6 and Isa 39:2), here in Matt and Luke and once in (Acts 15:3). That this very rare expression occurs within the birth-of-Jesus narrative, even more narrowly within the visitor narrative in both accounts, and even narrower still within the context of the revelation of the child's birth strongly suggests, if not demonstrates, dependence.

And as with the rest of the birth narrative, Luke also relies upon expressions from the Septuagint within his birth-of-Jesus-and-visitors narrative. Luke begins his birth narrative of Jesus by claiming that a census went out from Augustus "in these days" (ἐν ταῖς ἡμέραις ἐκείναις, 2:1), which is a prepositional phrase that does not occur in Greek literature prior to the Septuagint, but occurs therein over fifty times. In 2:5, Joseph travels to register in the "city of David" (πόλιν Δαυὶδ), which occurs numerous times in the Septuagint[47] but only here in the New Testament. "The days were fulfilled for Elizabeth to give birth" (ἐπλήσθησαν αἱ ἡμέραι τοῦ τεκεῖν αὐτήν) is essentially identical with the expression in Gen 25:24 for Rebecca to give birth (ἐπληρώθησαν αἱ ἡμέραι τοῦ τεκεῖν αὐτήν) and occurs only in these two passages in Greek literature. When the angel appeared to the shepherds, the "glory of the Lord" (δόξα κυρίου) shone round them. "Glory of the Lord" occurs twenty-six times in the Septuagint,[48] including Exod 16:10 where it appeared in a cloud and Num 14:10 where it also appeared in a cloud that also indicates the presence of the Hebrew God who then spoke to Moses. Luke 2:9 is its only occurrence in the New Testament. Upon seeing the glory of God, the shepherds "feared a great fear" (ἐφοβήθησαν φόβον μέγαν, 2:9), an expression that occurs only four times in Greek literature—two in the Septuagint (1 Macc 10:8 and Jonas 1:10), one in Mark (4:41), and here.

As noted above and in the previous chapter, Brown, Fitzmeyer, Lincoln, and others have advocated or accepted the idea that a *hypothetical* source/tradition that included many of the narrative features of the

---

47. See 2 Kgs 6:10, 12, 16; 3 Kgs 2:35; 5:14; 12:24; 1 Chr (1 Para) 11:7; 13:6, 13; 1 Macc 1:33; 7:32.

48. These include Exod 16:10; Lev 9:6, 23; Num 14:10, 21; 16:19; 17:7; 20:6; 3 Kgs 8:11; 2 Chr (2 Para) 5:14; 7:1, 2, 3; Ps 103:31; 137:5; Ps Sol 5:19; Isa 24:15; 40:5; 60:1; Ezek 3:13, 23; 8:4; 10:4, 18; 11:23; and 43:4.

foretelling-of-Jesus's-birth narratives (Matt 1:18–25 and Luke 1:27–38) was available to Matthew and Luke and that these two incorporated the material from this hypothetical document into their respective narratives completely independently of one another. Yet, upon careful examination, the themes, narrative order, and verbal similarities within these two narratives are strikingly similar. Moreover, when the narrative themes, narrative order, and verbal similarities from the birth-of-Jesus-and-visitors narratives (Matt 1:18–2:12 and Luke 2:1–20), for which there is no hypothetical source or tradition, are combined with the foretelling-of-the-birth-of-Jesus narratives, the numerous identical themes, almost identical narrative arrangement of those themes, and the verbal similarities combine to mount a formidable challenge to the hypothetical source hypothesis that Brown, Fitzmeyer, Lincoln, and others advance. Table 22 combines Tables 17 and 20 so as to demonstrate the extent of the similarities:

Table 22: The extent of Luke's structural imitation of Matthew

	Matthew	Similarity of event or theme	Luke
1	1:18–25	Foretelling-of-Jesus's-birth narrative	1:26–38
2	1:16; 1:18–25	Mary as Jesus's mother	1:26–2:52
3	μνηστευθείσης (1:18)	Mary engaged to Joseph	ἐμνηστεθμένην (1:27)
4	1:23	Mary as παρθένος	1:26
5	Ἐν γαστρὶ ἔχουσα (1:18)	Mary is pregnant	Συλλήμψῃ ἐν γαστρὶ (1:31)
6	1:18–25	Joseph and Mary live together before Jesus is born.	1:27; 2:1–7
7	Joseph as a righteous man (1:19)	Joseph and Mary's standing	Mary "found favor with God" (1:30)
8	1:19	Joseph contemplates "putting Mary away" (1:19).	Luke omits.
9	An "angel of the Lord" speaks to Joseph in a dream (1:19–21).	Angelic appearance (annunciation)	Gabriel speaks face-to-face with Mary (1:26–38).

	Matthew	Similarity of event or theme	Luke
10	"Do not fear to take Mary as your wife, for (γὰρ) that which is in her" (1:20).	Angel's reassurance/ explanation	"Do not fear, Mary, for (γὰρ) you have found favor with God" (1:30).
11	She was found to be pregnant from a spirit which is holy (ἐκ πνεύματος ἁγίου, 1.18, 20).	The sprit's role	A spirit which is holy will come upon you and the power of the most high overshadow you, (Πνεῦμα ἅγιον ἐπελεύσεται ἐπὶ σὲ καὶ δύναμις ὑψίστου ἐπισκιάσει σοι, 1.35).
12	Μὴ φοβηθῇς to Joseph (1:20).	"Do not fear"	Μὴ φοβοῦ to Mary (1:30).
13	τέξεται [Mary] δὲ υἱὸν (1:21).	"Bear a son"	Τέξῃ [Mary] υἱὸν (1:31).
14	καλέσεις τὸ ὄνομα αὐτοῦ Ἰησοῦν, "You [Joseph] will call him, Jesus" (1:21).	"You will call him"	καλέσεις τὸ ὄνομα αὐτοῦ Ἰησοῦν, "You [Mary] will call him, Jesus" (1:31).
15	1:22, by citing Isa 7:14.	In order that it might fulfill a prophecy	1:54 – 5, 70, 73; 2:29, but no explicit citation of Isa 7:14.
16	Save (σώσει) his people from their sins (1:21).	Jesus will:	be a savior (σωτὴρ) (2:11).
17	οὐκ ἐγίνωσκεν αὐτήν (Joseph did not know her 1:25).	"Knowing"	ἄνδρα οὐ γινώσκω Mary: "I am not knowing a man" (1:34).
18	Κάλεσεν τὸ ὄνομα αὐτοῦ Ἰησοῦν Joseph names the child: ("He (Joseph) called his name, Jesus," 1:25).	Naming the child	Gabriel tells Mary, "you will call (first-person singular) his name Jesus (1:31); ἐκλήθη τὸ ὄνομα αὐτοῦ Ἰησοῦν ("His name was called Jesus" 2:21).
19	Joseph did what he was told (1:24).	Response to angelic annunciation	Mary: "Let it be to me according to your word" (1:38).
20	2:1–23	Birth-of-Jesus-and-visitors narrative	2:1–52
21	ἐν ἡμέραις Ἡρῴδου τοῦ βασιλέως ("In [the] days of Herod the king 2:1).	When these events occurred	ἐν ταῖς ἡμέραις Ἡρῴδου βασιλέως ("In the days of Herod the king 1:5; 2:1).

	Matthew	Similarity of event or theme	Luke
22	Bethlehem in Judea (2:1–12).	Joseph and Mary's hometown	Nazareth in Galilee (2:1–7).
23	Bethlehem (2:1).	City where Jesus is born	Bethlehem (2:4).
24	τὴν οἰκίαν ("the house" of Joseph and Mary" 2:11).	Place where Jesus was born	ἐν τῷ καταλύματι ("in their accommodation" 2:7).
25	Magi (2:1–12).	Revelation of Jesus's birth to a group who were not in Bethlehem	Shepherds (2:8–15).
26	2:2–12.	These groups become the center of the narrative	2:8–15.
27	Via a star (2:2).	That group's journey to Bethlehem via revelatory intervention	Via an angel of the Lord (2:9).
28	Χαρὰν μεγάλην (2:10).	The groups are "overjoyed."	Χαρὰν μεγάλην (2:10).
29	In response to the visitors' question, Herod called the priests and scribes together to ask where the messiah would be born (2:4).	Jesus as Messiah within context of groups' narrative	The angel explains to the shepherds, "Today, there has been born for you in the city of David a deliverer—the messiah" (2:11).
30	And, coming into the house, they [the magi] see the child with Mary his mother (2:11).	The groups find the child with Mary or with Mary and Joseph.	And, hurrying off, they came and found Mary and Joseph and the child lying (2:16).
31	Then they returned to their own country (2:12).	After seeing the child, the groups return to where they came.	The shepherds returned, (2:20).

In summing up these similarities, from a probability perspective, what are the odds that two completely independent authors, writing at different times and in different places and for different reasons and without any knowledge whatsoever of the other's work, would take a pre-existing (hypothetical) source something like what Brown, Fitzmeyer, Lincoln, and others advocate for the foretelling-of-Jesus's-birth narrative (Matt 1:18–25 and Luke 1:26–38) and arrange the material from that hypothetical source into such strikingly similar thematic and narrative order and then also essentially work from scratch independently to craft birth-of-Jesus-and-visitors narratives (Matt 2:1–23 and Luke 2:1–20) both of which include a brief account of the birth followed by accounts of groups from out of the area who visit the new born child that share numerous and specific details? Thomas L. Brodie's observation concerning such narrative similarities seems to support the implausibility of the independence hypothesis:

> When random elements occur in two documents in the same order the similarity requires explanation. Similarity of order does not occur easily. If two people, independently of each other, arrange the numbers 1 to 5 at random, the chance that they will arrange them in the same order is less than one in a hundred. If the numbers are 1 to 10, the chance is less than one in a million.[49]

I have identified at least thirty-one similar narrative themes or events between the foretelling-of-Jesus's-birth narratives and the birth-of-Jesus in Matthew and Luke. I am not a statistician, but the odds that two writers writing independently of one another, without any knowledge of the other's narrative, would share so many theme, order, and verbal similarities would be astronomical, implausibly astronomical. To be sure, there are differences, often significant differences, between each author's accounts, and reasonable explanations for these differences will be discussed below, but these differences do not change the fact of the close, often strikingly close, similarities. These numerous and striking similarities must be explained. Moreover, and this is extremely important, when one acknowledges the narrative fact that Luke has imitated much of his birth narrative from 1 Samuel (1 Kgs LXX) and also used, often verbatim, a plethora of passages from the Septuagint, it becomes even more understandable and evident that he used Matthew in mimetical, rhetorical, and compositional ways very similar to how he used 1 Samuel (1 Kgs LXX). In short, the claim that Luke used Matthew as his primary source for his foretelling-of-Jesus's-birth narrative and for his birth-of-Jesus-and-visitors narrative is as strongly supported, if not more strongly supported, by the evidence as is his use of 1 Samuel (1 Kgs LXX) as a model for his birth narrative, the latter of which is widely acknowledged.

---

49. Brodie, *Birthing*, 45.

Jesus's Circumcision

Luke then states briefly that the "eight days were fulfilled for him to be circumcised" (2:21), fulfilling the covenant requirement that the Hebrew God established with Abraham in Gen 17.[50] It is important to note that it is only the author of Luke who has Jesus circumcised, a point to be discussed below in considering Luke's objectives in the birth narrative.

Presentation in the Temple

Jesus's presentation in the temple narrative (2:22–40) invokes many Old Testament themes. The purification-presentation scene (vv. 22–24) combines and confuses the two rituals. Without getting into the problems, my interest here is to show Luke's interest in establishing Jesus within Jewish traditions/practices (recognizing Luke's misunderstanding of these) and that the purification-presentation narrative is an imitation of 1 Kgs (LXX) 1:22–24. Therein, Elkana and Hannah took the young Samuel, after he was weaned, to the "house of the Lord at Selom" with their appropriate sacrifices to "lend him to the Lord for as long as he lives," thus fulfilling her earlier vow. Scholars agree that Luke is imitating 1 Kgs (LXX) here in 2:22–24[51] and that his discussion is confused, but, as confused as it is, Luke's aim is to stress the parents' fidelity to the Mosaic law and the extent to which Jesus was Jewish and raised under the law, which is one of Luke's objectives in the birth narrative to be discussed below.

Simeon is then introduced as an upright and devout man, who does not appear to be a priest, but who, scholars agree, evokes Eli in 1 Samuel (1 Kgs LXX) 2:19–24.[52] Simeon, we are told, was waiting for the "consolation of Israel" (παράκλησιν τοῦ Ἰσραήλ) and it was revealed to him that he would not die until he had seen the Lord's Messiah (2:25–27). Though the precise

---

50. Gen 17:12 has the Hebrew God speaking to Abraham, "And this is the covenant, which you shall keep, between me and you and between your offspring after you throughout their generations: Every male of yours shall be circumcised, and you shall be circumcised in the flesh of your foreskins, and it shall exist as a covenant sign between me and you. And a youngster of eight days shall be circumcised among you—every male—throughout your generations." See also Lev 12:3. For a discussion of the importance of the covenant of circumcision, see Hall, "Circumcision."

51. See Burrows, *Gospel of Luke*, 17–19; Creed, *Gospel According to St. Luke*, 39; Brown, *Birth*, 447–51; Fitzmeyer, *Luke*, 419–25, including his comment that "this scene has become a presentation in imitation of the presentation of Samuel in 1 Sam (1 Kgs LXX) 1:22–24" (421); and Bovon, *Luke*, 96–99.

52. Following Burrows, *Gospel of Luke*, 31; Fitzmeyer, *Luke*, 421; and Pervo, *Luke* 34.

phrase "consolation of Israel" does not occur in the Old Testament, it alludes to, or imitates, several passages in Second and Third Isaiah, including:

- "Comfort, O comfort [παρακαλεῖτε παρακαλεῖτε] my people, says God. O priests speak to the heart of Jerusalem" (Isa 40:1);
- "As a mother will comfort [παρακαλέσει] someone, so also I comfort you, and you shall be comforted in Jerusalem" (Isa 66:13); and
- "The Lord has comforted his people; he redeemed Jerusalem; he has bared his holy arm before the eyes of all the Gentiles" (Isa 52:9).

Upon taking the child Jesus in his arms, Simeon sings his Nunc Dimittis, which, like the Magnificat and Benedictus, is composed of passages from the Septuagint as Table 23 indicates.

Table 23: Septuagint sources for the Nunc Dimittis

Simeon's Nunc Dimittis (Luke 2:29–32)	Passages from the Septuagint
Now, master, release your servant in peace, according to your word (29), because my eyes have seen your salvation (30), which you prepared before the sight of all the people (32),	Then, the glory of the Lord shall appear, and all flesh shall see the salvation of God, because the lord has spoken. (Isa 40:5)
	He has bared his holy arm before the eyes of all the Gentiles; all ends of the earth will see the salvation of our God (Isa 52:10).
a light unto revelation for the Gentiles and glory to your people (32).	See, I have made you a light of nations that you may be for salvation to the end of the earth (Isa 49:6).
	I have given you as a covenant to a race, as a light to the Gentiles, to open the eyes of the blind (Isa 42:6).
	I have provided salvation in Zion, to Israel for glorying (Isa 46:13).

In addition to the thematic and verbal similarities noted in the Nunc Dimittis above, the phrase "according to your word" (κατὰ τὸ ῥῆμά σου) in v. 29 does not occur in Greek literature prior to the Septuagint where it occurs about fifty times and then in the New Testament only twice—here and Luke 1:38. The Simeon narrative closes with his warning to Mary after he blesses "them"[53] (καὶ εὐλόγησεν αὐτοὺς Συμεών, v. 34), which is an imitation of Eli's blessing Elkana and Hannah (καὶ εὐλόγησεν Ἠλι τὸν Ἐλκανα καὶ τὴν γυναῖκα) in the parallel scene in 1 Kgs (LXX) 2:20; the verb does not occur in this form prior to the Septuagint, where it is common, and, then, only a few times in the New Testament, primarily in Luke.[54]

After the Anna narrative (2:36–38) and after Joseph, Mary, and Jesus return to Nazareth (2:39–40), we are told that it was the parents' practice to attend the Passover festival every year, another indication of Luke's interest in depicting Joseph and Mary as devout and practicing Jews. After the episode in the temple when Jesus was twelve (2:41–50), the birth narrative ends with their return once again to Nazareth where Jesus grew and "advanced in wisdom and in favor with God and men" (καὶ Ἰησοῦς προέκοπτεν σοφίᾳ καὶ ἡλικίᾳ καὶ χάριτι παρὰ θεῷ καὶ ἀνθρώποις, 2:52), an appropriate imitation of 1 Samuel (1 Kgs LXX) 2:26—"And the boy Samuel kept going and became great and was in favor both with the Lord and the people" (καὶ τὸ παιδάριον Σαμουηλ ἐπορεύετο καὶ ἐμεγαλύετο καὶ ἀγαθὸν καὶ μετὰ κυρίου καὶ μετὰ ἀνθρώπων)—for concluding a birth narrative that is so reliant upon 1 Samuel for its overall structure.

Luke's Genealogy of Jesus

Before considering possible explanations as to why Luke so radically transformed Matthew's birth narrative, a few comments concerning any possible relationship between Luke's and Matthew's genealogies are in order. In Table 24 below, I reverse the order of Luke's genealogy so as to align it more with Matthew's for easier comparison, and, for space considerations, the names from Abraham through Adam are omitted. The *italics* indicate agreement among Old Testament (LXX) sources, Matthew, and Luke, while the underlined indicate differences and/or names that are not attested in the Old Testament.

---

53. The Greek is not clear whether Simeon's blessing includes Jesus or is limited to Joseph and Mary. If Luke is following 1 Sam (1 Kgs LXX) 2:20, the blessing would be limited to Joseph and Mary.

54. The verb occurs in this form in the NT in Mark 6:41; Matt 14:19; Luke 2:28, 34, 9:16, 24:30, 50; and Heb 11:20, 21.

Table 24: Comparison of the genealogies of Matthew and Luke[55]

Matt 1:1–16	1 Chr (1 Para LXX) 1:28, 34; 2:1–15; Ruth 4:18–22	Luke 3:23–37
Abraham	*Abraham*	*Abraham*
Isaac	*Isaac*	*Isaac*
Jacob	*Jacob*	*Jacob*
Judah	*Judah*	*Judah*
Perez (whose mother was Tamar)	*Perez*	*Perez*
Hezron	*Hezron*	*Hezron*
Aram	Ram (Aram, Arran in LXX)	Arni
		Admin
Amminadab	*Amminadab*	*Amminadab*
Nahshon	*Nahshon*	*Nahshon*
Salmon	Salma (Salmon in LXX)	Sala (Salmon)
Boaz (whose mother was Rahab)	*Boaz*	*Boaz*
Obed (whose mother was Ruth)	*Obed*	*Obed*
Jesse	*Jesse*	*Jesse*
David (the king)	*David*	*David*
	Kings of Judah from 3&4 Kings (LXX)	
Solomon (son of Bathsheba)	Solomon (961–922 BCE)	Nathan
Rehoboam	Rehoboam (922–915)	Mattatha(n)
Abijah	Abijah or Abijam (915–913)	Menna
Asaph	Asa (913–873)	Melea
Jehoshaphat	Jehoshaphat (873–849)	Eliakim

55. This table is adapted from Brown, *Birth*, 77–79.

Matt 1:1–16	1 Chr (1 Para LXX) 1:28, 34; 2:1–15; Ruth 4:18–22	Luke 3:23–37
Joram	Jehoram or Joram (849–842)	Jonam
	Ahaziah (842)	Joseph
	Queen Athaliah (842–837)	Judah
	Jehoash or Joash (837–800)	Simeon
	Amaziah (800–783)	Levi
Uzziah	(Uzziah or Azariah (783–742)	Mathhat
Jotham	Jotham (742–735)	Jorim
Ahaz	Ahaz or Jehoahaz I (735–715)	Eliezer
Hezekiah	Hezekiah (715–687)	Jesus (Joshua)
Manasseh	Manasseh (687–642)	Er
Amos	Amon (642–640)	Elmadam (Elmodam)
Josiah	Josiah (640–609)	Cosam
Jechoniah and his brothers	Jehoahaz II (609)	Addi
	Jehoiakim (609–598)	Melchi
	Jeconiah (597)	Neri
	Zedekiah (597–587)	
	Post-Monarchical Davidids (with approximate birth dates)	
Shealtiel	Sheenazzar or Sheshbazzar (595)	*Shealtiel*
Zerubbabel	Zerubbabel (570)	*Zerubbabel*
		Rhesa
Abiud	Hananiah (545)	Joanan
		Joda

Matt 1:1–16	1 Chr (1 Para LXX) 1:28, 34; 2:1–15; Ruth 4:18–22	Luke 3:23–37
Eliakim	Shecaniah (520)	Josech
		Semein
Azor	Hattush (495)	Mattathias
		Maath
Zadok	Elioenai (470)	Naggai
		Hesli
Achim	Anani (445)	Nahum
Eliud		Amos
		Mattathias
Eleazar		Joseph
		Jannai
Matthan		Melchi
		Levi
Jacob		Eli
Joseph, the husband of Mary		Joseph, of whom was the supposed son,
Jesus		Jesus

The difficulties with reconciling the two genealogies are many:

- Luke's genealogy is not included in his birth narrative or seemingly connected to it in any meaningful way; Matthew's precedes his birth narrative and is intrinsically related to it.
- Matthew begins with Abraham and lists names in a descending order to Jesus whereas Luke begins with Jesus and traces his lineage back to Adam in an ascending order.
- The syntactic structure is different in that Matthew uses an "A begat [γεννάω] B" format whereas Luke uses the "A son of [τοῦ] B."
- Matthew organizes his generations in a 3 x 14 format whereas Luke lists seventy-seven generations.
- Matthew lists forty-one names whereas Luke lists seventy-seven.

- While the names between the two genealogies are identical between Abraham and David, Shealtiel and Zerubbabel, and Joseph and Jesus, the rest are completely different.

- Matthew follows Jesus's lineage through Solomon whereas Luke follows it through Solomon's older brother Nathan, for whom there is no genealogical lineage in the Old Testament. Matthew lists nine names between Zerubbabel and Joseph; Luke lists seventeen, and none from either list has any historical attestation.

- Finally, in Matthew, Jacob is Jesus's grandfather, whereas in Luke it is Eli.

Do these many and significant differences preclude the possibility that Luke could have known and used Matthew's genealogy as his primary source for his own? I offer five points for consideration that they do not.

First, James Drury noted that the fact that Luke "had a genealogy at all shows his loyalty to Matthew."[56] I would add that the fact that both Luke and Matthew include a foretelling-of-Jesus's-birth narrative, a birth-of-Jesus-and-visitors narrative, and a genealogy of Jesus's birth is much more than a series of coincidences. That Luke knew, used, and radically rewrote Matthew's foretelling-of-Jesus's-birth and birth-of-Jesus narratives, as I demonstrated above, and that he knew Matthew's account of Jesus's relationship with his family, as I demonstrated in chapter 3, is compelling evidence that Luke knew Matthew's text.

Second, Bovon, Fitzmeyer, and Pervo speak to the distinction between Matthew's 3 x 14 organizational structure for his generations and Luke's more straight-forward list. Pervo's observation is representative: "Matthew's and Luke's genealogies cannot be reconciled: they exhibit different data, structure, and purposes. The former has forty-two names arranged in three groups from Abraham to Jesus, while the latter's reciprocal list has seventy-six entries from Jesus back to God."[57] In contrast, Goulder understands Luke's organization of his generations as a further development of Matthew's, for whereas Matthew offered a 3 x 14 organizational scheme, Luke, according to Goulder, constructed a 7 x 11 scheme, adding Admin just before Amminadab (3:33), to bring the number of names to seventy-seven.[58] This need to get to seventy-seven names may also explain why Luke

---

56. Drury, *Tradition and Design*, 125.

57. Pervo, *Luke* 44; Fitzmeyer, *Luke*, 496, and Bovon, *Luke*, 135.

58. Goulder, *Luke*, 289. For problems with patterns of seven, see Brown, *Birth*, 91–92.

includes eighteen names in his list from Zerubbabel to Joseph whereas Matthew has only nine.

Third, Luke departs from Matthew and follows (or creates) Jesus's lineage through Nathan before returning to Matthew with Shealtiel and Zerubbabel before offering his list of eighteen names between Zerubbabel and Joseph. His returning to Shealtiel and Zerubbabel aligns with Matthew's as does his creation of fictitious names between Zerubbabel and Joseph. These are exceptionally similar coincidences if Luke did not know Matthew's genealogy.

Fourth, Goulder suggests that Luke used at least three of the names from Jesus's list (none of whom is attested in the Old Testament) in his own: Mathat (μαθθὰτ, Luke 3:24; Matt 1:15); Amos (Ἀμὼς, Luke 3:25; Matt 1:10); and Eliakim (Ἐλιακὶμ, 3:30; Matt 1:13).

The fifth and perhaps weightiest similarity between the two lists is that both Matthew and Luke qualify Joseph's relationship to Jesus and, perhaps more striking, both qualify Joseph's relationship to Jesus by significantly altering the syntax in their genealogies. As noted in the last chapter, Matthew consistently writes that "A begat [ἐγέννησεν] B" thirty-nine times, employing the aorist active indicative form of the verb γεννάω before then going out of his way to alter this syntactical construction by inserting a relative clause governed by the feminine relative pronoun ἧς, the antecedent of which is Mary, thus bypassing Joseph altogether and claiming only that Jesus was begotten by Mary (1:16). The structure of Luke's qualification is extremely similar to Matthew's, as seventy-six times in his genealogy he writes, "A [is the] son of [τοῦ] B," but with Jesus, he writes, Jesus, "being the son, as it was thought, of Joseph" (ὢν υἱός, ὡς ἐνομίζετο, Ἰωσὴφ, 3:23). Similar to the unusualness of Matthew's qualifying construction, Luke's ὡς ἐνοίζετο ("as it was thought") is extremely rare, and this is its first occurrence in Greek literature.⁵⁹ Bovon suggests that the clause "as it was considered to be" can be read with two different meanings:

1. "He was considered to be Joseph's biological son" (but I, Luke, know this is not true); and

2. "He was rightfully declared to be Joseph's son" (and I, Luke, agree with this).⁶⁰

Bovon reasonably dismisses option (1) for two reasons. First, he cites three passages where Luke makes reference to Joseph as Jesus's "parent" or "father":

---

59. According to a *TLG* search, the expression occurs in Appian's *Mithridatic* 263.4 (ca. 150 CE) and then when later Christian writers cite Luke 3:23.

60. Bovon, *Luke*, 136.

when "the parents" (τοὺς γονεῖς) brought Jesus into the temple (2:27), where it was "his parents' [οἱ γονεῖς] practice" to go to Jerusalem for the Passover (2:41), and where Mary refers to Joseph as Jesus's father (ὁ πατὴρ σου, 2:48). To these we can add the question that Luke places in the mouths of the crowd within the "Rejection at Nazareth" narrative, "Is this not Joseph's son" (Οὐχὶ υἱός ἐστιν Ἰωσὴφ οὗτος, 4:22). Second, Bovon notes that as one of the genealogy's objectives was to demonstrate that Jesus is the "son of God," the genealogy would lose its significance if Joseph was the biological/physical father of Jesus. But, another possibility that Bovon does not consider is that Luke's qualification of Joseph's relationship to Jesus here is a response to Matthew's structurally similar qualification in his genealogy. This third option would read, "[Jesus] was the son, as was thought (by some, but not by others), of Joseph." That Luke adds this qualification of Jesus's relationship to Joseph within his genealogy just as Matthew added a qualification of Jesus's relationship within his genealogy strongly suggests that Luke's qualification must be understood in respect to Matthew's.

These points of contact with Matthew's genealogy, some stronger than others, need an explanation. Advocates of the view that the Matthew and Luke did not know each other's genealogy but that *somehow* these authors wrote independently of each other and *coincidentally* included all of these similarities not only do not provide any evidence to support their view, but they cannot explain these similarities. These similarities, some stronger than others, between Matthew's and Luke's genealogies offer compelling evidence that Luke knew and used Matthew's genealogy.

Luke's Objectives in the Birth Narrative: Explanations for the Differences between Luke and Matthew

While scholars have suggested a variety of objectives that the author of Luke was attempting to achieve in his birth narrative, I will briefly argue that two of these include that Luke was 1) responding to Matthew's claim that Mary was pregnant when she should not have been and 2) that he used Matthew's birth narrative as a model for crafting his own birth narrative that would serve as a response to the Marcionite claims that Jesus had no relationship with the Hebrew God or the Jewish scriptures and that Jesus was not born of a woman.

Concerning the first response, Matthew's foretelling-of-the-birth-of-Jesus narrative opens with authorial acknowledgement that Mary is pregnant when she should not have been. It is because of Joseph's suspicions as to how Mary became pregnant that the angel is dispatched to Joseph *after the fact* that Mary is pregnant, and the angel then *explains* the supernatural origin of her pregnancy. Goulder recognizes that Matt 1 is the substance of the content for Luke's annunciation narrative and states, "Luke does not mean to deny the truth of Matthew's story."[61] I disagree and suggest that Luke categorically rejects the implication in Matthew's narrative that Mary is pregnant when she should not have been. In sharp contrast, while Luke retains that Mary is engaged to Joseph, using the same verb (μνηστεύ-), he makes perfectly clear that Mary is not yet pregnant, that she is still a virgin, by referring to her as παρθένος twice in 1:27, and he completely eliminates any suspicion of the cause of her pregnancy—suspicion that was so obvious in Matthew's narrative and that prompted the angel's visit—by deleting Joseph's contemplation of what to do about Mary's pregnancy. How better to eliminate all suspicions of Mary's pregnancy than to, essentially, delete Joseph's role from the annunciation narrative—which was the source of the suspicion in Matthew? No, Luke will have no part of such suspicion. Instead, Gabriel is sent to Mary (rather than to Joseph) *prior* to her pregnancy to *inform* her (rather than *explain*) *ahead of time* (rather than *after the fact*) that she will conceive and bear a son. By such a recasting of Matthew's narrative, Luke completely exonerates Mary from any suspicion of wrongdoing. Moreover, Luke's elimination of the suspicion surrounding Mary's pregnancy could also explain why he excludes Matthew's women—Tamar, Rahab, Ruth, and Bathsheba, all of whom were involved or implicated in an inappropriate sexual relationship in Matthew's genealogy—from his own genealogy. In addition to eliminating such suspicion, Luke significantly elevates Mary's prominence throughout his birth narrative. Gabriel informs her that she is the "most favored one" (κεχαριτωμένη), a *hapax*, and here "designates Mary as the recipient of divine favor; it means 'favored by God' . . . . [s]he is favored by God to be the mother of the descendant of David and the Son of the Most High."[62] Gabriel continues informing Mary that "the Lord is with you" (1:28) and that "God has been gracious to you" (1:30). Elizabeth explains to Mary, "God's blessing is on you above all women" (1:42), and, in the Magnificat, Mary exclaims, "All generations will count me blessed, for the mighty God has done great things for me!" (1:48-49). In short, Luke has thoroughly transformed Matthew's portrayal of Mary as an adulterous woman to God's most favored (κεχαριτωμένη) and blessed.

A second objective of the author of the birth narrative in Luke would seem to be related to the author's extensive imitation, use of, or emphasis upon the Jewish scriptures (structure, content, style, and language, via the

---

61. Goulder, *Luke*, 221.
62. Fitzmeyer, *Luke*, 345.

Septuagint), as such extensive dependence needs an explanation. Joseph Tyson, in his *Marcion and Luke-Acts: A Defining Struggle*, has offered what seems to be a reasonable polemical context to which Luke's septuagintalizing birth-narrative would be a fitting counter-narrative: the birth narrative was added to an earlier version of Luke so as to counter Marcion's views that Jesus had no relationship whatsoever to the Hebrew God and Jewish scriptures and that Jesus was not born of a woman.

We do not know much about the historical Marcion. BeDuhn suggests that his life spanned ca. 95–165 CE;[63] he was born and raised in Pontus in North East Asia Minor (north coast of Turkey), and he was in the shipping business, possibly a ship owner. He may have moved onto and been active within the Christian church in Rome, a church to which he contributed a substantial amount of money, but he and the leaders of the church had a falling out over his, from their perspective, controversial views concerning Jesus's nature and Jesus's relationship with the Hebrew God, the Jewish religion, and the Jewish scriptures. As a result of this disagreement, the (proto-orthodox) church returned his contribution(s) and Marcion established his own church, which taught from the canon of texts that he claimed were the only authoritative texts—a text similar in many ways to our canonical Luke (excluding the birth narrative and much of chapter 24) and many of the letters attributed to Paul (which were pruned to remove references to the Hebrew God or Hebrew scriptures).[64] Most ancient testimony places Marcion's teaching activity toward the middle of the second century;[65] Tyson situates his teaching earlier, around 115–120. Marcion understood Paul literally—that the law is dead. Consistent with this view, he made a clear distinction between the God that Jesus and Paul advanced and the God of the Hebrew scriptures—as Tyson understands it, "between a God who enacted laws and judged humans in accordance with their obedience or disobedience of them and a God who justified sinners."[66]

---

63. BeDuhn, *First New Testament*, 12–13. See also Tyson, *Marcion*, 31–35; and Clabeaux, "Marcion."

64. In addition to his version of something like our canonical Luke, Marcion's canon included Gal, 1 and 2 Cor, Rom, 1 and 2 Thess, Eph, Col, Phil, and Phil. Many scholars now agree that Marcion's canon was the first NT canon. See, most recently, BeDuhn, *First New Testament*.

65. Tertullian refers to what is understood to be components of the first line of Marcion's gospel, "In the fifteenth year of Tiberius, Christ Jesus came from heaven, as the spirit of saving health" (*Against Marcion* 3.1.19). He then adds that there are 115 years and 6 ½ months between Jesus's appearance and Marcion. Tiberius began his reign in 14 CE, which would place Tertullian's reference to Marcion's text and teaching around 144. Irenaeus places Marcion in Rome around 140 (*Against Heresies* 1.27.1–2).

66. Tyson, *Marcion and Luke-Acts*, 31.

Because the God of Jesus was totally unknown before Jesus's sudden appearance in the "fifteenth year of Tiberius," which is also the first verse of Marcion's gospel, "Marcion concluded that there could be no connection between Jesus and the Hebrew Scriptures," which also means that there was no connection between Jesus and the Hebrew prophets. In addition to separating Jesus from the Hebrew God, their prophets, and scriptures, Tyson emphasizes that Marcion taught "that human procreation is vile and objectionable," and that "sexual acts and birth are regarded as contemptible and to be avoided."[67] Thus, Marcion's Jesus was not born, would not have been subjected to such a vile and contemptible act such as birth, but just appeared as a man "in the fifteenth year of Tiberius." Marcion's teaching was well received, for, as Clabeaux notes, "[s]cholars conjecture that in numbers alone the Marcionites may have nearly surpassed non-Marcionites in the decades of the 160s and 170s."[68]

In Tyson's text, he is reviving and further developing the work of his teacher, John Knox, claiming that our canonical Luke-Acts is a product of the second century, and, in many ways, a response to views espoused by Marcion. Tyson contends that our Luke is the result of a three stage compositional process. The first stage would be something like our Luke 3–23 (and a few versus from our chapter 24), without a birth narrative and without some of the post-resurrection appearances of Jesus that are now in our chapter 24. The second stage would be the composition of Marcion's gospel; Marcion would have used this earlier text as his model for his own but would have removed passages that indicate any relationship whatsoever to the Hebrew God or the Jewish scriptures, editing for which he was severely criticized by Irenaeus and Tertullian.[69] Then, the final author/editor of our Luke, (who, in Tyson's reconstruction, is also the author of canonical Acts) would have used the pre-Marcion text as his source but then also included our chapters 1–2 (the birth narrative) and much of chapter 24 (the post-resurrection appearances) as a response to the views espoused by Marcion.

Considering the contents of the Lukan birth narrative, one can see how its author could have crafted this narrative as a response to these Marcionite views. As noted above in detail, the overall structure, style, and language of

---

67. Ibid., 34–35.

68. Clabeaux, "Marcion," 515.

69. Concerning Marcion, Irenaeus (ca. 180 CE) writes, "Besides this, he mutilates the Gospel which is according to Luke, removing all that is written respecting the generation of the Lord, and setting aside a great deal of the teaching of the Lord, in which the Lord is recorded as most clearly confessing that the maker of this universe is his father" (*Against Heresies* 4.2), which Tertullian (ca. 207 CE) echoes, "Marcion seems to have singled out Luke for his mutilating process" (*Against Marcion*, 4.2).

the birth narrative is dependent upon the Septuagint, especially 1 Samuel (1 Kgs LXX). Tyson observes "The Septuagintal style has influenced the writing throughout Luke and Acts, but it is most prominent in the first two chapters" and he cites Cadbury and Fitzmyer to support his point before suggesting, "It is worthwhile to note that the Septuagintal language and tone of Luke 1:5–2:52 would be subtle but effective antidotes to Marcionite claims about the separation of Jesus from Hebrew prophecy and would serve to provide links between the reader and the Hebrew Scriptures."[70] The birth narrative begins with an introduction to John the Baptist's parents, who "blamelessly obeyed all the covenants and ordinances" of the Law. Zechariah was a Jewish priest and serving in an honorable position in the temple cult. The angel Gabriel appeared to Zechariah during his temple service and informed him that his son will "bring back many Israelites to the Lord their God and that he will be a forerunner in the "power of Elijah." Gabriel is one of only two angels named in the Hebrew Bible and one of the four archangels who, as such, guards the very throne of the Hebrew God.[71] The author of Luke could not have chosen a more Hebrew messenger to announce Jesus's birth.

Next, this same Gabriel appeared to Mary to inform her of her impending pregnancy. In his announcement to Mary, Gabriel informs her that her son "will be called the Son of the Most High, that the Lord God will give him the throne of his ancestor David, and he will be king over the house of Jacob forever" (1:32–33). As noted above, Luke's diction here is noteworthy. "Most High" and "Lord God" occur as references to the God of Israel hundreds of times in Jewish canonical and non-canonical literature and only rarely outside of Jewish literature. And the reference to "David" and the "house of Jacob" accentuate the Jewish emphasis. Concerning Gabriel's announcement to Mary, Tyson notes,

> The language that the angel Gabriel uses in addressing Mary in Luke 1:31 seems to have been selected specifically to offend the Marcionites—Mary is to conceive in her womb and produce a son (καὶ ἰδοὺ συλλήμψῃ ἐν γαστρὶ [sic] καὶ τέξῃ υἱὸν καὶ καλέσεις τὸ ὄνομα αὐτοῦ Ἰησοῦν, Luke 1:31). Anatomical references are also stressed in the meeting between Elizabeth and Mary (Luke 1:39–45), when the child of Elizabeth leaps in her womb (Luke 1:41, 44). Throughout the infancy narratives Jesus is referred to as a baby (βρέφος, Luke 2:12, 16) or a child (παιδίον, Luke 2:17, 27, 40; παῖς, Luke 2:43; τέκνον, Luke 2:48).... The language throughout Luke 1:5—2:52 emphasizes

70. Tyson, *Marcion*, 97.
71. See Dan 10:13, 21; 12:1; and *1 Enoch* 9:1; 40.

the humanity of Jesus, his proximity to his family, and his similarities with John.[72]

Tyson does not mention this, but that much of the language he cites here is directly from the Septuagint could also be understood as an additional stinger aimed at the Marcionites.

Luke then has Mary visit Elizabeth, who is pregnant with John the Baptist, from which we learn that Jesus is physically related to this soon-to-be Nazarite, information that would have been astounding news to the authors of Mark and Matthew, but Luke is attempting here to depict Jesus's Jewishness by aligning him with the very Jewish portrayal of John the Baptist. In Mary's "Magnificat," she sings that the God of the Hebrews has looked upon her with favor (1:48) and that he has "helped his servant Israel as he promised to our forefathers" (1:54–55), another connection between Jesus, the God of Israel, and Jewish ancestors. In Zechariah's Benedictus, he extols the Lord God of Israel, who sent a deliverer from the house of David as stated by the prophet, while recalling the covenant sworn to Abraham (1:67–73). These are surely explicit and intentional allusions to key themes of the Hebrew religion from the Jewish scriptures. That Jesus was born of a woman and swaddled and that the birth was witnessed by shepherds could be a direct counter to Marcion's views of the vileness of the birth process and that Jesus was only a spiritual being. Only Luke among our gospel authors has Jesus (and John the Baptist) circumcised—who has his parents obediently follow what is the foremost commandment of the Abrahamic covenant:

> God said to Abraham, 'For your part, you must keep my covenant, you and your descendants after you, generation by generation. This is how you are to keep this covenant between myself and you and your descendants after you: circumcise yourselves, every male among you. You must circumcise the flesh of your foreskin, and it will be the sign of the covenant between us.' (Gen 17:9–11)

Simeon then conjoins the Hebrew God to Jesus, who is "a light that will bring revelation to the Gentiles and glory to your people Israel" (2:32); Anna the prophetess then extolled Jesus to "all who were looking for the liberation of Jerusalem" (2:38); Joseph and Mary "completed everything required of them by the Law" before they returned to Nazareth, and, finally, when Jesus was twelve, his parents traveled to Jerusalem for the Passover and he remained in Jerusalem and, upon their return, they found him "sitting in

---

72. Tyson, *Marcion*, 99.

the temple surrounded by the teachers, listening to them and putting questions, and all who heard him were amazed at his intelligence and the answer he gave" (2:46–47).

There is a rhetorical and compositional reason why Luke emphasized the Jewishness of Jesus in his birth narrative via a septuagentalizing organizational structure, style, and language. Tyson offers a reasonable explanation for this material—a response to a competing group of early followers of Jesus recognized as followers of Marcion.

Conclusion: Luke Mimetically Imitated Matthew and the Septuagint

Scholars have long recognized Luke's mimetic dependence upon the Septuagint for his birth narrative but most of them have either ignored or dismissed, because of a preconceived view of independence, the possibility that he also imitated Matthew's birth narrative just as he imitated much material from the Septuagint. The striking similarities between the foretelling-of-Jesus's-birth narrative and the birth-of-Jesus-and-visitors narrative, and the inclusion of a genealogy in Luke that shares many striking features with Matthew's genealogy are undeniable and demand a reasonable explanation that is free of any preconceived bias and that is grounded in rhetorical and literary practices of the period. Luke 1–2 satisfies all of the criteria set out in chapter 2 for identifying imitated texts, with the lone possible exception of whether Luke's birth narrative post-dates Matthew's. Most scholars agree that it probably does, and the trajectory of Matt > Luke seems to make more developmental sense than Luke > Matt, as, it is difficult to imagine that Matthew would transform Luke's highly extolled Mary into a woman embroiled in inappropriate controversy. To be sure, there are differences, substantial differences. I have suggested here that there are reasonable explanations for these differences—Luke disagreed with much of what Matthew wrote concerning Mary while he may have also been responding to views advanced by the followers of Marcion. The evidence presented here that Luke imitated Matthew seems exceptionally strong. If my argument above is correct, the implications for understanding the birth narratives are significant. First, just as Matthew's genealogy and birth narrative were determined to be artificial and fictitious, so is Luke's for similar reasons. Yet, these are much more than merely works of fiction; they are carefully crafted works of polemical or rhetorical fiction that are offered as counter-narratives to earlier views.

PART 3

The Petrine-Pauline Controversy and Luke's Mimetic Transformation

Chapter 6

Establishing the Pauline-Petrine Controversy

A Prelude to Luke's Mimetic Transformation of Galatians 1–2

IN THE PREVIOUS CHAPTER, I argued that the author of the infancy narrative in Luke knew, used, and radically transformed the Matthean infancy narrative by means of Greco-Roman mimetic compositional conventions similarly to how he adapted material from the Septuagint and similar to the mimetic compositional conventions identified in Virgil's *Aeneid*. In the next chapter, I am going to argue that the author of Acts (who, most scholars agree, is also the author of the infancy narrative in Luke) knew and used Galatians 1–2 as his primary source for Acts 7:58—15:30 and that he mimetically and radically transformed what Paul wrote in Galatians, similarly to how he mimetically transformed Matthew 1–2, so as to depict a harmony and unity between Paul and the Jerusalem leaders of the followers-of-Jesus movement, including Peter, that, historically never existed. In short, there was intense controversy between Paul and these Jerusalem leaders, and it is necessary to establish the context of this controversy so as to gain a clearer understanding of the extent of Luke's mimetic whitewashing of this controversy in Acts. To this end, what I propose to do in this chapter is to present evidence of the controversy between Paul and the Jerusalem leaders (including Peter) from early Christian texts and offer a detailed summary of Paul's controversies in Galatians 1 and 2, setting the stage for the next chapter's discussion.

Evidence for the Controversy between Paul and the Jerusalem Leaders

There is a significant amount of evidence in early Christian literature of a conflict between Paul and Peter or between Pauline Hellenistic Christianity and Petrine Jewish Christianity and New Testament scholars have wrestled with identifying the extent of the controversy for over 150 years.[1] Again, the literature on the issue is vast, and only an outline of the controversy can be offered here.

One group of early Christians who were acutely aware of this conflict between Peter and Paul were those who may have been responsible for the composition of the *Kerygmata Petrou* (*Proclamations of Peter*), a document dated perhaps as early as 200 CE but that is also thought to reflect earlier views,[2] and is often attributed to the Ebionites, a Jewish Christian and anti-Pauline group who, some suggest, were the descendants of the earliest followers of Jesus. In his *Against the Heresies* (ca. 180 CE), Irenaeus writes that "the so-called Ebionites . . . . use only the gospel according to Matthew and reject the apostle Paul, saying that he is an apostate from the law. . . . They circumcise themselves and continue in the practices which are prescribed by the law and by the Judaic standard of living, so that they worship Jerusalem as the house of God."[3] In the *Kerygmata Petrou*, the anonymous author pits Peter against a Simon Magus, who is unquestionably a veiled cover for Paul, and has Peter engage Paul's account of the controversy between the two in Galatians:

> [Peter:] And if our Jesus appeared to you also and became known in a vision and met you as angry with an enemy, yet he has spoken only through visions and dreams or through external revelations. But can anyone be made competent to teach through a vision? And, if your opinion is, "that is possible," why then did our teacher spend a whole year with us who were awake? How can we believe you even if he has appeared to you, and how can he have appeared to you if you desire the opposite of what you have learned? But, if you were visited by him for the space of an hour and were instructed by him and thereby have become an apostle, then proclaim his words, expound what he has taught,

---

1. For a discussion of the problems with the terms used to identify the parties involved in this controversy, see Sumney, "Paul and Christ-Believing Jews." The literature on the Pauline-Petrine controversy is vast; see notes 6 and 7 below for some of the most relevant sources.

2. Strecker, "Pseudo-Clementines," 493.

3. Irenaeus, *Against the Heresies*, 90.

be a friend to his apostles and do not contend with me, who am his confidant; for you have in hostility withstood me, who am a firm rock, the foundation stone of the church. If you were not an enemy, then you would not slander me and revile my preaching in order that I may not be believed when I proclaim what I have heard in my own person from the Lord, as if I were undoubtedly condemned and you were acknowledged. And, if you call me condemned, then you accuse God, who revealed Christ to me, and disparage him who called me blessed on account of the revelation. But if you really desire to cooperate with the truth, then learn first from us what we have learned from him, and as a learner of the truth, become a fellow-worker with us.[4]

This excerpt from the *Kerygmata Petrou* demonstrates that people who considered themselves to be right-thinking Christians living in the second to early third century denied, or at least questioned, the legitimacy of Paul's claims about the nature of his so-called revelation (Gal 1:12) and his apostleship, and understood Peter to be the leader of the followers-of-Jesus movement. In contrast, the Marcionites, as noted in the previous chapter, adopted Paul's antinomianism and rejected Peter and the Hebrew Bible.[5]

Questions about Paul's position as an apostle and his teachings are also evident in New Testament texts, enough evidence to lead some scholars to suggest that many of the texts in the canonical New Testament were crafted to reflect one side of the controversy over the other.[6] The evidence concerns Paul's status as an apostle and his relationship with the leaders of the early Jesus movement.

One example of such tensions is in 1 Corinthians 1–4. In the opening lines of the letter, Paul reproves the recipients that "you should be united in the same mind and the same purpose, for there are quarrels among you," as each one says, "'I belong to Paul,' or 'I belong to Apollos,' or "I belong to Kephas[7] [Peter],' or 'I belong to *Christ*'" (1:10–13). Conflict, though

---

4. Strecker and Irmscher, trans., *Kerygmata Petrou*, "Homily 17."

5. Knox, *Marcion and the New Testament*; Tyson, *Marcion* (especially 24–49), and BeDuhn, *First New Testament*, 11–25.

6. In addition to Baur's *Paul the Apostle*, see Goulder's *St. Paul versus St. Peter* and *Paul and the Competing Mission*, Lüedemann, *Opposition to Paul*; Jackson-McCabe, ed., *Jewish Christianity Reconsidered*; and Nanos, ed., *Galatians Debate*.

7. That the names Kephas (Κηφᾶς) and "Peter" (Πέτρος) occur in Paul's letters has vexed scholars for many years. "Kephas" occurs in Paul's letters eight times (1 Cor 1:12; 3:22; 9:5; 15:5; Gal 1:18; 29; 2:11; and 2:14) whereas "Peter" only twice in Gal 2:7–8. One explanation is that Peter and Kephas are two different people and that Paul's angry outburst in Gal 2:11–14 was against Kephas not Petros; this dates from about the third century and is most recently supported by Ehrman ("Kephas and Peter") but refuted

undefined, is present. In 1 Corinthians 3, Paul seems to be using rhetorical comparison (σύγκρισις[8]) in a building metaphor to compare himself to an unnamed "other" builder.[9] Paul claims that he laid (ἔθηκα, aorist tense,) a foundation *as an expert builder* (σοφὸς ἀρχιτέκτων, a Pauline neologism[10]); but (δὲ) an other (ἄλλος, masculine, singular) is currently building (ἐποικοδομεῖ, present tense) upon it. Paul's use of ἄλλος here seems significant, as he does not use the indefinite pronoun τις ("someone"), but the singular adjective pronoun ἄλλος, which, as Smyth notes, "strictly means *other*."[11]

Yet, in Matthew, probably written about forty to fifty years after 1 Corinthians and often understood as written from a Petrine perspective, after Peter's confession that Jesus is the *Christos*, the author has Jesus say to Peter, "Blessed are you Simon Barjona, because flesh and blood did not reveal [that] to you, but my father who is in the heavens. You are Peter, the rock, and on this rock I will build my church" (σὺ εἶ Πέτρος, καὶ ἐπὶ ταύτῃ τῇ πέτρᾳ οἰκοδομήσω μου τὴν ἐκκλησίαν, 16:17–18). It is important to note that Matthew's source for this narrative is Mark, often considered a Pauline gospel, 8:29, which does not include Jesus's response to Peter; Matthew adds it himself, arguably as a counter to Paul's claim in 1 Corinthans that he laid the foundation.

---

by Allison ("Peter and Kephas"), who uses much the same evidence as Ehrman and counters that "Peter and Kephas were one and the same" (495). For further discussion see Lake, "Simon, Kephas, Peter"; La Piana, "Kephas and Peter in the Epistle to the Galatians"; Barnikol, "Non-Pauline Origin"; and Elliott, "Κηφᾶς: Σίμων Πέτρος: ὁ Πέτρος." Another explanation is that Gal 2:7–8, the only passages that include "Petros" in Paul's letters, is a later non-Pauline interpolation, which is most recently articulated by W. O. Walker, "Galatians 2:7b–8 as a Non-Pauline Interpolation." Because a lengthy discussion of the interpolation view would digress from my primary concern of this chapter, see Appendix 2 for an argument that the interpolation should include 2:7–9.

8. Anderson notes that σύγκρισις "involves the presentation of a parallel case/item which may be compared in some detail with the subject in hand in order to show how the one is better, worse, or equal to the other" (*Glossary of Greek Rhetorical Terms*, 110). For contrasting views as to whether Paul is familiar with and invoking rhetorical σύγκρισις in the letters to the Corinthians, see Forbes, "Comparison, Self-Praise, and Irony"; and Schellenberg, *Rethinking Paul's Rhetorical Education*, especially his chapter "Synkrisis in Corinth" (149–68).

9. Conzelmann does not even suggest that the "other" here is Peter. Rather, he seems to understand that those to whom Paul is comparing himself are "fellow-workers" (plural), but the Greek is clear throughout that the subject is singular (*1 Corinthians*, 74–75). Goulder (*Paul and the Competing Mission in Corinth*, 21–23) and Lüedemann (*Opposition*, 76–78) understand the one compared as Peter.

10. According to *TLG*, σοφὸς ἀρχιτέκτων is not attested prior to Paul's use here.

11. Smyth, *Greek Grammar*, 311. His emphasis.

Another indication that Matthew is engaging Paul is evident in Matt 5:17–19, where, within the Sermon on the Mount, Matthew has Jesus say,

> Do not think that I have come abolish the law or the prophets; I have not come to abolish but to fulfill. For truly I tell you, until the heaven and the earth pass away, not one letter, not one stroke of a letter, will pass from the law until all is accomplished. Therefore, whoever breaks one of the least of these commandments, and teaches others to do the same, will be called least in the kingdom of heaven, but whoever does and teaches [them] will be called great in the kingdom of heaven.

The author of Matthew presents Jesus here as an orthodox, Torah-abiding, Jew. That Matthew thought it necessary to have Jesus make this statement indicates that claims were in circulation that "Jesus's coming nullified the law." In Romans 10:4, Paul clearly states such a view, "*Christos* [is] the end of the law unto righteousness to all who believe" (τέλος γὰρ νόμου Χριστὸς εἰς δικαιοσύνην παντὶ πιστεύοντι). Paul's views of the Mosaic Law are scattered throughout his letters, and include these from Galatians:

- "We ourselves are Jews by birth and not Gentile sinners; yet we know that a person is justified not by the works of the law but through faith in Jesus Christ" (2:15–16);
- "All who rely on the works of the law are under a curse; for it is written, 'Cursed is everyone who does not observe and obey all the things written in the book of the law.' Now it is evident that no one is justified before God by the law" (3:10–11);
- "There is no longer Jew or Greek, there is no longer slave or free, there is no longer male and female; for all of you are one in Christ Jesus. And if you belong to Christ, then you are Abraham's offspring, heirs according to the promise" (3:28–29);
- "You [Galatians] are observing special days, and months, and seasons, and years. I am afraid that my work for you may have been wasted" (4:10–11);
- "Mark my words! I, Paul, am telling you that if you let yourselves be circumcised, Christ will be of no benefit to you. Once again I testify to every man who lets himself be circumcised that he is obliged to obey the entire law. You who want to be justified by the law have cut yourselves off from Christ" (5:2–4).

As Sim notes, Matthew's "anti-Pauline perspective is apparent."[12]

In 1 Corinthians 9, Paul offers a convoluted argument in which he claims that, as an apostle, he has the right to be supported by the community in Corinth, and he then offers several lines of argumentation—concerning the support of other apostles, soldiers, planters, shepherds, and plowmen—in an attempt to bolster his claim. It is his first claim, that he is an apostle at all, let alone the apostle of the status he claimed to be, that will be considered here, as there were questions within the Corinthian community as to whether, in fact, Paul was an apostle, and whether he had the rights of financial support that other acknowledged apostles assumed because he himself knew that he was not an apostle as these others, in fact, were. 1 Corinthians 9:1–6 will establish the context, wherein Paul writes,

> ¹Am I not free? Am I not an apostle? Have I not seen Jesus our Lord? Are you not my work in the Lord? ²If I am not an apostle to others, at least I am to you; for you are the seal of my apostleship in the Lord. 3 This is my defense to those who would examine me. ⁴Do we not have the right to our food and drink? ⁵Do we not have the right to be accompanied by a believing wife, as do the other apostles and the brothers of the Lord and Kephas (Peter) [the "Petrines"]? ⁶Or is it only Barnabas and I who have no right to refrain from working for a living?

While recognizing others as apostles, Paul refers to himself as a "called apostle" (κλητὸς ἀπόστολος, 1 Cor 1:1; Rom 1:1), as an apostle "through the will of God" (2 Cor 1:1), and as an apostle "sent not by men nor from men, but by Jesus *Christos*" (Gal 1:1), designations he does not attribute to any of the other apostles. Paul's two uses of "called apostle" (κλητὸς ἀπόστολος, Rom 1:1 and 1 Cor 1:1) are the only two occurrences of the verbal adjective κλητὸς in all of Greek literature, and, as Schmidt notes, "in Greek literature, there is attestation for the sense of 'called by God' only where Paul has exerted an influence."[13] Thus, for Paul, κλητὸς is a moniker that, it seems, he coined for his own understanding of his unique position as an apostle. Moreover, because of his understanding of this calling, he distinguished himself from the rest of those he also understood to be apostles, who were not "called apostles." It will be argued here that Paul's references to himself as a "called apostle" are apologetical and polemical. That is, his elevated status of himself as an apostle of Jesus was under attack by others who were apostles before

---

12. Sim, *Gospel of Matthew*, 208. See also Betz, *Sermon on the Mount*, especially 172–74.

13. Schmidt, "κλητὸς," *TDNT*, 3:495.

he was, and one aspect of his defense of his apostleship was to claim that he, and only he, had been "called" by God.

That Paul here is defending himself against such attacks is further indicated by the conditional clause in verse 2: "If to others I am not an apostle, at least I am to you" (εἰ ἄλλοις οὐκ εἰμὶ ἀπόστολος, ἀλλά γε ὑμῖν εἰμι). As a simple conditional clause, the protasis (the "if" clause) can simply "state a supposition with no implication as to its reality or probability"[14] but can also emphasize the reality of the condition; as Blass and DeBrunner note, "the condition is considered 'a real case.'"[15] That the latter is the case here is supported by Paul's use of ἀλλά γε in the apodosis (the "then" clause), for this rare combination denotes an "emphatic meaning" to be translated as "at least."[16] Thus, 9:2 can be rendered: "*Since, as is in fact the case*, I am not an apostle to others, *at least* I am to you,"[17] which is an emphatic acknowledgement of claims against his apostleship by some within the Corinthian community.

In 2 Corinthians 10–13 Paul provides several lines of comparative argument (σύγκρισις) in defense of his equality with the "super apostles." In 11:2–5, he writes,

> ²I joined you [the Corinthians] to one man to present a pure virgin [παρθένου ἁγνὴν] to *Christos*, ³but I fear that as the serpent, in its trickery, utterly deceived Eve, your mind has been corrupted/perverted from the sincere and pure devotion that you have[18] in *Christos*. ⁴For, if the one who is coming is proclaiming another ["an other" ἄλλον] Jesus whom we have not proclaimed, or [if] you receive a different spirit, which you did not [previously] receive, or a different gospel which you did not accept, you willingly endure it easily enough. ⁵For I consider myself not in any way inferior [ὑστερηκέναι] to the super [ὑπερλίαν]-apostles.

The imagery in 11:2–3 is striking. Rather than presenting the Corinthians as a "pure virgin" (παρθένου ἁγνὴν[19]) who had a "singleness of devotion

---

14. Smyth, *Greek Grammar*, 516.

15. BDF, 188.

16. Ibid., 226. See also Smyth, *Greek Grammar*, 633 for the emphasis that ἀλλά γε conveys in an apodosis.

17. So also Lüedmann, *Opposition*, 67.

18. I am adopting Malherbe's rendering of 11:3 here, which includes the understanding that ἀπὸ τῆς ἁπλότητος καὶ τῆς ἁγνότητος is the superior text. ("Through the Eye of the Needle," 121), which is also adopted by Dewey et al. (*Authentic Letters of Paul*, 133).

19. According to *TLG*, other than a possible occurrence in a fifth-century BCE

to *Christos*," their minds/faculties of understanding (τὰ νοήματα ὑμῶν) have been (from Paul's perspective) utterly deceived—similar to the serpent's corruption of Eve—in respect to Paul's gospel and Paul's understanding of who Jesus is. The term Paul uses for deceived here is ἐξηπάτησεν, which is a compound of ἐκ + ἀπατεύω. Whereas ἀπατεύω denotes "deceived" and is the term used in the Septuagint's rendering of Genesis 3:13 where Eve explains to God that "the serpent deceived me" (ὁ ὄφΙς ἠπάησέν με), the compound intensifies the meaning to "utterly deceived," "thoroughly deceived," or, in reference to a woman, can also mean "seduced."[20] Thus, rather than presenting a *purified virgin* to *Christos*, the Corinthians, from Paul's perspective, have been *utterly deceived, utterly corrupted* as the serpent *utterly deceived* Eve. The contrast between "holy virgin" and "utterly deceived" could not be more striking.

The reason that (γὰρ, v. 4) the Corinthians' minds have been utterly deceived is that, if we take Paul literally, one person is in the community, "the one coming" (ὁ ἐρχόμενος), who is proclaiming a different Jesus than the one Paul presented to them—a different gospel than that which Paul proclaimed to them, and, worse yet from Paul's perspective, the Corinthians are willingly enduring (ἀνέχεσθε) it. Paul's use of ὁ ἐρχόμενος is worth noting here, as this participial construction does not occur in Greek literature outside of two occurrences in the Septuagint.[21] This is also Paul's only use of the construction, the first occurrence of the construction among authors now recognized to be Christian, and the only occurrence of the construction within the canonical New Testament texts that seems to be referring to a specific, individual person (aside from the oft cited Psalms 117:26 (LXX), "The one who comes [ὁ ἐρχόμενος] in the name of the Lord."[22] Thus, it is again possible that Paul is referring to a specific individual here.

Verse 5 is Paul's first explicit statement concerning his relationship with a group of people who seem to be related to ὁ ἐρχόμενος in verse 4 who are proclaiming a different gospel:[23] I do not think that I am inferior (ὑστερηκέναι) to the "super-apostles" (ὑπερλίαν ἀποστόλων). First, it is noteworthy that ὑστερηκέναι and ὑπερλίαν are both Pauline neologisms, for the former is the first occurrence in Greek literature in this verbal form

---

fragment (Choerilus Epic. Samius, *Fragmenta epica*), this is the first occurrence in Greek literature of παρθένου ἁγνὴν.

20. For ἀπατεύω, LSJ, 181; and for ἐξαπατάω, LSJ, 586.

21. 2 Kgs (LXX) 2:23 and Ps 117:26 (LXX).

22. Mark 11:9; Matt 21:9; 23:39; Luke 6:47, 13:35; 19:38; John 12:13.

23. The only other option here would be that Paul is now referring to a different, a second, group of people who are also creating problems in Corinth, to whom he has not yet referred.

(a perfect infinitive) and this is the first occurrence for the latter in all of Greek literature. Moreover, by combining the preposition ὑπέρ (*over* or *above*) with the adverb λίαν (*very, exceedingly, very much*), Paul formed what Smyth terms a "determinative compound" whereby the modifier, the first term, "determines" the second term.[24] In this case, Paul is angrily or sarcastically identifying a "particular kind" of apostle, which is difficult to translate into English, but something like: *the overly exceedingly apostles*. As Lampe notes, "Paul must have had a wily smile on his lips when he made up this word."[25] Here, Paul is not claiming superiority to these "super apostles," but only that he is not inferior, which suggests that he is claiming equality with them. If this is the case, it is difficult to understand that Paul, who considers himself *the unique, called apostle called by God*, would consider any other apostles equal to him than those he recognizes as the original leaders of the followers-of-Jesus movement.

In 2 Cor 11:13-15, Paul's outrage against these apostles intensifies:

> [13]For such as these are pseudo-apostles [ψευδαπόστολοι[26]], deceitful workers [ἐργάται δόλιοι[27]], disguising themselves as apostles of Christ [μετασχηματιζόμενοι εἰς ἀποστόλους]. [14]And no wonder, for Satan himself disguises himself as a messenger of light; [15]therefore, it is not great if his servants [διάκονοι αὐτοῦ] also disguise themselves as servants of righteousness, whose end will be according to their works.

There is no contextual reason to think that Paul is referring to a different group of people here than those in vv. 2-5 above. Rather, these verses suggest that Paul is in the fiercest of competition with his opponents. He is hopeful that his continued work in the region of Achaia will completely eradicate (*wipe out, cut off*) his opponents' (which seem to be the "super apostles" and "the one who is coming") base of operations. Rather than referring to them as the "overly exceeding" apostles of v. 5, they are now "false" apostles and crafty, deceitful workers. Paul's imagery of Satan disguising or transfiguring himself as an angel of light is, like the imagery of the serpent deceiving Eve above, similar to that found in the *Life of Adam and Eve*, possibly composed

---

24. Smyth, *Greek Grammar*, 252. As for the adverb serving as an adjective here, Smyth notes, "In the attributive position an ordinary adverb may serve as an adjective" (284).

25. Lampe, "Can Words Be Violent," 227.

26. According to a *TLG* search, the term does not occur in Greek literature prior to its occurrence here.

27. This combination of terms does not occur in Greek literature prior to Paul's use here.

about the end of the first century CE, wherein Satan came to Eve in the form of an angel (ὁ σατανᾶς ἔγενετο ἐν εἴδει ἀγγέλου, *Apoc.*, 17.1) to deceive her a second time, but perhaps even closer to the Latin version, "Satan transformed himself into the brilliance of an angel" (Satanas et transfiguravit se in claritatem angelorum, *Vita*, 9.1).[28] The common imagery to denote cunning deception is apparent. Paul employs/creates the strongest language and imagery yet—false apostles, cunning/deceitful workers, and servants of Satan himself—to denounce his opponents/accusers from Corinth. Lampe has offered compelling argumentation that "the expressions in 11:13–15, ψευδαπόστολοι [false apostles], δόλιοι μετασχηματιζόμενοι εἰς ἀποστόλους [disguising themselves as apostles], διάκονοι τοῦ Σατανᾶ [servants of Satan] are apotropaic invectives"[29] and, as such, are to be "regarded as violent—and dangerous."[30] He rightly concludes that the conflict with [his opponents] "was not about compromising and integrating; it was about expelling, about winning or losing."[31]

In 11:22—12:1a, Paul boastfully compares his credentials to those that his opponents are boasting about in Corinth.

> But that about which someone might boast, I am speaking as a fool, I also boast.
>
> [22]Are they Hebrews? So am I.
>
> Are they Israelites? So am I.
>
> Are they the seed of Abraham? So am I.
>
> [23]Are they servants of *Christos* (διάκονοι χριστοῦ)? I more so (ὑπερ ἐγώ).

While recognizing that many commentators distinguish this group from those in vv. 2–5 and 12–15 above because this group is here explicitly identified as "servants of *Christos*" and difficulties arise in reconciling these "servants of *Christos*" with "servants of Satan" in 11:14, there is no indication within the context of this passage here that these opponents should in any way be distinguished from the opponents to whom he refers anywhere else in chapters 10–13. That Paul does not deny that his fierce opponents are Hebrews of the seed of Abraham who are also "servants

---

28. *Life of Adam and Eve*, 277, 260. The Greek text (*Apoc.*) of the *Life of Adam and Eve* is from the *TLG*; the Latin text (*Vita*) is from the Institute of Advanced Technology in the Humanities (http://www.iath.virginia.edu).

29. Lampe, "Can Words Be Violent," 223–24.

30. Ibid., 232.

31. Ibid., 223.

of *Christos*"³² strongly indicates that the opponents in Corinth are practitioners of Judaism who are also followers of Jesus. Goulder elaborates: "The missionaries are not just Jewish (Ἰουδαῖοι) but belong to the elect people of God, which Gentile Christians need to join. They are authorized 'ministers of *Christos*,' the spiritual power that possessed Jesus through his ministry, and neither Paul nor Apollos nor any other self-appointed preacher has any right to such a title."³³ Goulder identifies these as Petrines, and, as such, they "do not speak of themselves here as 'authorized ministers of Christ,' in contrast with the unauthorized Paul; they are the only ones there are."³⁴ If Goulder is right (and I think he is), then Paul's incessant claims of the divine authority of his apostleship and gospel seem all the more apologetic, even indefensibly so.

Yet, it is in reference to "servants of *Christos*" that Paul (almost hyperbolically) compares himself to these opponents in detail. While in the previous three questions, "Are they Hebrews?, Israelites?, the seed of Abraham?," Paul responds with the very common contraction κἀγώ ("I also"), in response to "Are they servants of *Christos*?," he combines ὑπερ + ἐγώ and creates a combination that does not occur in all of Greek literature prior to this occurrence to fervently emphasize the extent to which he is "better" or "excels or surpasses" or is "to a higher degree"³⁵ a "servant of *Christos*" than they are.³⁶

In attempting to identify Paul's opponents more specifically in 2 Corinthians, Lüedemann aligns 2 Cor 11:7-9 and 2 Cor 12:13 with 1 Cor 9. In 1 Cor 9, Paul renounces what he understands to be his apostolic right to be supported by the Corinthian congregation as the "rest of the apostles and Jesus's brothers, and Kephas" are (9:5-6). His renunciation of support is closely related to the Corinthians' understanding that Paul was not an apostle, as these others were (9:1-4), as discussed above. Paul is responding to the same problem in 2 Cor 11 and 12:

". . . was this my offense, that I made no charge for preaching the gospel? . . . . I robbed other congregations by accepting support from them to

---

32. It is worth noting here that the only other time that Paul uses the plural διάκονοι (servants) is 1 Cor 3:4-6: "For when someone says, 'I am of Paul,' but another, 'I am of Apollos,' are you not [literally] men? What is Apollos? What is Paul? Servants [διάκονοι] through whom you believed." The contrast between the "servants of Satan" in 2 Cor 11 and the "servants through whom you believed" is suggestive.

33. Goulder, *Paul and the Competing Mission*, 209-10.

34. Ibid., 210.

35. As noted in BDF, 121.

36. Wellborn suggests that the expression "is the verbal counterpart of the chest thumping gesture of the leading slave" in the Roman theater ("Runaway Paul," 121).

serve you.... Is there any way in which you were treated worse [by me] than the other congregations—except this, that I was never a charge on you?" (11:7–9; 12:12–13). Because Paul was attacked in 2 Corinthians for the same issue (renunciation), it must also be that Paul's opponents were apostles whom the Corinthian church was financially supporting. Moreover, if Paul's opponents in 2 Corinthians are the same as his opponents in 1 Corinthians 9 (as seems plausible), and, because Paul specifically refers to "the apostles and Jesus's brothers, and Kephas" and not other apostles in 1 Corinthians 9, it seems reasonable to infer that the Corinthians must at least know who "the apostles and Jesus's brothers, and Kephas (the Petrine party)" are and that it was the Petrine party who informed the Corinthians that Paul was not an apostle.[37]

In the Corinthian correspondences, Paul is responding to specific attacks against his self-proclaimed position as an apostle, his gospel, and him personally. In Galatians, we find more of the same. The crux of the controversy in Galatians is often understood to be 2:11–14, Paul's conflict with Kephas (Peter) in Antioch. As such, the focus of the discussion here will be on 1:1—2:14, excluding 2:7–9 because of the possibility that it is a non-Pauline interpolation. (See Appendix 2.) To be sure, there is considerable evidence of Paul's opponents in Galatians after 2:14—Paul castigates the "foolish Galatians" for being "bewitched" by his opponents (3:1) and for observing Jewish festivals and traditions (4:10–12); he complains that, because of his opponents' representation of him, he has "become their [the Galatians'] enemy" (4:16–17); he warns them that circumcision will not only not benefit them, but also will cut them off from the *Christos* (5:4) and that their progress has been thwarted (5:7); and he wishes that those "agitating" the Galatians would "castrate themselves" (5:12). But it is the controversy in Galatians 2 between Paul and the Jerusalem leaders, especially Peter, that so vexed second- and third-century Christian writers, especially the author of Acts who, it will be argued in the next chapter, used Galatians 1–2 as his primary source for Acts 7:58—15:30 and who mimetically transformed what Paul wrote in Galatians.

After his opening greeting in which Paul asserts that his apostleship is "neither from men nor through mankind" but through Jesus and God, Paul gets right to one of the more pressing points of the letter:

---

37. Lüedeman concludes that Paul's opponents in 2 Corinthians are members of the Kephas (or Petrine) party (*Opposition*, 91–92), and Goulder also identifies the opponents as those "authorized by the mother church in Jerusalem" (*Paul and the Competing Mission*, 40–41).

> ⁶I am astonished [θαυμάζω] that you are so quickly deserting [μετατίθεσθε] in this way the one who called you in grace unto a different gospel—⁷which is not another, except that some people [τινές] are agitating you and desiring to pervert the gospel of the *Christos*. ⁸But, even if we or an angel from heaven proclaim [to you] that which is contrary to that which [παρ' ὅ] we proclaimed to you, let him be accursed. ⁹As we said before, I also say again now, if anyone proclaims to you that which is contrary to what you received, let him be accursed. (1:6-9, My rendering.)

The verb that Paul uses (only) here to express his astonishment (θαυμάζω) is widely attested in ancient Greek literature, especially within rhetorical/polemical contexts[38] and denotes the sense of "wonder," "marvel," and "astonishment." His astonishment is that the Galatians are in the process (present tense) of abandoning (μετατίθεσθε) his gospel for another gospel. A parallel to Paul's use of μετατίθεσθε here is Diogenes Laertius's account of Dionysius (ca. 330–250 BCE) who became a "turncoat"[39] (ὁ μεταθέμενος) or "renegade"[40] by abandoning one philosophical school (and school of thought) for another.[41] Paul's concern here that the Galatians are abandoning the gospel he previously proclaimed to them for another closely parallels his concern expressed in 2 Corinthians: "If the one who is coming proclaims another Jesus [ἄλλον Ἰησοῦν] whom we have not proclaimed or you are receiving a different spirit which you did not receive or a different gospel [εὐαγγέλιον ἕτερον] which you did not accept, you endure it well enough" (11:4).

The Galatians have been introduced to a gospel "contrary to that which" [παρ' ὅ] Paul previously proclaimed, which is also similar to Paul's concern in 1 Corinthians that an "other" is building upon his foundation where he uses the same syntactical construction, παρα + the accusative, to emphasize his claim that "No one is able to lay a different foundation *contrary to that which has already been laid*" (παρὰ τὸν κείμενον, 3:11).[42] As in Corinth, Paul's gospel is facing a serious challenge in Galatia and enough

---

38. This term is exceptionally common in ancient Greek rhetors: Antiphon, Isocrates, Isaeus, Lysias, Demosthenes, Aeschines, Hyperides, Thucydides, Plato, and Xenophon. See also Betz, *Galatians*, 46–47; and Bertram, "Θαῦμα," *TDNT* 3.27–42.

39. BDAG, 513.

40. Hicks, *Diogenes Laertius*, 2.149, 271.

41. BDAG, 513; and Betz, *Galatians*, 48–49.

42. For "contrary to" with παρά + accusative, see Smyth, *Greek Grammar*, 383 and BDF, 123.

of a challenge to evoke from Paul a curse that those who are advancing the opposing gospel be damned—even, for rhetorical effect, doubly damned.

After asserting the supernatural origin of his position as apostle, denouncing the different gospel, and casting a double curse upon those who proclaim it, Paul declares the origin of his own gospel:

> ¹¹For I am making known to you, brothers, the gospel that is proclaimed by me is not according to man [οὐκ ἔστιν κατὰ ἄνθρωπον]; ¹²for I did not receive it from man, nor was I taught it, but [ἀλλὰ] through a revelation of Jesus the *Christos* [δι ἀποκαλύψεως Ἰησοῦ χριστοῦ].

Paul claims here to have received his gospel through a revelation of/from Jesus the *Christos* (δι ἀποκαλύψεως Ἰησοῦ χριστοῦ). Thus, if we combine his claim in 1:1 that his "gospel is not according to man" and his claims here, Paul is contending that neither his apostleship nor his gospel is derived in any way from man; neither men nor mankind confirmed apostleship upon him, and no human being was the source of, or taught him, his gospel. Rather, the direct source of his apostleship and gospel is Jesus through some meta-historical (revelatory) means, any details of which are not provided, but more likely invoking "revelation" as a rhetorical device. Again, such strong arguments for legitimacy are indicative of claims of illegitimacy. Moreover, it appears that Paul did not reveal/disclose to the Galatians the information that he received his gospel via a revelation during an earlier visit, and it is probably safe to assume the same about his supernatural claims to his apostleship. That Paul did not provide such seemingly important information when he initially established the congregations in Galatia but does so now when his gospel is clearly under attack by others suggests that Paul's claims here are apologetic/polemical reactions to some kind of accusations about his claims to his apostolic position and his gospel made by others.

Next, Gal 1:13–23 offers further support for Paul's claim that he had no contact with any of those who were leaders of the Jesus movement until several years after his conversion. Beginning at 1:13, Paul reminds the Galatians of his former life in Judaism, and makes very brief reference to his revelation of/from Jesus (lacking any details) instructing him to proclaim Jesus to the Gentiles (15–16). Rather than conferring with any "flesh and blood" or any who were apostles before he was, he claims that he traveled to Arabia and then Damascus, and three years later (from when it is not clear) to Jerusalem where he then met with Kephas (Peter), for apparently the first time, for fifteen days and saw no other apostle there but James, Jesus's brother, before heading off to the regions of Syria and Cilicia (17–20a). To convince the Galatians that this account of his actions after his conversion—that he did not meet with any others within the movement who may have conferred apostleship upon him and/or taught him the gospel—is a truthful account, Paul invokes an oath, "before the presence of God, I am not lying" (20b), similar to his oaths in 2 Corinthians 10–13.[43] As Price notes, this oath is obviously "a rebuttal to another account, widely known, in which Paul was a delegate of mortal agencies and had at once submitted himself to the previous apostles"[44]—another indication that Paul is engaged in a fierce controversy concerning the legitimacy of his apostolic status and his gospel.

Paul then claims that, after an interval of fourteen years (from when we do not know), he went up[45] to Jerusalem with Barnabas and Titus and privately laid before those to whom he referred as "having a reputation" [τοῖς δοκοῦσιν] the gospel that he proclaims to the Gentiles "lest in some way [or, for fear that, μή πως] I am running or had run in vain" (2:1–2). This creates an inconsistency with 1:1 and 1:11–12 above, where Paul could not be any more adamant and confident that his apostleship and his gospel are not in any way derived from mankind/men, but from some supernatural means, and, because of this origin, they command a divine authority and legitimacy. In 1:6–7, Paul is adamant that he does not allow for or accept a "different gospel" than his own, any of which would only be a perversion of his, *the authentic, the revealed*, gospel. It does not follow from these earlier claims that Paul would now humble himself and submit his gospel to "those who have a reputation" for approval as the text here states, fearful that his gospel (which, he claims, was supernaturally revealed) may not measure up to theirs, especially since he had been proclaiming his revealed gospel for at least fourteen or seventeen (14 + 3) years (1:18 + 2:1). When, in 1:18–19, he met with Kephas and James, which the text leads us to think occurred prior to 2:1–2, what did they talk about? The verb used in 1:18 of Paul's meeting with Kephas is ἱστορῆσαι, which denotes *to examine* or *to inquire of*; thus, Paul inquired of Kephas. What did Paul inquire about? Did they discuss Paul's and/or Kephas's and James's gospel(s)? Were not Kephas and James considered "those of reputation" (τοῖς δοκοῦσιν) at that time? Surely, Paul would have presented his gospel ("the gospel which is preached by me" 1:11) to Kephas and James during the earlier meeting of 1:18–19. Did Paul's

---

43. Paul's oaths in 2 Corinthians include "the truth of the Anointed is in me" (11:10); "I do not lie" (11:31); "I speak the truth" (12:6), and "We are not able [to do] anything against the truth" (13:8).

44. Price, *Pre-Nicene New Testament*, 18.

45. According to *TLG*, the only other occurrences of this form of the verb, συμπαραλαβών, in Greek literature are in Acts 12:25; 15:37; and 15:38, which will be discussed in the next chapter.

gospel change between 1:18–19 and 2:1–2 and lose its revealed status that may have led Paul to be compelled to submit his gospel (once again) to those of reputation in Jerusalem? These are important questions that the text not only does not address, but actually raises.

These problems aside, the narrative continues in 2:3 that Titus, a Hellene, and thus a Gentile follower of Jesus, was not compelled [ἠναγκάθη] to be circumcised [περιτμηθῆναι]. That Titus was not "compelled" to be circumcised suggests that someone or some group of people did, in fact, encourage or compel him to be circumcised. This reading of 2:3 is supported by the use of ἀναγκάζεις (same verb) in 2:14 below when Paul narrates his censure of Kephas in Antioch: "If you, a Jew, are living as a Gentile and not as a Jew, how do you compel the Gentiles to live like Jews (ἀναγκάζεις Ἰουδαΐζειν)?" Those who compelled Titus were those deemed by Paul to be "false brothers" [ψευδαδέλφους] who had sneaked in "in order that they might enslave [καταδουλώσουσιν] us" (2:5). These "false brothers" seem to have been a group of the followers of Jesus who thought that circumcision was a requirement of the movement, and it would seem that they would have been at least a subset, if not members, of "those who have a reputation," for it is difficult to understand that Paul would have been meeting with two different opposing groups of early followers of Jesus at the same time, in the same place, and considering the same issue(s). It appears as though Paul coined ψευδαδέλφους as it is attested in no other Greek text prior to the letters attributed to him,[46] and the term occurs only one other time, in 2 Corinthians 11:26 within his list of hardships. As discussed above, in 2 Corinthians, Paul is comparing himself to his opponents in Corinth and claims that he was in "dangers with false brothers" [ψευδαδέφοις]. These are "false brothers" only from Paul's perspective, for Betz is probably right that these "undoubtedly thought they were orthodox and conscientious Christians, and . . . simply understood the nature of their Christian existence in different terms" than Paul did.[47] It is also interesting that Paul here in Galatians 2 claims that these false brothers attempted to "enslave [καταδουλώσουσιν] us" by compelling Titus to be circumcised. The only other occurrence of καταδουλ- in the canonical New Testament is in 2 Corinthians 11:20 where Paul criticizes the Corinthians because they are enduring being enslaved (καταδουλοῖ) by his opponents.

Another problem in Galatians 2 concerns conflicting perspectives as to the esteem rendered toward "those of reputation." In verse 2, Paul claims that he laid his gospel before "those thought to have a reputation"

---

46. According to a *TLG* search.
47. Betz, *Galatians*, 90.

(τοῖς δοκοῦσιν), a common phrase[48] that is often used with sarcasm. Commentators are split as to whether its use here should be considered to suggest sarcasm or sincerity. Then, in verse 6, "those who are supposed to be somebody" (ἀπὸ δὲ δοκούντων εἶναί τι) are further characterized by "what sort they once were[49] makes no difference to me; God does not choose from man's appearance." This is a rare syntactical construction; τῶν δοκούντων εἶναί τι occurs only once prior to Paul's letters.[50] While the exact syntactical phrasing is rare, the practice of censoring those who claim to be something they are not was more common.[51] Warner understands this "nigh scornful phraseology" in Galatians 2:6 in negative terms,[52] as does Betz, noting that Paul uses "it as a principle here for the purpose of relativizing the authority of the Jerusalem apostles."[53]

The transition between Gal 2:6–10 and 2:11 is abrupt—all of a sudden the narrative jumps from Paul's account of his trip to Jerusalem to his account of his conflict with Peter in Antioch. As the Galatians narrative presents it, the Antioch incident chronologically follows the Jerusalem visit. Paul writes that he and Kephas were in Antioch together and that Kephas was eating

48. According to a *TLG* search, constructions referring to "those of reputation" or "those thought to be somebody" are widely attested in Euripides, Sophocles, Isocrates, Xenophon, Plato, Aristotle, Demosthenes, Polybius, Dionysius of Halicarnassus, Philo, Josephus, and Plutarch, but only one other occurrence within the canonical NT (Mark 10:42) other than these here in Galatians 2.

49. The problems generated by the past tense—"What sort they once were [ποτε ἦσαν]"—are discussed in Betz, *Galatians*, 92–95.

50. In Plato's *Gorgias*, Socrates is engaging Polus about the problems with the Athenian law courts. Socrates contends that his accusers' witness accounts are "worth nothing in regard to the truth, for on some occasions someone would be borne down by the false witness of many who seem to be somebody [τῶν δοκούντων εἶναί τι]." I adapted Nichols's (*Gorgias* 57, 471e) translation of the passage to reflect Dodds's rendering of τῶν δοκούντων εἶναι as "supposed to be somebody" (Dodds, *Gorgias*, 244).

51. Plato has Socrates conclude his apology with this request:

> However, I make this request of them: when my sons grow up, gentlemen, punish them by troubling them as I have troubled you; if they seem to you to care for money or anything else more than for virtue, and if they think they amount to something when they do not [καὶ ἐὰν δοκῶσί τι εἶναι μηδὲν ὄντες], rebuke them as I have rebuked you because they do not care for what they ought, and think they amount to something when they are worth nothing. If you do this, both I and my sons shall have received just treatment from you. (*Apology*, 145)

52. Warner, "Galatians ii. 3–8," 380.

53. Betz, *Galatians*, 94. Price offers a harsher assessment in his claim that Paul "seeks to hide the fact that this Torah faction was part of the core group of Pillars, 'those of repute.' He implies that no one knew them at the time for what they turned out to be: Judaizing hardliners" (*Pre-Nicene New Testament*, 319nr).

with Gentiles (having adopted Paul's practice it seems), until "certain men from James" (τινας ἀπὸ Ἰακώβου) arrived, at which time, he "drew back and began to hold aloof "fearing those from the circumcision" (φοβούμενος τοὺς ἐκ περιτομῆς), which seems to be an indication that those pressing for Titus's circumcision earlier in Galatians 2 were also from James, the leader of the Jerusalem followers of Jesus. The rest of the Jews who were there followed Kephas's lead—even Paul's close associate Barnabas, who "was led astray in their hypocrisy" (συναπήχθη αὐτῶν τῇ ὑποκρίσει). Paul writes that this conduct did not square with (*his* understanding of) "the truth of the gospel" (τὴν ἀλήθειαν τοῦ εὐαγγελίου), which led to Paul's angry rebuke of Kephas, "If you, a Jew, live like a Gentile and not like a Jew, how to you compel the Gentiles to live like Jews?" (2:14).

This conflict between Paul and Kephas created such angst within the early followers-of-Jesus movement that later Christian writers attempted to minimize the controversy in at least three ways. One was to add an interpolation into Galatians 2 (vv. 7–8 or 9) that depicted a unity between Paul and the Jerusalem leaders and a second was to argue that Kephas and Peter were two different people and that Paul rebuked Kephas instead of Peter. (See Appendix 2.) A third was to mimetically transform this event so that the controversy never took place at all and depict a harmony and unity between Paul and the Jerusalem leaders that, historically, never existed. This mimetical transformation is in our canonical book of Acts, 7:58—15:30, to be considered next.

Chapter 7

Luke's Mimetic Transformation of Galatians 1–2

A Rhetorical Analysis of Acts 7:58—15:30

IN CHAPTER 5, I argued that Luke mimetically transformed Matthew's birth narrative, and, in chapter 6, I established the context of the Petrine-Pauline controversy in early Christian literature and explained Paul's controversy with this group in Galatians 1–2. In this chapter, I am going to argue that the author of Acts, who is also the author of the birth narrative in Luke, knew and used Galatians as his primary source for Acts 7:58—15:30 and radically transformed what Paul wrote in Galatians so as to suppress or whitewash the controversy between Paul and the Jerusalem leaders similarly to how he mimetically transformed Matthew 1–2. Before launching into a dense and detailed rhetorical analysis of Acts 7:58—15:30, it is necessary to provide a brief background of the controversy as to whether Luke could have known and used Paul's letters, especially Galatians.

It is also necessary to state that the following discussion works from the understanding that Acts was written during the early decades of the second century (ca. 120–130 CE) and as such I do not accept the traditional attribution of the authorship of Acts to Paul's companion Luke, but instead understand that our canonical Acts is an anonymous text.[1]

Could the Author of Acts Have Known and Used Paul's Letters?[2]

One reason offered as to why the author of Acts could not have known Paul's letters is similar to those discussed in earlier chapters as to why

---

1. See Pervo, *Dating Acts*; Tyson, *Luke*; and Smith and Tyson, *Acts and Christian Beginnings*, 1–10.

2. Contemporary scholars credit Baur with originally articulating the problems

Luke could not have known Matthew—there are simply too many discrepancies between Galatians and Acts, similar to the claim that there too many discrepancies between Matthew's and Luke's birth narratives. A few of these discrepancies include whether Paul made two trips to Jerusalem (Gal 1:18–20; 2:1) or four (Acts 9:26–30; 11:30–12:25; 15:1–30; 21:17–40); whether Paul conferred with others immediately after his 'conversion' (Acts 9:15–21) or not (Gal 1:16); whether he went to the so-called Jerusalem Council because of a revelation (2:1) or because he was sent by others (Acts 11:29–30); whether he presented his gospel to the leaders of the Jerusalem community privately (Gal 2:2) or not at all (as there is no account of such in Acts); whether Titus accompanied Paul to Jerusalem (Gal 2:1) or not (as Titus is not mentioned in Acts); whether nothing was added to Paul's gospel (Gal 2:10) or whether the "decree" from James was added (Acts 15:24–29); and whether Paul had an angry confrontation with Peter in Antioch (Gal 2:1–14) or not (as Peter is never in Antioch in Acts and Paul and Peter, contrary to Galatians, never say one word to one another in Acts), just to mention a few. That advocates of the view that Luke could not have known and used Paul's letters simply cannot accept the possibility that the author of Acts contradicted Paul on any of these (or other) narrative events is expressed by C. K. Barrett's representative claim, "Luke was far too great an admirer of Paul to think of contradicting him."³

A second reason why scholars have maintained that Luke could not have known Paul's letters is because of a perceived absence of any verbal similarities between Acts and Galatians. John Knox explains the problem,

> As a matter of fact, in the absence of adequate evidence of *verbal* dependence (and this, it will be agreed, we do not have in the case of Acts), can there ever be, in a situation like this, any certainty of dependence at all? Indeed, the lack of verbal conformity may have the effect of reversing the argument. Can it be supposed that Luke used the letters of Paul as source for

---

between Acts and the Pauline letters, especially in his *Paul, the Apostle of Jesus Christ*. Therein, Baur wastes no time getting to his thesis, as in the "Preface" he writes, "[T]he harmonious relation which is commonly assumed to have existed between the Apostle Paul and the Jewish Christians with the older Apostles at their head, *is unhistorical*, and the conflict of the two parties whom we have to regonise [sic] upon this field entered more deeply into the life of the early Church than has been hitherto supposed" (vi). See also, Pervo, *Dating Acts*; Tyson, *Marcion and Luke-Acts*; Knox, "Acts and the Pauline Letter Corpus;" Enslin, "Once Again, Luke and Paul"; Barrett, "Acts and the Pauline Corpus"; Walker, "Acts and the Pauline Corpus Reconsidered"; Lüedemann, *Opposition to Paul*, especially 1–34; Johnson "Luke-Acts, Book of"; Trobisch, "Council of Jerusalem in Acts 15"; and Leppä, *Luke's Critical Use of Galatians*.

3. Barrett, "Acts and the Pauline Corpus."

facts or *data* but succeeded in avoiding (or would even have tried to avoid!) any trace of their actual language? In a word, so important is verbal reminiscence that one is almost justified in saying that *in the absence of it* every possible piece of evidence of Luke's having used the letters increases the probability that he did not use them.[4]

Because of this absence, Knox concludes, "So far as the actual evidence goes, then, I should say that no convincing case can be made for Luke's reliance on the letters of Paul or for his knowledge of them at all."[5]

Engaging those who contend that there is no evidence of direct verbal dependence between Galatians and Acts, Heikki Leppä, in his 2002 Ph.D. dissertation, *Luke's Critical Use of Galatians*, claims to have identified 10 specific examples of Greek terms or phrases that occur in similar contexts in both Acts and Galatians. These include:

1. συμπαραλαμβάνω (*to take or bring along with*, Gal 2:1; Acts 12:25; 15:37);

2. οἱ ἐκ περιτομῆς (*those from the circumcision*, Gal 2:12; Acts 11:2);

3. πορθέω (*destroy/maul*, Gal 1:13, 23; Acts 9:21);

4. ζηλωτὴς ὑπάρχων (*zealous for the law*, Gal 1:14; Acts 21:20; 22:3);

5. ἀφορίζω and προσκαλέω (*separate and called*, Gal 1:15; Acts 13:2);

6. τῆς Συρίας καὶ Κιλικίας (*of Syria and Cilicia*, Gal 1:21; Acts 15:23, 41);

7. ζυγός (*yoke*, Gal 5:1; Acts 15:10);

8. ὃ καὶ ἐποίησαν (*that which also I do*, Gal 2:10; Acts 11:30);

9. ἀκροβυστία and συνεσθίω (*uncircumcision* and *eat with*, Gal 2:7; Acts 11:3); and

10. διαταγεὶς δι' ἀγγέλων (*given through angels*, Gal 3:19; Acts 7:38, 53).

In addition to these close verbal similarities, Leppä outlines in some detail several structural similarities between Gal 1:13—2:14 and Acts 8:1—15:2a; he makes a compelling case that these verbal and structural agreements point "the way to literary dependence between Acts and Galatians,"[6] and, for Leppä "[t]he fact that Luke's story is different than Paul's story does not change these verbal similarities."[7] As for Luke's motive in changing the story,

---

4. Knox, "Acts and the Pauline Letter Corpus," 282.
5. Ibid., 282.
6. Leppä, *Luke's Critical Use*, 59.
7. Ibid., 60.

Leppä suggests that the "most plausible way to solve the tensions between Acts and Galatians is to assume that Luke wanted to criticize and correct Paul's information in Galatians 2"—for, "if the men from James in Gal 2:11–14 demanded circumcision of the Gentiles and Peter accepted their requirements, then Luke wrote Acts 15:1–15:30 [the so-called "Jerusalem Council" narrative] in order to cover an ancient scandal."[8]

Richard Pervo's 2006, *Dating Acts: Between the Evangelists and the Apologists* further advances Lëppa's work, as he examines over eighty passages that contain verbal similarities to passages in Acts, twenty-five of these are from Galatians, and eleven of these from Galatians 2.[9] He also identifies what he terms "eight items of narrative sequence," by which he means that there are eight similar (and dependent) points of contact between the narrative sequence of Galatians 2 and Acts 15. Pervo's argumentation concerning the verbal and narrative similarities is compelling and I will refer to it in more detail throughout my discussion below. As for imputing a motive to Luke for his use of Galatians in Acts, Pervo contends, "the author of Acts quite intentionally revised what Paul said in [Galatians] in order to create a construction more conducive to Christian unity."[10] That is, "[t]o put it rather sharply, in the matters of the dispute at Antioch, Luke has turned Galatians 2 upside down. Galatians appears to be his major source, but what he claims is quite opposed to what Paul says in Galatians."[11] In his 2009 commentary on Acts, he is more candid still, stating that the purpose of Acts 15 "is to paper over the rift between Paul and Peter, and the tension between Paul and James."[12]

This brief review of previous scholarship on Luke's knowledge and use of Galatians suggests that there is considerable evidence for the claim that Luke knew and used Galatians. I will build upon this earlier work and "add meat to the bones" that they have established by demonstrating the extent to which the entire narrative of Acts 7:58—15:30 is dependent upon, and mimetically and radically transforms, Galatians 1–2. One point that is important to note is that not one of these scholars who has recognized conceptual, structural, narrative, and verbal similarities between Galatians and Acts has suggested the possibility that Luke imitated Paul in the Greco-Roman sense of mimesis. This is especially surprising of Richard Pervo, for, as I noted

---

8. Ibid., 114.
9. Pervo, *Dating Acts*; see his ch. 4, especially "Statistical Summary" (139–43).
10. Ibid., 74.
11. Ibid., 92.
12. Pervo, *Acts*, 368.

in previous chapters, he observed that "Mimesis is what writers did;"[13] he acknowledged that the author of the gospel of Luke's greatest "facility is an ability to 'write like the Bible,' that is, to imitate the language of the LXX [Septuagint], most notably in Luke 1 - 2. He can suit style to matter,"[14] and, in his brief commentary on Luke notes,

> The story of Jesus opens [in Luke] like one of the Hebrew Bible's stories of remarkable births; much of Luke 1–2 is written in 'biblical language,' i.e., the language of the LXX. Language and content are two forms of imitation. Mimesis, to use the familiar Greek term, was a major component of ancient education. Just as you will see art students copying paintings in museums, students in the Greco-Roman world learned by imitating the masters. Imitation [also] extends to narrative units.[15]

If it can be shown that Luke used Greco-Roman compositional techniques in Galatians that are similar to those acknowledged mimetic compositional techniques he used in his imitation of the Septuagint and Matthew in his birth narrative in Luke 1–2, then the claim that Luke imitated Paul similarly to how he imitated Matthew and the Septuagint will be demonstrated.

Acts

Even though Acts opens with a second account of Jesus's alleged ascension that cannot be reconciled with the account at the end of Luke 24, Acts is intended as a sequel to Luke. Following this account of the alleged ascension, the eleven disciples/apostles (minus Judas) return to Jerusalem with Peter (not Kephas) as the indisputable leader. Paul is not yet in the narrative. Peter tells the others that they must choose a replacement for Judas, and citing the Septuagint version of Psalms 69 and 109, establish the following criteria for an apostle: one who accompanied the other followers of Jesus the whole time of Jesus's ministry—from his baptism until his ascension (1:21–22). Such a definition of an apostle, coming from Peter, eliminates Paul as an apostle. The Pentecost event follows, wherein devout Jews "from all nations" gather in Jerusalem, which gives Peter an opportunity to proclaim the gospel to them with the result that 3,000 of these devout Jews converted (2:41). Such immense growth is an important theme in Acts. Peter and the others then encountered opposition from the

---

13. Pervo, "Flattery," 11.
14. Pervo, *Acts*, 28.
15. Pervo, *Gospel of Luke*, 7.

Jewish leaders and the Sadducees, another central theme. We are told that "the whole company of believers was united in heart and soul" (4:32), that they shared their resources, and that a Barnabas, surely Paul's companion to be, sold his property and dropped the proceeds at "the apostles' feet" (4:36–37). This Barnabas was clearly not an apostle, contrary to Paul's representation of such in 1 Corinthians 9. Peter performs "many signs and wonders," faced more opposition from the high priest and Sadducees; the apostles were arrested; an angel freed them; they proclaimed in the Temple, were arrested again, flogged, and released. All this resulted in the "disciples growing in number" (6:1). Stephen is introduced; he performs "signs and wonders," and speaks in the "Synagogue of Freedman" comprised of Jews or converts to Judaism from all over the Mediterranean who disputed with Stephen and accused him of blasphemy. Before the Council, Stephen offers a speech suspiciously similar to Peter's earlier speech and other speeches in Acts, leading scholars to recognize that the speeches are Luke's and not the speakers to whom they are attributed.[16] For Stephen's efforts, he is led out of the city and stoned. "Witnesses laid their coats at the feet of a young man named Saul" (7:58) (and renamed Paul later in the narrative).

Scholars still debate what sources, if any, Luke might have used to craft Acts 1—7:57. That he relied upon the Septuagint is certain, but any others in addition to that have not received scholarly consensus.[17] As for 7:58—15:30,

16. Among the reasons for attributing the speeches in Acts to Luke are the following:

(1) Greco-Roman antiquity presumed that speeches included in works of literature, including history, were the work of the author rather than the putative speaker. (2) The speeches in Acts are Lukan in language, style, and thought. (3) The speeches often play a role in the narrative. (4) The majority of the speeches are interdependent: they build upon and depend upon one another. (5) The speeches establish the unity of the narrative of Acts and the continuity of its plot and thought. (6) The speeches are directed to the readers of the book rather than to the dramatic audiences in the text. (7) In the ancient world, means and motives for preserving speeches did not exist. (Pervo, "Speeches in Acts," 45–46.)

After briefly reviewing the problems with trusting the attribution of speeches in antiquity, George Kennedy concludes,

All of this, as well as the existence of prosopopoeiae in Luke's gospel, suggest that he would have felt free to compose speeches for participants in the events described in Acts on the basis of what they were likely to have said. What was 'likely' was determined by the demands of the situation, the character and beliefs associated with the speaker in Luke's mind, the rhetorical conventions of the setting, and what would seem appropriate to Luke's readers. (*New Testament Interpretation*, 114)

17. For the most recent discussion of sources in Acts, see Pervo, *Dating Acts*, 1–15 and, for a thorough review of recent scholarship on the sources in Acts, his "Appendix

although the majority consensus is still that Luke did not know or use Paul's letters (especially Galatians), there is a growing awareness that such use may, in fact, be the case. I will further demonstrate Luke's dependence on Galatians considering the overall conceptual and structural similarities along with the narrower thematic and verbal similarities between Galatians 1–2 and Acts 7:58—15:30 and then by identifying specific similarities and differences between Paul's account of the so-called Jerusalem Council and Luke's account of the same in Acts 15.

Table 25 depicts Acts' conceptual and structural dependence upon Galatians. The table aligns the relevant sections from each text in parallel (synoptic) columns, which will serve as an outline for the subsequent discussion, as the headings in the sections below will correspond with the "Event" headings in this outline and I will begin each section with an expanded outline of the material to be covered within that section.

Table 25: Synoptic outline of Galatians 1–2 and Acts 7:58—15:30[18]

Galatians	Event	Acts
1:13b	Paul as persecutor	7:58—8:3; 9:4–5; 22:7–8; 26:1, 14, 15
1:14	Paul's zeal	22:3
No corresponding narrative	Interlude 1	Acts 8:4–40
1:15–16	Paul's conversion	9:3–19
[2 Cor 11:33]	Paul's evangelism in Damascus and escape	9:20–25
1:18–19	Paul's first trip to Jerusalem	9:26–30
No corresponding narrative	Interlude 2	9:31—11:24
2:1–10	Paul's second trip to Jerusalem	11:25—12:24a

1: Scholarship on the Sources of Acts" (347–58).

18. While I have departed from Leppä's (*Luke's Critical Use*) and Pervo's (*Dating Acts*) tables depicting structural similarity, theirs have influenced and contributed to mine. I also adopt Pervo's term "Interlude" over Lëppa's "Long Period of Silence" for its brevity and conciseness.

Galatians	Event	Acts
No corresponding narrative	Interlude 3: Paul and Barnabas return to Antioch and "first missionary journey"	12:24b—14:23
2:11–14	Conflict in Antioch	14:27—15:3
Luke adapts material from throughout Gal 2:1–14	Jerusalem Council	15:4-35

Four observations from this table are that 1) Luke follows Galatians' conceptual and narrative (structural) order from Gal 1:13–2:10; 2) the themes and events are similar; 3) Luke adds three *Interludes* into his narrative that have no corresponding narrative in Galatians, and 4) Luke's material in his "Jerusalem Council" narrative is not derived solely from Paul's account (2:11–14), but drawn from several different passages from Galatians 2:1–14.

Table 26: Paul as persecutor

Galatians	Acts
For you heard about my former life in Judaism, that I <u>aggressively persecuted</u> [ὑπερβολὴν ἐδίωκον] the assembly of God and <u>ravaged</u> [ἐπόρθουν] it (1:13b).	[Saul] was harrying the church; he entered house after house, seizing men and women and sending them to prison (7:58—8:3).
	"Saul, Saul, why are you persecuting [διώκεις] me?" (9:4; cf. 9:5; 22:7-8; 26; 26:11, 14, 15).
I was still unknown by sight to the congregations in Judea; they had simply heard it said, 'Our former persecutor [ὁ διώκων] is preaching the good news of the faith which once he <u>tried to destroy</u> [ἐπόρθει] (1:22-23).	All who heard were astounded. 'Is this not the man, they said, who wreaked havoc [πορθήσας] among those in Jerusalem who invoke this name?' (9:21).
	And so I <u>persecuted</u> [ἐδίωξα] this movement to the death (22:4).

These are the only occurrences of the verb (πορθεῖν) in the canonical New Testament, and Leppä and, more recently, Pervo have argued compellingly—because of the rarity of the word and its use within similar contexts—that the author of Acts is dependent upon Paul's use of the term.[19] As Pervo observes,

> In the range of material covered by the standard lexicon of the New Testament and other early Christian literature (*BDAG*) it appears three times: Acts 9:21 and Galatians 1:13, 23. One may therefore narrow the range and say that in the New Testament πορθεῖν is used to describe a *single event*: Paul's persecution of the Jesus movement. This uniqueness increases the probability that Luke took the verb from Galatians.[20]

A second verbal similarity related to Paul's persecution of the followers of Jesus is the word for "persecution" itself, διώκειν, which denotes "pursue, chase, in war or hunting" or, in a legal sense, "prosecute," and is a very common verb in Greek literature. It occurs about forty-five times in the canonical New Testament and about half of these are in those Pauline letters considered to be authentic. Paul is explicit about his former persecution of the Jesus movement. In Philippians, for example, Paul writes that as far as his zeal goes, he was a "persecutor" [διώκων] of the church (3:6). In 1 Corinthians, he claims that he is not fit to be an apostle because he persecuted [ἐδίωξα] the church of God (15:9), which is reiterated in Galatians, "I aggressively persecuted [ὑπερβολὴν ἐδίωκον] the church of God" (1:9), and in 1:23, Paul conveys the converts of Judea's amazement that "our former persecutor [ὁ διώκων] is proclaiming the good news." The author of Acts employs the verb διώκειν nine times. While one of these is toward the end of Stephen's speech (7:52), the other eight are specific to Paul's persecution of the Jesus movement (9:4,5; 22:4; 22:7-8; 26:11,14,15):

- "'Saul, Saul, why are you persecuting [διώκεις] me?' 'Tell me, Lord,' he said, 'who are you?' 'I am Jesus whom you are persecuting [διώκεις]'" (9:4-5).

- "'Saul, Saul, why are you persecuting [διώκεις] me?' I answered, 'Tell me, Lord, who are you?' 'I am Jesus of Nazareth, whom you are persecuting [διώκεις]'" (22:7-8).

- "'Saul, Saul, why do you persecute [διώκεις] me? It hurts to kick like this against the goad.' I said, 'Tell me Lord, who are you,' and the Lord replied, 'I am Jesus, whom you are persecuting [διώκεις]'" (26:14-15).

---

19. Leppä, *Luke's Critical Use*, 40-44; and Pervo, *Dating Acts*, 74-75.
20. Pervo, *Dating Acts*, 75.

- "And so, I persecuted [ἐδίωξα] this movement to the death, arresting its followers, men and women alike, and committing them to prison" (22:4).

- "In all the synagogues I tried by repeated punishment to make them commit blasphemy; indeed my fury rose to such a pitch that I extended my persecution [ἐδίωκον] to foreign cities" (26:11).

Luke's repetitive, and even emphatic, use of διώκειν within the same narrative contexts within which Paul repeatedly uses the term suggests dependence upon Paul's claims of his persecution of the movement throughout his letters. Moreover, Luke's use of διώκειν within the same narrative context within which πορθεῖν occurs with διώκειν in Galatians strongly suggests dependence upon Paul's claim in Galatians.

Table 27: Paul's zealousness

Galatians	Acts
And progressed in Judaism beyond many of my age, as I was <u>far more zealous</u> [ζηλωτὴς ὑπάρχων] of my *forefathers' traditions* (14).	"I am a Jew," he began, 'a native of Tarsus in Cilicia. I was brought up in this city, and as a pupil of Gamaliel I was thoroughly trained in every point of *our ancestral law*, <u>exceedingly zealous</u> [ζηλωτὴς ὑπάρχων] for God (22:3).

In Galatians 1:13b, Paul referred to his former life of persecuting the followers of Jesus and Luke begins his narrative about Paul with this information (Acts 7:58—8:3). Following 1:13b, Paul, in v. 14, refers to the enthusiasm with which he embraced the Jewish traditions, "I progressed in Judaism beyond many of my age, as I was far more zealous [ζηλωτὴς ὑπάρχων] of my *forefathers' traditions*." This expression does not occur in all of Greek literature prior to Paul's use of it here. As Luke constructed his narrative of Paul, it was too soon, too early in his narrative as he conceived it to speak of Paul's zealousness for his ancestral traditions in Acts 8–9. This reference to Paul's zealousness was to be used later, on two occasions in Acts, where Luke thought its use would be more appropriate. The first is after Paul arrived in Jerusalem on his final visit. At that time and according to the narrative in Acts, Paul met with James and "all the elders" and explained to them what God had done in respect to the Gentiles through him. Luke has the elders respond by exhorting Paul to observe the "thousands of converts among the Jews, all of whom are "exceedingly zealous of the law" (πάντες ζηλωταὶ τοῦ νόμου ὑπάρχουσιν)" and who also have heard that Paul teaches Jews to disregard the law (21:20–22).[21] Whereas the context of the passage in Galatians refers to Paul's education and progress within Judaism and the context of Acts 21:20–22 places the zealousness among other Jews, both contexts include the two terms ζηλωτ- and ὑπάρχ- and Luke's use of these two terms in this context sets the stage for his second use of the expression in Acts 22:3. According to the narrative, Paul, while in the temple in Jerusalem, is accosted by Jews who then incite the crowd against him, which eventually leads to his arrest, at which point he is granted permission to speak to the crowd in, our narrative claims, the Hebrew dialect (Aramaic): "I am a Jewish man, born in Tarsus of Cilicia, brought up in this city where, at the feet of Gamaliel, I was thoroughly trained in our ancestral laws, exceedingly zealous [ζηλωτὴς ὑπάρχων] for God, just as all of you are today" (22:3). Here in 22:3, the content of the speech placed in Paul's mouth (as Paul did not make this speech) is identical to what he wrote in Galatians—his education, training, and zealousness, a zealousness he claims here to share with these Jews. As Leppä points out, the expression ζηλωτὴς ὑπάρχων is exceptionally rare,[22] as within all of Greek literature through the second century CE, this exact expression occurs only in Galatians 1:14 and Acts 22:3. The contexts and content of both passages within which the expression is used are the same. The most reasonable explanation for the use of the exact expression within both passages (Gal 1:14 and Acts 22:3) is that Paul coined the expression and Luke, using Galatians as his source, lifted the expression from one context and inserted it into a chronologically later context within Acts where it would better serve his rhetorical ends similar to how he relocated material from the LXX to craft portions of his birth narrative.

Interlude 1: Acts 8:4–40

Luke sandwiches his first interlude between his account of Paul's persecution of believers and his conversion (9:3–19). In this interlude, Philip is evangelizing in Samaria where he performed many signs and healed and converted many. He then inexplicably disappears from the narrative and Peter and

---

21. Betz notes that "zeal for the Torah is a general ideal of the time" and cites Josephus's account of the call of Mattathias as an example: "Whoever is zealous for our ancestral laws and the worship of God, let him follow ... me! (εἴ τις ζηλωτής ἐστιν τῶν πατρίων ἐθῶν καὶ τῆς τοῦ θεοῦ θρηκείας, ἐπέσθω ... ἐμοί" (*Galatians*, 68). The passage cited is from Josephus's *Antiquities* 12:271, quoted from Josephus, *Works*; Greek text from *TLG*.

22. Leppä, *Luke's Critical Use*, 45. See also Pervo, *Dating Acts*, 76.

John are dispatched from Jerusalem to finish the work there before Philip returns to the narrative, explicates Isaiah 53:7–8 for the Ethiopian official, and then converts and baptizes him. From a narrative perspective, one of the reasons why Luke inserted these narratives between Paul's persecution of the followers of Jesus and Paul's conversion is to make the point that the movement was spreading beyond Jerusalem to both Jews and Gentiles (even to inhabitants of foreign lands), by others, under the authority of the apostles from Jerusalem before Paul was even converted.

Table 28: Paul's conversion (Galatians 1:15–17 and Acts 9:1–19)

Galatians	Acts
But, when it pleased the one who separated me from my mother's womb ... to reveal his son in me, in order that I might proclaim him to the Gentiles ... I went to Arabia and then returned to Damascus (1:15–17).	While still on the road nearing Damascus, suddenly a light from the sky flashed all around him. He fell to the ground and heard a voice saying, 'Saul, Saul, why are you persecuting me?' (9:3–4).

That Paul's conversion narrative (9:1–19a) is closely linked to the earlier persecution narrative and the first interlude is supported further by the author's opening statement, "Saul, still breathing [ἔτι ἐμπνέων] threat and murder. . ." (9:1). The present participle "breathing" (ἐμπνέων) with its adverb "still" denotes that "a given situation is continuing *still, yet*."[23] That is, Saul's violent persecution of the followers of Jesus described in 8:3 has been ongoing during the two episodes with Philip in 8:4–40 and is ongoing still, as Saul seeks authorization, via the unnamed high priest, to track down and arrest followers of the movement in Damascus and extradite them to Jerusalem. Our narrator does not inform us why Saul is interested in those followers of Jesus in Damascus, as following upon 8:4–40, he could have sought out such followers in Samaria, or toward Gaza, or anywhere else where they may have scattered. The reason why Luke has Saul seek authorization for arrests in Damascus is because he is returning to his source, Galatians, wherein Paul claimed to have had his conversion revelation of Jesus near Damascus, "I did not confer with flesh and blood, neither did I go up to Jerusalem to those who were apostles before me, but I went unto Arabia and, again, returned to Damascus" (1:16–17). It seems important that "Damascus" occurs sixteen times in the canonical New Testament: three times in Paul's letters—his conversion narrative

23. BAGD, 315.

(Gal 1:17) and escape from Damascus narrative (2 Cor 11:32, 33)—and the other thirteen in the conversion and escape narratives in Acts. Thus, "Damascus" in Gal 1:17 corresponds with the term's use in Acts 9:2, 3, 8, and 10, along with its use in the other two reiterations of the conversion narratives (22:5, 6, 10, and 11; 26:12, 20), and "Damascus" in 2 Cor 11:32–33 corresponds with the use of "Damascus" in the escape narrative of Acts 9:19, 22, and 27. While this verbal similarity may be considered to be of a different kind than some of the other verbal similarities others have found between Galatians and Acts, the fact that the word occurs in the New Testament only in Paul and Acts and within the exact same narrative contexts in each suggests narrative and verbal dependence.

Luke's narrative of Saul seeking letters authorizing him to arrest followers of the Jesus movement in Damascus and then return them to Jerusalem is a literary device intended to get Paul near Damascus so that he can then have his revelatory vision because his source, Galatians, necessitates it. That this narrative of Saul's pursuit of the followers of Jesus to Damascus is Luke's rhetorical creation and unhistorical is further supported by the fact that neither the high priest nor any other religious body in Jerusalem would have had the authority to arrest citizens of Damascus and then expedite them back to Judea.[24]

As for the conversion account itself and as I mentioned in the previous chapter, Paul's claim of a revelation is a rhetorical device that, within an apocalyptic genre, grants divine authority to the person who makes the claim and legitimacy to that person's message. While Paul does not provide any details about the alleged metaphysical event anywhere in his letters, there are several narrative or thematic similarities between some things that Paul states in Galatians and the description of the event in Acts 9, as Table 29 indicates.

---

24. Pervo notes, "That Saul had access to the chief priest and that this official can issue warrants authorizing apprehension of persons in Damascus and their extradition to Jerusalem are both Lucan fictions" (*Acts*, 240). Haenechen, likewise, notes that the Sanhedrin "certainly did not have" the right "to secure the arrest of Jews in foreign states and their extradition to Judaea [sic]" (*Acts of the Apostles*, 321n24). Lüdemann adds, "No historical support can be adduced for Paul's journey from Jerusalem to Damascus on the warrant of the high priest in order to arrest Christians there and bring them back to Jerusalem. In fact, the jurisdiction of the high court did not extend as far as Damascus, but was limited to Judea" (*Acts of the Apostles*, 129). Levin also notes, "The *synedrion* does not appear as an independent, authority-wielding, body" (*Jerusalem*, 269).

Table 29: Similar narrative themes between
Paul's conversion in Galatians 2 and Acts 9

Galatians	Narrative event	Acts
"I <u>persecuted</u> the church of God and tried to destroy it" (1:13).	While a persecutor	"Saul, <u>still breathing threat and murder</u> against the Lord's disciples" (9:1)
Paul did not go to Jerusalem after his revelation but to Arabia, and then <u>returned to Damascus</u> (1:17).	Near Damascus	"While on the road and <u>nearing Damascus</u>, suddenly a light from the sky flashed all around him" (9:3).
"When the one who separated me from my mother's womb and who called [me] through his grace <u>revealed</u> his son in me" (1:15).	Meta-physical experience	"... <u>suddenly a light from the sky flashed all around him. He fell to the ground and heard a voice saying</u>" (9:3).
"When <u>the one who separated me from my mother's womb and who called</u> [me] through his grace revealed his son in me" (1:15).	Chosen	"The Lord said to [Ananias], "Go, because this one is my <u>chosen instrument</u>" (9:15).
"When the one who separated me from my mother's womb and who called [me] through his grace revealed his son in me <u>in order that I proclaim him among the Gentiles</u>" (1:15).	For a purpose	"The Lord said to [Ananias], "Go, because this one is my chosen instrument <u>to bear my name before Gentiles</u>, kings, and the sons of Israel" (9:15).

In both Galatians 1 and Acts 9, the text claims that Saul/Paul had a metaphysical/supernatural experience while he was still persecuting the followers of Jesus and while he was near Damascus. In both accounts, Paul is said to be chosen or called—"called" (ὁ.... καλέσας) in Galatians and a chosen instrument (σκεῦος ἐκλογῆς) in Acts, and in both respectively for the purpose of "proclaiming [Jesus] among the Gentiles" (Gal 1:15) or "bearing [Jesus's] name before Gentiles, kings, and the sons of Israel" (Acts 9:15). These narrative/thematic similarities strongly suggest literary dependence, but there are also significant differences.

In the conversion narrative in Acts, Luke writes that a light flashed all around Saul, that he fell to the ground and heard a voice (of Jesus), that Jesus spoke to him and commanded him to go into Damascus, that Saul had companions who assisted him into Damascus, that he was struck blind and took no food or drink for three days, and that an Ananias attended to

Saul in Damascus, laid hands on him, and baptized him. That Paul does not mention any of these events or people in Galatians or any other letter attributed to him does not in itself indicate that Luke's narrative is not historically trustworthy. However, other differences provide indications that Luke's account of Saul's conversion is another example of his rhetorical and fictitious reconstruction.

Paul's Conversion: Problem 1—Paul's Audience

For example, Luke narrates that Ananias had a vision in which Jesus informed him that he was to go to Saul and convey to him that he (Saul) was Jesus's "chosen instrument to bring my name before the Gentiles, *kings, and sons of Israel*" (9:15). As noted above, this differs from Paul's account in Galatians in that therein Paul is to proclaim Jesus among the "Gentiles" only, whereas in Acts "kings and sons of Israel" is added, which fits very nicely with the account in Acts where Luke has Paul proclaim before kings and Jews.[25] This revision fits one of the Luke's narrative themes, as he has Paul proclaiming to the Jews in synagogues in nine different communities—in Damascus (9:20), Salamis (13:5), Pisidian Antioch (13:14-43), Iconium (14:1), Thessalonica (17:1), Berorea (17:10), Athens (17:17), Corinth (18:4-17), and Ephesus (18:19-26); yet, in those letters thought to be authentic, Paul not only never enters a synagogue but, strikingly, the word "synagogue" (συναγωγή) does not occur even once in any of them.

Paul's Conversion: Problem 2—Ananias

Moreover, even though Ananias played such an instrumental role in Paul's conversion (according to Acts), there is no mention of Ananias in any of the letters attributed to Paul. Again, this in itself does not undermine the historicity of the Ananias narrative in Acts, but it does raise questions. The first is to ask how Ananias would have heard that Saul received the authority to track down, arrest, and extradite followers of Jesus, people like himself. Since Paul does not mention Ananias, who was so instrumental in his "conversion," in any of his letters, it is probably safe to think that Paul did not know him and, thus, would not have communicated this information to him. It is also doubtful that Saul would have advertised such an expedition, as doing so would surely jeopardize its success. More important (and problematic) though is that it is through Ananias, instead of Jesus, that Paul "received the Holy Spirit," for the text claims that Ananias "laid his

---

25. Luke has Paul defend himself before "King" Agrippa (25:13-26) and appeal to Caesar in Rome (25:6-12).

hands on him and said, 'Saul, my brother, the Lord Jesus, who appeared to you on your way here, has sent me to you so that you may recover your sight and be filled with the Holy Spirit" (9:17). There are two issues here. The first is the "laying on of hands," which plays such an important role in Acts. The apostles laid hands on the "Seven" to authorize their service, (service that never materialized, 6:6); it was through Peter and John's "laying on of hands" that those in Samaria received the Holy Spirit (8:17–19); later in Acts, it will be the prophets and teachers in Antioch who "lay their hands" on Barnabas and Paul to send them on their way on their so-called "first missionary journey" (13:1—14:26); later still, Paul "lays his hands" on the disciples in Ephesus who then receive the Holy Spirit and speak in tongues (19:6), and, finally, Paul lays his hands on Publius's father and heals him (28:8). In Acts, the "laying on of hands" clearly signifies a spiritual pecking order—that one in a higher sense of spiritual or supernatural authority has the power to then convey something spiritual to someone who is lower in the spiritual pecking order. In the case of Saul as it is narrated here in Acts, it is not Jesus, not an apostle, but Ananias, a mere, previously unknown disciple (μαθητής, 9:10) in Damascus who then disappears from the narrative, not to be heard from again, who lays hands upon Saul, who, as a result, receives the Holy Spirit. It is also important to note that the expression "laying on of hands" or any linguistic expression similar to it does not occur in the letters of Paul thought to be authentic. This seems to be an expression and practice with which he was not at all familiar, as it seems completely inconceivable that Ananias would have "laid his hands" on Paul (through which Paul would have received the Holy Spirit) and that Paul would then have laid his hands on disciples in Ephesus (through which they would receive the Holy Spirit), but that the practice or even mention of "laying on of hands" would then not appear anywhere, or play any role, in any of his letters, but do occur and play a role in 1 and 2 Timothy, which are recognizably later and not written by Paul.

Ananias's role in Paul's conversion raises another question, the source of Paul's gospel. In Galatians, Paul claims, "the gospel that is proclaimed by me is not according to man; for I did not receive it from man, nor was it taught [to me], but through a revelation" (1:11–13a). As I mentioned earlier, this seems to be an apologetical retort offered in response to claims against Paul to the contrary. Pervo states that "Luke is loyal to Galatians in avoiding any reference to human teachers of Paul,"[26] a view that Haenechen shares.[27] While I agree that Luke does not have Ananias explicitly teach Saul anything during their brief meeting, the text does state that, after Saul was bap-

---

26. Pervo, *Acts*, 246.

27. Haenechen notes that "here Luke cannot be said to conflict with Paul" (*Acts of the Apostles*, 328).

tized and regained his strength, "he was in Damascus with the disciples for a period of time [ἡμέρας τινάς] and, immediately [εὐθέως],[28] he proclaimed in the synagogues that Jesus is the son of God" (9:19-20). The expression "for a period of time" (ἡμέρας τινάς) occurs only four times in the canonical New Testament, all of which are in Acts,[29] and denotes an indefinite (and vague) period of time. In 10:48, for example, Cornelius's people ask Peter and those with him to stay "for a period of time" and in 16:12, Paul stays with Philip in Caesarea for "a period of time." Any reader would expect that Paul and Ananias,[30] the one through whom Paul received the Spirit, and the other disciples in Damascus would have discussed, among other things, the gospel; it seems inconceivable that they would not. Paul's account in Galatians gives the impression that his conversion event was more solitary than what Luke describes here in Acts, and Luke's account at least allows for the possibility that such conversations could have taken place.

Table 30: Paul's evangelizing in Damascus and his escape

Galatians and 2 Corinthians	Acts
But when the one who separated me from my mother's womb and who called [me] through his grace was well pleased to reveal his son in me, in order that I might proclaim him among the Gentiles, I did not immediately confer with flesh and blood, neither did I go to Jerusalem to those who were apostles before me, but I went to Arabia and again returned to Damascus (Gal 1:16–17).	He was with the disciples in Damascus for a period of time and immediately he proclaimed Jesus, in the synagogues, that this one is the son of God (9:19b–20).
[In Damascus, the ethnarch of King Aretas watched the city of Damascus to arrest me, and I was dropped down [ἐχαλάσθην] in a rope basket, through a window, over the wall [διὰ τοῦ τείχους] and I escaped his hands (2 Cor 11:32).]	But after many days had passed, the Jews plotted to kill him (9:23) . . . . but one night, some disciples took him and, lowering him [χαλάσαντες] in a basket, let him down over the wall [διὰ τοῦ τείχους] (9:25).

---

28. It is interesting to note that Luke uses the adverb εὐθέως (immediately) here and that the only occurrence of εὐθέως in Paul is in Gal 1:16, where he states within the same context, "I did not immediately [εὐθέως] confer with flesh and blood."

29. In addition to 9:19, ἡμερέρας τινάς occurs at 10:48; 16:12; and 24:24.

30. The context is not clear as to whether Ananias is to be included as one of the "disciples" in 9:19b. However, because he is referred to as a "disciple" (μαθητὴς) earlier in the narrative (9:10), it makes contextual sense that he could be included as one of the "disciples" (μαθητῶν) in 9:19b.

If, then, Luke does not consider Paul to be an apostle in the sense that he considers the Twelve in Acts 1 to be apostles, what does he understand Paul to be and does this relate to Paul's claims about his revelation/conversion in Galatians? In this section, I will argue that, like the narrative of Saul's conversion, the narrative of his activity in Damascus is dependent upon Galatians 1 and that Luke considers Paul to be, not an apostle, but an evangelist who proclaims that Jesus is the son of God because, in Galatians, Luke's source, Paul makes the same claim of himself. Then, because Paul, in Galatians, does not provide any details whatsoever about his departure from Damascus, the author of Acts moves from Galatians to 2 Corinthians as the source for his material for his narrative of Paul's escape from Damascus to Jerusalem.

Again, in Galatians 1, Paul writes, "But when the one who separated me from my mother's womb and who called me through his grace thought it good to reveal his son (τὸν υἱὸν αὐτοῦ) in me in order that I might proclaim him among the Gentiles (ἵνα εὐαγγελίζομαι αὐτὸν ἐν τοῖς ἔθνεσιν) (1:16). Paul claims that his purpose (ἵνα) is to *evangelize* (εὐαγγελίζομαι), to proclaim "his son" to the Gentiles. Similarly, in Acts 9:20, following immediately upon Saul's conversion and while he is with the disciples in Damascus, Luke narrates that Saul "proclaimed Jesus, that this one is the son of God" (ἐκήρυσσεν τὸν Ἰησοῦν ὅτι οὗτός ἐστιν ὁ υἱὸς τοῦ θεοῦ). For Luke, the verbs κηρύσσω (proclaim) and εὐαγγελίζω (proclaim, proclaim good news) are synonymous.[31] Aside from the Lukan alteration that has Paul proclaim to the Jews in the synagogues whereas Paul claims that he is to go to the Gentiles, the similarities in context, expression, and wording are striking, and suggest dependence, especially since it follows Saul's conversion, which, as has been argued, is dependent upon Galatians 1.[32] For Luke, Paul is not an apostle in the same sense that the Twelve of Acts 1, who were witnesses to Jesus's alleged resurrection, are apostles. Rather, he is an evangelist, one whose primary purpose is to proclaim (εὐαγγελίζομαι), as Paul said of himself in Galatians 1.[33] This can be demonstrated by how many times Luke uses the term in reference to Paul in Acts:

31. For example, in Acts 8:4–5 Luke writes, "Now those who were scattered went about preaching [εὐαγγελιζόμενοι] the word. And Philip went down to the city of Samaria and proclaimed [ἐκήρυσσεν] the Christos to them."

32. It is also interesting to note that this is the only passage in Acts where "son of God" occurs.

33. Other passages in Paul's letters that may have influenced Luke's understanding of Paul as an evangelist include: ". . . thus, my eagerness to proclaim the gospel [εὐαγγελίσασθαι] to you in Rome" (Rom 1:15); "and so counting it an honor to proclaim [εὐαγγελίζεσθαι] not where Christos has been named, in order that I might not build upon another's foundation" (Rom 15:20); "If I were to proclaim the gospel

- In the synagogue in Pisidian Antioch, Luke has Paul claim, "We proclaim (εὐαγγελιζόμεθα) to you the announcement made to your fathers (13:32);

- In Lystra and Derbe, Paul and Barnabas were continually proclaiming (εὐαγγελιζόμενοι ἦσαν) (14:7; 15, 21);

- Upon their return from their so-called "first missionary journey," Paul and Barnabas remained in Antioch proclaiming (εὐαγγελιζόμενοι) with many others the word (14:35); and

- In Troas, Luke narrates Paul's vision wherein a Macedonian is asking him to come to his land, and Paul becomes convinced that God has called him to "evangelize" (εὐαγγελίσασθαι) them (16:10).

Luke is following his source, Galatians 1, while retaining some of the material but transforming other.

Moving from Paul's purpose, Luke remains close to his source. In Galatians, Paul travels from Damascus to Jerusalem in just a few words—"Then, after three years, I went to Jerusalem" (1:18), but without any explanation as to his reason for the departure. Luke fills in the void by first offering a timeline, then creating a narrative of conflict in Acts between Paul and the Jews, and then incorporating material from 2 Corinthians.

First, Paul states that "after three years, I went to Jerusalem" (Gal 1:18). Luke seems to recognize this chronological marker, as he writes, "And when many days [ἡμέραι ἱκαναί] were fulfilled, the Jews decided to kill him" (9:23). The expression "many days" (ἡμέραι ἱκαναί) is very rare, occurring only three other times in Greek literature up to the fifth century CE[34] The addition of the adjective ἱκανός with a term representing time denotes "considerable time" or "long time."[35] Its use in Luke-Acts with other terms representing time seems to indicate a longer period of time than other expressions of length of time. For example, in the gospel of Luke, the Gerasene demoniac had not worn clothes or lived in a house "for a long time" (χρόνῳ ἱκανῷ, 8:27), and the man who planted a vineyard went abroad "for a long time" (χρόνους ἱκανούς) (20:9). In Acts, Peter stayed on in Joppa "for some time" (ἡμέρας ἱκανάς, 9:43), and Paul stayed on in Corinth "for some time" (ἡμέρας ἱκανάς, 18:18). Perhaps, along with the indefinite period of time

---

[εὐαγγελίζωμαι, it is no credit to me; for it is necessary for me; for it would be agony for me if I were not to proclaim [εὐαγγελίσομαι]" (1 Cor 9:16); "I laid before them the gospel which I proclaim [εὐαγγέλιον ὃ κηρύσσω] among the Gentiles" (Gal 2:2).

34. It occurs in the Hippocrates corpus (*De articulis* 14.91), then Galen cites the Hippocrates passage, and then John Chrysostum cites this passage in Acts 9:23 (*TLG*).

35. LSJ, 825, II.

(ἡμέρας τινάς) in which Paul stayed with the disciples in Damascus (9:19b), his use of "many days" here in 9:23 is intended to indicate the three-year period between Paul's relocating from Damascus to Jerusalem in Galatians 1. Luke fills in Galatian's unexplained void with Paul spending time with the Damascus disciples, proclaiming Jesus, and his escape. Whether "many days" indicates the three years precisely or not, Luke, like Paul, provides a chronological marker prior to Paul's trip to Jerusalem.

Next, in order to get Paul to Jerusalem, Luke needs a narrative device, much like the device of Paul hunting down followers of Jesus to get him from Jerusalem to, following his source, Damascus so that Saul could be (following Galatians) converted near Damascus. Luke explains that in his proclaiming of Jesus as the son of God, Saul confounded the Jews, which led to them creating a plot to kill him. Luke's escape narrative, his device to get Paul from Damascus to, following Galatians, Jerusalem, is dependent upon Paul's escape-from-Damascus narrative from 2 Corinthians 11, as depicted in Table 31.

Table 31: Paul's escape

2 Corinthians	Acts
In Damascus, the ethnarch of King Aretas watched the city of Damascus to arrest me, and I was <u>dropped down [ἐχαλάσθην] in a rope basket, through a window, through the wall [διὰ τοῦ τείχους]</u> and I escaped his hands (2 Cor 11:32).]	When many days were fulfilled, the Jews decided to kill him, but their plan became known to Saul. And they were watching the gates night and day so that they might kill him. But one night, some disciples took him and, <u>lowering him [χαλάσαντες] in a basket, let him down over the wall [διὰ τοῦ τείχους]</u> (9:23–25).

Table 32 depicts the similarities and differences in the two accounts.

Table 32: Similarities and differences in the escape narratives

2 Corinthians 11:32-33	Narrative theme	Acts 9:23-25
Within the broader context of Paul's boasts. This is Paul's third boast, and it pertains to his own weakness. It is used here in 2 Cor as a parody. He does not offer a word of explanation as to when this escape occurred.	Context	While Paul was proclaiming Jesus in the synagogues in Damascus.
An official of king Aretas.	Who was looking for Paul?	The Jews.
Watching (ἐφρούει) the city for him.	What were they doing?	Watching (παρετηροῦντο) the gates.
Damascus	Where?	Damascus
To arrest him (πιάσαι με).	Why were they looking for Paul?	To kill him (ἀνελεῖν αὐτόν).
No mention of the time.	Time of day	At night.
No mention of who lowered him.	Who lowered him?	[His] disciples lowered him.
Lowered (ἐχαλάσθην) in a basket (ἐν σαργάνῃ).	Lowering	Lowering (χαλάσαντες) him in a basket (ἐν σπυρίδι).
Through a window.	Window	No window is mentioned.
Over the wall (διὰ τοῦ τείχους).	Wall	Over the wall (διὰ τοῦ τείχους).

Paul's brief mention of his escape from Damascus in 2 Corinthians is couched within a broader discussion of his boasts pertaining to his weaknesses (11:16—12:10). He offers this episode only as an example of his weakness, escaping at night down the city wall, in contrast to the courage a soldier demonstrates in scaling an enemy's city wall. In order to avoid arrest by king Aretas's official, for what he does not state, he was shamelessly lowered to his freedom by others. That Luke lifted this narrative out of 2 Corinthians' context seems undeniable. In addition to the identical, yet altered, narrative themes, there are exact verbal similarities. The phrase "over the wall" (διὰ τοῦ τείχους) occurs only three times in Greek literature prior to Paul's use of it here[36] and then only in these two passages in the New Testament, and

---

36. It occurs twice in Polybius's *Historiae* (8:6.1 and 8.7.3) and in 2 Kgs LXX (2

the only difference with "lower" is that in Galatians it is an aorist passive (ἐχαλάσθην) whereas in Acts it is an aorist participle (χαλάσαντες) of the same verb. Moreover, these are the only two occurrences of the combination χαλάω- (lower) + διὰ τοῦ τείχους (over the wall) in all of Greek literature prior to its occurrence in 2 Corinthians and Acts.[37]

In lifting this passage, Luke significantly transformed it for his own use. Instead of a government official watching to arrest Paul, Luke has "the Jews" watching in order to kill him because he was proclaiming Jesus in the synagogues—a practice that I have already noted is foreign to Paul's letters, but is useful for Luke's rhetorical themes of Paul going to the Jews first and of the Jews' hatred of Paul throughout Acts. In the process of incorporating Paul's escape narrative into Acts 9, Luke leaves traces of a narrative seam: Why would Paul go from Damascus where "the Jews" are seeking to kill him to Jerusalem where there would be, presumably, many more Jews than there were in Damascus? This problem aside, Luke, following his source, gets Paul back to Jerusalem.

Table 33: Paul's first trip to Jerusalem

Galatians	Acts
[18]Then, after three years, I went up to Jerusalem to inquire of Kephas, and I stayed with him fifteen days. [19]I did not see [any] other of the apostles, except James, the brother of the lord. [20]These things that I write to you, I say before God, I am not lying. Then, I went to the regions of Syria and Cilicia [in Tarsus]. (1:18–20)	[26]When he came to Jerusalem, he attempted to join the disciples, and they were all fearful of him, not believing that he was a disciple. [27]But Barnabas, taking him, led him to the apostles and explained to them how he saw the lord along the road and that he (the Lord) spoke to him and how, in Damascus, he spoke boldly in the name of Jesus. [28]And he was with them going in and out to Jerusalem, speaking boldly in the name of the Lord, [29]and he spoke and disputed with the Hellenists, but they were attempting to kill him, [30]but when the brothers learned of this, they led him to Caesarea and they sent him off to Tarsus. (9:26–30)

Sam) 20:21.

37. According to a *TLG* search, the only other occurrences of this combination are in later Christian writers, beginning with Origen, who cite one or the other of the passages.

Table 34: Similarities and differences in the accounts of Paul's first trip to Jerusalem

Galatians	Narrative event	Acts
After three years (1:18).	Time?	He was with the disciples in Damascus for a period of time (9:19b) + After many days had passed (9:23).
To inquire of Kephas (1:18).	Reason for visit to Jerusalem?	To join the disciples (9:26).
"I" (seemingly alone; no mention here of Barnabas) (1:18).	Accompanied?	Barnabas led Paul to the disciples and the apostles (9:27).
Only Kephas and James, no other apostles (1:18–19).	Who did Paul see?	The "disciples," Barnabas, "the apostles," "the Hellenists." The text gives us no reason to think that Paul met with Kephas (Peter) or James (9:27–28).
Fifteen days (1:18).	How long was he in Jerusalem?	Not stated specifically, but "he was going in and out."
Not stated.	Why did he leave Jerusalem?	The Hellenists were attempting to kill him.
Syria and Cilicia.	Where did Paul go?	Tarsus (a chief city or capital of eastern Ciclicia).

There are only two definite similarities in these passages. In both, Paul went from Damascus to Jerusalem and then from Jerusalem to Cilicia. It is also reasonable to think that Luke's "for a period of time" (19b) and "after many days" (9:23) could roughly correspond with Paul's "after three years" (1:18). Other than these, there are no similarities. Rather, Luke radically transforms Paul's account, and in doing so, he creates more narrative problems.

According to Paul, this is his first trip to Jerusalem, and the impression we get from Galatians is that Paul went by himself, independently, to Jerusalem to seek out Kephas (Peter) but also saw Jesus's brother, James. In Acts 9, Luke does not have Paul meet either Kephas or James. Rather, he has Paul return to Jerusalem, from whence he earlier departed for Damascus, and Luke narrates that Barnabas led Paul to unnamed disciples and unnamed apostles. From a narrative perspective, where does Barnabas come from? The last time he appeared in the narrative was in 6:9 where he was introduced as a Cypriot Levite who sold his property and laid the proceeds at the feet of the apostles. Are readers to think that Barnabas remained in Jerusalem while Paul was in Damascus? If that is the case, then how did Barnabas know the details of Paul's conversion event and bold proclamations in Damascus? If word of Paul's transformation and bold speaking in Damascus reached Barnabas *in Jerusalem*, then it would also seem that it would have reached "the [other] disciples" who feared Paul (9:26) and, especially, "the apostles" to whom Paul is introduced by Barnabas, thus excluding the need for Barnabas to speak on Paul's behalf. It would also seem reasonable to think that if Barnabas accompanied Paul on his first trip to Jerusalem, Paul would have mentioned Barnabas in Galatians 1, as he does when Barnabas accompanies him on his second trip to Jerusalem in Galatians 2:1, or as he mentions him specifically at the controversy in Antioch wherein Barnabas was, according to Paul, led astray by the Jewish Christians from James (2:13), or as he refers to him specifically as a fellow-worker in 1 Corinthians 9:6. Luke transforms what Paul claimed to be his independence as an apostle and his individual or personal visit to Jerusalem to seek out Kephas into an event in which Paul attempted to join [ἐπείραθεν κολᾶσθαι] mere "disciples" who rejected him before being "led" [ἤγαγεν] by another disciple (Barnabas) to the unnamed "apostles," who accept him, the narrative leads us to believe, only after Barnabas, a trusted disciple, speaks on his behalf. The coherence and credibility of Luke's narrative is crumbling, and it is difficult to disagree with Haenechen's assessment that "the ground on which this entire Lucan edifice is erected will bear no weight, and all must come toppling down."[38]

Further evidence that Luke is radically transforming Galatians 1 here is his explanation for Paul's departure from Jerusalem. Whereas in Galatians Paul does not say anything about why he departed for Syria and Cilicia, Luke states that the "Hellenists" were continually attempting to kill him. The term "Hellenist" (Ἑλληνιστής) occurs four times in the New Testament, three of which are in Acts.[39] In 6:1, the "Hellenist" disciples are distinguished from the "Hebrew" (Ἑβραίους) disciples and in 21:37 the Roman officer, after Paul spoke to him in Greek, referred to him as a "Hellenist." Thus, a "Hellenist" is a Greek-speaking Jew as opposed to an Aramaic-speaking Jew,[40] and whereas Luke wrote that it was "the [Aramaic-speaking] Jews" who attempted to seize Paul in Damascus because of his bold proclamations, here, in Jerusalem, it is the Hellenistic Jews who were also those who engaged and ultimately stoned Stephen.

---

38. Haenechen, *Acts of the Apostles*, 335.

39. The other is John 19:20.

40. See Pervo, *Acts*, 158. Haenechen adds that the Greek-speaking Jews would be natives of the Diaspora, whereas the Aramaic-speaking Jews would have been born in Palestine (*Acts of the Apostles*, 267).

In Galatians 1, Paul gives the impression, if not explicitly states, that, from the beginning, he was working independently of his opponents from Jerusalem, that he considered himself equal with these apostles, and that, in his first visit to Jerusalem, he met Kephas and James. In Acts 9, Luke radically alters this impression. Paul is not an independent apostle, but he is dependent upon Barnabas, a disciple, for his contacts in Jerusalem; he is not a leader, but one of the disciples who works along side other unnamed apostles, and he does not meet or speak with Kephas and James. Moreover, whereas in Galatians it is other followers of Jesus who embrace principles and practices of Judaism who are his opponents, in Acts, Luke radically alters this by making the Aramaic- and Greek-speaking Jews his opponents. Again, Lucan narrative themes and his rhetorical intentions are behind these transformations of Galatians 1, and he, following Galatians, ends Paul's visit to Jerusalem situating him in Cilicia (9:31), and this will be the last that we hear of Paul in Acts until Barnabas departs Antioch to track him down in Tarsus (11:25).

Table 35: The "Silent Period" (Acts 9:31—11:24)

Galatians	Acts
No corresponding material in Galatians.	"Silent Period" 9:31—11:24
	• Church enjoyed a time of peace and grew (9:31).
	• Peter in Lydda and Joppa; Aeneas and Dorcas (9:32-43).
	• Cornelius (10:1—11:18).
	• Growth continues (11:19-24).
	– Scattered believers travel as far as Antioch and proclaim message only to Jews.
	– Believers in Antioch proclaim to Greeks.
	– News of this reaches Jerusalem.
	– Barnabas sent to Antioch.
	[Barnabas] then went off to Tarsus to look for Saul; and when he had found him, he brought him to Antioch. For a whole year the two of them lived in fellowship with the church there, and gave instruction to large numbers. It was in Antioch that the disciples first got the name of Christians. (11:25-26).

Leppä identifies Acts 9:31—11:24 as a "Long Period of Silence" and does not discuss how the material in this section of Acts does or does not fit into Luke's use of Galatians 1 and 2. From this silence, it is possible to conclude that Leppä does not see a relationship.[41] In *Dating Acts,* Pervo follows Leppä's understanding of the "Long Period of Silence," but identifies it as an "Interlude," about which he writes, "Acts interrupts the story of Paul to report a mission of Peter, including the conversion of a Gentile, the acceptance of that act in Jerusalem, and the beginnings of a mission in Antioch that included Gentiles,"[42] and then briefly suggests its relevance to Galatians 2,[43] to be considered below. In his commentary, he addresses the Pauline influence in Peter's sermon,[44] the similarity between Peter's revelation that God shows no partiality (10:34–5) and the similar sentiment expressed in Galatians 2:6,[45] and notes that Peter's sermon is a "bridge between the mission of Peter and the work of Paul, between the mission to the Jews and proclamation to the Gentiles."[46] In continuing my interest in understanding how Luke, *qua* author, used Galatians rhetorically and compositionally, my approach to this material in 10:1—11:24 will address three questions:

- What was Luke trying to tell his readers by creating these stories?

- Why did Luke include this material here between Paul's conversion and his second trip to Jerusalem (where he picks up his source, Galatians, once again)?

- Are there close narrative and/or rhetorical relationships between Acts 10:1—11:24 and Galatians 1 and 2 and, if so, what are they?

The primary focus of Acts 10 is the conversion of Cornelius in Caesarea and Peter's role therein. Yet, the last we saw of Peter in the narrative, he and John were returning to Jerusalem from their evangelistic efforts in Samaria (8:20). Luke needs a literary device to get Peter from Jerusalem (assuming the narrative still places him there) to Caesarea, which is located on the shores of the Mediterranean about 75 miles northwest of Jerusalem. So after he sends Paul off to Tarsus, he explains that the "church throughout all of

---

41. Leppä, *Luke's Critical Use,* 63. After his discussion of Paul's departure for Syria and Cilicia, Leppä moves on to consider the collection in Antioch (Acts 11:27–30), without any consideration of the intervening material.
42. Pervo, *Dating Acts,* 143.
43. Ibid., 90.
44. Pervo, *Acts,* 277.
45. Ibid., 277.
46. Ibid., 278.

Judea, Galilee, and Samaria had peace" and was growing (9:31).[47] Amid this growth, Peter, now on his own, would visit the "saints" in these communities and his first stop is in Lydda, about 35 miles northwest of Jerusalem and about half way to Caesarea. There, he heals the paralytic Aeneas, a curious name,[48] and as a result "all" (πάντες) those living in Lydda and the surrounding Plain of Sharon believed. Peter then travels to Joppa, about 10 miles northwest of Lydda, on the coast, and about 30 miles south of Caesarea, where he revives Tabitha (Greek, Dorcas); word spreads, and, as a result, "many" (πολλοί) in Joppa are converted. In addition to serving as a literary device to get Peter closer to Caesarea for the conversion-of-Cornelius narrative, these brief narratives further develop Luke's theme of growth and further showcase Peter's role, power, and authority over nature as the leading apostle and, has now, if not somewhat awkwardly, established a context for this narrative.

It is no accident that Luke situates the conversion of Cornelius in Caesarea. This seaport and its famous harbor were built during Herod the Great's reign (40–4 BCE.) between 22–10/9 BCE.[49] Josephus informs us that the city included a temple dedicated to Caesar—which, Josephus notes, "was excellent both in beauty and largeness,"[50] within which were statues of Caesar, Rome, and Jupiter Olympius—a theater, and an amphitheater "capable of holding a vast number of men,"[51] all of which many of Herod's conservative Jewish constituents surely viewed with the utmost contempt. Luke probably could not have chosen a more fitting Gentile setting for the conversion of Cornelius and his family.

---

47. The growth of the movement is one of the primary themes of Acts: 2:41; 2:47; 4:4; 5:14; 6:1; 6:7; 9:31; 11:24; 12:24; 13:49; 16:5; 19:20; and 21:20.

48. Aeneas was a Trojan leader in the *Iliad* who battled with Diomedes (5.217–353) and Achilles (20.153–353). This is the Aeneas who is then the hero of Virgil's *Aeneid*. Aside from this occurrence in the *Iliad*, the name occurs in Pindar (*Olympia* Ode 6.88), Thucydides (4.119.2), Euripides (*Rhesus* 90 and 585), and Xenophon's *Hellenica* (7.3.1). That Luke uses it here is curious and probably symbolic. Smith and Tyson suggest that the name is "synonymous with Rome itself," and that its use here is a "subtle symbol for the power of the gospel to heal a 'crippled' Rome" (*Acts and Christian Beginnings*, 120). Another possibility may be that "Aeneas" refers simply to the Roman people, when considered along with the translation of the Aramaic Tabitha into the Greek "Dorcas" in the following narrative, the names can be understood as symbolic for the Greek and Roman people—the gospel is going to the Gentiles, and going before Paul, the apostle to the Gentiles, is even converted.

49. Hohlfelder, "Caesarea," *ABD* 1:799.

50. Josephus, *Wars* 1.22.414.

51. Josephus, *Antiquities* 15.9.341.

In Caesarea, Cornelius, a Roman centurion,[52] had a vision (ὅραμα, 10:3) in which he was asked to send for Peter in Joppa. The next day, as Cornelius's men were closing in on Simon the Tanner's home in Joppa, Peter fell into a trance and saw his vision (ὅραμα, 10:17) in which it was explained to him that he "must not call any man profane or unclean." As Peter pondered over this vision (ὅραμα, 10:19), Cornelius's messengers arrived at Simon's home and Peter was advised to welcome them, after which they returned to Caesarea. Peter advised Cornelius and his guests that even though it is the custom of Jews not to associate with those of other races,[53] he, because of his mind-changing vision, was willing to hear Cornelius out, which led to Peter baptizing him and his household. Upon his return to Jerusalem, he recounted his vision (ὅραμα, 11:5) to "those from the circumcision" (οἱ ἐκ περιτομῆς) who took issue with him about associating with the uncircumcised (ἄνδρας ἀκροβυστίαν ἔχοντας[54]).

The meaning of Peter's vision—that "a major component of the purity code has been abolished,"[55] and its interpretation and application—that God is no respecter of person are clear enough. Luke also makes it very clear that it is Peter, rather than Paul (who according to our narrative is somewhere in the regions of Cilicia and Syria doing what we do not know), who initially takes the gospel to the Gentiles. This is reiterated later in Peter's contribution to the discussion at the so-called Jerusalem Council, "Men and brothers, you know that, from the earliest days, God decided among you that through my mouth [διὰ τοῦ στόματός μου] the Gentiles would hear the word of the gospel and believe" (15:7). According to Luke, it is Peter rather than Paul, contrary to what Paul claims in Galatians, who is the human catalyst behind the Gentile mission. In addition to these obvious expressions of what the author of Acts intends here, there are two others worthy of consideration—whether the visions in Acts 10 relate to Paul's conversion vision in Acts chapter 9 and the relationship between Acts 10—11:18 and Galatians 2:11-14.

---

52. Haenechen notes that "no Roman troops can have been stationed in Caesarea while that city was still under the jurisdiction of Herod Agrippa I, (i.e., up to year 44) (*Acts of the Apostles*, 359).

53. Haenechen notes that "diaspora Jews were not hermetically sealed off from dealings with the Gentiles" (*Acts of Apostles*, 350n4), which Pervo echoes, "There was no specific commandment against intercourse with Gentiles. Observance of purity codes prevented the strictly observant from such activities as eating in Gentile homes" (*Acts*, 274).

54. Literally, "those men who have the foreskin."

55. Pervo, *Acts*, 269.

As noted above, the term "visions" (ὅραμα) occurs four times in Acts 10:1—11:5, three in reference to Peter's vision, and, on two occasions, Peter, like Paul, heard a voice during his vision (though noting that the text states this occurred three times, 10:16). In addition, Luke has Peter reiterate his vision and its interpretation to the Jerusalem congregation. What is Luke emphasizing by repeating Peter's vision in Acts 10 and does this relate to Paul's vision in chapter 9? In response to this question, many years ago, F.C. Baur argued that Peter's visions in Acts 10 legitimized the authority of Paul's vision in Acts 9.[56] Paul's claim to have "seen Jesus" through a vision generated controversy that is evident in second century Christian literature (*Kerygmata Petrou*), as was considered in the last chapter, and this controversy may have its origin much earlier. One way of quelling the controversy between Paul and the Jerusalem leaders that the author of Acts pursues is to create a vision narrative for Paul's conversion, in which his mission to the Gentiles is initiated by the voice of the risen Jesus himself through the vision. Then, in response to the criticism of Paul's claims from the Jewish followers of Jesus, which seems to be still current at the time that Acts was written, Luke creates this vision narrative for Peter that legitimizes and advances Paul's position concerning the Gentile movement. When understood within the context of the fierce controversy between Paul and Jerusalem, it seems significant that the author of Acts invokes divine authority, taking Peter by the ear so to speak, to instruct, even demand, Peter, the leader of the Jerusalem community, to accept the abolishing of much of the purity code (10:11–16), to not call anyone profane or unclean (10:28), and to accept that "God has no favorites, but in every nation those who are God-fearing and do what is right are acceptable to him" (10:34). As Baur notes, "[t]hese words stand in opposition to Jewish exclusiveness"[57]—in stark opposition to the positions held by the Jerusalem congregation. Moreover, it is then Peter, when he returns to Jerusalem and is confronted by "those of the circumcision" for "visiting the uncircumcised and sitting at table with them," who retells his tale that leads to this Jerusalem congregation enthusiastically conceding "that God has granted life-giving repentance to the Gentiles also" (11:18). That the author of Acts has Peter repeat his vision and its interpretation to the Jerusalem congregation and then has them concede this point reflects that this—supporting the distinction between Jewish and Hellenistic followers of Jesus—is evidence of the historical conflict with the Jerusalem community. Baur's understanding of the

---

56. This paragraph is dependent upon Baur's argument in *Paul the Apostle of Jesus*, 80–87.

57. Ibid., 84.

rhetorical relationship between Paul's vision and Peter's vision in chapter 10 and its reiteration in chapter 11 seems right on:

> Paul must be represented as entering upon his apostolic work among the Gentiles under the shield of the Apostle Peter, who himself converted the first Gentile, and the heavenly appearance on which alone Paul grounds the proof of his apostolic calling, becomes legitimized in the most authentic manner, by a similar vision to that sent to the apostle Peter.[58]

In addition to the thematic parallels between Paul's vision in Acts 9 and Peter's in Acts 10, there are also verbal and thematic parallels between Galatians 2 and Acts 10—11:18. The three possible parallels are embedded within Galatians 2:7; 2:12; and Acts 11:2–3.

Table 36: Parallels between visions

Galatians	Acts
I had been entrusted to take the gospel to the uncircumcised [τῆς ἀκροβυστίας], Peter to the circumcised (2:7).	The apostles and the brothers in Judea heard that the Gentiles received the word of God. When Peter went to Jerusalem, those of the circumcision [οἱ ἐκ περιτομῆς] confronted him saying, 'You went to the uncircumcised [ἀκροβυστίαν] and ate with [συνέφανες] them (11:1–3).
Before certain men came from James, [Kephas] ate [συνήσθιεν] with the Gentiles; but when they came, he pulled away and separated himself, fearing those from the circumcision [τοὺς ἐκ περιτομῆς] (2:12).	

The first parallel concerns "the uncircumcised" in Galatians 2:7 and Acts 11:2. "Uncircumcised" (ἀκροβυστία) occurs twenty times in the New Testament, sixteen in Paul (eleven in Romans, twice in 1 Corinthians, and three in Galatians) but only here in Luke-Acts. Leppä contends that because Galatians 2:7 "is the only time when Paul used this word in connection with Peter," Luke's use of the word here in Acts 11 resembles most Paul's use in Galatians.[59] Pervo concurs, "As Leppä notes, it refers to Peter, thus evoking Gal 2.7."[60] I am not so sure. First, as I suggested in the previous chapter (and Appendix 2), there is good reason to think that Gal 2:7–9 is a later non-Pauline interpolation that was probably inserted either

---

58. Ibid., 87.
59. Leppä, *Luke's Critical Use*, 55.
60. Pervo, *Dating Acts*, 90.

contemporaneous with the composition/publication of Acts or shortly thereafter. If that were the case, then 2:7 would not have been in Luke's version of Galatians. And, as noted above, Paul uses the term ἀκροβυστία in several passages in Romans and 1 Corinthians by which Luke could have been familiar with his use of the term.

The next two possible parallels have more to recommend them. The expression "those from the circumcision" occurs only six times in the New Testament: twice in Paul's letters (Gal 2:12 and Rom 4:2), twice in Acts (10:45 and 11:2), Col 4:11, and Tit 1:10. It is only in Gal 2:12 and Acts 11:3 that "those from the circumcision" (οἱ ἐκ περιτομῆς) refers to followers of Jesus who are Jews, who are associated with Jerusalem, who also engage Kephas/Peter concerning his intermingling with Gentiles. The major differences between these two passages, and they are significant, are that in Galatians the incident described takes place in Antioch where Paul accuses Kephas of acting hypocritically in his conduct with Gentiles whereas in Acts the incident takes place in Jerusalem and "those from the circumcision" accuse Peter of acting toward the Gentiles as Paul initially accused him of in Galatians. This important distinction will be considered below, but I agree with Leppä that the expression "those from the circumcision" has "exactly [the] same meaning,"[61] and Pervo that "the context makes it apparent that Luke derived the phrase from Galatians."[62] In addition, the verb "ate with" (συνήσθιεν and συνέφανες) provides further evidence of dependence. The verb in both passages is the same, συνεσθίω; the difference in form is due to the tenses used—the imperfect in Galatians and aorist in Acts. This, too, is a rare verb, occurring only five times in the New Testament, three in Luke-Acts and two in Paul's letters.[63] To find this verb with οἱ ἐκ περιτομῆς in identical contexts, except for the location, "provides," as Leppä notes, "additional evidence that Acts 11:3 is literarily dependent on Galatians 2:12."[64] Pervo is more to the point: "The dependence is not trivial or incidental. Luke is revising the story of Peter. To put it rather sharply, in the matters of the dispute at Antioch Luke has turned Galatians 2 upside down. Galatians appears to be his major source, but what he says is quite opposed to what Paul says in Galatians."[65]

To expand upon Pervo's observation, the author of Acts is undoubtedly familiar with Galatians 2 and the conflict between Paul and Peter

61. Leppä, *Luke's Critical Use*, 39.
62. Pervo, *Dating Acts*, 90.
63. It occurs in Luke 15:2; Acts 10:41; 11:3; Gal 2:12; and 1 Cor 5:11.
64. Leppä, *Luke's Critical Use*, 56.
65. Pervo, *Dating Acts*, 92.

recorded therein that, according to Paul, took place in Antioch. The author of Acts completely erases the conflict in Antioch between Paul and Kephas by completely recasting/reframing it in two parts; this is the first; the second is 14:26—15:2 (to be considered later in this chapter). Here:

- In Galatians, the incident took place after Paul's second visit to Jerusalem. In Acts, it took place between Paul's first and second visits to Jerusalem, while Paul was out of the narrative picture in Syria and Cilicia, and before Paul even began his Gentile mission and before he even set foot in Antioch.

- In Galatians, the confrontation took place in Antioch. In Acts, Peter received his vision in Joppa, then confirmed/applied it in Caesarea, and was then confronted by "those from the circumcision"—which surely included the other eleven apostles of Acts 1—in Jerusalem. Moreover, in Acts, Peter is not only never in Antioch, but he and Paul never say a single word to one another.

- In Galatians, the issue was between Paul and Kephas (Peter). In Acts, the issue was between "those from the circumcision" and Peter—that is, among members of the Jerusalem congregation themselves.

- In Galatians, Paul accuses Kephas of hypocrisy. In Acts, "those from the circumcision" accuse Peter of eating with Gentiles, which Paul states Peter was doing in Antioch before his hypocrisy.

- In Galatians, the conflict concludes with Barnabas siding with Kephas and "those from James" leaving the impression that Paul's position was completely rejected. In Acts, "those from the circumcision" were silenced and glorified God, acknowledging, "to the Gentiles also God has granted repentance unto life" (11:18), thus enthusiastically adopting Paul's position.

By recasting Galatians as he does here in Acts 10:1—11:18, Luke completely abolishes any possibility that the conflict in Antioch could have occurred as recorded in Galatians 2, for, before Luke even mentions Antioch, he has Peter and the Jerusalem community—the community that sends "those from the circumcision" to Antioch in Galatians—learn and enthusiastically accept that God himself makes no distinction between Jews and Gentiles, has legitimized the Gentile mission, and has abolished key components of the purity code. This narrative fact also indicates that Luke either knew nothing of or did not accept the distinction made in Galatians 2:7–9.

To say that Luke radically transformed Galatians, while accurate, does not do justice to recognizing the author's rhetorical and compositional skills. This author inserted this material where he did in his narrative in order both to legitimize his narrative of Paul's conversion and mission and to show that the Gentile mission that Paul was about to embark upon was a mission that was already in full swing—a mission that Peter and the Jerusalem congregation, Paul's opponents in Galatians, had already enthusiastically embraced and initiated, in striking contrast to Paul's version of the events in Galatians (and 2 Cor 10–13). Moreover, that it is Peter and the Jewish Christians in Jerusalem who are identified in Acts (and not some other group) who acknowledge and accept Paul's position clearly indicates that, for Luke, it was these who were Paul's opponents in Galatians and not some other group of early followers of Jesus.

Growth Continues; Antioch (11:19–24)

As the last section of the "Silent Period" or "Interlude," Acts 11:19-24 serves as an awkward and problematic device to advance the narrative from Peter's and the Jerusalem leaders' acceptance of the Gentile mission to Luke's account of Paul's second trip to Jerusalem (11:25-30). Because there is an overlapping of content between 11:19-24 and 11:25-30, I will conclude this section of the "Silent Period" by considering the problems that these passages raise and then attempt an explanation for the problems in the next section, "Paul's Second Trip to Jerusalem (Acts 12)."

Luke begins by explaining that those (disciples) who scattered after Stephen's execution made their way to Phoenicia (on the coast of the Mediterranean, north-west of Jerusalem), the island of Cyprus, and to (Syrian) Antioch speaking only to Jews. The narrative is now situated in Antioch where, following the growth theme, "a great many" (πολύς τε ἀριθμὸς) were converted (11:21), so much so that word of this growth reached the Jerusalem congregation—including, presumably, the other eleven apostles—who, in turn, sent the disciple Barnabas to Antioch. Why Luke has Barnabas sent to Antioch instead of someone else, we are not told. If this section is a literary device to set the stage for retrieving Paul from Tarsus, where Luke sends him in 9:30, it serves its purpose in a way similar to Peter's intermediary journeys along the way to Caesarea, as Barnabas is now about three-quarters of the way to Tarsus, as Antioch is about 300 miles north of Jerusalem and about 90 miles southeast of Tarsus. We are also not told why Paul is brought to Antioch, but, once there, he and Barnabas spend a "whole year" teaching the "large numbers" (ὄχλος ἱκανὸν) who have joined the congregation there (11:26).

While Paul and Barnabas were teaching in Antioch, prophets made their way up from Jerusalem, leading to Agabus's prophecy of a world-wide famine that the author informs us came to pass during the reign of Claudius (41–54 CE). This sentence is replete with problems. First, earlier in our narrative (as noted above), we were told that "all" except the apostles scattered because of Stephen's persecution, followed by the report that Barnabas and Paul mingled with disciples upon their arrival to Jerusalem, and now we are told that prophets had been in Jerusalem after the "scattering" as well. Luke does not tie these loose ends together. A second problem is Agabus's prophecy of a "great famine" (λιμὸν μεγάλην) upon "the whole world" (ὅλην τὴν οἰκουμένην) and its confirmation. Lüdemann cites Wellhausen's observation that the famine "extending over the whole world was as universal as Quirinius's census,"[66] and notes that there were many famines during the reign of Claudius "but they were as local as the census,"[67] and, like others, offers Josephus's *Antiquities* (20.51, 101) as a likely source for Luke's notion of a famine. Therein we read that between 46–48 CE, during the reign of Claudius, Queen Helena of Adiabene (in modern Iraq) visited Jerusalem and, seeing the extent of a local famine, provided many provisions and "great sums of money to the principal men in Jerusalem" (20:51).[68] Pervo notes that Josephus's summary of Helena's generosity (20:101) shares several verbal similarities with Luke's account of the famine in Acts 11:27–29, the most notable of which is "great famine" (μέγαν λιμὸν in *Antiquities* 20:101 and λιμὸν μεγάλην in Acts 11:28).[69] It is also interesting to note that these are the only two occurrences of λιμὸν μεγα- in all of Greek literature,[70] which may further support the suggestion that Josephus influenced Luke's creation of the famine narrative.

The problems continue as Luke has the congregation in Antioch contribute to a collection that Barnabas and Saul are to deliver to Jerusalem. Why are Barnabas and Paul chosen to escort the collection down to Jerusalem instead of those prophets who hailed from Jerusalem in the first place? It would seem reasonable to think that it makes more sense that these prophets would simply take the collection back with them upon their return. Why Paul and Barnabas? If it is a world-wide famine, why are those in Antioch

---

66. Lüdemann, *Early Christianity*, 135, citing Julius Wellhausen, *Kritische Analyse der Apostelgeschichte* (Berlin, 1914), 21.

67. Ibid., 135. See also for details of other local famines. Pervo adds, "There is ample evidence for local famines in the eastern Mediterranean in the late 40s (during the reign of Claudius" (*Dating Acts*, 193 and 421n230 for references).

68. Josephus, *Antiquities*, in *Works*, 528–31.

69. Pervo, *Dating Acts*, 193; and *Acts*, 295–97.

70. According to a *TLG* search.

not concerned about their own situation or about those in Samaria or Phoenicia or any of the other communities to which the movement has spread? Most interestingly, why do we not hear another word about the famine or the collection after Barnabas and Paul arrive in Jerusalem other than that they "accomplished their mission" (πληρώσαντες τὴν διακονίαν, 12:24)? One would think that such a famine and collection for its relief would at least be mentioned. Is Paul and Barnabas's trip to Jerusalem recorded here, Paul's second in Acts, intended to correspond with Galatians 2:1–10, which Paul claims was his second trip to Jerusalem?

These questions and others contribute to the difficulties of understanding what the author of Acts wants his reader to understand from these passages (11:19–30). I am hopeful to have demonstrated that what Leppä identifies as the "Silent Period" is, from a narrative perspective, not silent at all, as the author, through the Cornelius narrative, legitimizes Paul's conversionary vision and the Gentile mission through Peter's vision and his reiteration of that vision to the Jerusalem congregation. It is crucial to emphasize that the author of Acts invokes divine authority and that this divine authority is addressed to Peter and the Jerusalem congregation—Paul's opponents—and that the author of Acts begins to deconstruct the Antioch incident as Paul explains it in such a way that the controversy between Paul and Peter and "those from James" in Antioch could not have occurred as Paul explains it. The narrative awkwardly moves on so as to depict the burgeoning growth, expanding to both Jews and Gentiles, as far away now as Antioch—more evidence that Paul was not the initial or primary human agent through whom the Gentiles received the word, as he is still out of the narrative picture and exponential (if not embellished) growth of the Gentile movement is occurring without him, the apostle to the Gentiles. News of the reception and of the message and growth of the movement in Antioch reaches Jerusalem, so the leaders there dispatch Barnabas, who then retrieves Paul back into the narrative where the two are positioned to deliver famine relief to the leaders of the Jerusalem congregation. Thus, from a narrative perspective, Pervo's identification of this material as an "Interlude" seems more fitting than Leppä's "Silent Period," except that instead of "interrupting the story of Paul," I would argue that in Acts 10:1—11:24, Luke both creates a narrative that legitimizes Paul's visionary claim in Galatians (and perhaps 1 Corinthians), that qualifies (if not undercuts) Paul's claim that he (primarily if not exclusively) is "the apostle to the Gentiles," and that begins to deconstruct Paul's account of the conflict in Antioch as recorded in Galatians 2.

Paul's Second Trip to Jerusalem
(Gal 2:1–10 and Acts 11:25—12:24)

Table 37: Paul's second trip to Jerusalem

Galatians	Acts
¹Then, after fourteen years, [2:1a; Acts 9:31—11:24], I went up to Jerusalem with Barnabas and taking Titus along. ²I went according to a revelation, and I laid before them the gospel that I proclaim to the Gentiles, but privately, to those who have a reputation, for fear I was running or had run in vain. ³But not even Titus, the one with me, while being a Hellene, was compelled to be circumcised. ⁴But because of the false brothers brought in secretly, some sneaked in to spy out our freedom which we had in Christ Jesus, in order that they might enslave us; ⁵to whom we did not yield in submission for an instant in order that the truth of the gospel might continue unchanged. ⁶But, from those who seem to be something—what sort they once were makes no difference to me; ⁶God does not choose from man's appearance—for those of reputation added nothing to me.... [except] ¹⁰that we should keep in mind the poor, the very thing I have always made it my business to do.	²⁷During this period, some prophets came down from Jerusalem to Antioch, ²⁸and one of them, Agabus by name, was inspired to stand up and predict a severe and world-wise famine, which in fact occurred in the reign of Claudius. ²⁹So the disciples agreed to make a contribution, each according to his means, for the relief of their fellow-Christians in Judaea. ³⁰This they did, and sent it off to the elders [in Jerusalem], entrusting it to Barnabas and Saul (11:27–30). • Herod's attack on church; beheading of James (12:1–2) • Herod imprisons Peter and his escape (12:3–19) • Herod's death (19b–23) • Meanwhile, the word of God spread, and after Barnabas and Paul fulfilled their mission, returned from Jerusalem [to Antioch], taking John Mark with them. (12:24)

I have been arguing that Luke followed Galatians 1 very closely as his structural and conceptual narrative source for the material beginning at Acts 7:58. If this is the case and if Luke continued this practice, which I think he did, then he intends his account of Paul's second trip to Jerusalem (11:30—12:24) to coincide with Paul's account of his second trip to Jerusalem in Galatians 2:1–10. To be sure, there are significant inconsistencies, conflicts, and contradictions between the content in the two texts, so many conflicts that the majority of scholars cannot accept that 11:30—12:24 describes the same trip that Paul describes in Galatians 2:1–10. On the other hand, we have seen how Luke radically alters/mimetically transforms Galatians to advance his own rhetorical reconstruction. He does the same thing with Galatians 2:1-10 in Acts 11:30—12:24. A few of the similarities will be considered first.

Beginning with locations, in Galatians 1:21, Paul writes that after his first trip to Jerusalem, he set out for Syria and Cilicia, and this is the last location we have for him before 2:1, when, "fourteen years later, I went up again to Jerusalem with Barnabas, taking Titus along." We do not know whether or not he spent that entire intervening period in Syria and Cilicia only, but the text could be read that way. And, it can be argued that the author of Acts read Galatians this way, for, after narrating Paul's first visit to Jerusalem, he ships Paul off to Tarsus, the capital of Cilicia (9:30). Luke then narrates a series of events that span over an indefinite period of time—the church was left in peace and grew; Peter traveled to Lydda, Joppa, and then Caeseraea where he stayed with Cornelius "for a period of time" (ἡμέρας τινάς, 10:48) before he returned to Jerusalem; another narrative of believers travel to Phoenicia, Cyprus, and Antioch; Barnabas is dispatched from Jerusalem to Antioch, then to Tarsus to bring Paul back to Antioch, (which, is in Syria, following Galatians 1:21) where they stay for a year before making their trip to Jerusalem. As is his practice, Luke does not provide a specific timeline for these narrative events. If, however, he is following Galatians as his structural source, it seems reasonable to think that the narrative material between Acts 9:30 and 11:30 could be designed to fill in the fourteen-year gap that Paul mentions in Galatians 2:1. That Luke situates Paul during this interval in both "Syria [Antioch] and Cilicia [Tarsus]"—coinciding with Galatians 1:21—before his second trip into Jerusalem further supports this possibility.

Two other possible similarities include the impetus for Paul's trip to Jerusalem and equating the collection that Paul and Barnabas delivered to Jerusalem with Paul's collection in his letters.

As for the impetus for Paul's trip, Pervo is an advocate of the position that the meeting Paul describes in Galatians 2:1-10 is also the so-called Jerusalem Council of Acts 15,[71] wherein, men came up from Jerusalem to Antioch claiming that circumcision was necessary and either they (τινες) or the brothers (τοὺς ἀδελφοὺς) ordered Paul and Barnabas and others to go to Jerusalem to resolve this issue. Thus, Paul was ordered to go to Jerusalem by others, and Pervo suggests that "[t]here is no necessary conflict between this 'revelation' [Gal 2] and a request or order from some human authority" [Acts 11:30].[72] He does not provide any discussion to support this suggestion and, because of this, his claim is not very convincing. Trobisch, on the

---

71. Pervo, *Dating Acts*, 79.
72. Ibid., 395n155.

other hand, acknowledging the difficulty interpreters have had of relating Galatians 2:1–10 with the book of Acts, suggests that "a plausible reading does not seem very difficult from a canonical perspective. Paul's comment that he left for Jerusalem *'in response to a revelation'* (Gal 2:2) is explained by Luke as a reference to the prophet Agabus (11:28), who had predicted a famine. The Christians of Antioch had organized a collection and they sent it with Paul and Barnabas to Jerusalem, thus representing Paul's visit as a response to Agabus's revelation."[73] To further support his interpretation, Trobisch equates Luke's "during the reign of Claudius" (Acts 11:28) with Paul's "after fourteen years" in Galatians 2:1, and the collection of Acts 11 with Paul's expressed intention to "remember the poor"—"that which also I was eager to do [ὃ καὶ ἐσπούδασα αὐτὸ τοῦτο ποιῆσαι]" in Gal 2:10.[74] In assessing Trobisch's interpretation, his equating of Agabus's prophecy with Paul's revelation does fit Acts' narrative chronology and it is possible that Luke could understand a prophecy as a revelation of some kind,[75] and his equating the Antioch collection with Paul's concern for the poor is a view represented by many, including Pervo.[76] There are, however, at least two problems with correlation between Claudius and Paul's fourteen years. First, we get the impression from Acts 11 that Paul and Barnabas departed from Antioch for Jerusalem immediately after Agabus's prophecy of the famine rather than waiting fourteen years, and, second, the Claudius explanation does not take into account the considerable narrative material from Acts 9:30—11:30, which could account for some, if not all, of this fourteen-year period. Thus, while recognizing that both views could be wrong, Trobisch's position has more to recommend it than Pervo's view that there is no conflict between Paul's revelation and Paul and Barnabas being ordered to Jerusalem in Acts 15. It is not that Paul equated this revelation with Agabus's prophecy, but only that Luke, in need of a literary device to get Paul to Jerusalem from Syria (Antioch), chose to align Paul's claim that he went to Jerusalem via a revelation with Agabus's prophecy (revelation).

As for the collection, the issue is whether the collection made by the community in Antioch is to be equated with the collection Paul mentions several times in his letters including his statement in Galatians 2:10 that he will remember the poor. The earliest reference that we have of Paul's collection

---

73. Trobisch, "Council of Jerusalem in Acts 15," 336. His emphasis.

74. Ibid.

75. In his birth narrative, Luke closely aligns prophetic announcements with revelations of new knowledge. See especially Luke 1:25–38. It is important to remember here that we are not concerned with what Paul means by "revelation" in Gal 2:2, but with how Luke could read, interpret, and use "revelation" for his own narrative purpose.

76. Pervo, *Dating Acts*, 79.

is probably in 1 Corinthians where Paul encouraged the Corinthians to do as he instructed those in Galatia—to put aside what each person could afford every Sunday and that he would then gather the collection and either have trusted associates deliver it to Jerusalem or take it himself" (16:1–4).[77] What are probably his last words on the collection before he attempted to deliver it to Jerusalem are probably recorded in Romans: "I appeal to you, brethren, . . . to strive together with me in your prayers to God on my behalf that I may be delivered from the unbelievers in Judea, and that my service for Jerusalem may be acceptable to the saints" (15:30–31). It is important to note here that Paul claims to have initiated his collection with the Galatians, but, here in Acts 11, Paul and Barnabas are sent to Jerusalem with a collection *before they even begin their so-called first missionary journey*, which is into the province of South Galatia and which does not begin until Acts 13. The chronology simply does not work. This is not to say that Luke is not thinking about the Pauline collection here, as he could be. The Greek word, διακονία, is the same,[78] and, as Pervo suggests, Luke could have "invented the 'famine relief' offering to diffuse allegations about the Pauline 'collection for Jerusalem,'"[79] or he could have invented the collection narrative and placed it here in order to distract readers from the likely fact that the Jerusalem congregation did not accept Paul's collection, as the collection is not mentioned anywhere else in Acts, and this silence suggests rejection.

In addition to the possible thematic similarity of the collection, Leppä, following Enslin, identifies two possible verbal similarities. The first is between Acts 11:27–30 and Galatians 2:10—both passages include the rare expression, "which also" (ὃ καὶ) as the object of the verb "do" (ποιέω):

Table 38: "This they did" (Galatians 2:6, 10 and Acts 11:29–30)

Galatians	Acts
Those of reputation added nothing to me . . . only that we might remember the poor, <u>that same thing which I also desired to do (ὃ καὶ ἐσπούδασα αὐτὸ τοῦτο ποιῆσαι</u>, 2:6–10).	The disciples determined that according to their ability, each would send relief to the believers living in Judea; <u>this they did (ὃ καὶ ἐποίησαν)</u>, sending it to the elders by Barnabas and Saul (11:29–30).

This construction of ὃ καὶ as the object of ποιέω occurs only one other time in the New Testament, in Acts, where Luke has Paul explain his persecuting

77. 1 Cor 16:1–4; see also 2 Cor 8–9.
78. The Greek is the same except for 1 Cor 16:11–12, where it is λογείας.
79. Pervo, *Dating Acts*, 79.

activities in Jerusalem: "This I did [ὃ καὶ ἐποίησα] in Jerusalem, and many of the saints I locked in prisons" (26:10). Leppä explains that ὃ καὶ "is a very Pauline phrase" in the New Testament (1 Cor 11:23, 15:3; Gal 2:10; Phil 2:5) and that Luke adopts it twice—"once when he is talking about action close to what Paul describes in Galatians [2:10] and the other time when he is putting the words in Paul's mouth [Acts 26:10]."[80] Pervo concurs, "Dependence is probable here."[81]

The second possible verbal similarity is with the verb συμπαραλαμβάνω ("take with"), which is, as Leppä notes, "an ordinary, but seldom used, word with a wide range of meanings,"[82] which occurs only four times in the New Testament:

Table 39: "Taking along" (Galatians 2:1 and Acts12:25 and 15:37–38)

Galatians	Acts
Then, after fourteen years, I went up again to Jerusalem with Barnabas, taking [συμπαραλαμβανών] Titus along also (2:1).	Having fulfilled their mission, Barnabas and Saul returned to Jerusalem, taking along [συμπαραλαβόντες] John, who is also called Mark (12:25).
	Barnabas wanted to take [συμπαραλαβεῖν] also John, who is called Mark, but Paul insisted that the man who had deserted them in Pamphylia and had not gone on to share in their work was not the man to take with them [συμπαραλαμβάνειν] (15:37–38).

In Galatians 2:1, Paul employs συμπαραλαμβανών within the context in which he is in Jerusalem for his second time, along with Barnabas, and they are taking Titus along with them. In Acts 12:25, Luke employs συμπαραλαβόντες for the first time within the context of Paul's second trip to Jerusalem, along with Barnabas, and they are taking John Mark with them, in this case from Jerusalem to Antioch. Then, in Acts 15, the context is again with Barnabas and Paul and they dispute over taking (συμπαραλαμβάνειν) John Mark with them on their so-called second missionary journey. Leppä concludes that the same word used within very

---

80. Leppä, *Luke's Critical Use*, 54. He cites Enslin, "Luke and Paul," 88 (54n127) as the one who initially pointed out this similar use of ὃ καὶ in Galatians and Acts.

81. Pervo, *Dating Acts*, 79.

82. Leppä, *Luke's Critical Use*, 36.

similar contexts in only Galatians and Acts suggests dependence. Again, Pervo concurs, "συμπαραλαμβάνω in Acts 12:25; 15:37–38 very probably derives from Galatians 2:1."[83]

It can be argued that the possible thematic similarities of location, time, Agabus's prophecy/Paul's revelation, the collection, and the possible verbal similarities of διακονία, ὃ καὶ + ποιέω, and συμπαραβαμβάνω strongly suggest that the author of Acts was familiar with Galatians 2 and adopted some of Paul's verbiage therefrom as he penned Acts 11:27—12:25. A consideration of the author's overall structure of the passage and his intent may further support the case for familiarity and dependence.

That the author of Acts intended to convey that Acts 12 is closely related to 11:27–30 is evident by its chiastic narrative structure:[84]

- A   This they did and sent [the collection] off to the elders, entrusting it to Barnabas and Saul (11:30).

-   B   (Herod[85]) Agrippa's persecution of the church (1–5)

-     C   Peter's imprisonment (7–10)

-     C   Peter's escape and departure (12–17)

-   B   (Herod) Agrippa's death (19–23)

- A   Barnabas and Saul, their task fulfilled, returned from Jerusalem, taking John Mark with them (12:25).

David E. Aune contends that the recognition of "chiastic structures in texts enables the interpreter to appreciate comparisons and contrasts, to apprehend the emphasis of the textual unit defined by the chiasmus, to understand the point being made, and to determine the point or purpose of a composition."[86] If Aune is right, then the most noticeable emphases within this passage from a broader narrative perspective include that:

---

83. Pervo, *Dating Acts*, 90.

84. Lüdemann equates the narrative structure of chapter 12 with the author of Mark's "technique of interweaving stories"—often referred to as "sandwiching" and understands the chapter as a "parenthetical continuation of the previous episode" (*Acts of the Apostles*, 156). Longenecker ("Lukan Aversion") identifies the rhetorical structure with Quintilian's understanding that transitions "overlap" and Lucian's chain-link transitions.

85. Pervo notes, "There is no evidence that Agrippa I ever bore the name 'Herod'" (*Acts*, 303).

86. Aune, *Westminister Dictionary*, 94.

- the content within 11:30—12:25 is to be understood within the time that Paul and Barnabas set out from Antioch for Jerusalem (11:30) and return to Antioch from Jerusalem (12:25);
- Barnabas and Paul were in Jerusalem during Agrippa's persecution of the church (1–5);
- Barnabas and Paul would have (seemingly) been aware of James's death and Peter's imprisonment, escape, and departure (7–17), (but Paul never says anything about this in any of his letters), and
- Barnabas and Paul were non-players in the events described while they were in Jerusalem as there is not a single reference to either one of them between 12:1 and 12:24; yet, they must have also delivered the collection to the "elders" of 11:30, as 12:25 claims that they returned from Jerusalem "after" (πληρώσαντες—aorist tense) completing their mission.

Within this broader narrative structure are two stories about Agrippa and within these are two stories about Peter, and it is these two about Peter that seem to serve as the core or kernel of the chapter.

Adopting this overall structure, the following discussion will attempt to answer three questions: What did Luke mean to communicate here? Why did Luke place this material (chapter 12) here?, and What, if any, relationship is there between this material and Paul's second trip to Jerusalem in Galatians 2?

Chapter 12 begins with Agrippa's persecution of "some" (τινας, indefinite) of the congregation in Jerusalem; only two of its leaders are specified, James and Peter. Luke tells us that Agrippa beheads James, whom he identifies specifically as "the brother of John" (τὸν ἀδελφὸν Ἰωάνου), but he does not explain a reason for his execution or why it was the apostle James who was executed and not someone else. Wall suggests that the fact that James is not replaced indicates "an early indication of the Twelve's waning role,"[87] a view shared by Bruce Longenecker.[88] This is possible, but any apostle would have served this purpose and Peter would have been a better candidate. John Painter offers what seems to be a more fitting possibility: "Mention of the execution makes clear the identity of the James in Acts 12:17 by removing the other notable James from the scene."[89] Agrippa saw that James's execution was "pleasing to the Jews," so he also arrested Peter for no other reason, it seems, than their gratification, which, in Acts, inten-

---

87. Wall, "Successors to 'the Twelve,'" 61.
88. Longenecker, "Lukan Aversion," 198.
89. Painter, *Just James*, 42–43.

sifies the conflict between the followers of Jesus in Jerusalem and the "the Jews." By constructing such a narrative, Luke is not only indicating that the peace of 9:31 is over but also advancing his theme of conflict between "the Jews" and the new movement, and (though cryptically) clearing the way for James, Jesus's brother, taking the lead of the growing movement.

Peter's imprisonment and escape narrative are the stuff Greco-Roman comedy.[90] His cryptic, "Tell these things to James and the brothers" (12:17) and his unexplained removal "to an other place" (εἰς ἕτερον τόπον)[91] are at the core of Luke's narrative structure and, as such, seem to be the most important points that Luke wants to convey in this narrative. James receives no introduction; now that James the apostle is dead, Luke seems to assume that the readers will know that this James is Jesus's brother. From this point on, Peter has only a minor role in Acts, reappearing (from where we are not told) at the so-called Jerusalem Council (15:6-11) before completely vanishing from the narrative. Like Peter, the role of "the apostles" also diminishes, as in addition to not replacing the apostle James after his execution, the term "apostle" is only used eight times, six times during the narrative of the "Jerusalem Council," but not again after 16:4.

The diminishing of the roles of Peter and the apostles, the abrupt introduction of James, and the roles that James and Paul (beginning at 13:1) will play in the rest of Acts has led Robert Wall to conclude "that the evangelist's purpose is to narrate and indeed authorize the transition of leadership within earliest Christianity from 'apostolic' rule, symbolized by Peter, to the second generation of Christian leaders symbolized by James in Jewish Christianity and especially by Paul in Gentile Christianity." According to Wall, the legitimation of the transition of authority to James and Paul is symbolized through Peter's imprisonment, escape, and departure, which is to be understood as parallel to Jesus's passion, resurrection,

---

90. Harrill demonstrates that Rhoda's character corresponds "to those of a *servus currens*, the comic 'running slave' familiar from Greek New Comedy" whose function "is to intensify the anticipation of the reader, to develop irony, . . . and to provide comic relief at a critical juncture in the narrative when all seems lost" ("Dramatic Function," 151). See also Pervo, *Acts*, 306-7.

91. Commentators have noted that Luke's enigmatic reference to Peter going "to another place" (εἰς ἕτερον τόπον) can suggest Peter's death. The same phrase is used by Plutarch (ca. 45-120 CE): "So, even if it be likely that death transports us into another place [εἰς ἕτερον τόπον], it is not an evil" ("Letter to Apollonius," 108d, LCL). In *1 Clement*, there is a similar phrase: "Peter, . . . having given his testimony, went to his appointed place of glory" (εἰς τὸν ὀφειλόμενον τόπον τῆς δόξης) (*Apostolic Fathers*, 5.4). But Peter's (re-)appearance at the so-called Jerusalem Council in Acts 15 seems to argue against understanding this phrase as referring to Peter's death in Acts 12:17 for the simple reason that if Peter died and went to "the other place" in Acts 12, he could not have then reappeared in Acts 15.

and ascension."[92] Pervo argues for a similar symbolic understanding of the passage,[93] acknowledges that Peter's escape marks the end of his mission, and that the passage represents the end of the apostolic age and the succession of James and Paul.[94]

Neither Wall nor Pervo (but see below) discusses whether Luke intended the reader to understand whether Paul and Barnabas were in Jerusalem while the events described in chapter 12 were taking place.[95] Longenecker addresses this issue by responding to the view represented by Haenechen, who, because of the chiasmic structure framed by 11:30 and 12:25 and chapter 12's opening phrase "At that time" (κατ'ἐκεῖνον δὲ τὸν καιρὸν), writes, "[I]n this note, in itself indefinite, Luke has in view the days when Barnabas and Saul were staying in Jerusalem because of the collection."[96] Commenting upon 12:25, which closes the chiasmic frame, Haenechen notes, "The continual presence of the Antiochian delegation in Jerusalem throughout the persecution served Luke as a demonstration of the heartfelt communion between the mother church and the daughter congregation."[97] Thus, for Haenechen (and the outline offered above), Luke had Barnabas and Paul in Jerusalem during the events described in chapter 12. Longenecker argues that Haenechen's view is "not wholly compelling" because the phrase "at that time" (κατ'ἐκεῖνον δὲ τὸν καιρὸν) is vague, and while this vagueness allows for Haenehen's interpretation, it is also this vagueness that, for Longenecker, "counts heavily against that interpretation."[98] Instead, Longenecker claims, Luke, "a master of transitional linkages," can overlap two episodes to show "simultaneity" at will, if he so chooses, and he provides two examples to support this claim. The first connects Acts 17:16–34 with 17:10–15 with the phrase "While Paul was waiting for them in Athens, . . ." (ἐν δὲ ταῖς Ἀθήναις ἐκδεχομένου αὐτοὺς τοῦ Παύλου, 17:16) and the second connects 19:1 with 18:24–28 with a similar construction, "While Apollos was in Corinth" (ἐν τῷ τὸν πολλῷ εἶναι ἐν Κορίνθῳ, 19:1).[99] From these two examples, Longenecker concludes, "[I]t is clear that, had Luke intended for his audience to envisage Barnabas and Saul in Jerusalem when the events of

92. Wall, "Successors to the 'Twelve,'" 632–35.

93. Pervo argues "that the narrative is a symbolic portrayal of Peter's 'passion' 'resurrection,' and vindication that through initiatory language, makes it a paradigm of Christian experience" (*Acts*, 302).

94. Ibid., 301–88.

95. Wall, "Acts," 173–83; and Pervo, *Acts*, 299–315.

96. Haenechen, *Acts of the Apostles*, 381n1.

97. Ibid., 385n5.

98. Longenecker, "Lukan Aversion," 192.

99. Ibid., 192.

12:1–24 occurred, we would expect him to have made this important point explicitly."[100] For Longenecker, the problem with understanding that Barnabas and Paul were in Jerusalem during the events described in chapter 12 is, "[O]ne might arrive at the conclusion that Paul had become a relatively insignificant figure by the time that he arrived in Jerusalem"—that "Paul's stature had significantly diminished in the time since his previous visit to Jerusalem."[101] As for 12:25, which closes Haenechen's narrative frame (and the chiasmic structure offered above), Longenecker acknowledges that it closes the 11:27:30 unit, but not within a chiasmic type structure, but what he terms, drawing on Quintilian and Lucian, a "chain-link," "overlapping" structure by which "Luke is seen simply to have reserved the conclusion of the Antiochene collection story for the very end of the text unit (i.e., 12:25) in order to draw further attention to the fact that a text-unit transition is underway."[102] That is, for Longenecker, "[t]he somewhat surprising continuation of the Antiochene collection story in 12:25 alerts the audience to the fact that something new is happening. Their expectations are fulfilled in the narrative that follows."[103]

Three points can be offered in response to Longenecker's argumentation. The first is that Longenecker's interpretation is clearly driven by theological, rather than historical, interests. He claims that the view that 11:27–30 and 12:25 are the outside frames of a chiasmic type narrative that would then result in understanding 12:1–24 as inextricably linked to these outside frames (as represented by "Haenechen and others") is "for both stylistic and literary—*theological* reasons" "not compelling,"[104] but theological presuppositions cannot drive historical research. The second point, a "stylistic" point, concerns the phrase that opens 12:1, "at that time" (κατ'ἐκεῖνον δὲ τὸν καιρὸν), which Longenecker asserts is "vague" without, curiously, any further discussion. This phrase occurs only here in the New Testament. However, it occurs twenty-five times in Josephus's *Antiquities*, which was "published" ca. 94 CE, and which seems to be a source for some of Luke's material in Acts, even Herod's death narrative in 12:19c–23.[105] In every occurrence in the *Antiquities*,[106] κατ'ἐκεῖνον δὲ τὸν καιρὸν denotes

---

100. Ibid., 192.
101. Ibid., 192–93.
102. Ibid., 200.
103. Ibid., 200–201. Emphasis mine.
104. Ibid., 194.
105. For Luke's use of Josephus, see Pervo, *Dating Acts*, 149–200; and *Acts*, 312–13.
106. See *Antiquities* 2.205; 5.121; 6.30; 8.155, 206 232, 262, 400; 9.88, 97, 229; 10.228; 11.32, 77; 12.169, 223; 13.304; 15.225, 425.

synchronicity. A few examples include "Jehoshaphat called prophets as to whether they should make an expedition *at this time* (κατ'ἐκεῖνον δὲ τὸν καιρὸν, 8.400);" Menaham, who was *at that time* [κατ'ἐκεῖνον δὲ τὸν καιρὸν, in the city of Tirzah (9.229);" and "Philostratus says that this king [Nebuchadnezzar] besieged Tyre thirteen times, while *at the same time* [κατ'ἐκεῖνον δὲ τὸν καιρὸν], Ethbaal reigned at Tyre (10.228). The phrase also occurs once in the Septuagint: "When [Simon] could not prevail over Onias, he went to Apollonius of Tarsus, who *at that time* [κατ'ἐκεῖνον δὲ τὸν καιρὸν] was governor of Coelseyria and Phoenicia" (2 Macc 3.5). While the phrase *may possibly* denote a vague conception of time on occasion, it can also denote explicit simultaneity, as it does here in Acts 12:1. The third point follows from the second. Because Longenecker cannot allow for Barnabas and Paul to be in Jerusalem during the events of chapter 12, he divorces 11:27–30 and 12:25 from 12:1–24, which I suggested above serve as the outside framing of the chiasmic structure. For Longenecker, 12:25 concludes 11:27–30, but only as "the continuation of the story told in 11:27–30,"[107] not as the closing frame of a chiasmic narrative structure that includes 11:27 *through* 12:25, for, he claims, "it is curious that Luke should have interrupted the journey(s) of Barnabas and Paul with a long intervening narrative," which "is a somewhat unusual manner of story telling, with a transitional unit being split into two parts separated by a significant block of text."[108] Longenecker's argumentation here in an attempt to support his divorcing 11:30 and 12:25 from 12:1–24 is weak, but necessary for him to try to maintain that Paul and Barnabas were not in Jerusalem during the events described.

Longenecker claims that Luke does not place Barnabas and Paul in Jerusalem during the events described in Acts 12 because doing so would minimize Paul's status—that "Paul's stature had significantly diminished." In sharp contrast to this view, I argue 1) that the chiasmic structure of Acts 11:27—12:25 demands that Luke placed Barnabas and Paul in Jerusalem during the events described in 12:1–24; 2) that Luke places Paul and Barnabas in Jerusalem because his source, Galatians, places them in Jerusalem, and 3) that the controversy between Herod, "the Jews," and the members of the Jerusalem congregation in Acts 12 is a Lukan creation meant to redirect or deflect the controversy away from Paul and the leaders of the Jerusalem congregation that is evident in Galatians 2:1–10.

I addressed 1 (the unity of the chiasmic structure) and 2 (that Luke is following Galatians 1 and 2) above. As for 3, in Galatians 2:1–6, and as I

---

107. Longenecker, "Lukan Aversion," 190.
108. Ibid., 191.

discussed in detail in the previous chapter, there is heightened tension between Paul and the "false brothers" and "those of reputation in Jerusalem." Thus, the conflict Paul narrates in Galatians 2 is clearly between himself and leaders within the Jesus movement in Jerusalem and concerns at least a sharp exchange concerning circumcision, but it is a narrative habit of the author of Acts not to allow any of Paul's controversies with other followers of Jesus to "soil [his] portrait of the nascent church."[109] So while Luke places Paul and Barnabas in Jerusalem, adhering to his source, he not only completely distances Paul from any controversy, but creates another controversy as a smokescreen of sorts that both distracts the readers' attention from Paul's controversy but also serves as a transition to Paul's and James's leadership positions. This means that Luke (almost) completely rewrites Galatians 2:1–6. Luke's revision of, or omission of, material in Galatians 2 includes:

- In Galatians, Paul, Barnabas, and Titus make the trip to Jerusalem. In Acts, only Paul and Barnabas make the trip; Titus is not mentioned anywhere in Acts.

- In Galatians, Paul's purpose in going to Jerusalem is to lay before those of reputation "the gospel that I proclaim to the Gentiles (2:2);" in Acts, Paul and Barnabas are sent to deliver the collection for famine relief.

- In Galatians, there is no mention of a famine; in Acts, the "worldwide" famine is the reason why Paul and Barnabas are sent (11:27–30), but the famine is not only not mentioned in Acts 12, but there is no indication that those in Jerusalem are dealing with any of the effects of a famine.

- In Galatians, Paul meets privately with "those of reputation;" in Acts, Paul does not speak with anyone while in Jerusalem.

- In Galatians, Paul becomes engaged in a controversy with the "false brothers" concerning circumcision; in Acts, Paul and Barnabas do not talk to anyone in Jerusalem during their stay and there is no controversy with the "false brothers" or any other followers of Jesus.

- In Galatians, there is no mention of Antipas's persecution or Peter's imprisonment; in Acts, Herod's persecution of the followers of Jesus, Peter's imprisonment, and Herod's death make up the content of chapter 12.

- In Galatians, Paul mentions that those of reputation encouraged him to remember the poor; in Acts 12, we are told that Paul and Barnabas

---

109. Pervo, *Dating Acts*, 88.

delivered the collection from Antioch, but no details for this transaction are mentioned.

There may be some reasonable explanations for some of these revisions/omissions. Luke may have omitted Titus, who is not mentioned anywhere in Acts, because of his association with the problems in Corinth, the controversy in Galatians 2 concerning circumcision, and his association with the Pauline collection.[110] Luke would not have included anything about Paul "presenting his gospel in private to those of reputation" for at least two reasons. First, in Acts, Paul advances the (Pauline) gospel first proclaimed by Peter rather than advancing his own; second, in Acts, Paul is subservient to the Jerusalem leaders, and, third, Paul does not set out on his so-called "first missionary journey" in which he would have an opportunity to proclaim *his* gospel to the Gentiles until the next chapter in Acts, chapter 13. The famine in Acts that is not in Galatians could serve as Luke's literary device to get Paul and Barnabas to Jerusalem (following Gal 2:1). That there is no mention of the famine or collection in chapter 12 further supports the suggestion that these are Lucan constructions to serve as a rhetorical device to get Paul and Barnabas to Jerusalem, again, following his source. Luke does not mention Paul's meeting with "those of reputation" but does have Paul and Barnabas tacitly deliver the collection to the "elders." Luke does not mention anything about the controversy concerning circumcision here as Paul does, but moves this controversy to 15:1–2 and rewrites Paul's opponents from the "false brothers," who in Galatians 2 are closely associated with the Jerusalem congregation, to the indefinite "some who came down from Judea" (15:1, drawing on Gal 2:11) who are later identified as "some to whom we gave no instruction" (15:24), indicating that these were not, in sharp contrast to Galatians, associated with the leadership of the Jerusalem congregation.

There is one other similarity between Acts 12 and Galatians 2 that needs to be considered that suggests dependence or recognition of some kind. In Galatians 2:9, our text reads, "and knowing the grace that was given to me, James and Kephas and John, those considered to be pillars, gave the right hand of fellowship to me and Barnabas in order that we [might go] to the Gentiles, they to the circumcised." Acts 12 and Galatians 2:9 are the only passages in the New Testament in which Paul, Barnabas, James, Peter

---

110. See especially Walker, "Timothy-Titus Problem Reconsidered," wherein he suggests that there may be good reasons why the author of Acts did not mention Titus, as he is closely associated with the collection, the controversies in Corinth (2 Cor 12:12–13; 7:5–15, 8:6, 16–23; and 12:17–18) in addition to the controversy concerning circumcision in Gal 2 (232).

(Kephas), and John are mentioned together. They are also the only passages that place these five men together in Jerusalem at the same time. Moreover, this is John the apostle's last appearance in Acts; he is not at the so-called Jerusalem Council in Acts 15, so, according to Galatians, Acts 15 could not be the meeting where the "pillars"—James, Kephas, and John—"extended the right hand of fellowship to Paul and Barnabas." It may be a mere coincidence that these men are mentioned together in Jerusalem in Galatians 2:9 and Acts 12, but combined with the several other indications that the author of Acts intended chapter 12 to be understood as coinciding with Galatians 2, it seems reasonable to think that the author of Acts crafted chapter 12 with James, Peter, John, Paul, and Barnabas in Jerusalem at the same time in order to help the readers understand that they were to associate Galatians 2 with Acts 12, to read and understand Galatians 2 in light of Acts 12, and that the conflicts in Galatians 2 are to be understood to be more in line with the conflicts in Acts 12—between the congregation and "the Jews"—than between Paul and the Jerusalem leaders.

In sum, the cumulative evidence that the author of Acts intended 11:30—12:25 to correspond to Galatians 2:1-10 is compelling. This evidence includes that Luke has been using Galatians as his primary source since 7:58 (and will continue to use it through 16:3); the chiasmic structure of 11:30—12:25—that Barnabas and Paul are in Jerusalem during the time the events are described in Acts 11:30—12:25; the similarity of the presence of James (Jesus's brother), Peter, and John—the "pillars" of Galatians 2:9—with Paul and Barnabas in Jerusalem at the same time and during Paul's second trip to Jerusalem in both Galatians and Acts; the locations of Syria and Ciclicia; Paul's "revelation" and Agabus's prophecy; the collection; and the verbal similarities of ὃ καὶ ("that which also") as the object of the verb ποιέω ("do") (Acts 11:30 and Galatians 2:10) and συμπαραλαμβάνω ("take with") (Acts 12:25 and Galatians 2:1). If it is accurate that Acts 11:30—12:25 corresponds with Galatians 2:1-10, then the author of Acts radically transformed his source, shifting the controversy between Paul and the Jerusalem congregation to "the Jews," supported by Agrippa, versus the church, while also cryptically indicating that there is a change in the movement's leadership. As Pervo notes, Luke "will suppress persons and events when the circumstances require, but he is aware that the superior tactic is to revise or redirect."[111] What he does with Acts chapter 12 is a superb example of such mimetic redirecting.

---

111. Pervo, *Dating Acts*, 135.

Table 40: Paul and Barnabas return to Antioch;
the so-called "First Missionary Journey"

Galatians	Acts[112]
(But when Kephas came to Antioch . . .) (2:11).	And Barnabas and Saul, their task fulfilled, returned from Jerusalem [to Antioch], taking John Mark with them (12:24b).
	Barnabas and Paul set apart: to Cyprus and Jewish synagogues (13:1–12).
	To Pisidian Antioch; Jewish synagogues. (12:13–52).
	To Iconium; Jewish synagogue; Lystra and Derbe (14:1–23).

Luke has Barnabas and Paul return to Antioch in Acts 12:25 because his source, Galatians, next situates them in Antioch in 2:11–14 after they were in Jerusalem in 2:1–10. However, between Galatians 2:10 and the controversy related in Galatians 2:11–14, Luke inserts Paul and Barnabas's so-called "first missionary journey" in Acts 13–14, in which they travel into the regions of southern Galatia before returning to Syrian Antioch in 14:26. The author of Acts situates the material in our Acts 13–14 between Peter's passing of the torch in chapter 12 and Acts 15 in order to set the stage for the arrival of "some men from Judea" and the ensuing controversy of 15:1–2.

As Luke narrates it, Barnabas and Paul are sent out by the Antiochean congregation after the "laying on of hands," a practice, which, again, would be foreign to the historical Paul. Knox notes that Paul's *ordination* by the laying on of hands here denotes a subjugation to others that does not correspond with Paul's view of himself in his letters, especially in Galatians.[112] Moreover, the impression we get from Paul's letters is that he, primarily, is the "apostle to the Gentiles." Yet, here, Barnabas and Paul are depicted as equal partners in the effort. These problems aside, Barnabas, Paul, and John-Mark travel from Antioch to Seleucia, Antioch's seaport about 16 miles west of Antioch-on-the-Orontes,[113] before sailing to Cyprus's eastern city of Salamis, where they "proclaimed the word of God in the Jewish synagogues (ἐν ταῖς συναγωγαῖς τῶν Ἰουδαίων, 13:5)."[114] Luke's claim

---

112. Knox, *Chapters in a Life of Paul*, 15.

113. Hoppe, "Seleucia," 5:175.

114. Josephus indicates that there was a considerable Jewish population in Cyrpus, which may explain Luke's plural "synagogues" (*Antiquities* 13.284).

that Paul spoke in synagogues in Salamis is the only evidence we have of a synagogue (or, of synagogues) in Salamis. To date, there is no evidence from archaeological sites or inscriptions to support Luke's claim. Neither Stephen Catto[115] nor Paul Trebilco[116] mention Cyprus or Salamis in their respective discussions of diaspora synagogues. Runesson, Binder, and Olsson mention only that "[v]ery little is known about the Jewish community on Cyprus, but according to Luke there existed more than one synagogue in Salamis, the most important city on the island at this time."[117] Regardless of the problem, Luke situates Paul's—the apostle to the Gentiles—first proclamations of the gospel to the Jews in their synagogues (even though such a practice does not occur in Paul's letters), not to Gentiles.

Paphos, about 140 miles west of Salamis, is their next stop, where Luke has Paul engage and prevail over "the sorcerer" (ὁ μάγος, 13:8) Elymas similar to how he had Peter prevail and overcome Simon and his magical powers (μαγεύων, 8:9). Paul's encounter with Elymas somehow leads to the conversion of the proconsul (governor) Sergius Paullus, an experience that Luke seems to associate with Paul's name change from Saul to Paul. The problems of associating the historical Sergius Paullus with Paul range from Loisy's "Sergius Paulus, the proconsul of Cyprus, was never converted by Paul, for the simple reason that he never met him"[118] to Stephen Mitchell and Mark Waelkens's "elementary inference" that Paullus was not only converted by Paul in Cyprus but because he had family in Pisidian Antioch, Paullus "advised and encouraged Paul to make the trip up-country into Asia Minor, following the *via Sebaste* from Perga, where Paul and Barnabas docked, to Antioch" in order to share his message with them.[119] The view accepted here is that neither the Elymas nor Paullus narrative reflects historical reality,[120] but that both are literary/rhetorical devices that serve at least three narrative goals. First, both episodes align Paul closely with

---

115. See especially Catto, *Reconstructing the First-Century Synagogue*, 154–64 for a review of the debate concerning Luke's use of "συναγωγή" in Acts.

116. Trebilco, *Jewish Communities in Asia Minor* and "Jews in Asia Minor."

117. Runesson et al., *Ancient Synagogue*, 163.

118. Loisy, *Les Actes des Apôtres*, 518, cited in Haenechen, *Acts of the Apostles*, 403.

119. Mitchell and Waelkens, *Pisidian Antioch*, 12.

120. With Pervo, "If it is conceded that there is no visible traditional basis for a mission of Paul and Barnabas to Cyprus, it follows that the entire episode is, as it stands, unhistorical" (*Acts*, 323); and Lüdemann's conclusion that Acts 13:6–12 "is a Lukan creation cobbled together from such traditional elements as Baranabas's Cypriot origin, his mission on Cyrpus with John Mark [Acts 15:39], and the joint activities of Barnabas and Paul" (*Acts of the Apostles*, 167). See also Lake, "Proconsulship of Sergius Paulus" for thorough discussion of the evidence that problematizes any historical connection between Paul and Sergio Paullus.

Peter—each encountered and prevailed over a μάγος, thus demonstrating that the new movement is to be distinguished from practitioners of magic. Second, both Peter and Paul converted Roman officials of position—Peter a centurion and Paul a proconsul—thus, demonstrating that Rome was sympathetic to the movement and that the movement could be appealing to men of insight, such as Luke's Sergius Paullus. The third follows from the first two—that Paul and Peter share similar experiences, authority, and power, and are in all respects like-minded. This like-mindedness is evidenced further in Paul's first sermon in Pisidian Antioch.

From Paphos, Paul, Barnabas, and John Mark sail to the region of southern Galatia—first into the port city of Perga (in Pamphylia),[121] then Pisidian Antioch,[122] Iconium,[123] Lystra,[124] Derbe,[125] and then reversing their route on their return adding Atalia. It is important to note that all of these cities are within the province of (south) Galatia[126] and equally important to note that Paul does not refer to any one of them in his letters. That Paul does not refer to any of these cities in his letters raises suspicions as to the historicity of Luke's account. The fact is we simply do not know whether Paul was in any of these communities; our only source is Luke and it has been demonstrated throughout this chapter that he is more interested in crafting a narrative to meet his rhetorical interests than recording accurate history. What is imperative for us to understand, however, is that Luke, *qua an author and organizer of this narrative and as one who is rewriting Paul's account in Galatians*, has Paul travel to communities within south Galatia in Acts 13–14 just prior to the controversy of Acts 15:1–2, wherein "some men from Judea" come to Antioch contesting claims that Paul makes in his letter addressed *to the Galatians* (2:11–15). Thus, Luke is an advocate of the "South Galatia" view and he is establishing his desired context for the controversy of Acts 15.

They begin their Galatian journey by landing in Perga (13:13), an important port city adorned with statues of the imperial family, a stadium that could accommodate up to 14,000 spectators, and a gymnasium with statues dedicated to Claudius (reigning from 41–54 CE)[127]—an appropriate beginning for a mission to the Gentiles. Luke does not have anything to say

---

121. Gasque, "Perga."
122. Idem, "Pisidian Antioch."
123. Idem, "Iconium."
124. Potter, "Lystra."
125. Wineland, "Derbe."
126. Mitchell, "Galatia."
127. Gasque, "Perga," 228.

about their activities in Perga other than that John Mark left them, possibly to set the stage for Paul and Barnabas's argument about him in 15:37–40, to return to Jerusalem. Pisidian Antioch is their next destination, where Luke has Paul offer his first sermon in the book of Acts.

Founded in the third-century BCE, Caesar Augustus annexed the Galatian province (of which Pisidian Antioch was a part) in 25 CE[128] In the first century CE, the community covered only about 115 square acres and its population was probably between 6,000–10,000.[129]

Like the existence of the synagogue in Salamis, there is no archaeological evidence of a Jewish synagogue in Pisidian Antioch for the first century CE; Acts is our only extant source of evidence. Mitchell, who treats the account in Acts very generously, speculates that the synagogue referred to in Acts 13 may have been constructed during the Hellenistic period.[130] This uncritical view of Acts is common in the literature. Elaine Gazda and Diana Ng, for example, claim, "It is clear from the account of Paul's visit to Antioch recorded in the book of Acts, chapter 13, that there was a Jewish synagogue in the city in the mid-1st century."[131] Similarly, Taşlialan, while acknowledging that there is no archaeological evidence for the existence of a Jewish synagogue in Pisidian Antioch in the first century CE, contends that the Church of St. Paul, constructed in the fourth century, was built upon the site of the Jewish synagogue,[132] which leads Gazda and Ng to surmise that it is "tempting to think" that the Chruch of St. Paul was constructed from reused blocks from the same non-existent synagogue.[133] Such speculation without a shred of corresponding physical evidence is not helpful for trying to understand what the author of Acts is attempting to accomplish in the narrative. It may be that there was a Jewish synagogue in Pisidian Antioch in the first century CE, but the unhistorical nature of the Acts narrative as demonstrated thus far and the unhistorical nature of Paul's discourse to the Pisidian Antioch Jews, to be considered next, raise suspicions about the historical accuracy of the entire narrative.

Like the other speeches and narratives in Acts, Paul's sermon in chapter 13 is a Lukan construction and the similarities between Paul's sermon in

---

128. Mitchell, "Antioch of Pisidia."

129. Catto, *Reconstructing the First-Century Synagogue*, 191.

130. Mitchell, "Antioch of Pisidia."

131. Gazda and Ng, eds., *Building a New Rome*, 127.

132. Taşlialan, "Excavations at the Church of St. Paul," cited in Gazda and Ng, *Building a New Rome*, 127.

133. Gazda and Ng, *Building a New Rome*, 127.

Acts 13 and other speeches in Acts have been recognized for many years.[134] Table 41 identifies several of these similarities:

Table 41: Similarities between Paul's sermon in Acts 13 and other sermons in Acts

Paul's sermon in Acts 13	Similarity	Other sermons in Acts
Paul stood up (13:16).	Standing to speak	Peter stood up before the assembled brothers (1:15; cf. 2:14).
Paul to those in attendance at the synagogue in Pisidian Antioch, "Men of Israel and god-fearers, listen" (Ἄνδρες Ἰσραηλῖται καὶ οἱ φοβούμενοι τὸν θεόν, ἀκούσατε, 13:16).	"Men of Israel, listen."	Peter to the fellow Jews, "Men of Israel, hear these words" (Ἄνδρες Ἰσραηλῖται, ἀκούσατε τοὺς λόγους τούτους, 2:22; cf. 3:12 and 5:35).
Paul: "The God of this people, Israel, chose our forefathers (τοὺς πατέρας, 13:17; cf. v. 32 and 36).	Reference to "the fathers"	Peter to the men of Israel: "You are the heirs of the covenant that God made with your forefathers (τοὺς πατέρας, 3:25; cf. 7:2, 11, 12, 15, 19, 39, 45, 51, 52).
This [David] is the man from whose descendants God has brought Israel a savior (13:23).	Jesus as David's descendant	David was a prophet who knew that one of his descendants would sit on the throne (2:29–31).
John made ready for his coming by proclaiming a baptism in token of repentance to the whole people (13:27). (Yet, there is no mention of John the Baptist in Paul's letters.)	John's Baptism	Peter to the brothers: "Therefore, one of those who bore us company all the while the Lord Jesus was going about among us, from his baptism by John until the day when he was taken up" (1:22). Peter to Cornelius and his household: "I need not tell you what has happened lately all over the land of the Jews, starting from Galilee after the baptism proclaimed by John" (10:37; cf. 11:16).
The people of Jerusalem and their rulers did not recognize Jesus or understand the words of the prophets which are read Sabbath by Sabbath; indeed, they fulfilled them by condemning him" (13:27).	The people of Jerusalem and their rulers did not recognize Jesus.	Peter to the "men of Israel," Now my friends, I know that you acted in ignorance, as did your rulers (3:17; cf. 4:5–10).

---

134. For discussion, see Haenechen, *Acts of the Apostles*, 405–18; Lüdemann, *Acts of the Apostles*, 169–75; Soards, *Speeches in Acts*, 79–88; Catto, *Reconstructing the First-Century Synagogue*, 190–94; and Pervo, *Acts*, 334–44.

Paul's sermon in Acts 13	Similarity	Other sermons in Acts
The leaders and the people of Jerusalem condemned Jesus (13:27).	Jews condemned/killed Jesus	Peter to the men of Israel: "You killed him" (2:23; cf. 7:52).
The people of Jerusalem and their leaders did not recognize Jesus and handed him over to Pilate to be executed (13:28). (Yet, there is no reference to Pilate in Paul's letters.)	Pilate	Peter to the men of Israel: "You disowned the hold and righteous one when Pilate wanted to release him" (3:13). Peter: "Herod and Pilate conspired, by your decree, to accomplish all that was foreordained" (4:27).
David suffered corruption (13:37).	David is dead.	David is dead; we have his tomb. (2:24).
Jesus did not suffer corruption (13:37).	Jesus's body did not suffer corruption (i.e., Jesus did not die).	The one about whom [David] spoke (Ps 116) did not suffer corruption. (2:24–28).
God raised him (13:32–33).	Jesus raised from the dead.	God raised Jesus from the dead (2:24, 32).
But God raised him from the dead; and over a period of many days he appeared to those who had come up with him from Galilee to Jerusalem, and they are now his witnesses before our people (13:30).	Witnesses	"Of this [Jesus's resurrection], we are witnesses" (2:32).

Through these shared themes, Luke not only propagates his version of salvation history but also further advances his contention that Paul, Stephen, and especially Peter share one understanding of the gospel, that they proclaim one and the same unified message.

There are a few problems though. First, with Pervo, we must question the verisimilitude that the leader(s) of the Jewish synagogue would invite perfect strangers to proclaim in their synagogue[135] and, even more, that Paul and Barnabas would be invited back the following Sabbath after Paul concludes his sermon with:

> Be it known to you therefore, brethren, that through this man [Jesus] forgiveness of sins is proclaimed to you; and from all

---

135. Pervo, *Acts*, 331.

things of which you could not by the law of Moses be exonerated, by this man every believer is exonerated. Beware therefore, that what was said in the prophets may not come upon you: 'Behold, despisers, and marvel, and perish; for I work a work in your days, a work which you will not believe, if one declare it to you' (13:38–41).

In the next verse, Luke continues, "While they were leaving, they were exhorted that these matters be spoken to them on the next Sabbath" (Ἐξιόντων δὲ αὐτῶν παρεκάλουν εἰς τὸ μεταξὺ σάββατον λαληθῆναι αὐτοῖς τὰ ῥήματα ταῦτα, 13:42). Would members of a Jewish synagogue really invite such a speaker who identifies a weakness in the Mosaic Law and offends his Jewish audience back the following week? One of the problems with this passage, which is evident in the translations, is determining who it is who is exhorting Paul and Barnabas to return and speak further. Haenechen, for example, translates vs. 42 as, "And as they went out, people asked that these things might be spoken about to them the next Sabbath,"[136] understanding and supplying "people" as the subject of the verb "asked" (παρεκάλουν). Pervo, on the other hand, renders it, "As they were leaving, Paul and Barnabas were urged [παρεκάλουν] to say more about their message on the following sabbath,"[137] understanding παρεκάλουν as "probably intentionally impersonal,"[138] which explains his omission of a subject for "urged" (παρεκάλουν). Attempts to address the ambiguity are also evident in the manuscript tradition,[139] as the scribes/editors responsible for the manuscripts behind the Textus Receptus tradition make two emendations. First, to clarify who was "leaving," some of the manuscripts add, "from the synagogue of the Jews" (ἐκ τῆς σναγωγῆς τῶν Ἰουδαίων), which can be construed as "the Jews were leaving the synagogue." But to avoid the possibility that "the Jews" could also be understood as the subject of παρεκάλουν, making "the Jews" those who extended a second invitation to Paul and Barnabas, some of these same manuscripts also added "the Gentiles" as the subject of παρεκάλουν (παρεκάλουν τὰ ἔθνη εἰς τὸ μεταξὺ σάββατον), as Metzger speculates, "probably because it was considered necessary that the request to speak again should be ascribed to the Gentiles, in view of the hostility of

---

136. Haenechen, *Acts of the Apostles*, 413. Metzger also supports this rendering (*Textual Commentary*, 416).

137. Pervo, *Acts*, 330.

138. Ibid., 341. Smyth notes that impersonal verbs, "have a grammatical subject in the personal ending; but the real subject is properly an idea more or less vague that is present to the mind of the speaker" (*Greek Grammar*, 256).

139. For discussion, see Metzger, *Textual Commentary*, 416–18; and Pervo, *Acts*, 341–42, especially n104.

the Jews" expressed against Paul and Barnabas in v. 45.[140] Another possible, and in my view more likely, interpretation of the passage is to understand the "synagogue leaders" of 13:15 as the subject of παρεκάλουν. Παρεκάλουν is the third person plural, imperfect form of the verb παρακαλέω. The nearest plural subject for this verb is the "synagogue leaders" who extended the offer to Paul and Barnabas to speak in v. 15, "After the reading of the law and the prophets, the synagogue leaders [οἱ ἀρχισυνάγωγοι—nominative, masculine, plural] sent to them saying, 'Men, brothers, if there is some word of exhortation within you for the people, speak." It is possible, maybe even likely, that the earliest readers of Acts would have understood the "synagogue leaders" in 13:15 to have been the subject of παρεκάλουν in 13:42, and it could have been this reading that motivated later scribes/editors to emend the text, realizing that the leaders of the synagogue would not invite Paul and Barnabas for another sermon. This then leaves us with the historical unlikelihood that the "god-fearers" would have the authority to invite Paul and Barnabas back to the synagogue the following week. Thus, both possibilities—that the Jewish leaders or the Jewish audience invited Paul and Barnabas back or that the "god-fearers" invited them back—lack historical credibility, and further demonstrate the unhistorical character of the passage.

A second problem with the narrative of Paul's sermon in Acts 13 concerns many of the themes in the sermon that are not in Paul's letters. Luke has Paul refer to the "fathers" (vv. 17, 32, 36), the Egypt-David narrative that includes references to Egypt, Samuel, Saul (vv. 17-23), and to the Jewish rulers who did not recognize but killed Jesus (13:27). While these echo sentiments expressed in Peter's and Stephen's speeches earlier in Acts and demonstrate Luke's unifying intent, they are foreign to those letters thought to be penned by Paul, as there is not one reference to any of these people or themes in those letters that share the sentiment expressed in Acts 13:17-23, with the exception of one reference to Jesus as the descendant of David in Romans 1:3[141] Luke also has Paul invoke the John the Baptist narrative (13:24-25) and the Pilate narrative (13:28), both of which would not only require Paul's knowledge of the gospel narratives (presumably about thirty years before the first was written) but are also completely foreign to Paul's letters. Perhaps the most egregious statement that Luke has Paul make is, "But God raised him from the dead; and over a period of many days he ap-

---

140. Metzger, *Textual Commentary*, 416.

141. The only other references to David in those letters thought to be authentic are Rom 4:6 and 11:9, wherein David is cited as the author of our Pss 32 and 69, respectively. There are no references to "Egypt," "Samuel," "Saul," or "the Jerusalem leaders." In 1 Cor 10, Paul does refer to the "fathers" in the wilderness, but allegorically.

peared to those who had come up with him from Galilee to Jerusalem, and they are now his witnesses before our people" (13:30–31). As Haenechen notes, "The real Paul would not have appealed to the Christophanies before the Twelve without referring to his own vision!"[142]

Despite these problems, upon Paul and Barnabas's return the following sabbath, controversy erupts and "the Jews," seeing the crowds, "were filled with jealousy and were contradicting [ἀντέλεγον] Paul's claims with violent abuse [βλασφημοῦντες]" (13:45). This is the second of six episodes that Luke offers in Acts 13–14 of Jewish opposition to Paul. The first was the Jewish "sorcerer" Elymas who "opposed" (ἀθίστατο) Paul and Barnabas in 13:8. Then, in 13:50, after Luke has Paul divorce Judaism from the gospel by proclaiming to the Jews in Pisidian Antioch, "It was necessary that the word of God should be declared to you first. But since you reject it and judge yourselves unworthy of eternal life, we now turn to the Gentiles" (13:46), he sets these Jews against Paul for the third time, "The Jews incited [παρώτρυναν] the god-fearing women of high standing and the leading men of the city and incited persecution [ἐπήγειραν διωγμὸν] against Paul and Barnabas and expelled them from their district" (13:50–51). The fourth incident occurs as soon as Paul and Barnabas arrive at the synagogue in Iconium, for which there is, again, not a shred of physical evidence other than this lone reference.[143] Here the experience is similar to that which occurred in Pisidian Antioch—Paul and Barnabas speak, many Jews and Gentiles believe, some do not, and, here, those "non-believing Jews" [ἀπειθήσαντες Ἰουδαῖοι] again "incited" the Gentiles and "poisoned their minds against the brothers" (14:2). (It seems worth noting here that the expression "non-believing Jews" occurs only one other time in Greek literature prior to Luke's use of it here in Acts 14, and this is Paul's use of a very similar expression in Romans where Paul implores his readers to pray for him that he "might be saved from the unbelievers in Judea [ἀπειθούντων ἐν τῇ Ἰουδαίᾳ] and that my errand to Jerusalem may find acceptance with God's people" (15:30),[144] suggesting dependence. In time, the fifth episode of opposition occurs, as the non-believing Jews and Gentiles connived to "maltreat" Paul and Barnabas and stone them, but the two (somehow!) learned of the plan and made their escape to Lystra, Derbe, and the surrounding area (14:4–6). In Lystra, after Paul heals a cripple from birth (similar to Peter's healing in Acts 3) and after Barnabas and Paul are hailed as gods (similar to Peter's experience with

---

142. Haenechen, *Acts of the Apostles*, 411. Knox also notes that here Luke "places in his mouth words that Paul himself would have repudiated with scorn" (*Chapters in a Life of Paul*, 99).

143. Runesson et al. cite only this passage as any evidence for the synagogue in Iconium (*Ancient Synagogue*, 218).

144. According to a *TLG* search for "ἀπειθ" + "Ἰουδαι," where the former term occurs within four words prior to the latter.

Cornelius in Acts 10[145]), we are told, "The Jews from [Pisidian] Antioch and Iconium came on the scene and won over the crowds. They stoned Paul and dragged him out of the city, thinking him dead" (14:19), which is the sixth occurrence of Jewish opposition to Paul in Acts 13–14. Developing this theme of Jewish (only) opposition against Paul is an important component of Luke's organizational strategy leading up to chapter 15.

Before summarizing how Luke has revised Galatians 1–2 in chapters 7:58—14:28 and then discussing the problems in Acts chapter 15, there is one more point to be made from chapter 14 that further demonstrates the rhetorical and unhistorical character of the chapter. In 14:21–22, the text states that Paul and Barnabas returned to Antioch by way of Derbe, Lystra, and Iconium, encouraging the disciples, and "appointing elders in each church" (χειροτονήσαντες δὲ αὐτοῖς κατ' ἐκκλησίαν πρεσβυτέρους, 14:23). The problem is that πρεσβυτέρος, in any case form, does not occur in any of those letters attributed to Paul that are considered to be authentic, and nowhere in these letters does Paul appoint leaders. As Haenechen notes, "That Paul and Barnabas everywhere appointed elders agrees indeed with Titus 1:5, but not with the community organization which emerges from the genuine Paulines. Luke has simply taken for granted that the ecclesiastical constitution of his own day already existed in the time of Paul."[146] Pervo reiterates, "Verse 23 is anachronistic and certainly un-Pauline, for Paul makes no reference to presbyters. The pastoral perspective is that of Titus 1:5 and 1 Clement 42:4."[147] Luke is writing at a much later time and possibly using Titus and perhaps 1 Clement as source material.[148]

---

145. In Acts 10, upon Peter's entrance in Cornelius's home, Cornelius falls at Peter's feet, to which Peter responds, "I am only a man" [ἐγὼ αὐτὸς ἄνθρωπος εἰμι], whereas here in 14:15 Luke has Paul claim, "We too are only men" [ἡμεῖς ὁμοιοπαθεῖς ἐσμεν ὑμῖν ἄνθρωποι].

146. Haenechen, *Acts of the Apostles*, 426.

147. Pervo, *Acts*, 362.

148. Titus 1:5 reads, "The reason I left you in Crete was that you might straighten out what was left unfinished and appoint elders in every town, as I directed you." *1 Clement* 42:4, in advancing apostolic succession, reads, "So, preaching both in the country and in the towns, they [the apostles] appointed their first fruits, when they had tested them by the Spirit, to be bishops and deacons for the future believers" (*Apostolic Fathers*, 101).

Summary of Events in Acts 7:58—14:28 Leading Up to the Issues in Acts 15

With Philip's evangelistic activity in Samaria and the conversion of the Ethiopian (8:4–40), Luke began the mission beyond Jerusalem and to non-Jews in earnest, but it is during the (not-so) "Silent Period" (9:31—11:24) that he begins to insert material concerning the mission to the Gentiles as it relates directly to Galatians 1–2 and Acts 15. On his journey toward Caesarea, Luke has Peter meet and heal an Aeneas (9:32–35), most likely a Gentile, and, after reviving Tabitha, whose Greek name we are told is Dorcas, Luke narrates Peter's vision, encouraging him to "kill and eat," in which he is told "not to call impure that which God has made clean" (10:15). After Peter meets Cornelius, he informs the Roman centurion, "You are well aware that it is against our Law for a Jew to associate with a Gentile or visit him. But God has shown me that I should not call any man impure or unclean" (10:28). The requirements of *kashrut* and the association of Jews with Gentiles—the two issues central to the Antioch incident described by Paul in Galatians 2:11–14—were resolved in Acts 10–11, as Luke had Peter and the Jerusalem leaders (Paul's opponents in Galatians) accept the Gentile mission before Paul even begins his so-called "first missionary journey." Then in Acts 12, Luke, following Galatians, has Paul make his second trip to Jerusalem, which Luke intends to correspond with Paul's account of his second trip to Jerusalem in Galatians 2:1–10, but Luke radically transforms the content of his source, probably in an attempt to suppress or omit the controversy that Galatians 2:1–10 cryptically describes. After the bewildering change of leadership episode in Acts 12, wherein Peter's leadership role fades into the background, Paul and Barnabas, in Acts 13–14, make their so-called "first missionary journey" into the province of south Galatia where Luke narrates/establishes harsh opposition to Paul not by other followers of Jesus, as Paul describes in Galatians, but, primarily, by the Jews. This (at times) ruthless opposition stems not from any explicit criticism of the Jewish Law that Paul espoused (for Paul only mentions the Law once during his south Galatian journey, 13:39), but (seemingly) because of his claim that Jesus is the Messiah—the same gospel advanced by Peter, John, and Stephen earlier in Acts. So by the time the Acts narrative arrives at chapter 15, the controversy concerning Jewish/Gentile relations in Galatians 2:11–14 has already been addressed, but perhaps not as explicitly resolved as Luke thought it could be. In addition, and following the narrative sequence in Galatians 2, there was still the intense conflict in Antioch between Peter and Paul (2:11–14) to deal with. Thus, in chapter 15, Luke will juxtapose and conflate material from Galatians 2:1–10 and 11–14 into one event to finally resolve both the Jewish/Gentile relationship issue (already addressed in chapters 10 and 11) and the conflict in Antioch between Peter and Paul by completely deleting or erasing it.

Acts 15, Paul's Third Trip to Jerusalem in Acts, the So-Called "Jerusalem Council"

I have been arguing that Luke is both using Galatians as his narrative-framework source and following (for the most part) Galatians' narrative sequence for the material beginning at Acts 7:58 while also creating and inserting sections of narrative material (interludes) into this framework that are not in Galatians. Just prior to Interlude 3 (the so-called "first missionary journey" to South Galatia), Luke has Paul and Barnabas return to Antioch following their second visit to Jerusalem (Acts 12:25 following Gal 2:1–10). Luke is aware that the troubling Antioch incident that Paul describes in Galatians 2:11–14 follows 2:1–10, but he needs to establish a context that will set the stage for his revision of the incident, so he creates the "first missionary journey" narrative in which he sends Paul and Barnabas into Jewish synagogues (for which there is no physical evidence of their existence in the first century CE nor textual evidence from Paul's letters) in the province of south Galatia and inserts this narrative between 12:25 and 15:1 as Interlude 3. It is not a narrative accident that Luke, *qua* author, has Paul (and Barnabas) traveling through the south Galatia province (Acts 11–14) just prior to his transformation of the Antioch incident—a transformation that concerns itself, primarily, with issues raised in Paul's letter *to the Galatians*—and then has Paul serve as an overseer of the delivery of the "decree" to the communities in Antioch, Syria, and Cilicia (areas of Paul's travels,[149] 15:23 and Gal 1:21) just prior to Paul's (and Timothy's) return to the province of Galatia (16:6). In other words, Luke, *qua* author, sandwiches his discussion of the so-called "Jerusalem Council" between Paul's two excursions to the regions of Galatia, the intended audience for Galatians. Luke, *qua* author, has established that Acts 15 is to be situated/understood within the broader context of Paul's travels within the province of Galatia.

The secondary literature supporting the prevailing view concerning the relationship between Acts 15:1–29 and Galatians 2:1–10 is vast and this

---

149. While the combination of "Syria and Cilicia" is common in Greek literature, it seems worth noting that the only occurrences of this combination in the NT are in Galatians, when Paul, after his first visit to Jerusalem, left for "the regions of Syria and Cilicia" (1:21); in Acts 15:23, where Paul (Barnabas and others) deliver the "apostolic decree" "to Antioch, Syria, and Cilicia"; and Acts in 15:41, where Paul (and Timothy) traveled through "Syria and Cilicia strengthening the churches."

view is represented most recently by Pervo, "With most scholars I hold that they refer to the same meeting and that Galatians is generally the more 'accurate' of the two."[150] For this discussion, I am not going to concern myself with whether Paul's account or Luke's account is more accurate. Rather, my concern here is to demonstrate that Luke knew the Galatians account and significantly transformed it. To be sure, there are a few similarities between the two narratives, but they are very few, and even these are problematic, but there are many points of contact between the two that Table 42 identifies.

Table 42: Narrative differences between Galatians 2 and Acts 15[151]

	Galatians	Acts 15
1	The so-called "Jerusalem Council" occurs *before* (2:1–10) the Antioch incident (2:11–14).	The so-called "Jerusalem Council" (15:5–29) occurs *after* the Antioch incident (15:1).
2	The explanation that Paul provides for his trip to Jerusalem in Gal 2 is to present his gospel that he proclaims to the Gentiles to "those of reputation" (2:2).	It is the Antioch incident (15:1–2) that creates the need for the so-called "Jerusalem Council" and the reason for Paul and Barnabas to go to Jerusalem.
3	Paul and Barnabas travel to Jerusalem with Titus after 14 years. There is no mention of from where they came (2:1).	Paul, Barnabas, and some others go to Jerusalem from Antioch (15:2). *Titus is not mentioned in Acts.*
4	They go to Jerusalem in response to a revelation (2:2).	Paul and Barnabas are sent to Jerusalem by the community in Antioch as its representatives to discuss issues raised by "certain men from James" (15:2).
5	Paul went to present his gospel that he proclaims to the Gentiles (2:2).	Paul does not present or explain his gospel to anyone in Acts.
6	Paul presents his gospel to those of reputation in a private meeting (2:2).	There is no private meeting between Paul and those of reputation in Acts; Paul does not present or explain his gospel to anyone in Acts.

150. Pervo, *Dating Acts*, 79. Cousar ("Jerusalem, Council of") offers a helpful overview of other views and the related difficulties, and Taussig ("Jerusalem as Occasion for Conversation") offers a helpful analysis of the similarities and differences between the two passages.

151. Taussig ("Jerusalem as Occasion for Conversation," 89) and Pervo (*Dating Acts*, 86) offer tables with fewer points of contact.

	Galatians	Acts 15
7	Titus is not compelled to be circumcised (2:3).	Titus is not mentioned in Acts; Paul circumcises Timothy (16:1-3).
8	Paul refers to "false brothers" in Jerusalem who were spying and apparently demanding circumcision (2:4).	There are no "false brothers" in Acts. There are "some who came down from Judea who were teaching the brothers that 'if you are not circumcised in the custom of Moses, you will not be able to be saved,'" (15:1) and there are "believers from among the Pharisees" demanding circumcision and compliance with the Law (15:5).
9	Paul refers to "false brothers" and their claim that circumcision was necessary. This occurred in Jerusalem (2:3-4).	"Some from Judea" (not "false brothers") came to Antioch and were teaching the necessity of circumcision. This occurred in Antioch (15:1). Then, in Jerusalem, "some believers from the Pharisaic party claimed that it is necessary that Gentiles be circumcised and observe the Law of Moses (15:5).
10	Paul expresses an antagonistic attitude toward "those of reputation"—"What sort they were makes no difference to me; God does not choose from man's appearance" (2:6).	Paul does not express any antagonism against James or Peter in Acts. Rather, he is compliant, submissive.
11	"Those of reputation" "added nothing to me" except that "I care for the poor" (2:6, 10).	The "decree," penned by James, adds restrictions from meat offered to idols, blood, anything that has been strangled, and fornication (15:29)—restrictions that, scholars agree, Paul would not have accepted. There is no hint of Paul's concern for the 'poor' in Acts 15. The only reference that could possibly be construed as Paul remembering the poor in Acts is the contribution that he and Barnabas carry to Jerusalem from Antioch (at the behest of the Antioch community, not from "those of reputation" (11:25-30).
12	If 2:7-9 is not an interpolation, there is an acknowledged distinction between Paul's and Peter's apostleships (2:7-9).	There is no such distinction in Acts.

	Galatians	Acts 15
13	If 2:7–9 is not an interpolation, Paul and Barnabas meet with James, Kephas (Peter), and John, the "pillars" (2:9).	A "pillar" named John is not mentioned in Acts. James and Peter are never identified as "pillars" in Acts. The only time that Paul and Peter are together in Acts is in chapter 15, but they do not speak one word to each other.
14	If 2:7–9 is not an interpolation, there is an extension of the "right hand" between "pillars" and Paul and Barnabas (2:7 – 9).	There is no such extension in Acts. Paul and Barnabas have been a part of the group since chapter 9.
15	"When Kephas came to Antioch" (2:11).	Kephas (Peter) is never in Antioch in Acts. Paul and Peter are never in Antioch together in Acts.
16	Paul opposed Peter to his face, as he was eating with Gentiles but backed off when "those from James" arrived (2:11–12).	(Peter) is never in Antioch in Acts. Paul and Peter are never in Antioch together in Acts. There is no confrontation between the two in Acts.
17	"Some men from James" [τινας ἀπὸ Ἰακώβου] went to Antioch (2:12).	"Some men" [τινες] came down from Judea (15:1).
18	Peter retracts for fear of "those of the circumcision" (2:12).	Peter is never in Antioch in Acts. Peter met with "those of the circumcision" in Acts 11 and was instrumental in demonstrating to them that God makes a distinction between Jew and Gentile.
19	Barnabas is carried away by "those sent from James" (2:13).	Paul and Barnabas part ways because of John Mark, not because of any conflict in Antioch. In fact, in Acts, Barnabas accompanies Paul to Jerusalem *after* the Antioch incident, which is inconceivable if he would have been "carried away" as Gal 2:13 claims.
20	Paul to Kephas: "If you, a Jew, live like a Gentile, how do you compel the Gentiles to live like Jews?" (2:14).	Peter is never in Antioch in Acts and Paul and Peter never speak to one another rin Acts. Peter is instrumental in arguing against Jewish requirements for Gentiles because of his vision in chapter 10, and, in Acts, peter asserts that God established from the beginning that it was through his mouth that the Gentiles were to be saved.

There are five similar or parallel narrative themes in agreement between Galatians 2 and Acts 15:

1. Paul and Barnabas travel to Jerusalem and participate in a meeting there (Gal 2:1; Acts 15:2);
2. While in Jerusalem, circumcision is an issue (Gal 2:3-4; Acts 15:5);
3. There was an incident in Antioch (Gal 2:11-14; Acts 15:1);
4. "Some men" went from Jerusalem to Antioch (Gal 2:12; Acts 15:1); and
5. Paul and Barnabas have a dispute and go separate ways (Gal 2:13; Acts 15:36-41).

While recognizing these similar narrative themes, I suggest that Luke radically juxtaposed the sequential order of the two chronologically and thematically different events in Galatians 2 into one event in Acts 15. For example, whereas earlier in Acts, Luke closely followed the sequence of events in Galatians 1-2, here in Acts 15, he does not follow the account in Galatians 2:1-10 and 2:11-14 sequentially. In Galatians, the Jerusalem Council (2:1-10) occurs chronologically (or at least narratively) prior to the incident in Antioch (2:11-14), but in Acts, the incident in Antioch precedes (15:1) and is the cause or reason for the Council meeting in Jerusalem (15:2-29). A second example of Luke's juxtaposition is Baranbas's and Paul's dispute and separation. In Galatians, Paul seems to indicate that they separated immediately after the incident in Antioch and that the incident there was the cause for the separation (2:13). In Acts, Paul and Barnabas are both partners in Antioch in contending with "those from Judea" over the circumcision issue, travel companions to Jerusalem after the incident, and close collaborators during the Council, only to disagree and then separate later (after they return to Antioch with the "decree") because of a dispute over John Mark (15:36-41). A third example is that, in Galatians 2:1-10, the issue is circumcision *in Jerusalem* and, in 2:11-14, the issue is Jewish/Gentile relationships concerning kashrut *in Antioch*. Luke juxtaposes these by raising the circumcision issue initially *in Antioch* (15:1) only to be reiterated in Jerusalem (15:5) and by dealing with the kashrut issue *in Jerusalem* via the "decree," even though this issue had already been resolved through Peter's vision in chapter 10 and to the satisfaction of "those of the circumcision" in Jerusalem in chapter 11 who would, seemingly, also be in attendance at the Council in chapter 15.

Luke's radical transformation continues. Whereas in Galatians 2:2 Paul plans to present his own gospel (about which he so proudly boasts earlier in Galatians) to "those of reputation," in Acts 15, Paul does not have a gospel of his own, but he inherits and advances that (Pauline) gospel expressed by Peter in 15:9–11. Related to this is Paul's sense of working independently of the Jerusalem community in Galatians 1 and 2 and even treating them with a measure of antagonism (2:6), but in Acts he is working closely with and subservient to them. And, perhaps Luke's most significant transformation of Galatians 2 is the conflict in Antioch that, in Galatians, was between Paul and Peter and Paul and Barnabas. In Galatians, Paul "opposes Peter to his face" because prior to the arrival of "those from James," Peter would eat with the Gentiles, but, after their arrival, he drew back because of his "fear of the Jews." According to Galatians, Barnabas sided with Peter against Paul. In Acts, Peter is never in Antioch; Paul and Peter never disagree; Paul never opposes Peter; Paul and Barnabas are still partners in their work, and the conflict is between Paul and Barnabas as associates against "some who came down from Judea" (who are later in Acts said not to have been authorized by the Jerusalem leaders, 15:24), who are teaching that circumcision is necessary (15:1).

Conclusion: Applying Mimetic Criteria to Luke's Composition of Acts 7:58—15:30

It seems superfluous to align Luke's compositional conventions in Acts 7:58—15:30 with the criteria for imitated texts established in chapter 2. That the composition of Acts post-dates Paul is beyond reasonable dispute even if one does not accept a date range between 120–130 CE. In addition, while a few may date Matthew prior to Luke, I am not aware of any respectable scholar who would venture a date of Acts prior to Paul. Thus, the external plausibility criterion is satisfied. Significant similarities in regard to conception, narrative structure, themes, order, and linguistic details are patently evident, and there is no question that Luke scrutinized Galatians as meticulously as he scoured Matthew's birth narrative, so the intimate familiarity criterion is met. In significantly transforming Paul's account of Galatians 1–2, Luke completely whitewashes, or papers over, the controversy between Paul and the Jerusalem leaders and Paul and Barnabas that Paul describes in Galatians and that is evident in the Corinthian letters. Luke rivaled and overwhelmed his source. The intelligibility of differences criterion is certainly met. The weight of the criteria criterion suggests, without dispute it would seem, that the author of Acts mimetically transformed Galatians just as skillfully as he mimetically transformed Matthew's birth narrative and just as skillfully as Virgil, it could be argued, mimetically transformed Homer.

Chapter 8

Conclusion

In chapter 2, I provided evidence that demonstrates the prevalence of mimesis/imitatio in Greco-Roman education and literary culture. Ancient authors imitated other ancient authors in every genre in a wide variety of ways, and mimesis/imitation was the means by which students were taught to read, write, critically analyze a text, and prepare a speech. Some of the characteristics of mimesis/imitation that pertain to written texts include the importance of careful reading, internalizing and digesting the source text, scrutinizing every phrase of an author's text, dependence upon a source text as conceptual and narrative models, marshaling the material in a different way so as to *make it one's own*, and rivaling the source text(s), which seems to be the primary objective of imitating another's work. Adapting MacDonald's, Brodie's, and Winn's criteria, I incorporated these mimetic characteristics into the criteria adopted for this study:

1. *External plausibility* (recognizing the difficulty of dating some texts);
2. *Significant similarities* in compositional conventions with those identified in Virgil's *Aeneid* (in organizational and conceptual structures, action/theme/plot, order, and linguistic or verbal details, while avoiding parallels that "stretch credibility" or seem "far-fetched");
3. *Evidence of intimate familiarity with source* (evidence of careful scrutiny or "digesting" of the source);
4. *Intelligibility of differences* (understanding the importance of rivalry and transformation of previous texts); and
5. *Weight of the combined criteria.*

In chapter 3, I provided detailed literary evidence that demonstrated that Matthew knew, used, and significantly altered and rivaled Mark's Beelzebul narrative. Few scholars would disagree with this, but few would also attribute Matthew's revision to Greco-Roman mimesis. I think it is the best explanation. I then provided similar detailed literary evidence that demonstrated that Luke knew, used, and significantly revised both Mark and Matthew in rhetorical and compositional ways that are similar, if not identical, to how Matthew engaged and revised Mark. Luke rewrote Mark's and Matthew's Beelzebul narratives via Greco-Roman imitation just as Matthew's Beelzebul narrative is an imitation of Mark's. The differences between Mark's and Matthew's narratives can be reasonably explained—Matthew disagreed with Mark's implication that Jesus's mother and family members were not "insiders" but "outsiders" so he eliminated, or deleted, that implication. Similarly, while Luke recognized Matthew's effort, he was not satisfied with it, thought he could improve upon it, and, in his revision, further distanced Jesus's mother and family members from Mark's implication, and, in fact, transformed it so that it was they who "do the will of God," and, as such, would be included among Jesus's most intimate associates. I suggested there was a trajectory from Mark > Matt > Luke, and, to satisfy the *external plausibility* criterion, I relied upon the prevailing view that Matthew is chronologically prior to Luke. Similar, if not identical, rhetorical and compositional strategies are evident with Matthew's revision of the possible slurs in Mark 6 and then again with Luke's further development of Matthew's revision. Matthew, I argued, recognized Mark's reference to Jesus as a carpenter in negative terms and removed the reference to Jesus, transforming it to the "son of a carpenter." He then rewrote Mark's "son of Mary" in such a way to remove the connotation that could accompany the expression. In similar fashion to how he further distanced Jesus's family from the Beelzebul controversy than Matthew did, Luke completely removed any reference to "carpenter" in his revision, citing Jesus as merely the "son of Joseph," which also completely removes any possibility of the potential slur against Mary, who is not even mentioned. Matthew clearly satisfies all of these criteria. The only possible weak link with Luke satisfying all of the criteria is the question of whether Matthew's text is chronologically prior to Luke's. The prevailing view is that it is, and the case could be made that the trajectories argued for in chapter 3 provide supporting evidence, as a trajectory of Luke > Matthew does not seem to make narrative sense. Thus, the *weight of the combined criteria* strongly suggests, if not indicates, that Matthew imitated Mark and that Luke imitated Mark and Matthew.

In chapter 4, I argued that at least one of the objectives of Matthew's birth narrative was to respond to implications raised in Mark's gospel and that may have also been in wider circulation. In order to respond to these claims, Matthew had to craft a birth narrative that explains Mary's pregnancy after the fact—that explains why Mary is pregnant when she should not be and pregnant by someone other than her husband and that may also rebuff possible claims of Jesus's illegitimacy. No such birth narrative existed to serve as a model for Matthew, so he had to craft one by drawing upon and imitating passages from the Greek translation of the Hebrew Bible, the Septuagint. It is this deficiency of a model to which Matthew could respond that explains why Matthew's imitative practices in Matthew 1 are somewhat different than what we saw in his revising of Mark 3 and 6. In Matthew's use of the Septuagint, there is no question that he satisfies the *external plausibility* criterion. As for the *significant similarities*, Matthew demonstrates very well that he knew the genealogies in 1 Chronicles and Ruth, that he knew the narratives of the four women from Genesis 38 (Tamar), Joshua (Rahab), Ruth (Ruth), and 2 Samuel (Bathsheba), the Babylonian captivity, and birth annunciations, especially Isaiah 7:14. His use and recasting of these women to create a lineage for Jesus that also contributes to his explanation for Mary's pregnancy—that these other women were also involved in inappropriate sexual relationships—are rhetorically fascinating. Matthew's revision of Isaiah 7:14, if my argument above is correct, demonstrates creative (and deceptive) *linguistic details* and *complex coherence*. The differences between the narratives that Matthew adopts (and adapts) from the Septuagint and how these narratives fit within the Old Testament are extensive, radically extensive, but few scholars would deny that Matthew does not draw upon and recast these narratives—that these narratives in the Septuagint are Matthew's conceptual source for his genealogy and conception narrative. Thus, the *intelligible differences* criterion is met. The *weight of the evidence* indicates that Matthew imitated passages from the Septuagint to make something new.

Did Luke know and use Matthew's foretelling-of-Jesus's-birth (1:18-25) and Jesus's-birth-and-visitors (2:1–20) narratives? In chapter 5, I first reviewed the prevailing view that Matthew and Luke wrote independently of one another without one knowing the other's text and the scholarship that speaks to Luke's imitation of many passages from the Septuagint in his birth narrative, especially 1 Samuel (1 Kgs LXX) and the Psalms. I then presented detailed evidence that demonstrates beyond reasonable doubt that Luke knew, used, and imitated Matthew's foretelling-of-Jesus's-birth and Jesus's-birth-and-visitors narratives. The *significant similarities* are many. The first undeniable similarity is the existence of these two conception and birth narratives themselves in both gospels. Within these two narratives in both gospels, I identified *similar themes, structural similarities, narrative order, linguistic details,* and *complex coherence*, all of which can only be explained by one author using/imitating the other. There is no question of Luke's intimate familiarity with his source; Matthew's narrative was Luke's *conceptual source*. Luke "swallowed Matthew whole," to once again borrow and adapt Brodie's expression. I argued that there is also strong evidence of Luke's use of Matthew's genealogy. Again, the existence of the genealogy alone is strong evidence of dependence, and when we add that Luke's organizational structure may reflect Matthean influence, his returning to Shealtiel and Zerubabel just as Matthew did, his use of three of names found in Matthew, that Mathat is Jesus's ancestor in both, and especially the similarities of Luke's qualifications of Joseph as Jesus's father with Matthew's, a very compelling case can be made for Luke's knowledge, use, and dependence upon Matthew's genealogy, and Greco-Roman imitation. Yes, there are significant differences, but these differences do not alter the narrative fact of the similarities and they can be reasonably explained. First, Luke was not at all satisfied with Matthew's acknowledgement and explanation that Mary was pregnant when she should not have been. How can we explain Luke's elevated portrayal of Mary if not that he was responding to a representation of Mary that, in his mind, needed to be elevated? Matthew's portrayal of Mary in his birth narrative provided such an opportunity. Moreover, it does not seem to need much argumentation to determine that Luke followed Matthew rather than Matthew followed Luke, as a trajectory from Luke's elevated portrayal of Mary that is free of any scandalous behavior on her part to Matthew's account in which there is no question that Mary was pregnant when she should not have been seems extremely unlikely. Second, Luke's extensive use of Septuagentalisms in the birth narrative needs an explanation. Why would he do this? The answer is similar to his portrayal of Mary. Luke seems to be responding to claims that discounted or dismissed Jesus's relationship with the Hebrew God and the Jewish scriptures. Is there any evidence that such claims were in circulation within a timeframe when Luke's birth narrative might have been written? One possibility is Marcion, and Joseph Tyson has made the connection and dated Marcion's influence to the first fifth of the second century, about 120, which is earlier than when most scholars date Marcion's work. Yet, as Bellizoni has demonstrated, there is no evidence of knowledge of Luke as a text resembling ours until about the middle of the second century, so it may not be necessary to move Marcion's influence any earlier than when most scholars believe he was active—ca. 130–140.[1]

---

1. In his *Dating Acts*, Richard Pervo argues in significant detail for a date range of 110–120 for the composition of Acts. In his *Marcion and Luke*-Acts, Joseph Tyson accepts and works from Pervo's date range and contends that Marcion's views were probably known and in circulation by 115–120 (31) and dates the composition of Acts and Luke 1–2 (as a response to Marcion's views) at about this time. Arthur Bellinzoni had previously provided evidence that indicated that there "was apparently little or no significant use of the Gospel of Luke before 150" (in Justin Martyr), which would include any knowledge of Luke among the so-called Apostolic Fathers, and also notes that Matthew was the "more familiar and influential gospel" ("Gospel of Luke in the Second

A later date for Luke would provide even more evidence that it post-dates Matthew, which was the most popular gospel of the second century, and thus more evidence for satisfying the *external plausibility* criterion.

After establishing the narrative contexts of the controversy between Paul and the leadership of the followers-of-Jesus-movement in Jerusalem, after detailing Paul's elevated view of his position as an apostle and noting that other leaders within the movement rejected Paul's claim of his position, and after reviewing Paul's controversy with the Jerusalem leaders in Galatians in chapter 6, I argued in extensive detail in chapter 7 that Luke knew and used Paul's letter to the Galatians. While a majority of scholars acknowledge that Acts probably post-dates Paul's letters (even if not accepting a second-century date for the composition of Acts), satisfying the *external plausibility* criterion, it is still a minority position that Luke knew and used them. Pervo's contention that "with regard to Paul's letters the burden [now] lies on those who contend that Luke did not use them,"[2] has been further supported here, which also adds further support to the *external plausibility* criterion. Because of the many specific and detailed *conceptual*, *structural*, *thematic*, and *verbal similarities* between Galatians 1–2 and Acts 7:58—15:30, the weight of the evidence—especially when considering Luke's compositional activity in light of the prevalent compositional practices of Greco-Roman mimesis—seems incontrovertible that Luke knew, used, and radically transformed Galatians with very simlar rhetorical and compositional techniques to how he radically transformed Matthew 1–2. Moreover, just as he strongly disagreed with Matthew's attempt to explain Mary's situation, he just as strongly disagreed with Paul's account of his relationship with the Jerusalem leaders and completely erased or transformed the controversy from the historical record and offered, instead, his fictional account of a unity between them that simply never existed.

In considering the implications of this study, to understand the compositional practices of New Testament authors—especially the authors of Matthew, Luke, and Acts—within their (immediate) contemporary rhetorical and compositional contexts, rhetorical mimesis should receive much more scholarly attention than it has hitherto. Although this study was limited to certain portions of Matthew, Luke, and Acts, the mimetical compositional techniques identified herein are consistently evident throughout these three texts. Moreover, when it is considered that Matthew, Luke, and Acts

---

Century CE," 59–76, 61). Thus, there is no need to insist on a dating of Luke 1–2 (if it was a later addition to an earlier version of Luke, which seems reasonable) much earlier than Justin Martyr. And, the later Luke is dated, the more likely it post-dates Matthew.

2. Pervo, *Acts*, 12.

comprise a little over 40 percent of the canonical New Testament,[3] and arguably reflect the bulk of narrative material concerning the life of Jesus and the growth of the early church, an understanding that the authors of these texts are writing two or three times removed (at the least) from the events about which they write and that they are rivaling earlier accounts via rhetorical mimesis seriously challenges any notions that these texts reflect historical reality, and this intellectual challenge may be a reason why Greco-Roman mimesis has not received the attention it deserves. However, understood from the perspective of rhetorical mimesis, these texts reflect the conflicts, intense conflicts, within earliest Christianity and attempts by skilled writers to counter, transform, suppress, or whitewash them.

A second result from this study is the observation that Matthew and Luke demonstrate use of similar mimetic compositional techniques. It is unfortunate that early Christian authors and / or editors who are responsible for the form of the texts as they have come down to us decided to ascribe pseudonymous or forged authorship of these texts.[4] As a result, we do not know the actual names of these authors; we do not know where they lived or where they received their training; we do not know who their teachers were, and we do not know whether they were among the very few who completed a *rhetor's* training or just that of a *grammaticus*, although their skill with mimetic composition techniques would suggest the former. All that we have are their works in their canonical form, and careful examination of these works indicates very similar compositional practices. This may be more evident in Matthew's transformation of Mark's accounts of Jesus's relationship with his family than in his birth narrative, but what he does compositionally with Mark is very similar, if not identical, with what Luke then does with Mark and Matthew (and such compositional similarities are also obvious in both writers' accounts of Jesus's baptism, his temptation, and trial and resurrection accounts, just to mention a few). Such similar practices in compositional techniques suggest that Matthew and Luke had somewhat similar training—training that taught these mimetic compositional techniques. Moreover, when we acknowledge that Matthew's and Luke's compositional techniques are also very similar, if not identical to, those identified in Virgil's *Aeneid*, and when we recall the *Aeneid*'s place in Greco-Roman schools beginning shortly after his death (19 BCE), then the possibility presents itself that students were taught Virgilian mimetic compositional techniques. I am not suggesting that they were taught the *Aeneid* specifically, but only that

---

3. For the statistics, see Just, "New Testament Statistics," http://catholic-resources.org/Bible/NT-Statistics-Greek.htm.

4. In addition to David Trobish's *The First New Testament*, see Bart Ehrman's *Forged: Writing in the Name of God*.

they were taught mimetic compositional skills that are very similar to those that I identified in the *Aeneid* in chapter 2. Are Matthew's and Luke's similar mimetic compositional techniques unique to the two of these authors writing between the very end of the first century and middle of the second? Are there any other examples of similar mimetic techniques within this period that may help us to determine if such techniques are more widely used or limited to these Christian authors? What explains these similar techniques in the *Aeneid*, Matthew, Luke, and Acts? Are we aware of any rhetors during this period who may have taught these techniques? Were there any schools organized and/or funded by Christian rhetors or grammatici during this earliest period of Christian textual development that may have served as precurosrs to the later schools or textual laboratories of Origen and Eusebius? Finally, to use Jeffrey Walker's understanding of the *application* of the study of rhetoric, who or what training was influential in *cultivating* these two *rhetors—rhetors* whose persuasive skills and texts have had a profound influence on Western civilization for almost two thousand years?[5]

---

5. In the "Prologue" to his *The Genuine Teachers of This Art*, Walker explains that a third definition of rhetoric, an "art" that is "concerned with critical analysis and theory," while credible for academic enterprise, should not be the end of the academic enterprise of the study of rhetoric. He explains that while a student of the art "will be an appreciator, interpreter, analyst, judge, or theorist of discourse," he may not be "an excellent producer of it." It is this, Walker argues, the "*art of producing a rhêtôr*" that should be the end of rhetoric as an academic discipline, as it was for those who taught the art so many years ago (2).

Appendix 1

Ancient Greco-Roman Authors on Μίμησις/Imitatio

It may seem surprising that with scholars' growing understanding of the prevalence of mimesis/imitatio (imitation) within Greco-Roman education and among ancient Greek and Roman speakers, writers, and students that there is no single article, book chapter, or encyclopedia entry that attempts to collect into one place many (or most) of the primary passages from ancient Greek and Latin texts that speak directly to mimesis/imitation in its various forms and that clearly demonstrates its pervasiveness and importance for the teaching and practices of speaking, composition (in all its forms), and literary analysis. Thus, I offer below translations and paraphrases of many of the relevant passages in Greco-Roman texts (but by no means exhaustive), without much additional commentary, that speak to aspects of mimesis/imitation in their chronological order (as best as these can be determined) and within their narrative contexts in an attempt to provide readers with a sense of the importance and prevalence of the practice as the ancients themselves understood them to be. These are the texts upon which the summary comments in chapter 2 are based.

Isocrates (436–338 BCE)

In *Against the Sophists*, writing within the context of what students needed to learn to be able to "compose and present all discourses" effectively [ἐξ ὧν τοὺς λόγους ἅπαντας καὶ λεγόμενον καὶ συντίθεμεν], Isocrates continues,

> But to choose from these elements those which should be employed for each subject, to join them together, to arrange them properly, and also, not to miss what the occasion demands but appropriately to adorn the whole speech with striking thoughts and to clothe it in flowing and melodious phrase—these things, I hold, require much study and are the task of a vigorous and

> imaginative mind; for this, the student must not only have the requisite aptitude but he must learn the different kinds of discourse and practice himself in their use; and the teacher [διδάσκαλον], for his part, must so expound the principles of the art with the utmost possible exactness as to leave out nothing that can be taught, and, for the rest, he must in himself set such an example [παράδειγμα] that the students who have taken form under his instruction and are able to imitate [μιμήσασθαι] him will, from the outset, show in their discoursing a degree of grace and charm which is not found in others.[1]

In his introduction to his *Panegyricus* (ca. 380 BCE) he writes,

> If it were possible to present the same subject matter in one form and in no other, one might have reason to think it gratuitous to weary one's hearers by speaking again in the same manner as his predecessors; but since discourses [οἱ λόγοι] are of such a nature that it is possible to discourse on the same subject matter in many different ways—to represent the great as lowly or invest the little with grandeur, to recount the things of old in a new manner or set forth events of recent date in an old fashion—it follows that one must not shun the subjects upon which others have spoken before, but must try to speak better than they. For the deeds of the past are, indeed, an inheritance common to us all; but the ability to make proper use of them at the appropriate time, to conceive the right sentiments about them in each instance, and to set them forth in finished phrase, is the peculiar gift of the wise. And it is my opinion that the other arts and the philosophy concerning discourses [τὴν περὶ τοὺς λόγους φιλοσοφίαν] would make the greatest advance if we should admire and honor, not those who make first beginnings in their crafts, but those who are the most finished craftsmen in each, and not those who seek to speak on subjects which no one has spoken before, but those who know how to speak as no one else could.[2]

In his *Panathenaicus*, probably written toward the end of his long life, he responds to his detractors:

> But why wonder at those who are by nature envious of all superior excellence, when certain even of those who regard themselves as superior and who seek to emulate me and imitate [ζηλούντων ἐμὲ μιμεῖσθαι] my work are more hostile to me than

---

1. Isocrates, *Soph.* 17–18.
2. Idem, *Paneg.* §7–10.

is the general public? And yet where in the world could you find men more reprehensible—for I shall speak my mind even at the risk of appearing to some to discourse with more vehemence and rancor than is becoming to my age—where, I say, could you find men more reprehensible than these, who are not able to put before their students even a fraction of what I have set forth in my teaching but use my discourses as models and make their living from so doing, and yet are so far from being grateful to me on this account that they are not even willing to let me alone but are always saying disparaging things about me?[3]

'Demetrius' (ca. Second Century BCE[4])

In the *On Style*, the author notes that poetic vocabulary adds grandeur to prose but prose writers "imitate" [μιμήσει] the poets quite crudely, or rather, they do not imitate but plagiarize [οὐ μιμήσει ἀλλὰ μεταθέσει] them, as Herodotus has done. Contrast Thucydides. Even if he borrows vocabulary from a poet, he uses it in his own way and makes it his own property [ἰδίως αὐτῷ χρώμενος ἴδιον]. He then provides an example as to how Thucydides imitated Homer:

> Homer says of Crete: 'There is a land [γαῖ] of Crete, in the midst of the wine-dark sea, beautiful, fertile, wave-surrounded [περίρρυτος].' Now, Homer used the word 'wave-surrounded' to be impressive. Thucydides, for his part, thinks it right that the Sicilians should act in unity, as they belong to one single 'wave-surrounded [περιρρύτου] land [γῆς].' He uses the same words as Homer, 'land' [γῆν] instead of 'island' and 'wave-surrounded [περίρρυτον],' yet he seems to be saying something different. The reason is that he uses the words not to impress but to recommend unity.[5]

---

3. Idem, *Panath.* §16.

4. Russell dates the text and author to the "late Hellenistic or early Roman period," which is probably as close as the current evidence suggests ("Demetrius," 450).

5. 'Demetrius,' *On Style* (*Eloc.*) §112–13.

Ad Herennium (ca. Mid 80s BCE)

The author of the *Ad Herennium* notes (or boasts) that he uses his own examples [exemplis][6] and, in so doing, has departed from the Greek teachers of rhetoric, and he sets out to explain the Greek practice before justifying his own. He makes three points. The first is that for each kind of embellishment, these Greek teachers, so the author claims, offer an example drawn from a reputable orator or poet. They claim that they do so out of modesty as they do not want to be perceived as showing themselves off. The second is that the "very prestige of the ancients" not only lends greater authority to their (the Greek teachers') doctrines but also sharpens in men the desire to imitate (to imitandum) them—"Yes, it excites the ambitions and whets the zeal of all men when the hope is implanted in them of being able by imitation [posse imitando] to attain to the skill of a Gracchus or a Crassus."[7] The author's third criticism of the Greeks is that they say,

> the highest art resides in selecting a great diversity of passages widely scattered and interspersed among so many poems and speeches, and doing this with such painstaking care that you can list examples, each according to its kind, under the respective topics of the art . . . . This, then, is the height of technical skill—in one's own treatise to succeed also in using borrowed examples [alienis exemplis]![8]

"Indeed," our author concludes, "if the ancient orators and poets should take the books of these rhetoricians and each remove therefrom what belongs to himself, the rhetoricians would have nothing left to claim as their own."[9]

In response to the Greeks' practice of, in his view, excessive imitation, the author contends that a better proof of a writer's mastery is that he write artistically himself: "For though the artistic writer will find it easy to discern what has been skillfully written by others, the facile chooser of examples will

---

6. *Ad Herennium* 4.1.1 reads: "Inasmuch as in the present book, Herennius, I have written about style, and wherever there was need of examples [exemplis], I have used those of my own making, and in so doing have departed from the practice of the Greeks on the subject, I must in a few words justify my method." The *OLD* notes that exemplum denotes "an example (for imitation), pattern, model" (639).

7. Ibid., 4.1.2. The Gracchus referred to is C. Sempronius Gracchus (ca. 151–121 BCE), who was tribune (123–122), a talented orator, and mentioned frequently in Cicero's *De Oratore* (1.38, 154; 2.106, 132, 169, 269; 3.214, 225–26) Crassus is Lucius Licinius Crassus (140–91 BCE), a consul (95), talented orator, and interlocutor in *De Oratore*.

8. Ibid., 4.2.3.

9. Ibid., 4.3.5.

not necessarily write with skill himself. And even if it is an especial mark of artistic skill, let them employ this faculty at another time, and not now when they themselves should be conceiving, creating, and bringing forth." Instead, he suggests, "let them devote their artistic power to this purpose— to win esteem as worthy themselves to be chosen as models by others, rather than as good choosers of others who should serve as models for them."[10]

The author then concludes this discussion by adding that even worse than the Greeks' faulty practice of borrowing examples, they "make a greater mistake in borrowing from a great number of sources." The author's preference, if he were to agree to borrowing sources at all, would be to borrow from only one, for, he explains, teaching students to borrow examples from a variety of orators, poets, and historians would give the students the impression that the totality of skills could only be obtained by imitating many and that no individual could master them all.[11]

Cicero

Quintilian informs us that Cicero (106–43 BCE) "devoted himself heart and soul to the imitation of the Greeks" [cum se totum ad imitationem Graecorum contulisset] and that he "succeeded in reproducing the force of Demosthenes, the copious flow of Plato, and the charm of Isocrates."[12] In *De Inventione* (ca. 80s BCE), attributed to Cicero, he explains that when he struck upon the idea of crafting a textbook of his own on rhetoric,

> I did not set before myself some one model [exemplum] which I thought necessary to reproduce in all details, of whatever sort they might be, but after collecting all the works on the subject I excerpted what seemed the most suitable precepts from each, and so culled the flower of many minds. For each of the writers who are worthy of fame and reputation seemed to say something better than anyone else, but not to attain pre-eminence in all points. It seemed folly therefore, either to refuse to follow the good ideas of any author, merely because I was offended by some fault in his work, or to follow the mistakes of a writer who had attracted me by some correct precept.[13]

---

10. Ibid., 4.4.7.
11. Ibid., 4.5.7.
12. Quintilian, *Inst.* 10.108.
13. Cicero, *De Inv.* 2.1.4.

In his *De Oratore*, Cicero has Antonius explain that upon initially hearing Sulpicius, when he was still young, there were problems with his delivery, so Antonius urged him to consider the law courts as his school and to choose a master, a teacher. Antonius recommended Crassus. A year later, Antonius noticed that the difference was incredible, and he attributes this improvement to Sulpicius's "careful imitation" [studio imitatione] of Crassus, which leads to Antonius's first counsel concerning whom to imitate—"that we show the student whom to imitate [quem imitetur], and to imitate in such a way [quem imitabitur] as to strive with all possible care to attain the most excellent qualities of his model."[14] Later, Cicero has Crassus remark, "Only let the intending speaker or writer, thanks to the training given by a liberal education in boyhood, possess a glowing enthusiasm as well as the assistance of good natural endowments, and, having had practice in the abstract discussions of general principles, have selected the most accomplished writers and orators for study and imitation" [ornatissimos scriptores oratoresque ad cognoscendum imitandumque].[15]

In *Brutus*, Atticus and Brutus are discussing Ennius's (epic poet, ca. 239–169 BCE) dependence upon his predecessor Naevius (ca. 264–201 BCE) and Cicero has Atticus acknowledge that

> Ennius is more finished, as undoubtedly he is; yet if Ennius had really scorned him [Naevius], as he professes, he would not in undertaking to describe all our wars have passed over that stubbornly contested first Punic War. But he tells us himself why he does so: 'Others,' he says, 'have written the theme in verse'—yes, and brilliantly too they wrote, even if with less polish than you, sir; and surely you ought not to think otherwise, you who from Naevius have taken much [sumpsisti], if you confess the debt, or if you deny it, much have stolen [surripuisti].[16]

For Cicero, the apparent difference between appropriate and inappropriate imitation (or plagiarism) is whether the person imitating an earlier author or text acknowledges the debt.

In his *De Finibus*, Cicero defends his right to insert his own translations from Greek philosophers into his works just as earlier Roman poets have done with Greek poets:

> Yet, even in supposing I gave a direct translation of Plato or Aristotle, exactly as our poets have done with the plays, would it

---

14. Cicero, *De or.* 2.89–90.
15. Ibid., 3.125.
16. Cicero, *Brut.* §76.

not, pray, be a patriotic service to introduce those transcendent intellects to the acquaintance of my fellow-country-men? As a matter of fact, however, this has not been my procedure hitherto, though I do not feel I am debarred from adopting it. Indeed, I expressly reserve the right of borrowing [transferam] certain passages, if I think fit, and particularly from the philosophers just mentioned, when an appropriate occasion offers for so doing; just as Ennius regularly borrows from Homer, and Afranius from Menander.[17]

In his *De Oratore*, Cicero has Crassus speak to what would become recognized as *paraphrase* and *translation*:

> For my part, in the daily exercises of youth, I used chiefly to set myself that task which I knew Gaius Carbo, my old enemy, was wont to practice: this was to set myself some poetry, the most impressive to be found, or to read as much of some speech as I could keep in my memory, and then to declaim upon the actual subject-matter of my reading, choosing as far as possible different words. But later, I noticed this defect in my method, that those words which best befitted each subject, and were the most elegant and in fact the best, had been already seized upon by Ennius, if it was on his poetry that I was practicing, or by Gracchus, if I chanced to have set myself a speech of his. Thus, I saw that to employ the same expressions profited me nothing, while to employ others was a positive hindrance, in that I was forming the habit of using the less appropriate. Afterwards, I resolved—and this practice I followed when somewhat older—to translate freely Greek speeches of the most eminent orators. The result of reading these was that, in rendering into Latin what I had read in Greek, I not only found myself using the best words—and yet familiar ones—but also coining by analogy certain words such as would be new to our people, provided only they were appropriate.[18]

Dionysius of Halicarnassus (60–7 BCE)

By the time that Dionysius of Halicarnassus was active in Rome (ca. 30–7 BCE), the principle of μίμησις had been "long firmly entrenched in the

---

17. Idem, *Fin.* 1.3.
18. Idem, *De or.* 1.154–55.

rhetorical schools."[19] Dionysius explicitly states that the examination of the Attic orators for the purpose of imitation was one of his primary interests in composing the *Attic Orators*, as he explains in his "Preface" to the work:[20]

> the subject I have chosen for my discourse ["The Ancient Orators"] is one of general interest and great potential benefit to mankind. It is this. Who are the most important of the ancient orators and historians? What manner of life and style of writing did they adopt? Which characteristics of each of them should we imitate and which should we avoid?[21]

Bonner notes that an equally important concern of Dionysius was determining authentic authorship of the texts attributed to these orators and that such work had considerable practical value, "for it was obviously of service to all students of oratory to know when they were dealing with a genuine speech of one of the great orators, and when they were merely being deceived by one of those servile imitators which circulated all too freely in the Hellenistic world, and brought no little profit to those who compiled them."[22] Thus, in addition to determining the authenticity of orations attributed to these orators, Dinonysius's primary purpose in crafting these essays is to provide examples/models for the purposes of imitation.

Within his introduction to his *Lysias*, for example, he outlines his plan through a series of questions: "What type of style did he employ? What qualities did he originate? In what respects is he superior to his successors, and in what respects inferior? Which of his qualities should be adopted?"[23] It is important to note that, for Dionysius, subject matter was just as important a component for study and imitation as a rhetor's style, as, in his *On Literary Composition*, he writes, "In virtually all kinds of discourse two things require study: the ideas and the words [τῆς περὶ τὰ νοήματα καὶ τῆς περὶ τὰ ὀνόματα]. We may regard the first of these as concerned chiefly with subject matter [τοῦ πραγματικοῦ], and the latter with expression [τοῦ λεκτικοῦ]; and all those who aim to become good rhetors pay close attention to both these aspects of discourse equally."[24] Thus in his essays on the rhetors, he considers what characteristics of both subject matter and style should or should not be studied, imitated, and adopted.

---

19. Bonner, *Literary Treatises of Dionysius of Halicarnassus*, 14.
20. Dionysius of Halicarnassus, *Critical Essays*, vii–xxvii, especially xxi.
21. Ibid., §4.
22. Bonner, *Literary Treatises of Dionysius of Halicarnassus*, 11.
23. Dionysius of Halicarnass, *Lys.* §1.
24. Dionysius of Halicarnass, *Comp.* §1.

For example, in the *Lysias*, he determines that "propriety of diction" (πρέπον τῆς λέξεως)—appropriate language for different characters, audiences, and different parts of a speech—and "persuasive style" are "qualities to be taken from Lysias."[25] Wrapping up his discussion of Lysias's style, he states, "I could mention many other fine qualities of Lysias's style which would improve the expressive powers of any who adopted and imitated them [καὶ μιμούμενος]," and concludes, that not one of Lysias's successors "imitated [ἐμιμήσατο] him with complete success."[26]

In his *Isocrates*, he praises Isocrates's subject matter, selection of material, arrangement and division of topics before noting,

> But most significant of all are the themes upon which he chose to concentrate, and the nobility of the subjects which he spent his time in studying. . . . I therefore affirm that the man who intends to acquire ability in the whole field of politics, not merely a part of that science, should make Isocrates his constant companion. And, anyone who is interested in true philosophy, and enjoys studying its practical as well as its speculative branches, and is seeking a carefree way by which he will benefit many people, not one which gives him a carefree life, would be well advised to imitate [μιμεῖσθαι] the principles which this rhetor adopts.[27]

In his *Thucydides*, Dionysius reminds his readers why he undertook his project on the rhetors, "that those who intend to become good writers and speakers [γράφειν τε καὶ λέγειν εὖ] should have sound and approved standards by which to carry out their individual exercises, not imitating all the qualities of these authors [μὴ πάντα μιμούμενοι τὰ παρ'ἐκείνοις κείμενα τοῖς ἀνδράσιν], but adopting their good qualities and guarding against their failings."[28] He then discusses examples of Thucydides's subject matter (πραγματικὸν)—including his discussion of Themistocles's virtues, Pericles's achievements and the encomium Thucydides crafted for Pericles (2.65), and the virtues of several generals and politicians—that are "admirable and worthy of imitation [καλὰ καὶ μιμήσεως ἄξια]."[29] Further along in his narrative, he again reminds the reader of his objective, "to reveal [Thucydides's] peculiar character, including all the noteworthy qualities that are to be found in his style. My aim in doing so is to assist those who may actually wish to imitate him

---

25. Dionysius of Halicarnassus, *Lys.* §9–10.
26. Ibid., §10, 13.
27. Dionysius of Halicarnassus, *Isoc.* §4.
28. Ibid., *Thuc.* §1.
29. Ibid., §8.

[μιμεῖσθαι τὸν ἄνδρα]."³⁰ Dionysius then notes that Thucydides's narrative of the sea battle in Syracuse harbor (7.69.4-72.1) "and narratives like it seemed to me admirable and worthy of imitation [ἄξια ζήλου τε καὶ μιμήσεως],"³¹ discusses a selection of his speeches "that should be emulated, and it is from these that I suggest writers of history should select their models for imitation [ταῦτα δὴ Θουκιδίδου ζηλωτὰ ἔργα, καὶ ἀπὸ τούτων τὰ μιμήματα τοῖς Ἱστοριογραφοῦσιν ὑποτίθεμαι λαμβάνειν],³² and identifies a concluding passage from one of Thucydides's speeches (6.80.3) "and others like it" that are "fine and worthy of emulation [καλὰ καὶ ζήλου ἄξια]."³³

Dionysius continues his discussion of Thucydides with a consideration of his imitators, noting that no historian had been successful at imitating him, and, among the rhetors, that only Demosthenes successfully "imitated Thucydides in many ways, just as he did all who seemed to him to have achieved greatness and distinction in their field; and he added to his political speeches many virtues that he derived from Thucydides."³⁴ It is with praise of Demosthenes that Dionysius concludes his discussion of Thucydides,

> I should not hesitate to suggest to students of political discourses—those, at least, who still try to keep their critical faculties unprejudiced—that they should take Demosthenes as their guide, as I am persuaded that he was the finest of the rhetors. They should imitate [μιμεῖσθαι] those specimens of his composition in which his brevity, rhetorical power, force, intensity, impressiveness and other related virtues are plain for all men to see; those which are allusive and difficult to follow, and require a commentary, and those which are full of tortured and apparently ungrammatical constructions deserve neither to be admired nor imitated [μήτε θαυμάζειν μήτε μιμεῖσθαι].³⁵

It is in his *Letter to Gnaeus Pompeius* that Dionysius refers to his work *Concerning Mimesis* (Περὶ τῆς Μιμήσεως), which, he explains, included three books: the first "considered the nature of imitation [τὴν περὶ τῆς μιμήσεως ζήτησιν];" the second discusses the question of which particular poets and philosophers, historians and rhetors should be imitated [τοῦ τίνας ἄνδρας μιμεῖσθαι δεῖ ποιητάς τε καὶ φιλοσόφους, Ἱστοριογράφους τε καὶ ῥήτορας], and the third how imitation should be done [πῶς δεῖ μιμεῖσθαι]."³⁶ All that

30. Ibid., §25.
31. Ibid., §27.
32. Ibid., §42.
33. Ibid., §48.
34. Ibid., §52.
35. Ibid., §55.
36. Ibid., *Pomp.* §3.

remains of this work is an epitome, mostly of the second book, that is included in sections 3–5 of this letter to *Pompeius*, along with a few other fragments.[37] In this excerpt from the second book, Dionysius explains that he discusses Herodotus, Thucydides, Xenophon, Philistus, and Theopompus, "writers whom I judged to be most suitable for imitation [ἔκρινον τοὺς ἄνδρας εἰς μίμησιν ἐπιτηδειοτάτους],[38] and Dionysius developed comparative criteria based upon his understanding of *mimesis* for evaluating each historian's subject matter and style and then began to assess each historian's work accordingly. Table 43 reflects his criteria for judging Herodotus's and Thucydides's mimetic style.

Table 43: Dionysius of Halicarnassus's criteria for judging Herodotus's and Thucydides's mimetic characteristics

Criteria	Judgment
Subject matter:	
• Choice of subject	• Herodotus is better.
• Where to begin and end	• Herodotus is better.
• Which events should be included and which omitted	• Herodotus is better.
• Arrangement of material	• Herodotus is better.
• Author's treatment of/attitude about the subject matter	• Herodotus is better.
Style (essential qualities)	
• Purity of Language	• Both are equally good.
• Lucidity	• Herodotus is better.
• Brevity	• Thucydides is better.
Style (ornamental qualities)	
• Vividness	• Both are good.
• Imitation of character and emotions	• Thucydides for emotion; Herodotus for character.
• Grandeur in composition (loftiness)	• Both are good.
• Force and intensity	• Thucydides is better.
• Charm and persuasiveness	• Herodotus is better.
• Propriety	• Herodotus is better.

37. Greek text is in Dionysius Halicarnassus, *On Imitation*, 197–217.

38. Dionysius of Halicarnassus, *Pomp.* §3. Philistus (ca. 430–356 BCE) wrote *The History of Sicily* and Theompus of Chios (fourth century BCE) was possibly a student of Isocrates and an exponent of rhetorical historiography ("Theompus," *OCD*, 1505).

Dionysius's consideration of Xenophon, Philistus, and Theopompus is much briefer and addresses only some of these criteria for each writer, but he notes that Xenophon emulated [ζηλωτὴς] Herodotus in both subject matter and language[39] and that his emulation [ζηλωτὴς] of Herodotus's subject matter, which Usher identifies as Herodotus's "chronological and geographical scope,"[40] is "worthy of praise [χάριν ἄξιος]."[41] Similarly, he remarks that Theopompus's selection and handling of his subject matter—the settlements of the tribes, his description of the foundation of the cities, his portrayal of the lives of kings, and narration of the peculiarities of customs—are qualities of the historian that should be "emulated [ζηλωτά]."[42]

In the *Dinarchus*, Dionysius characterizes him as an eclectic speaker—identifying and briefly discussing how Dinarchus imitates some aspects from Lysias, some from Hyperides, but most from Demosthenes.[43] Claiming that Dinarchus is neither uniform nor the inventor of an original style, Dionysius stresses that Dinarchus, like Isocrates's students and like Isocrates himself, "displays many examples of imitation and of difference from the original models of the speeches [πολὺ γὰρ ἐμφαίνει μιμήσεις τε καὶ αὐτῶν ὡς πρὸς τῶν]."[44]

It is also in the *Dinarchus* that Dionysius distinguishes between two kinds of μίμησις, but, before discussing these, there is a definition of *mimesis* in the fragments that, combined with his distinction between kinds of *mimesis*, may better reflect his understanding of these terms. *Mimesis* he defines as "a copying-the-model-by-means-of-theoretical-principles activity" [μίμησις ἐστιν ἐνέργεια διὰ τῶν θεωρημάτων ἐκματτομένη τὸ παράδειγμα].[45] With this definition of *mimesis*, he then distinguishes two kinds:

> Generally speaking, two different forms of imitation can be found with regard to ancient models: one is natural, and is acquired by intensive learning and familiarity; the other is related to it, but is acquired by following precepts of the art. About the first, what more is there to say? About the second, what is there to be said except that a certain spontaneous charm and freshness emanates from all the original models, whereas in the artificial copies, even if they attain the height of imitative skill,

39. Dionysius of Halicarnassus, *Pomp.* §4.
40. Ibid., 387 n. 3.
41. Ibid., §4.
42. Ibid., §6.
43. *Dinarchus*, §5.
44. Ibid., §6.
45. Dionysius of Halicarnassus, *On Imitation*, 200.

there is present nevertheless a certain element of contrivance and unnaturalness also?[46]

In Dionysius's first kind of imitation, the primary meaning of the word that he uses for "familiarity" (συντροφίας) denotes "common nurture" or "living together," suggesting that what he has in mind here is that the better, more natural, kind of imitation is one wherein the person doing the imitating has both carefully studied the source to be imitated and, in the process, become intimately familiar with it. Perhaps what Dionysius means by this kind of *mimesis* is explained by his definition of *zelos* (emulation), which follows his definition of *mimesis* in the fragments: "an intellectual activity driving oneself toward admiration of that which is considered to be fine" [ζῆλος δὲ ἐστιν ἐνέργεια ψυχῆς πρὸς θαῦμα τοῦ δοκοῦντος εἶναι καλοῦ κινουμένη].[47] We will consider examples below that reflect both of these kinds of imitation.

Horace (65–5 BCE)

In his *Art of Poetry*, Horace criticizes the meter and "unmusical verses" of Roman poets and exhorts his Roman readers to turn to the Greeks— "handle Greek models by night; handle them by day (vos exemplaria Graeca nocturna versate manu, versate diruna).[48] Earlier in the same poem, he addresses the problems of working with common or traditional material and making the imitated material "one's own":

> It is hard to treat in your own way what is common: and you are doing better in spinning into acts a song of Troy than if, for the first time, you were giving the world a theme unknown and unsung. In ground open to all you will win private rights [private iuris] if you do not linger along the easy and open pathway, if you do not seek to render word for word as a slavish translator, and if in your copying you do not leap into the

---

46. Dionysius of Halicarnassus, *Din.*, §7. On Dionysius's distinction, Jeffrey Walker notes, "one is 'natural' (*phusikos*) and is acquired 'by thorough instruction and familiarity' (*katechesis kai suntrophia*)—the disciplining of aesthesis and habit through guided experience and practice that he everywhere talks about—while the other is acquired 'from the precepts of the art'. . . . a superficial matter of following rules" (*Genuine Teachers*, 262–63).

47. Dionysius of Halicarnassus, *On Imitation*, 200.

48. Horace, *Ars*, lines 268–69 (472).

narrow well, out of which either shame nor the laws of your task will allow you to escape.[49]

Responding to his critics' complaints that his *Epodes* and *Odes* were slavish imitations, Horace, in *Epistle 19*, acknowledges the prevalent practice of imitation, criticizes what he understands to be false imitation, and contends that his practice of imitation relies upon the best Greek models but not slavishly so.[50] In his epistle to Julius Florus, in which he is inquiring about the activities of his younger literary colleagues, Horace expresses concerns about a Celsus's borrowing: "What, pray, is Celsus doing? He was warned, and must often be warned to search for home treasures, and to shrink from touching the writings which Apollo on the Palatine has admitted: lest, if some day perchance the flock of birds come to reclaim their plumage, the poor crow, stripped of his stolen colors, awake laughter."[51]

Seneca the Elder (54 BCE–39 CE)

Seneca the Elder, writing to his sons in the early first century CE, encourages them that they

> are doing something necessary and useful in refusing to be satisfied with models [exempla] provided by your own day and wanting to get to know those of the preceding generation too. For one thing, the more patterns one examines, the greater advantage to one's eloquence. You should not imitate [imitandus] one man, however distinguished: for an imitator [imitator] never comes up to the level of his model. This is the way it is; the copy always falls short of the reality.[52]

In his *Suasoriae* 3, Seneca the Elder provides an example of appropriate imitation: "Gallio said that his friend Ovid had very much liked the [Virgilian] phrase ['He's full of the god'] and that as a result the poet did something he had done with many other lines of Virgil—with no thought of plagiarism [subripiendi, stealing], but meaning that his piece of open borrowing should be noticed."[53]

---

49. Ibid., lines 128–135 (461).
50. Ibid., 381–85.
51. Horace, *Ep.*, 1.3, §14–20.
52. Seneca the Elder, *Cont.*, 1.6.
53. Idem, *Suasoriae*, 3.7.

'Longinus' (ca. First Century BCE to First Century CE)

The date for 'Longinus's' *On the Sublime* is still a matter of debate, so I situate it here in the first half of the first century CE while recognizing that some scholars date it a century in either direction. Herein, the author, in reference to Plato, speaks of *mimesis* as a path to sublimity.

Referring to Plato:

> Here is an author who shows us, if we will condescend to see, that there is another road, besides those we have mentioned, which leads to sublimity. What and what manner of road is this? Imitation and emulation of the great prose writers and poets of the past [τῶν ἔμπροσθεν μεγάλων συγγραφέων καὶ ποιητῶν μίμησις τε καὶ ζήλωσις]. That is the aim, dear friend; let us hold to it with all our might. For many are carried away by the inspiration of another, just as the story runs that the Pythian priestess on approaching the tripod where there is, they say, a rift in the earth, exhaling divine vapor, thereby becomes impregnated with the divine power and is at once inspired to utter oracles, so, too, from the natural genius of those old writers there flows into the hearts of their admirers as it were an emanation from those holy mouths. Inspired by this, even those who are not easily moved to prophecy share the enthusiasm of these others' grandeur. Was Herodotus alone Homeric in the highest degree? No, there was Stesichorus at a still earlier date and Archilochus too, and above all others Plato, who drew off for his own use ten thousand runnels from the great Homeric spring. We might need to give instances, had not people like Ammonius drawn up a collection.[54] Such borrowing is no theft; it is rather like the reproduction of good character by sculptures or other works of art. So many of these qualities would never have flourished among Plato's philosophic tenets, nor would he have entered so often into the subjects and language of poetry, had he not striven, with heart and soul, to contest the prize with Homer, like a young antagonist with one who had already won his spurs, perhaps in too keen emulation, longing as it were to break a lance, and yet always to good purpose; for, as Hesiod says, "Good is this strife for mankind." Fair indeed is the crown, and the fight for fame well worth the winning, where even to be worsted by our forerunners is not without glory.

---

54. Stesichorus (ca. 600–550 BCE) was a Greek lyric poet (*OCD*, 1442), Archilochus (ca. 650 BCE) was an elegiac and iambic poet (*OCD*, 145) and Ammonius (second century BCE) wrote, in addition to his work on Plato's imitations of Homer, a commentary on Homer (*OCD*, 74).

We too, then, when we are working at some passage that demands sublimity of thought and expression, should do well to form in our hearts the question: "How might Homer have said this same thing, how would Plato or Demosthenes or Thucydides have made it sublime?" Emulation [ζῆλον] will bring those great characters before our eyes, and their shining presence will lead our thoughts to the ideal standards of perfection. Still more will this be so, if we also try to imagine to ourselves: "How would Homer or Demosthenes, had either been present, have listened to this passage of mine? How would that passage have affected them?" Great indeed is the ordeal if we suppose such a jury and audience as this to listen to our own utterances and make believe that we are submitting our work to the scrutiny of such heroes as witnesses and judges. Even more stimulating would it be to add, "If I write this, how would all posterity receive it?" But if a man shrinks at the very thought of saying anything that is going to outlast his own life and time, then must all the conceptions of that man's mind be like some blind, half-formed embryo, all too abortive for the life of post-humous fame.[55]

Seneca the Younger (4–65 CE)

Seneca the Younger, in his Epistle 84, acknowledges that reading is indispensable but that continuous reading alone will "make our strength flabby and watery;" similarly, continuous writing "will cast a gloom over our strength and exhaust it." Thus he recommends alternating between the two, which he terms "study," so that the fruits of one's reading may be reduced to concrete form by the pen." To explain how this works, he adopts the metaphor of the bees—"who flit about and cull the flowers that are suitable for producing honey, and then arrange and assort in their cells all that they have brought in." Though he explains that it is uncertain how the honey is actually formed from the bees collecting, sifting, and storing (arranging) activities, the end result is that we have this "delicious object." So it is, he suggests, with our reading and writing—that "we ought to copy these bees," by sifting whatever we have gathered from our reading, "so blend those several flavors into one delicious compound," not concern ourselves with diverse origin, but revel in the "clearly different thing from that whence it came." Whether he is adopting Horace's view of "making it your own" or whether this concept was merely common practice that Seneca was following, he recommends that

---

55. 'Longinus,' *Subl.*, 209–15.

"whatever we have absorbed should not be allowed to remain unchanged, or it will be no part of us. We must digest it; otherwise it will merely enter the memory and not the reasoning power." This, he claims, is what the mind should do, "it should hide away all the materials by which it has been aided, and bring to light only what it has made of them." Anticipating criticism of such use of others' materials, he responds:

> "What," you say, "will it not be seen whose style you are imitating, whose method of reasoning, whose pungent sayings?" I think that sometimes it is impossible for it to be seen who is being imitated, if the copy is a true one; for a true copy stamps its own form upon all the features which it has drawn from what we may call the original, in such a way that they are combined into a unity.[56]

In *Epistle 79*, the younger Seneca encourages the letter's recipient not to be hesitant to revisit a topic that has already been covered thoroughly by others:

> Nay, what am I to offer you not merely to describe Aetna in your poem, and not to touch lightly upon a topic that is a matter of ritual for all poets? Ovid could not be prevented from using this theme simply because Virgil had already fully covered it; nor could either of these writers frighten off Cornelius Severus. Besides, the topic has served them all with happy results, and those who have gone before seem to me not to have forestalled all that could be said, but merely to have opened the way. It makes a great deal of difference whether you approach a subject that has been exhausted, or one where the ground has merely been broken; in the latter case, the topic grows day by day, and what is already discovered does not hinder new discoveries. Besides, he who writes last has the best of the bargain; he finds already at hand words which, when marshalled in a different way, show a new face. And he is not pilfering them, as if they belonged to someone else, when he uses them, for they are common property.[57]

Quintilian (35–100 CE)

Quintilian writes more about imitation (imitatio) than any of his predecessors (at least for texts that are extant). For Quintilian, imitation plays a

56. Lucius Annaeus Seneca, *Epistles*, Epistle 84.
57. Ibid., *Epistle 79*.

principal role in a child's education from very early on, as he recommends that the child's nurse should "speak correctly" because it is the nurse whom "the child first hears, and her words that he will first attempt to imitate [imitando]."[58] As soon as the child begins his studies, the teacher's first responsibility is to determine that student's ability and character. He specifies two indicators; the first is the power of memory and the second is imitation, "for this [imitation] is a sign that the child is teachable: but he must imitate merely what he is taught, and must not, for example, mimic someone's gait or bearing or defects. For I have no hope that a child will turn out well who loves imitation merely for the purpose of raising a laugh."[59] As the child progresses and begins submitting written exercises for the teacher's assessment, Quintilian suggests that the teachers should not be too harsh in correcting his faults, but perhaps himself alter the student's composition while explaining the reasons for the alterations, and, on occasion, even dictating whole themes to the student so that he may "imitate them and, for the time being, love them as if they were his own."[60]

When Quintilian gets to book 10 of his *Institutes*, he makes very clear that he is no longer considering "primary training," but presumes that students have learned how to conceive their subject and select and arrange their words, proceeding now to make the best use of the acquired knowledge. Echoing Dionysius of Halicarnassus, Quintilian proclaims that students' resources are "a copious supply of matter and words" [copia rerum ac verborum] and that these will be attained by "reading and listening to the best writers and orators," for, he claims, "in everything that we teach examples [exempla] are more effective even than the rules that are taught in the schools, so long as the student has reached a state when he can appreciate such examples without the assistance of a teacher, and can rely on his own powers to imitate them."[61]

It is within this context of the value of examples that Quintilian emphasizes the importance of careful reading, as one cannot imitate well if he has not read his source material very carefully:

> Reading, however, is free, and does not hurry past us with the speed of oral delivery; we can reread a passage again and again if we are in doubt about it or wish to fix it in the memory. We must return to what we have read and reconsider it with care, while, just as we do not swallow our food till we have chewed

---

58. Quintilian, *Inst.* 1.1.5. All quotations will be taken from this Loeb edition.
59. Ibid., 1.3.1.
60. Ibid., 2.4.12.
61. Ibid., 10.1.5.

APPENDIX 1: ANCIENT GRECO-ROMAN AUTHORS ON Μίμησις/IMITATIO   273

it and reduced it almost to a state of liquefaction to assist the process of digestion, so what we read must not be committed to the memory and imitation [imitationique] while it is still in a crude state, but must be softened and, if I may use the phrase, reduced to a pulp by frequent re-perusal.⁶²

Quintilian continues that this reading must be thorough—"as if we were actually transcribing what we read; nor must we study it merely in parts, but must read through the whole work from cover to cover and then read it afresh."⁶³

Quintilian's emphasis on the importance of reading segues into his discussion of whom students should read and imitate. This long discussion from 10.1.27–10.1.130 of models (60 pages in the Loeb edition) is a who's who of ancient Greek and Latin poets, historians, rhetors, and orators.⁶⁴ Homer, who has "given us a model and inspiration for every department of eloquence" heads the list, as his "similes, amplifications, examples, digressions, indications of fact, inferences, and all the other methods of proof and refutation [and arrangement] which he employs" . . . "are so numerous that the majority of writers on the principles of rhetoric have gone to his works for examples of all these things."⁶⁵ In his discussion of the Greek lyric poets, he identifies Pindar as one whom Horace hailed as "imitable [imitabilem],"⁶⁶ and, discussing the Greek tragedians, he notes that Menander (a Greek, new comedy poet) testifies in his works that he "had a profound admiration for Euripides, and imitated him, although in a different type of work." ⁶⁷ Herodotus and Thucydides possess qualities worth imitating, along with Philistus who "was an imitator of Thucydides."⁶⁸ Plato, Xenophon, Aristotle, and Theophrastus are next, and Quintilian notes that Cicero "acknowledges

---

62. Ibid., 10.1.15.

63. Ibid., 10.1.20.

64. It is unfortunate that Murphy's *Quintilian on the Teaching of Speaking and Writing* omits this material. Murphy explains, "Here begins a lengthy discussion of particular orators and writers. Since these figures would be virtually unknown to modern readers, his comments on them are omitted here" (131 n. 8). While one can understand Murphy's (or the editor's) decision to omit this lengthy discussion, readers whose only familiarity with Quintilian is this text miss out on the tremendous importance Quintilian attributes to reading, imitating, and emulating such a wide range of poets, historians, rhetors, and orators.

65. Quintilian, *Inst.* 10.1.49–50.

66. Ibid., 10.1.61.

67. Ibid., 10.1.69.

68. Ibid., 10.1.74.

that he derived such a large portion of his eloquence" from them.[69] Roman authors follow, and, as Virgil ranks second only to Homer, he must be carefully studied, as must Lucan (poet, first century CE), though he is "more suitable for imitation [imitandus] by the orator than by the poet."[70] For the Roman historians, Quintilian unhesitatingly equates Sallust's (86–35 BCE) compositional qualities with Thucydides's and Livy's (59 BCE–17 CE) with Herodotus's, both of whom are worthy of study.[71] Cicero heads the list of Roman orators, as "the name of Cicero has come to be regarded not as the name of a man, but as the name of eloquence itself. Let us, therefore, fix our eyes on him, take him as our pattern [exemplum], and let the student realize that he has made real progress if he is a passionate admirer of Cicero."[72] The first century-CE orator Cassius Severus, "if read with discrimination, will provide much that is worthy of imitation [dabit imitation digna]."[73] Other "consummate advocates of the present day are serious rivals of the ancients, while enthusiastic effort and lofty ideals lead many a young student to tread in their footsteps and imitate [imitatur] their excellence,"[74] except, perhaps, for Seneca, "as the young men loved him rather than imitated him . . . as he "pleased them for his faults alone, and each individual sought to imitate such of those faults as lay within his capacity to reproduce."[75] Quintilian concludes his discussion of models of imitation with what seems to be a theoretical perspective grounded in nature, which I cite in its entirety:

> It is from these and other authors worthy of our study that we must draw our stock of words, the variety of our figures, and our methods of composition, while we must form our minds on the model [exemplum] of every excellence. For there can be no doubt that in art no small portion of our task lies in imitation [imitation]. . . . it is expedient to imitate whatever has been invented with success. And it is a universal rule of life that we should wish to copy what we approve in others. It is for this reason that boys copy the shapes of letters that they may learn to write, and that musicians take the voices of their teachers, painters the works of their predecessors, and peasants the principles of agriculture which have been proved in practice, as models for their imitation. In fact, we may note that the elementary study

69. Ibid., 10.1.81.
70. Ibid., 10.1.91.
71. Ibid., 10.1.101–4.
72. Ibid., 10.1.112.
73. Ibid., 10.1.116.
74. Ibid., 10.1.122.
75. Ibid., 10.1.127.

of every branch of learning is directed by reference to some definite standard that is placed before the learner. We must, in fact, either be like or unlike those who have proved their excellence. It is rare for nature to produce such resemblance, which is more often the result of imitation [imitation].[76]

Having provided numerous Greek and Roman poets, historians, philosophers, and rhetors/orators who could serve as models for students to imitate, Quintilian moves on to explain that "imitation alone is not sufficient—if only for the reason that a sluggish nature is only too ready to rest content with the inventions of others."[77] In even stronger language, he adds that "it is a positive disgrace to be content to owe all our achievement to imitation," ... "for the man whose aim is to prove himself better than another, even if he does not surpass him, may hope to equal him. But he can never hope to equal him, if he thinks it is his duty merely to tread in his footsteps; for the mere follower must always lag behind."[78] Thus, Quintilian offers four crucial points. The first is the importance of considering whom to imitate, as "many" have imitated the "worst and most decadent of authors" and exaggerate the blemishes of those they copy rather than improve on the good.[79] The second is, for Quintilian, closely related to the first—that the student must know "what it is that he is to imitate, and know why it is good."[80] The third is that, although there may be authors' qualities and practices worthy of imitation, each individual student needs to "consult his own powers," as there are some things "that may be beyond the capacity of any given individual," as Quintilian recognizes that not even the ideal "teacher will waste his labor in attempting to develop qualities to the attainment of which he perceives nature's gifts to be opposed."[81] That imitation should not be confined merely to words is Quintilian's fourth point. In addition to words themselves, the student must consider how well the speaker handles circumstances and persons involved in cases, how well the material is arranged, and how well the speaker is focused upon securing victory.[82]

After lengthy consideration of whom, what, and why to imitate, Quintilian moves on to discuss means of imitating, which begins with the pen, "which brings the most labor and the most profit." Writing will be essential

76. Ibid., 10.2.1–3.
77. Ibid., 10.2.4.
78. Ibid., 10.2.7–10.
79. Ibid., 10.2.14–15.
80. Ibid., 10.2.18.
81. Ibid., 10.2.19–21.
82. Ibid., 10.2.27.

for two important exercises: translation and paraphrase. Translation of Greek into Latin is first, as the "purpose for this exercise is obvious. For Greek authors are conspicuous for the variety of their matter [rerum copia], and there is much art in all their eloquence, while, when we translate them, we are at liberty to use the best words available."[83] Paraphrasing from the Latin is also "of much assistance" and is especially valuable in respect to literature (poetry) for two reasons. First, a paraphrase should not be the bare

> interpretation of the original: its duty is rather to rival and vie [certamen atque aemulationem] with the original in the expression of the same thoughts .... For it is always possible that we may discover expressions that are an improvement on those which have already been used, and nature did not make eloquence such a poor and starveling thing that there should be only one adequate expression for any one theme.[84]

Second, paraphrase challenges the student, as

> The exercise is valuable in virtue of its difficulty; and again, there is no better way of acquiring a thorough understanding of the greatest authors. For, instead of hurriedly running a careless eye over their writings, we handle each separate phrase and are forced to give it close examination, and we come to realize the greatness of their excellence from the very fact that we cannot imitate them [quod imitari non possumus].[85]

Pliny the Younger (61–112 CE)

Pliny the Younger shares his sentiments concerning a method of study with Fuscus in *Epistle 9*.

> It is a very advantageous practice (and what many recommend) to translate either from Greek into Latin or from Latin into Greek. By this sort of exercise, one acquires noble and proper expressions, variety of figures, and a forcible turn of exposition. Besides, to imitate [imitation] the most approved authors, gives one aptitude to invent after their manner, and, at the same time, things that you might have overlooked in reading cannot escape you in translating and improve your judgment.
>
> It may not be amiss when you have read only so much of an author at once, as to carry in your head his subject and

---

83. Ibid., 10.5.3.
84. Ibid., 10.5.5.
85. Ibid., 10.5.8.

argument, to turn, as it were, his rival, and write something on the same topic; then compare your performance to his, and minutely examine in what points either you or he most happily succeeded. It will be a matter of very pleasing congratulation to yourself if you shall find that in some things you have the advantage of him, as it will be a great mortification if he should rise above you in all.

You may sometimes venture to pick out and try to emulate the most shining passages of an author. Such a context is, indeed, something bold; but as it passes in secret, it can be taxed with presumption. Not but that we see many persons enter this sort of list with great applause, and because they do not despair of themselves, advance before those whom they thought it sufficient to follow.[86]

Martial (40–102 CE)

Martial, an older contemporary of Pliny, accuses two writers of plagiarizing his works:

> To your charge, I entrust, Quintianus, my works—if, after all, I can call those mine which that poet of yours recites. If they complain of their grievous servitude, come forward as their champion and give bail for them; and when that fellow calls himself their owner, say that they are mine, sent forth from my hand. If thrice and four times you shout this, you will shame the plagiarist [plagiario].[87]
>
> There is one page of yours, Fidentinus, in a book of mine—a page, too, stamped by the distinct likeness of its master—which convicts your poems of palpable theft. So, when set among them, a Lingonian cowled cloak defiles with greasy wool the violent-purple robes of town; so crocks from Arretium degrade crystal glass; so a black raven, perchance wandering on Cayster's banks, is laughed at among Leda's swans; so, when a sacred grove is afire with the varied tones of the Athenian nightingale, an impudent jay jars on those Attic notes of woe. My books need no title or judge to prove them; your page stares you in the face, and calls, 'You are a thief" ['Fur es.'].[88]

---

86. Pliny, "To Fuscus," 23.
87. Martial, *Epig.* 1.52.
88. Ibid., 1.53.

Theon (First to Fifth Century CE)

The *Progymnasmata* attributed to a Theon (yet to be identified) is dated anywhere from the first century BCE to the fifth century CE,[89] so consideration of it is included here because its content could possibly reflect composition exercises dating to a period contemporary with the composition of the gospels and Acts. Theon's *Progymnasmata* is replete with instructions to students to rely upon examples from the ancients.

> Anagnosis (reading aloud) . . . is the nourishment of style; for we imitate [μιμησόμεθα] most beautifully when our mind has been stamped with beautiful examples [παραδείγματα]. And who would not take pleasure in *akroasis* (hearing a work read aloud), readily taking in what has been created by the toil of others? But just as it is no help to those wanting to paint to look at the works of Apelles and Protogenes and Atniphilus unless they themselves put their hand to painting, so neither the words of older writers nor the multitude of their thoughts nor their purity of language nor harmonious composition nor urbanity of sound, nor in a word, any of the beauties in rhetoric, are useful to those who are going to engage in rhetoric unless each student exercises himself every day in writing.
>
> Despite what some say or have thought, paraphrase (παράφρασις) is not without utility. The argument of opponents is that once something has been well said it cannot be done a second time but those who say this are far from hitting on what is right. Thought is not moved by any one thing in only one way so as to express the idea (φαντασία) that has occurred to it in a similar form, but it is stirred in a number of different ways, and sometimes we are making a declaration, sometimes asking a question, sometimes making an inquiry, sometimes beseeching, and sometimes expressing our thought in some other way. There is nothing to prevent what is imagined from being expressed equally well in all these ways. There is evidence of this in paraphrase by a poet of his own thoughts elsewhere or paraphrase by another poet and in the orators and historian, and, in brief, all ancient writers seem to have used paraphrase in the best possible way, rephrasing not only their own writing but those of each other.[90]

---

89. George Kennedy adopts scholars' consensus for an earlier dating (*Progymnasmata*, 1), whereas Malcolm Heath makes a compelling argument for a fifth century date ("Theon and the History of the Progymnasmata").

90. Kennedy, *Progymnasmata*, 5–6.

APPENDIX 1: ANCIENT GRECO-ROMAN AUTHORS ON Μίμησις/IMITATIO 279

Theon then provides numerous examples as to how later authors paraphrased earlier authors before noting,

> Indeed, Philistus [fourth century BCE historian] in his history of Sicily borrowed almost the whole account of the war with Athens from Thucydides, and Demosthenese in his speech *Against Meidias* borrowed from speeches about wanton violence by Lysias and Lycurgus and passages from Issaeus's speeches against the violence of Diocles. You may also find in Isocrates's *Panegyricus* some things from Lysias's *Epitaphius* and *Olympicus*.[91]

In section 2, "On the Education of the Young," Theon states that the "teacher should collect good examples of each exercise from ancient prose works and assign them to the young to be learned by heart," and specifies a passage from Plato's *Republic* as an example of *chreia*, examples of *fable* from Herodotus, Philistus, and Xenophon. He continues instructing his would be instructors that the "best examples" of mythical narration are to be found in selections of Plato's works, of factual narration from Herodotus and Thucydides, and so it goes for each of the following exercises to be considered, before he summarizes:

> These things are, as it were, the foundation of every kind of discourse, and depending on how one instills them in the mind of the young, necessarily the results make themselves felt in the same way later. Thus, in addition to what has been said, the teacher himself must compose some especially fine refutations and confirmations and assign them to the young to retell, in order that, molded by what they have learned, they may be able to imitate.[92]

In section 13, "Reading Aloud," Theon admonishes his charges, "Do not imitate only one model but all the most famous of the ancients. Thus we shall have copious, numerous, and varied resources on which to draw. It is wrong to limit imitation to a single author; those who imitate only Demosthenes become stiff, tiresome, and obscure, and those who want to imitate only Lysias are thin, weak, and clumsy."[93]

Without associating paraphrase as a kind of *mimesis* as does Dionysius of Halicarnassus, Theon writes that it "consists of changing the form of expression while keeping the thoughts; it is also called *metaphrase*, and he identifies four kinds: syntactical (vaguely explained as retaining the same

---

91. Ibid., 7.
92. Ibid., 13.
93. Ibid., 68.

words but transposing the parts), adding words to the original, subtracting words, and a combination of all three.[94]

Lucian (ca. 120–180 CE)

The last writer to be considered is the second century CE rhetor and satirist, Lucian. Of the seventy works attributed to him that are extant, only two will be considered here.

The first is his *A Professor of Public Speaking*, a satire on what he deems to be the current fad in public speaking and the current training required to become a rhetor. Lucian, in responding to an unnamed boy's request for advice on how to become a public speaker (ῥήτωρ), describes two roads to becoming a successful speaker. One he describes as a "rough road, or a steep and sweaty one," "toilsome, and, as a rule, hopeless," whereas the other is like a "leisurely stroll through flowery fields and perfect shade in great comfort and luxury," via a "sloping bridle-path that is very short as well as very pleasant."[95] If the young man were to follow this second path, his guide would be a "handsome gentleman with a mincing gait," a "honeyed voice," who "distils perfume," and carefully dresses his hair. The most important thing that the student must bring along this path is ignorance, followed by recklessness, effrontery, and shamelessness. "Modesty, respectability, self-restraint, and blushes may be left at home, as they are useless."[96] This guide will inform the student to emulate everything he does (ζῆλου πάντα) and not to be concerned he (the student) has not

> gone through all the rites of initiation preliminary to rhetoric, through which the usual course of elementary instruction guides the steps of the senseless and silly at the cost of great weariness. No, go straight in, ... and you will not fare any the worse for that, even if you are quite in the prevailing fashion and do not know how to write, for rhetors are beyond that![97]

In sharp contrast, the other path—the path Lucian pursued himself, foolishly believing that "blessings were engendered by toil"—is "narrow, briery, and rough, promising great thirstiness and sweat."[98] The guide for this path is a "vigorous man with hard muscles and a manly stride," who has a heavy tan, is "bold-eyed and alert." This burly guide will exhort the student to follow in the footsteps of Plato, Demosthenes, and other ancients, and "he

---

94. Ibid., 70.
95. Lucian, 4. *Professor of Public Speaking*, §3, in *Lucian*.
96. Ibid., §3–16.
97. Ibid., §14.
98. Ibid., §7.

will tell you to emulate [ζηλοῦν] those ancient worthies, and will set you fusty models [παραδείγματα] for your speeches, far from easy to imitate [μιμεῖσθαι]."⁹⁹ Moreover, this "old fogey" will display "dead men of a bygone age to serve as patterns, and expect you to dig up long-buried speeches as if they were something tremendously helpful, wanting you to emulate the son of a sword-maker [Demosthenes], and some other fellow, the son of a schoolmaster named Atrometus [Aeschines]."¹⁰⁰

Lucian's *How to Write History* is, perhaps, most often cited to reflect his insistence that the historian's primary objective is to record the truth— "history cannot admit a lie, even a tiny one;"¹⁰¹ "history has one task and one end, what is useful, and that comes from truth alone,"¹⁰² but he also offers a few comments on how contemporary historians misused imitation. For example, in the first part of his narrative, he provides specific examples of what, in his view, historians should not do. One of these is Crepereius Calpurnianus, a "keen emulator [ζηλωτὴς ἄκρος] of Thucydides." Lucian complains that Crepereius modeled himself "closely upon his original, [and] like him began with his own name." Lucian then reads from the first line of Crepereius's text, and Table 44 reflects how slavishly Crepereius imitated Thucydides's first line from his *Peloponnesian War*.

Table 44: Lucian's critique of Crepereius's imitation of Thucydides

Κρεπέρηος Καλπουρνιανὸς Πομπηϊυπολίτης συνέγραψε τὸν πόλεμον τῶν Παρθυαίων καὶ Ῥωμαίων, ὡς ἐπολέμησαν πρὸς ἀλλήλους, ἀρξάμενος εὐθὺς συνισταμένου.	Θουκυδίδης Ἀθηναῖος ξυνέγραψε τὸν πόλεμον τῶν Πελοποννησίων καὶ Ἀθηναίων, ὡς ἐπολέμησαν πρὸς ἀλλήλους, ἀρξάμενος εὐθὺς καθισταμένου . . .
Crepereis Calpurnianus of Pompeiopolis wrote the history of the war between the Parthians and the Romans beginning at its very outset.	Thucydides of Athens wrote the history of the war between Athens and Sparta, beginning at its very outset . . .

Lucian continues that Crepereius also incorporated a speech (from *Peloponnesian War* 1.32) into his narrative and that he also inserted a plaque (from 2.47 – 54) almost in its entirety upon the people of Nisbis that, historically, never befell them, and that he also lifted several phrases and other narratives before Lucian quit reading his work as he knew "just what he

---

99. Ibid., §9.
100. Ibid., §10.
101. Lucian, *How to Write History*, in *Lucian*, vol. 6, trans. K. Kilburn, §7.
102. Ibid., §9. See also, "the historian's sole task is to tell the tale as it happened" (§39); the historian "does not welcome fiction but is leaving to posterity the true account of what happened" (§42), and "what historians have to relate is fact" (§50).

was going to say after I had gone." To his dismay, Lucian notes that such imitation and writing is "quite a fashion just now, to suppose that you're following Thucydides's style if you reproduce, with some small alterations, his own expressions."[103] Yet, while criticizing this kind of imitation and after completing his criticism of contemporary historians, Lucian "maintain[s] then that the best writer of history comes ready equipped with these two supreme qualities: political understanding and power of expression [δύναμιν ἑρμηνευτικήν]; the former is an unteachable gift of nature, while the power of expression may come through a great deal of practice, continual toil, and emulation of the ancients [ζήλῳ τῶν ἀρχαίων]."[104] Lucian does not anywhere in the *History* explain what he means by either imitation or emulation, but, that he criticizes one form of it earlier but recommends it here suggests that there is a form of imitation or emulation to be learned that is essential for the aspiring historian.

103. Ibid., §15.
104. Ibid., §31.

Appendix 2

Galatians 2:7–9 as a Later, Post-Pauline Interpolation

Prolegomena

IN HIS "GALATIANS 2:7B-8 as a Non-Pauline Interpolation," William O. Walker, Jr., sets out to examine two competing hypotheses for explaining the problems within Galatians 2:7-8, the *protocol* hypothesis and the *interpolation* hypothesis. After concisely presenting arguments for and against the *protocol* position—that Πέτρος occurs in Galatians 2:7-8 instead of Κηφᾶς because "Paul is [therein] citing, directly or indirectly, some official or quasi-official record or 'protocol' of the division of labor worked out between himself and 'pillar' apostles' when they met in Jerusalem (2:1-10; cf. also Acts 15:1-35)"—Walker rejects the explanation as "unpersuasive."[1] Turning to the *interpolation* hypothesis—that Galatians 2:7b-8 is "a later, non-Pauline insertion"—Walker offers a summary of its advocates' argumentation, focusing primarily upon Ernst Barnikol's understanding that the interpolation in Galatians 2:7b-8 consists of the following: "for the uncircumcised, just as Peter had been entrusted with the gospel for the circumcised (for he who worked through Peter making him an apostle to the circumcised also worked through me in sending me to the Gentiles," τῆς ἀκροβυστίας καθὼς Πέτρος τῆς περιτομῆς. ὁ γὰρ ἐνεργήσας Πέτρῳ εἰς ἀποστολὴν τῆς περιτομῆς ἐνήργησεν καὶ ἐμοὶ εἰς τὰ ἔθνη). He then identifies six problems within Galatians 2:7b-8 as they relate to this interpolation hypothesis—the name Πέτρος instead of Κηφᾶς, the peculiar construction with ἐνεργεῖν, the distinction between Peter and Paul, the treatment of apostleship, and understanding Galatians 2:7b-8 within its immediate context—before concluding that the *interpolation* hypothesis is less problematic than the *protocol* hypothesis and that the "seeming awkwardness of the 'fit' between Gal 2:7b-8 and its immediate context

---

1. Walker, "Galatians 2:7b-8," 569 and 571.

suggests that this material was composed by someone other than Paul and somewhat arbitrarily inserted at its present location."[2]

While Barnikol's argumentation, further explained and supplemented by Walker, is compelling, I will argue that the proposed interpolation, ending at 2:8, does not go far enough, but that it should also include all of 2:9. Lines of argumentation to support this claim will include 1) brief consideration of the Κηφᾶς/Πέτρος problem; 2) that the text of Galatians 2:6–10 is more syntactically coherent if it excludes vv. 7b, 8, and 9; 3) "James, Kephas, and John" in v. 9 is a problem—that the "pillars" acknowledging the "grace that was given" to Paul and their extending a "right hand of fellowship" to Paul is inconsistent with Paul's view of his own apostleship and would eliminate any need for Acts' revisions of Galatians 2 and for any later anti-Pauline literature; and 4) incorporating and adapting David Trobisch's work on the New Testament canon, the "James and Kephas and John" in v. 9 and then v. 9 as a whole should be understood as a rhetorical/literary device that would indicate to the readers of the first edition of the New Testament that Paul's letters should be understood as in harmony with James's, Peter's, and John's letters that precede Paul's in an early edition of the New Testament.

Coherence of 2:6–10

Galatians 2:6–10 is widely recognized by grammarians as an anacoluthon—"a sentence by which a construction started at the beginning is not followed out consistently."[3] Verse 6 is a mess: "And from those who were supposed to be acknowledged leaders (what they actually were makes no difference to me; God shows no partiality)—those leaders contributed nothing to me" (ἀπὸ τῶν δοκούντων εἶναί τι—ὁποῖοί ποτε ἦσαν οὐδέν μοι διαφέρει πρόσωπον ὁ θεὸς ἀνθρώπου οὐ λαμβάνει—ἐμοὶ γὰρ οἱ δοκοῦντες οὐδὲν προσανέθεντο). It opens (6a) with what appears to be some kind of prepositional phrase construction (ἀπὸ) that is incomplete (literally—"from those who appear to be somebody"), then shifts to what appears to be (6b) a parenthetical (and invective) thought—ὁποῖοί ποτε ἦσαν οὐδέν μοι διαφέρει πρόσωπον ὁ θεὸς ἀνθρώπου οὐ λαμβάνει—("What sort they once were makes no difference to me; God does not choose from man's appearance") before beginning a new γὰρ (explanatory) clause (6c), ἐμοὶ γὰρ οἱ δοκοῦντες οὐδὲν προσανέθεντο ("for those of reputation added nothing to me") that is syntactically disconnected from 6a and that does not explain anything, that precedes or follows it (as γὰρ clauses do). Blass and Debrunner suggest that the author of Gala-

2. Ibid., 585.
3. Smyth, *Greek Grammar*, 671.

tians 2:6 "has either forgotten the opening clause, or deemed it convenient to replace it with a new form."[4] A.T. Robertson is more reverential of Paul's thinking process: "A more complicated kind of anacoluthon is where a digression is caused by an intervening sentence or explanatory clause. Those naturally occur mainly in the epistles of Paul where his energy of thought and passion of soul overlap all trammels."[5] A better explanation seems to be that v. 6 reflects the tension between Paul and "those who appear to be somebody" who are also to be understood as "those of reputation" in 2:2 who may have had a role in compelling Titus to be circumcised and "those of reputation who added nothing to me" in 6c. This view suggests that the syntactical awkwardness of v. 6 is due, not to Paul's "energy of thought and passion of soul," but to a later catholic editor deleting what may have been "angry and fierce" remarks by Paul against the Jerusalem leaders while still trying to retain much of the original sense of what Paul may have written.[6] If either a portion, or all, of 2:7–9 is an interpolation by a later catholic editor who is attempting to mend fences, then it is not unreasonable to think that said editor might also try to gloss over harsh language, though done so imperfectly in v. 6, while retaining 6c, which, in this editor's mind, could serve as a reasonable segue to vv. 7–9. Moreover, the best explanation for the many difficulties, both syntactic and interpretive, may be that, because of the problems Galatians 2 (especially 2:6–10 and 2:11–14) raised within early Christianity,[7] the reworking of the passage by a later editor (or editors?) resulted in the messy state that we now find it.

If vv. 7–9 are eliminated, vv. 6c and 10 read very coherently—"for those of reputation added nothing to me, only that we remember the poor, something I also make every effort to do." The meaning that begins in 6c that "they added nothing to me" is coherently completed in v. 10, "only that we remember the poor." It is this and only this, at least by Paul's account here, that was added to his gospel. In sharp contrast, if only 7b–8 is eliminated, then we read, "for those of reputation added nothing to me, *but to the contrary* [ἀλλὰ τοὐναντίον] ... they gave the right hand of fellowship to me and Barnabas ... we to the Gentiles ... only that we should remember the poor." The added material (7a–8) torturously interrupts what seems to be the clearer meaning that avails itself when 7a–9 is omitted. Rather than the contrast expressed between "they added nothing ... only that [μόνον ... ἵνα] we remember the poor," the stronger contrast

---

4. BDF, 245.
5. Robertson, *Grammar*, 437.
6. See Detering, *Original Version of the Epistle to the Galatians*, 31–32.
7. See the discussion in chapter 6.

ἀλλὰ τοὐναντίον is now between "they added nothing, but to the contrary [ἀλλὰ τοὐναντίον], they gave to me and Barnabas the right hand of fellowship" and then the "only that we remember the poor" is awkwardly tacked on—no longer the primary contrast it is with 6c, but seemingly linked to "we [go] to the Gentiles" of v. 9. It is worth noting here that, while the ἀλλὰ τοὐναντίον construction is common in ancient Greek, this is the only occurrence of this construction within the canonical New Testament texts. Here, in Galatians 2:7, its use seriously interrupts the syntax and meaning of 6c and 10. That is, ἀλλὰ τοὐναντίον denotes a sharp contrast. For example, in *Against Apion*, Josephus is discussing different points of view about the meaning of the word "Hyksos" (Υκσώς) where one text contends that it denotes "kings" but "in another it is said that this word does not denote 'kings' but, on the contrary [ἀλλὰ τοὐναντίον] denotes 'captive shepherds.'"[8] Similarly, in his *First Letter to Ammaeus* (late first century BCE), Dionysius of Halicarnassus argues that Demosthenes did not learn his rhetorical skills from Aristotle's *Rhetoric*, "but, on the contrary [ἀλλὰ τοὐναντίον] Aristotle wrote his *Rhetoric* with reference to the works of Demosthenes."[9] In both cases, a sharp contrast or comparison of opposites is in view. Here in our passage, "Those of reputation added nothing to me, but, on the contrary [ἀλλὰ τοὐναντίον], . . . they gave the right hand of fellowship to me and Barnabas" can be understood to offer a contrast of sorts (questionable though whether it is a contrast of opposites), but the contrast devastatingly interrupts the coherence of 6c and 10, for there would then be no syntactical connection between "Those of reputation added nothing to me" of v. 6c and "only that we remember the poor" of v. 10. Instead, as noted above, "only that we remember the poor" in v. 10 now seems to be awkwardly appended to "in order that we [go] to the gentiles" in v. 9.

"James, Kephas, and John"

Other problems with considering 2:9 as part of the original text revolve around four related issues: the appearance of Κηφᾶς instead of Πέτρος; the appearance of "James, Kephas and John;" James, Kephas, and John recognizing that a divine favor (γνόντες τὴν χάριν τὴν δοθεῖσάν μοι) had been bestowed upon Paul; and that James, Kephas, and John gave Paul and Barnabas the "right hand of fellowship" (δεξιὰς ἔδωκεν ἐμοὶ καὶ βαρναβᾷ κοινωνίας).

---

8. Josephus, *Against Apion* in *Works*, 1.83. Greek text from *TLG*.
9. Dionysius of Halicarnassus, *Dem.* 345.

Κηφᾶς/Πέτρος

As noted in chapter 6, the occurrence of the different names Κηφᾶς and Πέτρος in Gal 1 and 2, especially 2:7–14, has generated considerable scholarly discussion. One of the strongest lines of evidence to support Barnikol's/Walker's argumentation that 2:7b–8 is a later, non-Pauline interpolation is that only the name Πέτρος occurs in the manuscript history of Galatians 2:7–8 and because there was "no Latin or Greek rendering of the Aramaic title of honor" when Paul was writing in the mid 50's, Paul would have only have known Κηφᾶς (as in 1 Corinthians 1:12; 3:22; 9:5; and 15:5, if the latter is not an interpolation[10]), which leads to Barnikol's conclusion that Πέτρος "could not have been written by Paul."[11] It seems safe to suggest, though, that one of the reasons, if not the primary reason, why Galatians 2:9 has not received consideration as continuing the interpolation of 2:7b–8 is because, unlike 2:7b–8, both Κηφᾶς and Πέτρος are attested in the manuscript history and in every passage in Galatians where both names are attested editors have adopted Κηφᾶς. However, consideration of the fuller context of 2:6c–9 demonstrates that there are still serious ideational conflicts (Walker's fourth criterion for identifying interpolations[12]) in 2:9, that are similar to those in 2:7b–8, that are not resolved if the interpolation is limited to 2:7b–8.

"James, Kephas, and John"

The occurrence of "James, Kephas [Peter], and John" here seems very odd. While scholars are somewhat confident as to who Kephas (or Peter) is and about as confident that the James referred to here is Jesus's brother and the (traditional) leader of the Jerusalem church to whom Paul makes reference in Gal 1:19 and 2:11–14, there are more questions about who the John mentioned here might be. Unlike references to a Kephas and James in those letters thought to be written by Paul, he makes no reference to anyone named John. Despite this, Raymond Collins represents what may be the prevailing

---

10. It is often claimed that Paul would have only written Κηφᾶς, and, thus, if Κηφᾶς is the editor's preferred reading in passages where Πέτρος is also attested, then it is likely that Paul wrote that passage. However, if 1 Cor 15:3–11 is an interpolation as Robert Price has argued in "Apocryphal Apparitions," then the possibility exists that the interpolator(s) could have written Κηφᾶς, as it occurs in 15:5, just as easily as Paul himself.

11. Barnikol, "Non-Pauline Origin," 290.

12. Walker writes, "Ideational evidence for interpolation would be data suggesting that significant features of the substantive content of a passage are not characteristically Pauline or, in some cases, perhaps that they are even anti-Pauline" (*Interpolations*, 82).

view that the John referred to in Galatians 2:7–9 would be the John of the "James and John (the sons of Zebedee)" who are frequently mentioned in the synoptic gospels and early in Acts. Collins notes that while this John has no role at the so-called Jerusalem Council, "Nonetheless, in what appears to be a reference to those events, Paul (Gal 2:9–10) mentions John, along with James (the brother of the Lord) and Cephas as one of the "pillars" of the community of Christians in Jerusalem."[13] In the synoptic gospels, the three disciples "Peter, James, and John" (the latter two as the sons of Zebedee) appear together several times as Jesus's closest followers—as the earliest followers of Jesus (Mark 1:19, Matt 3:13, and Luke 5:1–11), witnessing Jesus resurrect Jairus's daughter (Mark 5:21–43 and Luke 8:49–56), at the transfiguration (Mark 9:2–13, Matt 17: 1–13, and Luke (9:28–36), and with Jesus while he prayed in Gethsemane (Mark 14: 32–42, Matt 26:36–46, and Luke 22:39–46). But, in Acts, while this disciple John initially accompanies Peter in evangelistic endeavors, his notoriety wanes after he and Peter return from Samaria (8:41), and the last reference to him is when Herod Agrippa beheads James, "the brother of John," in 12:2. As noted above, this John is not mentioned in the so-called Jerusalem Council in Acts 15. Thus, while this John was a companion, disciple, and then early apostle of Jesus, the narrative in Acts grants him no authoritative role in the early church that would lead readers to think that he was one of the "pillars" mentioned in Gal 2: 9.

The only other likely John mentioned in the New Testament who could possibly be recognized by Paul as a "pillar" would be the John of Acts who is surnamed Mark. This John is abruptly introduced in Acts 12 when, after miraculously being released from prison, Peter flees to a Mary's home, who is further identified as the "mother of John, surnamed Mark" (Μαρίας τῆς μητρὸς Ἰωάννου τοῦ ἐπικαλουμένου Μάρκου, 12:12). This John Mark (or John, 13:13) accompanies Paul and Barnabas from Jerusalem to Antioch (12:25), serves as their assistant in Cyrpus (13:5), accompanies them to Pamphylia, but then departs from them there and returns to Jerusalem, and after the Jerusalem Council, Barnabas wanted to include him on his and Paul's next journey, but Paul adamantly refused because John Mark abandoned them earlier in Pamphylia (15:37). This disagreement led to the split between Paul and Barnabas, after which Barnabas took Mark with him to Cyprus, and, other than a reference to him in 1 Peter 5:3, this is the last that we hear of a John Mark in the New Testament, unless one aligns him with the Mark mentioned in Col (4:10), Philem (24), and 2 Tim (4:11) as does Clayton Jefford.[14] But, because the author of Acts grants this John no au-

13. Collins, "John (Disciple)," in *ABD*, 3:885.
14. Nefford, "Mark, John," in *ABD*, 4:557–58.

thoritative role and even has Paul reject this John Mark, it seems extremely unlikely that Paul would then consider him to be a *pillar* of the Jerusalem community.

This problem with identifying this John aside for the moment, these three, James, Kephas, and John, are referred to as "pillars" (στῦλοι), which is the only occurrence of this word in those letters thought to be written by Paul; yet it occurs in later Christian literature in reference to Peter and other apostles (*1 Clem* 5:2) and in reference to the church (1 Tim 3:15).[15] That these "pillars" in Jerusalem "realized" (γνόντες) that Paul, who advocated against continuing traditional Jewish practices and customs, was granted any kind of divine favor (τὴν χάριν τὴν δοθεῖσάν μοι) is incomprehensible, especially if, as Betz suggests, in "the context of the letter, 'grace' [χάριν] is the content of the Pauline message of the gospel"[16]—just as incomprehensible as the claim in 2:7 that Paul would agree to or authorize two gospels, one to the Jews through Peter and one to the Gentiles through Paul. Much the same can be said for these Jerusalem "pillars" granting Paul the "right hand of fellowship." While the practice of extending the "right hand" (δεξιάς) as a peaceful gesture is common in the Maccabean and other Jewish literature,[17] the idea that the Jerusalem "pillars" would make peace with Paul, within the same context within which Paul is condemning Jewish practices and their influence upon his gospel, is not only inconceivable, but it would perfectly eliminate the need for the author of Acts to recast Paul and Galatians 1 and 2 and the later anti-Pauline literature that emerged after this purported peace-making event, as the problems would have been resolved.

How then is the appearance of "James and Kephas and John" in 2:9 to be explained? Incorporating material from David Trobisch, I suggest that a later catholic editor (or editors) added 2:9, if not 2:7b–9, in an attempt to present Paul as aligned with the "pillars" who are also the (alleged) authors of the Catholic/General epistles, which epistles, interestingly, are arranged in the earliest codices in the same order that we find here in Galatians 2:9—James, Peter, and John.

---

15. In *1 Clement*, the author writes, "Because of jealousy and envy the greatest and most righteous pillars [στῦλοι] were persecuted and fought to the death" (5:2, in Holmes, ed., *Apostolic Fathers*). Holmes allows that the traditional date for the composition *1 Clement* (ca. 95–98 CE) is "possible," but also adds the possibility that it could be "during the last two decades of the first century" (36). In 1 Timothy, the author writes that the church of the living God is "the pillar [στῦλος] and bulwark of the truth" (3:15).

16. Betz, *Galatians*, 99.

17. 1 Macc 6:58; 11:50, 62, 66; 13:45; 13:50; 2 Macc 4:35; 11:26, 30; 12:11, 12; 13:22; 14:19.

James, Peter, and John as Rhetorical/Literary Device

In *Paul's Letter Collection: Tracing the Origins,* Trobisch provides compelling argumentation that Paul edited Romans, 1 and 2 Corinthians, and Galatians as a "literary contribution" to his ongoing conflict with Peter and James. He argues that Romans 16 serves as the cover letter for this, the first edited collection of Paul's letters,[18] and equates "those who stir up quarrels and lead others astray, contrary to the teaching you received" (16:17) and the "unbelievers in Judea" (15:3–32) with Paul's opponents in 1 Corinthians 9, the "super apostles" in 2 Corinthians 11, and those of the circumcision party in Galatians—James, Kephas (or Petros), and John. Trobisch seems to understand Galatians 2:9 as evidence that these "pillars" had at one time granted Paul the "right hand of fellowship" but subsequently reneged on their agreement,[19] a point that I question below. In his "Postscript," he concludes, "It is this conflict between Paul and the Jerusalem authorities that pushed Paul to publish four of his letters," and seemingly looking ahead to his *The First Edition of the New Testament*, he adds, "it is this conflict that later editors may have had in mind when they prepared a collection of Christian writings for publication, a collection that came to be known as the New Testament."[20]

True to form, in *The First Edition of the New Testament* (2000),[21] Trobisch argues that the consistent use of *nomina sacra*, the "four collection units," the consistent number of texts, and the titles of the books in the New Testament indicate an "overall editorial concept." The *nomina sacra* (sacred names) are contracted terms in the earliest Greek codices whereby the words will be reduced to an abbreviated form with a horizontal line over the top of the letters, such as θεός is represented by θς, χριστός by χς, and πνεῦμα by πνα, each with a horizontal line over the letters. The "four collection units" are, according to Trobisch, the gospels (Matthew, Mark, Luke, and John), the Praxapostolos (Acts, James, 1 and 2 Peter, 1, 2, and 3 John, and Jude), all the letters attributed to Paul, and Revelation, and each of these units is present and usually arranged in the same way (Gospels, Praxapostolos, Paul, Revelation) in the earliest codices. As for the titles of the books, for the gospels, each name is preceded by Κατὰ (Κατὰ Μαθθαῖον, Κατὰ Μᾶρκον, Κατὰ Λουκᾶν, Κατὰ Ἰωάννην); the Praxapostolos includes Acts and then each of the Catholic/General epistles by its alleged/forged author's

---

18. Trobisch, *Paul's Letter Collection*. Trobisch suggests that later editions that included more of Paul's (and non-Pauline) letters were produced after his death (50).

19. Ibid., 87–95.

20. Ibid., 97.

21. Trobisch, *First Edition*.

APPENDIX 2: GALATIANS 2:7–9 AS A LATER, POST-PAULINE INTERPOLATION 291

name—James, 1 and 2 Peter, 1, 2, and 3 John, and Jude), whereas for the Pauline collection, each letter is titled by its recipient (Πρὸς Ῥωμαίους, Πρὸς Κορινθίους ά, Πρὸς Τίτον). This uniform structure suggests to Trobisch an "overall editorial concept,"[22] whereby the editors were "trying to unify the dissimilar material. As these collectors selected a certain number of writings, then edited and arranged them, they had a deliberate redactional strategy in mind," among other things, to harmonize the conflict between Peter and Paul.[23] According to Trobisch, these editors accomplished this harmonization by arranging Paul's letters "side by side" his opponents' (James's, Peter's, and John's) letters, as Paul's unit of letters would follow, in the codices, the Catholic/General Epistles, suggesting to the readers of the document (what became our New Testament) that all of these alleged authors were of one mind and even collaborated in a unified effort. Trobisch notices that "Galatians contradicts this image"—that the editors' redaction "suggests that the clashing parties had reconciled later, an interpretation that is not reconciled by the text of Galatians."[24] In this later work, Trobisch does not restate his earlier view expressed in *Paul's Letter Collection* that the Jerusalem "pillars" made peace with Paul (via extending the "right hand of fellowship") but then later reneged, and neither does he say anything about the possibility that any portion of Galatians 2:6–10 could be an interpolation.

What I suggest is that perhaps, in the process of collecting and editing the texts for their "Canonical Edition" (as Trobisch refers to this text), the editors, in keeping with their "overall editorial concept," added either Galatians 2:7b–9 or just 2:9 ("and knowing the grace that was given to me, James, and Kephas and John—those recognized to be pillars—gave to me and Barnabas [the] right hand of partnership in order that we [might go] to the gentiles, but they to the circumcised") in an attempt to recast the conflict between Paul and the Jerusalem "pillars" from opposition to harmonization and collaboration. What could be a more compelling way to revise this controversy than to have Paul himself state that these "pillars" recognized Paul's divine favor and extended to him the right hand of fellowship? That this could be the case may be further supported by the fact that the "James and Kephas and John" of Galatians 2:9 is also the order that the letters attributed to these three "pillars" appear in the Praxapostolos (James, 1 and 2 Peter, 1, 2, and 3 John), which preceded Paul's letters in the codices, and that these three (except perhaps for John as noted above) were also depicted as playing significant roles in the early church as presented by the author

22. Ibid., 41.
23. Ibid., 43.
24. Ibid., 46.

of Acts, a work that precedes their respective letters in the Praxapostolos. The editors are not only reconciling Paul with the Jerusalem pillars by having the latter extend to Paul the "right hand of fellowship," something that seems historically inconceivable, but also by associating Paul's contentious letter with theirs, suggesting to the readers of this unified collection of texts, that "Paul and the Jerusalem apostles finally made peace and collaborated."[25] One other editorial addition within this "Canonical Edition" may further support the claim that the editors of this now unified text are attempting to harmonize the controversy between Peter and Paul, as they craft a forged letter attributed to Peter himself in which they have Peter vouche for the integrity of Paul and his letters:

> Bear in mind that our Lord's patience is an opportunity for salvation, as Paul, our dear friend and brother, said when he wrote to you with the wisdom God gave him. He does the same in all his other letters, wherever he speaks about this, though they contain some obscure passages, which the ignorant and unstable misinterpret to their own ruin, as they do the other scriptures. (2 Pet 3:15–16)

Without identifying an editor or editors, Trobisch suggests that the editing of the "Canonical Edition" could have taken place by someone with ties to both Rome and Asia Minor and that, similar to Barnikol and Walker, it "reflects an anti-Marcionite attitude."[26] Then, in his 2008 "Who Published the New Testament?," Trobisch takes the "bold" step of identifying this editor as Polycarp of Smyrna, who had ties to both Asia Minor and Rome and who, according to Irenaeus, opposed Marcion to his face, calling him "the first-born of Satan,"[27] and he narrows the date range for the editorial work of the "Canonical Edition" to between 156–157.[28]

Trobisch's understanding that the editorial work of the "Canonical Edition" was a reaction to Marcionism and dated to the middle to latter half of the second century coincides with Barnikol's and Walker's views of the work of the catholic interpolator in response to Marcion in the second century prior to Irenaeus's *Against Heresies* (ca. 180), which is a date not too far removed from the chronologically first occurrence of Πέτρος in Galatians 2:9 in the manuscript history (P46, ca. late second to early third century). Trobisch offers a slightly narrower window and a possible specific person responsible for the editorial and/or interpolation effort, but, even if

25. Ibid., 61.
26. Ibid., 102.
27. Irenaeus, *Against Heresies* 3.3 (416).
28. Trobisch, "Who Published the New Testament?"

his suggested editor is questionable, it is especially his explanation of the "editorial concept" that links the editing of the previously independent texts into a unified whole that provides a reasonable context for understanding Galatians 2:7–9 as a catholic interpolation (either by one editor or an earlier and then later editor) into an earlier edition of Galatians.

I mentioned above that, in Acts, John was not present at the so-called Jerusalem Council. It is difficult to understand why the author of Acts would not have included him at this meeting if he used an edition of Galatians 2 that included v. 9 as his source for Acts 15. A possible explanation is this: Because the edition of Galatians that the author of Acts used as his source did not include 2:9, the author of Acts used Paul's references to his meetings with Peter (1:18) and James (1:19) as his source for depicting only these two as the leaders of the Jerusalem community. John was not, at the time that Paul wrote, a leader within the community or (alleged) author of several canonical works, and this could explain why Paul never refers to John in his letters (excepting Gal 2:9) and why the author of Acts did not include John in the proceedings of the so-called Jerusalem Council. Between the time that Paul wrote Galatians (ca. mid-50s) and the author of Acts wrote Acts (ca. 110–130?), writings attributed to this John became important texts to the author of Acts and the editor(s) of the "Canonical Edition." This "John" needed authority, credibility—ἦθος. The editor of the "Canonical Edition" develops this ἦθος by situating the texts attributed to Matthew, Mark, and Luke (wherein John is identified as a disciple of Jesus) before the gospel attributed to John and by situating this gospel attributed to John just before Acts. The author of Acts, who may or may not be the same person as the editor of the "Canonical Edition," portrays this same John as not only a disciple, but also as collaborating with Peter in healing a beggar (3:1–11), engaging the Jewish leaders and teachers in Jerusalem (4:5–22), and by evangelizing Samaria (8:14–25). Thus, once Acts is written, circulated, and included in the "Canonical Edition," John is established as a leading figure within the earliest development of what would become Christianity. Reading from this "Editorial Concept" perspective, it is only at this time, after Acts was written and circulating, that John could have been recognized as one of the Jerusalem "pillars," which is also about the same time that we find other occurrences of στῦλοι in Christian literature. It would have been at this time, after John would have been recognized as a "pillar" and author of texts within the "Canonical Edition," that an editor (or editors) would have inserted either 2:7b–8 or 2:7–9 into Galatians.

Conclusion

Could Barnikol's and Walker's interpolator(s) be Trobisch's editor(s) of his "Canonical Edition"? The evidence presented above makes a compelling case for an affirmative response. Reading 2:6c and 2:10 without 2:7–9 offers a much more syntactically coherent sentence; if "James and Kephas and John" in 2:9 would have "realized the grace that was given to" Paul and then extended to him the "right hand of fellowship," there would have been no need for much of Acts and the anti-Pauline literature that developed in the second century and beyond, including Acts. The evidence seems to suggest that it is better to understand that the "James and Kephas and John" passage in 2:9 individually or 2:7b–9 as a whole were added to Galatians after Acts was written in order to align Paul with those three "pillars" as they are depicted in Acts and as an attempt to harmonize Paul and his conflict with the Jerusalem pillars and the letters attributed to them that preceded Paul's in an early edition of the New Testament.

Bibliography

1 Enoch. Translated by E. Isaac. In *The Old Testament Pseudepigrapha,* edited by James H. Charlesworth, 1:5-90. Garden City, NY: Doubleday, 1983.
Ad Herennium. Translated by Harry Caplan. LCL. Cambridge, MA: Harvard University Press, 1989.
Adler-Goodfriend, Claire. "Adultery." In *ABD,* 2:82-86.
"Adultery." *Virtual Jewish Library,* Issues in Jewish Ethics. http://www.jewishvirtual library.org/adultery-2.
Alderink, L. J. "Baal Zebub." In *DDD,* 154-56.
Allison, Dale C. Jr. "Peter and Cephas: One and the Same." *JBL* 111/3 (1992) 489-95.
Anderson, R. Dean, Jr. *Glossary of Greek Rhetorical Terms Connected to Methods of Argumentation, Figures, and Tropes from Anaximenes to Quintilian.* Leuven: Peeters, 2000.
The Apostolic Fathers. Edited and translated by Michael W. Holmes. Grand Rapids: Baker Academic, 1999.
Atkins, J. W. H. *Literary Criticism in Antiquity: A Sketch of Its Development.* 2 vols. Gloucester, MA: Peter Smith, 1961.
Aune, David E., ed. *The Blackwell Companion to the New Testament.* Oxford: Wiley-Blackwell, 2010.
———. *The New Testament in Its Literary Environment.* Philadelphia: Westminster, 1989.
———. *The Westminster Dictionary of New Testament and Early Christian Literature and Rhetoric.* Louisville: John Knox, 2003.
Barnikol, Ernst. "The Non-Pauline Origin of the Parallelism of the Apostles Peter and Paul: Galatians 2:7-8." Translated by Darrell J. Doughty with B. Keith Brewer. *Journal of Higher Criticism* (Fall 1998) 285-300.
Barrett, C.K. "Acts and the Pauline Corpus." *ExpTim* 78/1 (1976) 2-5.
Barton, Stephen. *Discipleship and Family Ties in Mark and Matthew.* New York: Cambridge University Press, 1994.
Baur, F. C. *Paul, the Apostle of Jesus Christ: His Life and Work, His Epistles and His Doctrine.* Translated by A. Menzies. Edited by Eduard Zeller. 2 vols. London: Williams and Norgate, 1876.
———. *Paul the Apostle of Jesus Christ: His Life and Works, His Epistles and Teachings.* 2 vols. Peabody, MA: Hendrickson, 2003.
Beattie, D. R. G. *Jewish Exegesis of the Book of Ruth.* Sheffield: JSOT Press, 1977.
BeDuhn, Jason D. *The First New Testament: Marcion's Scriptural Canon.* Salem, OR: Polebridge, 2013.

Bellinzoni, Arthur J. "The Gospel of Luke in the Second Century CE." In *Literary Studies in Luke-Acts: Essays in Honor of Joseph B. Tyson*, edited by Richard P. Thompson and Thomas E. Phillips, 59–76. Macon, GA: Mercer University Press, 1998.

———. "The Gospel of Matthew in the Second Century." *Second Century* 9/4 (1992) 197–258.

Bertram, Georg. "Θαῦμα." In *TDNT*, 3:27–42.

Best, E. "Mark III.20–21, 31–35." *NTS* 22/3 (1976) 309–19.

Betz, Hans Dieter Betz. *Galatians: A Commentary on Paul's Letter to the Churches in Galatia*. 4th printing. Philadelphia: Fortress, [1979] 1988.

Black, C. Clifton. *The Rhetoric of the Gospel: Theological Artistry in the Gospels and Acts*. St. Louis: Chalice, 2001.

Bonner, Stanley F. *Education in Ancient Rome: From the Elder Cato to the Younger Pliny*. Berkeley: University of California Press, 1977.

———. *The Literary Treatises of Dionysius of Halicarnassus: A Study in the Development of Critical Method*. Cambridge: Cambridge University Press, 1939.

Bonz, Marianne. *The Past as Legacy: Luke-Acts and Ancient Epic*. Minneapolis: Fortress, 2000.

Borg, Marcus J., and John Dominic Crossan. *The First Christmas: What the Gospels Really Teach about Jesus's Birth*. New York: HarperOne, 2009.

Bovon, François. *Luke*. Vol. 1: *A Commentary on the Gospel of Luke 1:1—9:50*. Translated by Christine M. Thomas. Hermeneia. Minneapolis: Fortress, 2002.

Brodie, Thomas L. *The Birthing of the New Testament: The Intertextual Development of the New Testament Writings*. Sheffield: Sheffield Phoenix, 2004.

———. "Greco-Roman Imitation of Texts as a Partial Guide to Luke's Use of Sources." In *Luke-Acts: New Perspectives*, edited by C. H. Talbert, 17–46. New York: Crossroads, 1983.

Brown, Francis, S. R. Driver, and Charles A. Briggs. *The Brown-Driver-Briggs Hebrew and English Lexicon*. Peabody, MA: Hendrickson, [1906] 2008.

Brown, Raymond. *The Birth of the Messiah*. New York: Doubleday, [1997] 1999.

Brown, Raymond, Karl P. Donfried, Joseph A. Fitzmyer, and John Reumann, eds. *Mary in the New Testament*. New York: Paulist, 1978.

Burridge, Richard. "Gospels and Acts." In *Handbook of Classical Rhetoric in the Hellenistic Period, 330 B.C.–A.D. 400*, edited by Stanley F. Porter, 507–32. New York: Brill, 1997.

Burrows, Eric. *The Gospel of the Infancy and Other Biblical Essays*. London: Burn, Oates & Washbourne, 1940.

Cadbury, Henry. *The Making of Luke-Acts*. Peabody, MA: Hendrickson, [1927] 1999.

Campbell, Edward F., Jr. *Ruth: A New Translation with Introduction, Notes, and Commentary*. Anchor Bible 7. Garden City, NY: Doubleday, 1975.

Carlson, Stephen. "The Accommodations of Joseph and Mary." *NTS* 56/3 (2010) 326–42.

———. "Overview of Proposed Solutions." http://www.hypotposeis.org/synoptic-problem/2004/09/overview-of-proposed-solutions.html.

Casey, P. M. "In Which Language Did Jesus Teach?" *ExpTim* 108/11 (1997) 326–28.

Catto, Stephen K. *Reconstructing the First-Century Synagogue: A Critical Analysis of Current Research*. London: T. & T. Clark, 2007.

Charlesworth, James H., ed. *The Old Testament Pseudepigrapha*. 2 vols. New York: Doubleday, 1985.

Chartrand-Burke, Tony. Review of *The Birthing of the New Testament: The Intertextual Development of the New Testament Writings*. *CBQ* 68 (2006) 756–58.
Cicero. *Brutus, Orator*. Translated by G. L. Hendrickson. LCL. Cambridge, MA: Harvard University Press, 1939.
———. *De Finibus*. Translated by H. Rackham. LCL. Cambridge, MA: Harvard University Press, 1931.
———. *De Inventione*. Translated by H.M. Hubbell. LCL. Cambridge, MA: Harvard University Press, 1991.
———. *De Oratore*. Translated by E.W. Sutton and H. Rackham. 2 vols. LCL. Cambridge, MA: Harvard University Press, 1996.
Clabeaux, Jason. "Marcion." In *ABD*, 4:514–16.
Clark, Donald L. *Rhetoric in Greco-Roman Education*. Morningside Heights, NY: Columbia University Press, 1957.
Conway, Robert Seymour. "Vergil as a Student of Homer." *Martin Classical Lectures* 1 (1930) 151–81.
Conzelmann, Hans. *1 Corinthians: A Commentary on the First Epistle to the Corinthians*. Translated by James W. Leitch. Edited by George W. MacRae. Hermeneia. Philadelphia: Fortress, [1975] 1981.
Cousar, Charles B. "Jerusalem, Council of." In *ABD*, 3:766–68.
Creed, John Martin. *The Gospel According to St. Luke*. London: Macmillan, 1965.
Cribiore, Rafaella. *Gymnastics of the Mind: Greek Education in Hellenistic and Roman Egypt*. Princeton, NJ: Princeton University Press, 2001.
———. *Writing, Teachers, and Students in Graeco-Roman Education*. Morningside Heights, NY: Columbia University Press, 1996.
Crossan, John Dominic. "Mark and the Relatives of Jesus." *NovT* 15 (1973) 81–113.
D'Alton, J. F. *Roman Literary Theory and Criticism: A Study in Tendencies*. New York: Russell & Russell, 1962.
Daly-Denton, Margaret. Review of *The Birthing of the New Testament: The Intertextual Development of the New Testament Writings*. *Review of Biblical Literature*, August 12, 2006.
Damm, Adam. *Ancient Rhetoric and the Synoptic Problem: Clarifying Markan Priority*. Leuven: Peeters, 2013.
Davidson, Richard M. "Divorce and Remarriage in the Old Testament: A Fresh Look at Deut. 24: 1–4." *Journal of the Adventist Theological Society* 10/1–2 (1999) 2–22.
Davies, W. D., and D. C. Allison. *The Gospel According to Saint Matthew*. Vol 1. London: T. & T. Clark, [1988] 2009.
'Demetrius.' *On Style*. Translated by Doreen C. Innes. LCL. Cambridge, MA: Harvard University Press, 1995.
Derrenbacker, R. A., Jr. *Ancient Compositional Practices and the Synoptic Problem*. Leuven: Leuven University Press, 2005.
Detering, Hermann. *The Original Version of the Epistle to the Galatians: Explanations*. Translated by Frans-Joris Fabri. http://radikalkritik.de/DetGalExpl.pdf.
Dewey, Arthur. "The Family of Jesus: Family Feud or 'Dynasty Two'?" *Forum* (new series) 21 (1999) 81.
Dewey, Arthur, Roy W. Hoover, Lane C. McGaughy, and Daryl D. Schmidt, trans. *The Authentic Letters of Paul: A New Reading of Paul's Rhetoric and Meaning*. Salem, OR: Polebridge, 2010.

Dionysius of Halicarnassus. *Critical Essays.* Translated by Stephen Usher. 2 vols. LCL. Cambridge, MA: Harvard University Press, 1974.

Diogenes Laertius. *Lives of the Eminent Philosophers.* Translated by R. D. Hicks. 2 vols. LCL. Cambridge, MA: Harvard University Press, 1925.

Dionysius Halicarnassus. *On Imitation.* Edited by H. Usener and L. Radermacher. Stuttgart, Germany, [1899] 1965.

Dodds, E. R., trans. *Gorgias: A Revised Text with Introduction and Commentary.* Oxford: Clarendon, 1990.

Donahue, John R., and Daniel J. Harrington. *The Gospel of Mark.* Sacra pagina 2. Collegeville, MN: Liturgical, 2002.

Donatus, Aelius. *Life of Virgil.* Translated by David Scott Wilson-Okamura. 2008. http://virgil.org/vitae/.

Doulamis, Konstantin, ed. *Echoing Narratives: Studies of Intertextuality in Greek and Roman Prose Fiction.* Groningen: Barkhuis, 2001.

Downing, F. G. "Compositional Conventions and the Synoptic Problem." *JBL* 107/1 (1988) 69–85.

———. *Doing Things with Words in the First Christian Century.* London: T. & T. Clark, 2004.

———. "Markan Intercalation in Cultural Context." In *Narrativity in Biblical and Related Texts*, edited by G. J. Brooke and J. D. Kaestli, 105–18. Leuven: Leuven University Press, 2000.

Drury, John. *Tradition and Design in Luke's Gospel: A Study in Early Christian Historiography.* London: Longman and Todd, 1976.

Durousseau, Clifford H. "Isaiah 7:14B in New Major Christian Bible Translations." *Jewish Biblical Quarterly* 41/3 (2013) 175–80.

Edwards, James E. "Markan Sandwiches: The Significance of Interpolations in Markan Narratives." *NovT* 31/3 (1989) 192–216.

Ehrman, Bart D. *Forged: Writing in the Name of God: Why the Bible's Authors Are Not Who We Think They Are.* San Francisco: HarperOne, 2012.

———. *The New Testament: A Historical Introduction to the Early Christian Writings.* New York: Oxford University Press, 2004.

———. "Cephas and Peter." *JBL* 109/3 (1990) 463–74.

Elliott, J. K. "Κηφᾶς; Σίμων Πέτρος; ὁ Πέτρος: An Examination of New Testament Usage." *NovT* 14/4 (1972) 241–56.

Enslin, Morton S. "Luke and Paul." *Journal of the American Oriental Society* 53/1 (1938) 81–91.

———. "Once Again, Luke and Paul." *Zeitschrift FürDie Neutestamentlich Wissenschaft* 61 (1970) 253–71.

Finkelstein, Israel, and Neil Asher Silberman. *The Bible Unearthed: Archaeology's New Vision of Ancient Israel and the Origin of Its Sacred Text.* New York: Simon and Schuster, 2002.

Fiske, George Converse. *Lucillius and Horace: A Study in the Classical Theory of Imitation.* University of Wisconsin Studies in Language and Literature 7. Madison: University of Wisconsin, 1920.

Fitzmyer, Joseph A. *The Gospel According to Luke (I–IX).* Garden City, NY: Doubleday, 1983.

Flusser, David. *Jesus.* Jerusalem: Magnes Press, Hebrew University, [1997], 1998.

Forbes, Christopher. "Comparison, Self-Praise, and Irony: Paul's Boasting and the Conventions of Hellenistic Rhetoric." *NTS* 32 (1986) 1–30.
Fowler, Don P., and Peta G. Fowler. "Virgil." In *OCD*, 1605.
Franklin, Eric. *Luke: Interpreter of Paul, Critic of Matthew*. Sheffield: Sheffield Academic, 1994.
Freed, Edwin D. *The Stories of Jesus' Birth: A Critical Introduction*. St. Louis: Chalice, 2001.
Friedman, Richard E. *Who Wrote the Bible?* New York: Harper Collins, [1987] 1997.
Fronda, Michael P. "Imitation (*mimesis, imitatio*)." In *The Encyclopedia of Ancient History*, edited by Roger S. Barnall, Kai Brodersen, Craige B. Champion, Andrew Erskine, and Sabine R. Huebner, 3416–17. Malden, MA: Blackwell, 2013. http://onlinelibrary.wiley.com/doi/10.1002/9781444338386.wbeah08087/pdf.
Gasque, W. Ward. "Iconium." In *ABD*, 3:357–58.
———. "Perga." In *ABD*, 5:228.
———. "Pisidian Antioch." In *ABD*, 5:374–75.
Gazda, Elain E., and Diana Y. Ng, eds. *Building a New Rome: The Imperial Colony of Pisidian Antioch (25 BC–AD 700)*. Kelsey Museum Publication 5. Ann Arbor, MI: Kelsey Museum of Archaeology, 2011.
Ginzberg, Louis. *The Legends of the Jews*. 6 vols. Philadelphia: Jewish Publication Society of America, 1982.
Goodacre, Mark. *The Case Against Q: Studies in Markan Priority and the Synoptic Problem*. Harrisburg, PA: Trinity, 2002.
———. *The Synoptic Problem: A Way through the Maze*. London: Continuum, 2001.
Goodfriend, Elaine Adler. "Adultery." In *ABD*, 1:82–86.
Goulder, M. D. *Luke: A New Paradigm*. Sheffield: Sheffield Phoenix, [1989] 1994.
———. *Paul and the Competing Mission in Corinth*. Peabody, MA: Hendrickson Publishers, 2001.
———. *St. Paul versus St. Peter: A Tale of Two Missions*. Louisville: Westminster John Knox, 1994.
———. "Those Outside (Mk. 4:10–12)." *NovT* 33/4 (1991) 289–302.
Goulder, M. D., and Murray Sanderson. "St. Luke's Genesis." *Journal of Theological Studies* 8/1 (1957) 12–20.
Green, H.B. "The Credibility of Luke's Transformation of Matthew." In *Synoptic Studies: The Ampleforth Conferences of 1982 and 1982*, edited by C. M. Tuckett. Sheffield: JSNT, 1984.
Gundry, Robert H. *Mark: A Commentary on His Apology for the Cross*. Grand Rapids: Eerdmans, 1993.
Haenchen, Ernst. *The Acts of the Apostles: A Commentary*. Translated by Bernard Noble and Gerald Shinn. Philadelphia: Fortress, [1945] 1971.
Hall, Robert G. "Circumcision." In *ABD*, 1:1025–31.
Hardie, Philip. "Epic." In *OCD*, 530.
Harnack, Alfred. *Luke the Physician*. Translated by J. R. Wilkinson. London: Williams & Norgate, [1908] 1911.
Harrill, J. A. "The Dramatic Function of the Running Slave Rhoda (Acts 12:13–16): A Piece of Greco-Roman Comedy." *NTS* 46/1 (2000) 155–57.
Heath, Malcolm. "Theon and the History of the *Progymnasmata*." *GRBS* 43 (2002–2003) 129–60.

Heinze, Richard. *Virgil's Epic Technique*. Translated by Hazel and David Harvey and Fred Robertson. Berkeley: University of California Press, 1993.

Hohlfelder, Robert L. "Caesarea." In *ABD*, 1:798–803.

Homer. *Odyssey*. Translated by A. T. Murray and George E. Dimock. 2 vols. LCL. Cambridge, MA: Harvard University Press, 1998.

Hoppe, Leslie L. "Seleucia." In *ABD*, 5:1075–76.

Horace. *Satires, Epistles, and Ars Poetica*. Translated by H. Rushton. LCL. Cambridge, MA: Harvard University Press, 1991.

Hubbard, Robert L. *The Book of Ruth*. NICOT. Grand Rapids: Eerdmans, 1988.

Hunter, Richard. *Plato and the Traditions of Ancient Literature: The Silent Stream*. Cambridge: Cambridge University Press, 2012.

Ilan, Tal. "'Man Morn of Woman . . .' (Job 14:1): The Phenomenon of Men Bearing Metronymes at the Time of Jesus." *NovT* 34/1 (1992) 23–45.

Ingram, Helen. *Was Jesus a Magician?: Extracts from 'Driving Down Heaven: Jesus as Magician and a Manipulator of Spirits in the Gospels'*. Blog. Institute for Advanced Technology in the Humanities. http://wasjesusamagician.blogspot.com/.

Institute for Advanced Technology in the Humanities. University of Virginia. http://www.iath.virginia.edu.

"Interpolation." In *Westiminister Dictionary of New Testament and Early Christian Literature and Rhetoric*, edited by David E. Aune, 232–34.

Irenaeus. *Against Heresies*. Translated by Frederick Crombie. In *ANF*, vol. 4. Peabody, MA: Hendrickson, 1994.

———. *Against the Heresies*. Translated by Dominic J. Unger. New York: Newman, 1992.

Jackson-McCabe, Matt, ed. *Jewish Christianity Reconsidered: Rethinking Ancient Groups and Texts*. Minneapolis: Fortress, 2007.

Jobes, Karen H., and Moises Silva. *Invitation to the Septuagint*. Grant Rapids: Baker Academic, 2000.

Johnson, Luke Timothy. "Luke-Acts, Book of." In *ABD*, 4:404–8.

Johnson, Marshal D. *The Purpose of the Biblical Genealogies: With Special Reference to the Setting of the Genealogies of Jesus*. 2nd ed. Eugene, OR: Wipf and Stock, 2002.

Josephus. *The Works of Josephus*. Translated by William Whiston. Peabody, MA: Hendrickson, [1987] 2007.

Just, Felix. "New Testament Statistics." http://catholic-resources.org/Bible/Nt-Statistics-Greek.htm.

Kennedy, George. *New Testament Interpretation through Rhetorical Criticism*. Chapel Hill: University of North Carolina, Press, 1984.

———. *Progymnasmata: Greek Textbooks of Prose Composition and Rhetoric*. Atlanta: SBL, 2003.

Knauer, G. N. *Die Aeneis und Homer: Studien zur poetischen tichnik Vergils mit Listen der Homerzitate in der Aenis*. Göttingen: Vandenhoeck & Ruprecht, [1964] 1979.

———. "Vergil and Homer." *Aufstieg und Niedergang der römischen Welt* 31/2 (1980) 871–914.

Knox, John. "Acts and the Pauline Letter Corpus." In *Studies in Luke-Acts*, edited by Leander E. Keck and J. Louis Martyn, 279–87. Philadelphia: Fortress, [1966] 1980.

———. *Chapters in the Life of Paul*. Macon, GA: Mercer University Press, 1987.

———. *Marcion and the New Testament: An Essay in the Early History of the Canon*. Chicago: University of Chicago Press, 1942.

Korpel, Marjo C. A. *The Structure of the Book of Ruth*. Koninklijke: Vangorcum, 2001.
Lachs, Samuel Tobia. *A Rabbinic Commentary on the New Testament: The Gospels of Matthew, Mark, and Luke*. Hoboken, NJ: KTAV, 1987.
Lake, Kirsopp. "The Proconsulship of Sergius Paulus." In *The Beginnings of Christianity, Part 1: The Acts of the Apostles*, edited by F. J. Foakes Jackson and Kirsopp Lake, 455–59. London: Macmillan, 1933.
———. "Simon, Cephas, Peter." *HTR* 14/1 (1921) 95–97.
Lambrecht, J. "The Relatives of Jesus." *NovT* 16 (1974) 241–58.
Lampe, Peter. "Can Words Be Violent or Do They Only Sound that Way?: Second Corinthians Verbal Warfare from Afar as a Complement to Placid Personal Presence." In *Paul and Rhetoric*, edited by J. Paul Sampley and Peter Lampe, 223–39. New York: Continuum, 2010.
Landry, David. "Luke's Revision of Matthew's Birth Narrative." In *Reading Ideologies: Essays on the Bible and Interpretation in Honor of Mary Ann Tolbert*, edited by Tat-siong Benny Liew, 45–75. Sheffield: Sheffield Phoenix, 2011.
La Piana, G. "Cephas and Peter in the Epistle to the Galatians." *HTR* 14/2 (1921) 187–93.
Law, Timothy Michael. *When God Spoke Greek: The Septuagint and the Making of the Christian Bible*. New York. Oxford University Press, 2013.
Leppä, Heikki. *Luke's Critical Use of Galatians*. Finland: Dark Oy, 2002.
Levine, Lee. *Jerusalem: Portrait of the City in the Second Temple Period (538 B.C.E–70 C.E)*. Philadelphia: Jewish Publication Society, 2002.
Lewis, Theodore. "Beelzebul." In *ABD*, 1:638–40.
Life of Adam and Eve. Translated by M. D. Johnson. In *The Old Testament Pseudepigrapha*, edited by James H. Charlesworth, 2:249–95. New York: Doubleday, 1985.
Lincoln, Andrew. *Born of a Virgin?: Reconceiving Jesus in the Bible, Tradition, and Theology*. Grand Rapids: Eerdmans, 2013.
Longenecker, Bruce W. "Lukan Aversion to Humps and Hollows: The Case of Acts 11:27—12:25." *NTS* 50/2 (2004) 185–204.
'Longinus.' *On the Sublime*. Translated by W. H. Fyfe. LCL. Cambridge, MA: Harvard University Press, 1995.
Loubser, J. A. "Invoking the Ancestors: Some Socio-Rhetorical Aspects of the Genealogies in the Gospels of Matthew and Luke." *Neotestamenica* 39 (2005) 127–40.
Lucian. *Lucian*. Translated by K. Kilburn. LCL. Cambridge, MA: Harvard University Press, 2006.
Lüdemann, Gerd. *The Acts of the Apostles: What Really Happened in the Earliest Days of the Church*. Amherst, NY: Prometheus, 2005.
———. *Jesus after Two thousand Years*. Amherst, NY: Prometheus, 2001.
———. *Opposition to Paul in Jewish Christianity*. Translated by M. Eugene Boring. Minneapolis: Fortress, 1989.
———. *Virgin Birth?: The Real Story of Mary and Her Son Jesus*. Harrisburg, PA: Trinity, 1998.
Luz, Ulrich. *Matthew: A Commentary*. Translated by James E. Crouch. 2 vols. Hermeneia. Minneapolis: Fortress, 2007.
MacDonald, Dennis R. *Does the New Testament Imitate Homer?: Four Cases from the Acts of the Apostles*. New Haven, CT: Yale University Press, 2003.

———. *The Homeric Epics and the Gospel of Mark*. New Haven, CT: Yale University Press, 2000.

———. *Luke and Vergil: Imitations of Classical Greek Literature*. Lanham, MD: Rowman & Littlefield, 2015.

———, ed. *Mimesis and Intertextuality in Antiquity and Christianity*. Harrisburg, PA: Trinity, 2001.

———. "My Turn." http://iac.cgu.edu.drm/My_Turn.pdf.

Macrobius. *The Saturnalia*. Translated by Percival Vaughan Davies. New York: Columbia University Press, 1969.

Malherbe, Abraham. *Ancient Epistolary Theorists*. Atlanta: Scholars, 1988.

———. "Through the Eye of the Needle: Simplicity or Singleness?" *Restoration Quarterly* 5/3 (1960) 119–29.

Martial, *Epigrams*. Translated by Walter C. A. Ker. 2 vols. LCL London: William Heinemann, 1930.

McArthur, Harvey K. "'Son of Mary.'" *NovT* 15 (1973) 38–58.

Meier, John P. *A Marginal Jew: Rethinking the Historical Jesus*. Vol. 1, *The Roots of the Problem and the Person*. New York: Doubleday, 1991.

Metzger, Bruce, ed. *The Oxford Annotated Apocrypha: The Apocrypha of the Old Testament*. New York: Oxford University Press, 1977.

Metzger, Bruce., ed. *A Textual Commentary on the Greek New Testament*. Stuttgart: United Bible Society, 1975.

"Mimesis/Imitation." In *Encyclopedia of Rhetoric*, edited by Thomas O. Sloane, 381–84. New York: Oxford University Press, 2006.

Mitchell, Margaret M. "Homer in the New Testament?: The Homeric Epics and the Gospel of Mark." *Journal of Religion* 83/2 (2004) 244–60.

Mitchell, Stephen. "Antioch of Pisidia." In *ABD*, 1:264–65.

———. "Galatia." In *ABD*, 2:870–72.

Mitchell, Steven, and Mark Waelkens. *Pisidian Antioch: The Site and Its Monuments*. London: Duckworth, 1998.

Moore, Clifford H. "Latin Exercises from a Greek Schoolroom." *Classical Philology* 194 (1924) 317–28.

Morgan, Teresa. *Literate Education in the Hellenistic and Roman Worlds*. Cambridge: Cambridge University Press, 2007.

Moule, C. F. D. *An Idiom Book of New Testament Greek*. Cambridge: Cambridge University Press, [1953] 1984.

Moyise, Steve. *Was the Birth of Jesus According to Scripture?* Eugene, OR: Cascade, 2013.

Murphy, James J. *Quintilian on the Teaching of Speaking and Writing: Translation from Books One, Two, and Ten of the "Institutio Oratoria"*. Carbondale: Southern Illinois University Press, 1987.

Nanos, Mark D., ed. *The Galatians Debate: Contemporary Issues in Rhetorical and Historical Interpretation*. Peabody, MA: Hendrickson, 2002.

Nestle, Eberhard, Erwin Nestle, Barbara Aland, Kurt Aland, Johannes Karavidopoulos, Carlo M. Martini, and Bruce M. Metzger, eds. *Novum Testamentum Graece*. 28th ed. Stuttgart: Deutsche Bibelgesellschaft, 2014.

Nichols, James H., Jr., trans. *Gorgias*. Ithaca, NY: Cornell University Press, 1998.

Nolland, John. "The Four (Five) Women and Other Annotations in Matthew's Genealogy." *NTS* 43 (1997) 527–39.

Oepke, Albrecht. "Ἐξίστημι." In *TDNT*, 2:458–59.

Oosterhuis, David K. "The 'Catalepton': Myths of Virgil." PhD diss., University of Minnesota, 2007.
Origen. *Against Celsus*. Translated by Frederick Crombie. In *ANF*, vol. 4. Peabody, MA: Hendrickson, 1995.
Painter, John. *Just James: The Brother of Jesus in History and Tradition*. Minneapolis: Fortress, 1999.
Palmer, Darryl W. Review of *The Past as Legacy: Luke-Acts and Ancient Epic. Australian Biblical Review* 51 (2003). http://www.fbs.org.au/reviews/bonz51.html.
Parsons, P. J. "Stesichorus." In *OCD*, 1442.
Pervo, Richard. *Acts: A Commentary*. Edited by Harold W. Attridge. Hermeneia. Minneapolis: Fortress, 2009.
———. *Dating Acts: Between the Evangelists and the Apologists*. Santa Rosa, CA: Polebridge, 2006.
———. "Flattery in Its Sincerest Manifestation." *The Fourth R* 22/5 (2009) 11–14, 28.
———. *The Gospel of Luke*. The Scholars Bible 4. Salem, OR: Polebridge, 2014.
———. "Speeches in Acts: A Cameo Essay." In *Acts and Christian Beginnings: The Acts Seminar Report*, edited by Dennis E. Smith and Joseph B. Tyson, 45–46. Salem, OR: Polebridge, 2013.
Philo of Alexandria. *Hypothetica: Apology for the Jews*. Early Christian Writings. Edited by Peter Kerby. http://www.earlychristianwritings.com/yonge/book37.html.
Pietersma, Albert, and Bengamin G. Wright, eds. *A New English Translation of the Septuagint and the Other Greek Translations Traditionally Included under That Title*. New York: Oxford University Press, 2007.
Plato. *The Apology*. Translated by Harold North Fowler. LCL. Cambridge, MA: Harvard University Press, 1990.
Pliny the Younger. *Letters*. Translated by William Melmoth. LCL. Cambridge, MA: Harvard University Press.
Plutarch. "A Letter to Appollonius." In *Moralia*, vol. 2. Translated by Frank Cole Babbitt. LCL. Cambridge, MA: Harvard University Press, 1998.
———. *The Life of Demosthenes*. Translated by Bernadotte Perrin. LCL. Cambridge, MA: Harvard University Press, 1919.
Porter, Stanley F. "Did Jesus Teach in Greek?" *TynBul* 44/2 (1993) 193–235.
———, ed. *Handbook of Classical Rhetoric in the Hellenistic Period, 330 B.C.–A.D. 400*. New York: Brill, 1997.
———. "Jesus and the Use of Greek: A Response to Maurice Casey." *Bulletin for Biblical Research* 10/1 (2000) 71–87.
———. "Joseph, Husband of Mary." In *ABD*, 3:974.
Porter, Stanley. and Bryan Dyer, eds. *The Synoptic Problem: Four Views*. Grand Rapids: Baker Academic, 2016.
Potter, D. S. "Lystra." In *ABD*, 4:426–27.
Price, Robert M. "Apocryphal Apparitions: 1 Corinthians 15:3–11 as a Post-Pauline Interpolation." *Journal of Higher Criticism* 2/2 (1995) 69–99.
———. *The Pre-Nicene New Testament: Fifty-Four Formative Texts*. Salt Lake City: Signature, 2006.
Quintilian. *Institutes*. Translated by H. E. Butler. LCL. London: Heinemann, 1992.
Rahlfs, Alfred, ed. *Septuaginta*. Stuttgart: Deutsche Bibelgesellschaft, 2006.
Rajak, Tessa. *Translation and Survival: The Greek Bible of the Ancient Jewish Diaspora*. New York: Oxford University Press, 2009.

Rochette, Bruno. "Greek and Latin Bilingualism." In *A Companion to the Ancient Greek Language*, edited by Egbeert J. Bakker, 281–94. Oxford: Blackwell.

Runesson, Anders, Donald D. Binder, and Birger Olsson. *The Ancient Synagogue from Its Origins to 200 C.E.: A Source Book*. Leiden: Brill, 2010.

Russell, Donald A. "De Imitatione." In *Creative Imitation and Latin Literature*, edited by David West and Tony Woodman, 1–16. Cambridge: Cambridge University Press, 1979.

———. "Demetrius." In *OCD*, 450.

Russell, D. A. and M. Winterbottom, eds. *Ancient Literary Criticism: The Principal Texts in New Translations*. Oxford: Clarendon, 1972.

Sandnes, Karl Olav. "Imitatio Homeri?: An Appraisal of Dennis R. MacDonald's 'Mimesis Criticism.'" *JBL* 124/4 (2005) 715–32.

Sasson, Jack M. *Ruth: A New Translation with a Philological Commentary and a Formalist-Forklorist Interpretation*. Baltimore: Johns Hopkins University Press, 1979.

Satlow, Michael L. *Jewish Marriage in Antiquity*. Princeton, NJ: Princeton University Press, 2001.

Schaberg, Jane. *The Illegitimacy of Jesus: A Feminist Theological Interpretation of the Infancy Narratives*. Sheffield: Sheffield Phoenix, [1987] 2006.

Schellenberg, Ryan S. *Rethinking Paul's Rhetorical Education: Comparative Rhetoric and 2 Corinthians 10–13*. Atlanta: SBL, 2013.

Schlier, Heinrich. "δειγματίζω." In *TDNT*, 2:31–32.

Schmidt, K. L. "κλητὸς." In *TDNT*, 2:32.

Seneca the Elder. *Controversiae*. Translated by M. Winterbottom. LCL. Cambridge, MA: Harvard University Press, 1974.

Seneca, Lucius Annaeus. *Epistles*. Vol. 2. Translated by Richard M. Gummere. LCL. Cambridge, MA: Harvard University Press, [1920] 2014.

Sim, David C. *The Gospel of Matthew and Christian Judaism: The History and Social Setting of the Matthean Community*. Edinburgh: T. & T. Clark, 1998.

Smit, Peter-Ben. "Something about Mary?: Remarks about the Five Women in the Matthean Genealogy." *NTS* 56 (2010) 191–207.

Smith, Dennis E., and Joseph B. Tyson, eds. *Acts and Christian Beginnings: The Acts Seminar Report*. Salem, OR: Polebridge, 2013.

Smith, Morton. "Historical Method in the Study of Religion." *History and Theory* 8/1 (1968) 1–16.

Smyth, Herbert W. *Greek Grammar*. Revised by Gordon M. Messing. Cambridge, MA: Harvard University Press, [1920] 1984.

Soards, Marion. L. *The Speeches in Acts: Their Content, Context, and Concerns*. Louisville: Westminister John Knox, 1994.

Stauffer, Ethelbert. *Jesus and His Story*. Translated by Richard and Clara Winston. New York: Knopf, 1960.

Strecker, Georg. "The Pseudo-Clementines: Introduction." In *New Testament Apocrypha*, edited by Edgar Hennecke and Wilhelm Schneemelcher, translated by R. Wilson, 2:483–93. Louisville: Westminister John Knox, 2003.

Strecker, Georg, and Johannes Irmscher, trans. *Kerygmata Petrou*. In *New Testament Apocrypha*, edited by Wilhelm Schneemelcher, English translation edited by R. McL. Wilson, 2:531–41. Louisville: John Knox, 2003.

Suetonius. *Lives of Illustrious Men.* Translated by J. C. Rolfe. 2 vols. LCL. Harvard University Press, 1914.

Sumney, Jerry L. "Paul and Christ-Believing Jews Whom He Opposes." In *Jewish Christianity Reconsidered*, edited by Matt Jackson-McCabe, 57–80. Philadelphia: Fortress, 2007.

Swete, Henry Barclay. *Commentary on Mark.* Grand Rapids: Kregel, [1905] 1977.

Tanach: The Torah/Prophets/Writings: The Twenty-Four Books of the Bible, Newly Translated and Annotated. Edited by Rabbi Nosson Scherman. Brooklyn, NY: Mesorah, [1996] 2009.

Taşlialan, Mehmet. "Excavations at the Church of St. Paul." In *Actes du Ier Congres International sur Antioche de Pisidie*, edited by T. Drew-Bear, M. Taşliahan, and C. Thomas, 9–32. Paris: Université Lumigre, 2002.

Tatum, W. Barnes. "The Historical Quest for the Baby Jesus, Mt. 1–2." *Forum* (new series) 2 (1999) 7–23.

Taussig, Hal E. "Jerusalem as Occasion for Conversation: The Intersection of Acts 15 and Galatians 2." *Forum* (new series) 4 (2001) 89–104.

Tertullian. *Against Marcion.* Translated by Peter Holmes. In *ANF*, vol. 3. Peabody, MA: Hendrickson, 1995.

Thomas, Rosalind. "Genealogy." In *OCD*, 629.

Trebilco, Paul R. *Jewish Communities in Asia Minor.* Cambridge: Cambridge University Press, 1991.

———. "The Jews in Asia Minor, 66–235 C.E." In *The Cambridge History of Judaism*, edited by Steven T. Katz, 4:75–82. Cambridge: Cambridge University Press, 2006.

Trobisch, David. "The Council of Jerusalem in Acts 15 and Paul's Letter to the Galatians." In *Theological Exegesis: Essays in Honor of Brevard S. Childs*, edited by Christopher Seitz and Kathryn Greene-McCreight, 331–38. Grand Rapids: Eerdmans, 1999.

———. *The First Edition of the New Testament.* New York: Oxford University Press, 2000.

———. *Paul's Letter Collection: Tracing the Origins.* Minneapolis: Fortress, 1994.

———. "Who Published the New Testament?" *Free Inquiry* 28/1 (2008) 30–33.

Tyson, Joseph. *Marcion and Luke-Acts: A Defining Struggle.* Columbia: University of South Carolina Press, 2006.

Vegge, Tor. "The Literacy of Jesus the Carpenter's Son." *Studia Theologica* 59 (2005) 19–37.

Vermes, Geza. *Jesus the Jew: A Historians Reading of the Gospels.* Philadelphia: Fortress, 1973.

Virgil. *Eclogues, Georgics, Aeneid 1–6.* Translated by H. R. Fairclough and G. P. Gould. LCL. Cambridge, MA: Harvard University Press, 1999.

Walker, Jeffrey. *The Genuine Teachers of This Art: Rhetorical Education in Antiquity.* Columbia: University of South Carolina Press, 2011.

Walker, William O., Jr. "Acts and the Pauline Corpus Reconsidered." *JSNT* 24 (1985) 3–23.

———. "Galatians 2:7b-8 as a Non-Pauline Interpolation." *CBQ* 65/4 (2003) 568–87.

———. *Interpolations in the Pauline Letters.* JSNT Supplement Series 213. Sheffield: Sheffield Academic, 2002.

———. "The Timothy-Titus Problem Reconsidered." *ExpTim* 92 (1980–81) 231–35.

Wall, Robert W. "Acts of the Apostles." In *The New Interpreter's Bible*, 10:173–83. Nashville: Abingdon, 2002.

———. "Successors to 'the Twelve' According to Acts 12:1–17." *CBQ* 53 (1991) 628–43.
Warner, David. "Galatians 2:3–8 as an Interpolation." *ExpTim* 62/12 (1950–51) 628–43.
Watson, Duane Frederick. *The Rhetoric of the New Testament: A Bibliographic Survey*. Blandford Forum, UK: Deo, 2006.
Wellborn, L. L. "The Runaway Paul." *HTR* 92/2 (1999) 115–63.
Weren, W. J. C. "The Five Women in Matthew's Genealogy." *CBQ* 59 (1997) 288–305.
Wildberger, Hans. *Isaiah 1–12: A Commentary*. Translated by Thomas H. Trapp. Continental Commentaires. Minneapolis: Fortress, 1991.
Williams, R. D. "Virgil and the Odyssey." *Phoenix* 17/4 (1963) 266–74.
Wilson, Robert. "Genealogy." In *ABD*, 2:929–32.
———. "The Old Testament Genealogies in Recent Research." *JBL* 94/2 (1975) 166–89.
Wineland, John D. "Derbe." In *ABD*, 2:184–85.
Winn, Adam. *Mark and the Elijah-Elisha Narrative: Considering the Practice of Greco-Roman Imitation in the Search for Markan Source Material*. Eugene, OR: Pickwick, 2010.
Witherington, Ben, III. *New Testament Rhetoric: An Introductory Guide to the Art of Persuasion in and of the New Testament*. Eugene, OR: Cascade, 2009.
Xenephon. *The Memorabilia: Recollections of Socrates*. Translated by H. G. Dakyns. Project Gutenberg, August 24, 2008. http://www.gutenberg.org/files/1177/1177-h/1177-h.htm.
Yarbro-Collins, Adela. *Mark: A Commentary*. Hermeneia. Minneapolis: Fortress, 2007.
Yosef, Uri. "Isaiah 7:14—Part 1: An Accurate Grammatical Analysis." http://thejewishhome.org/counter/Isa714_1.pdf.
Young, George W. Review of *The Past as Legacy: Luke-Acts and Ancient Epic*. *JBL* 121/1 (Spring 2002) 178–81.

Subject Index

Acts 7:58—15:30 as mimetic transformation of Gal 1-2, 184-247
  Paul as persecutor, Acts 7:58—8:3 cf. Gal 1:14, 190-91
  Paul's zealousness, Acts 22:3 cf. Gal 1:14, 190-91
  Paul's "conversion," Acts 9:3-15 cf. Gal 1:15-17, 192-97
  Paul's evangelism in and escape from Damascus, Acts 9:23-29 cf. Gal 1:16-17 (and 2 Cor. 11:32), 197-202
  Paul's first trip to Jerusalem, Acts 9:26-30 cf. Gal 1:18-20, 202-205
  Acts 10:1—11:18 cf. Gal 2:11-14, 208-13
  Acts 11:25—12:24 cf. Gal 2:1-10, 216-240
  Acts 15 cf. Gal 2:11-14, 241-6
alleged multiple attestation, 92-94
annunciation, to Joseph, 104-6
  to Mary, 128-32
anonymous authorship of gospels, 13
atheistic historical method, 13
authorship of the gospels, 14

Benedictus, derived from Septuagint, 135-36
Beelzebul, in Mark, 54-55
  in Matt, 58-59
  in Luke, 59-62
betrothal, in 1st century CE, 92-96

Farrer, Goulder, Goodacre Hypothesis, 12

Galatians 1—2, Luke's mimetic transformation of, 183-247
Galatians 2:7-9, as a later, non-Pauline interpolation, 283-94
Galatians 2:11-14, deleted/recast in Acts 10:1—11:18, 208-13
Greco-Roman writers on mimesis/imitation, 17-25, 255-282

Historical verisimilitude of New Testament texts considered, 252

"James, Kephas, and John," 287-90
"James, Peter, and John" as rhetorical/literary device, 290-3
Jerusalem Council, 241-46
Jesus, as a "carpenter," 66-68
  as "son of Mary," 68-71
  illegitimacy of 68-71 and 76-118, as a "lunatic," 53-4
  language spoken, 54-6
  sermon in Nazareth, 64-71, 75
Jesus's relatives, in Mark, 53-58, in Matt, 58-59, in Luke, 59-64
  as "outsiders," 53-64, especially 56
Jesus's circumcision, derived from Septuagint, 146
Jesus's presentation in the Temple, derived from Septuagint, 146-48
John the Baptist, birth narrative in Luke derived from the Septuagint, 126-28

SUBJECT INDEX

Kerygmata Petrou, 164–65

laying on of hands, Paul's participation in in Acts but not his letters, 195–6, 230
Luke's alleged independence from Matthew, 88–94, 120–21
Luke's birth narrative, as a mimetic response to Matthew's and to Marcion, 154–60
Luke's genealogy, 148–54
  dependent upon Matthew's, 151–54
  Luke's Joseph dependent upon Matthew's, 153–54
  explanation of differences between Matthew's and Luke's birth narratives, 154–60
Luke's knowledge and mimetic use of Paul's letters, arguments against, 181–83
  evidence for, 183–247
Luke's mimetic use of Matthew, 60–64
Luke's mimetic use of the Septuagint, 125–29, 131–37
Luke's structural imitation of Matthew, 129–37, 142–44
Luke's structural imitation of the Septuagint and Matthew, 125–26

Magnificat derived from Septuagint, 131–34
Marcion, as one exigence for Luke's birth narrative, 154–60
Markan "sandwich" (intercalation), 51–52
Matthew 1–2, Luke's mimetic transformation of, 125–54
Matthew's foretelling-of-Jesus's-birth, as fictional and apologetical, 95–118, subjective omniscient narrative, 96–8
  derived from Septuagint, 98–118, *haalma/parthenos*, 108–18
  author of Matthew intentionally altered Isaiah 7:14, 114–18
Matthew's genealogy, rhetorical function of, 76
  artificiality of, 77–78
  Septuagint sources of, 76–94
  problems within, 78–80
  four women within, 80–7, Joseph as apologetic device in, 87–94
  haalma / parthenos, 108–18, debate between Christians and Jews concerning, 114–18
  Matthew's intentional alteration of Isaiah 7:14, 114–18
μίμησις (mimesis, imitation), dearth of in NT studies, 1–3
  defined, 17
  prevalence in Greco-Roman culture, 17–20
  whom to imitate, 20–21
  what to imitate, 21–22
  how to imitate, 22–25
  example of Greco-Roman imitation, 25–34
  contemporary applications and critiques of, 34–46
  adopted criteria, 46–47, 247
  Matthew's mimetic transformation of Mark, 58–59, 64–69, of the Septuagint, 76–119
  Luke's mimetic transformation of Mark and Matthew, 59–64, 69–71, of Matthew and the Septuagint, 125–54, of Galatians, 185–247

Nunc Dimittis, mimetically derived from Septuagint, 147

Paul, in conflict with the Jerusalem leaders, 168–80
  as an illegitimate apostle, 164–80
  and Matthew, 166–68
Paul's sermon in Acts 13, compared to other sermons in Acts, 234–37
  content within absent from his letters, 237–38
Peter, as Kephas, 165–66, 287
  or Paul as 'foundation', 166
Peter's vision, as legitimating Paul's vision in Acts, 209–11

SUBJECT INDEX

Q, a hypothetical source document, 12

Septuagint, as Matthew's source, 74–119
    as Luke's source, 120–61

synagogue, Paul's visits to in Acts but not in his letters, 230–39

synoptic problem, 12

Author Index

Alderink, I. J., 54n10
Allison, Dale, 165n7
Anderson, R. Dean, 166n8
Atkins, J.W.H., 18
Aune, David E., 2, 51n1, 52n2, 221n86

Barnikol, Ernst, 166n7, 287
Barrett, C.K., 182, 182n2
Barton, Stephen, 56n15, 57
Baur, F. C., 165, 209, 209n56
Beattie, D. R. G., 83, 84
BeDuhn, Jason, 156, 165
Bellinzoni, Arthur, 72
Bertram, Georg, 175n38
Best, E., 56
Betz, Hanz Dieter, 174n38, 178, 179, 179n49, 191n21, 289
Black, C. Clifton, 2
Bonner, Stanley, 18, 43, 262
Bonz, Marianne, 4, 6, 40–47
Borg, Marcus and Crossan, John Dominic, 91
Bovon, François, 124, 132n31, 146n51, 152, 153
Brodie, Thomas, 2, 3, 4, 6, 18, 32, 33–40, 47, 145
Brown, Raymond, 68n41, 75, 79, 80n12, 85n31, 88, 91, 96, 99n66, 104, 105n84, 120, 127, 132n31, 138, 139, 140, 146n51, 149n55
Brown, Raymond et al., 57n27
Burridge, Richard, 2–3
Burrows, Eric, 123, 128n27, 146n51, 146n52

Cadbury, Henry, 123
Campbell, Edward, 82, 83
Carlson, Stephen, 12, 137n36
Casey, P. M., 54n12
Catto, Stephen, 231, 233, 234n134
Chartrand-Burke, Tony, 40
Clabeaux, Tony, 156n63, 157
Clark, Donald, L.18
Collins, Raymond, F. 288
Conzelman, Hans, 166, 166n9
Creed, John Martin, 123, 132n31, 132, 133n33, 146n51
Cribiore, Rafaella, 18, 44
Crossan, John Dominic, 53n2

D'Alton, J. F., 18
Daly-Denton, Margaret, 40
Damm, Adam, 3
Davidson, Richard M., 103
Davies, W.D. and Allison, D.C., 77n6, 77n7, 79, 80, 85n31, 87, 97n63, 99n66, 104n82
Derrenbacker, R. A., 3
Detering, Hermann, 285n6
Dewey, Arthur, 56, 169n18
Dodds, E. R., 179n50
Donahue, John R. and Harrington, Daniel J., 68
Doulamis, Konstantin, 18
Downing, F. G., 2, 51n1
Drury, 121, 152
Durousseau, Clifford H., 110

Edwards, James E., 51, 56, 57
Ehrman, Bart D., 165n7, 254n4

AUTHOR INDEX

Elliott, J. K., 166n7
Enslin, Morton S., 182n2, 220n80

Fairclough and Goold, 27n61
Finklestein, Israel and Neil A. Silberman, 81n14
Fiske, George, C., 17
Fitzmyer, Joseph, 88, 88n46, 89, 120, 121, 124, 132, 132n31, 138, 139, 138, 139, 10, 146n51, 146n52, 152, 155
Flusser, David, 66, 68
Forbes, Christopher, 166n8
Franklin, Eric, 122
Freed, Edwin, D., 80n12, 84
Fronda, Michael, P., 17

Gasque, W. Ward, 232
Gazdn, Elaine E. and Diana Ng, 233
Ginzberg, Louis, 84
Goodacre Mark, 122
Goodfriend, Elaine A., 101
Goulder, M.D., 53n2, 56n15, 57, 59n31, 121, 138n40, 152, 155, 165n6, 173, 174n37
Goulder, M. D. and Murray Sanderson, 123
Green, H. B., 121
Gundry, Robert H., 66

Haenechen, Ernst, 193n24, 196n27, 204, 204n40, 208n52, 208n53, 224, 234n134, 236n136, 238, 239
Hall, Robert G., 146n50
Hardie, 44
Harnack, Alfred, 123, 132n31, 132n32
Harrill, J.A., 223
Heath, Malcolm, 278n89
Heinze, Richard, 25 n57
Hohlfelder, Robert, 207n48
Holmes, 289n15
Hoppe, Leslie I., 230
Hubbard, Robert L., 83, 83n20
Hunter, Richard, 18n3

Ilan, Tal, 68n43
Ingram, Helen, 89n52

Jackson-McCabe, Matt 165n6
Jobes Karen H. and Moises Silva, 115n100, 116
Johnson, Luke Timothy, 182n2
Johnson, Marshal D., 76, 85n31, 86n35, 86n39
Just, Felix, 252n3

Kennedy, George, 2, 29n.38, 186n16, 278, 278n89
Knauer, G. N., 25, 26, 32, 33, 37
Knox, John, 165, 182n2, 183, 230
Korpel, Marjo, 83

Lachs, Samuel Tobia, 68n42
Lake, Kirsopp, 166n7, 231n120
Lambrecht, J., 56
Lampe, Peter, 171, 172
Landry, David, 122
LaPiana, G., 166n7
Law, Timothy Michael, 115n100
Leppä, Heikki, 10, 182n2, 163-80
Levin, Lee, 193n24
Lewis, Theodore, 54n10
Lincoln, Andrew, 13, 80n12, 122
Longnecker, Bruce W., 222-26
Loubser, J. A., 80n12
Lüdemann, Gerd, 53n2, 56, 58n30, 68n41, 68n42, 88, 165n6, 166n9, 169, 174n37, 182n2, 193n24, 214, 221n84, 231n120, 234n134
Luz, Ulrich, 76n5, 85, 85n31, 86, 89, 90

MacDonald, Dennis, R., 2, 3, 4, 6, 18, 35-40, 43, 46
Malherbe, Abraham, 169n18
McArthur, Harvey K., 68n43
Meier, John P., 68n41, 68n43, 88n43, 89
Metzger, Bruce, 53n3, 55n14, 67n38, 236n139, 237
Mitchell, Margaret M., 39-40
Mitchell, Stephen, 232, 233
Mitchell, Steven and Mark Waelkens, 231
Moore, Clifford H., 43
Morgan, Teresa, 18, 22
Moyise, Steve, 13 n17
Murphy, James, 273n64

Nefford, Clayton N., 288
Nichols, James H., 179n50

Oepke, Albrecht, 53n6

Pagels, Elaine, 104n81
Painter, John, 222
Palmer, Darrel W., 45
Parsons, P.J., 19 n10
Pervo, Richard, 11, 19, 72, 124, 146n52, 152, 163–80
Porter, Stanley, 2, 54n12, 90–91
Potter, D. S., 232
Price, Robert M., 177n44, 179n53, 287n10

Rhalfs, Alfred, 115n100, 116n104
Robertson, A.T., 285
Rochette, Bruno, 44
Runnesson, Anders, et al. 231, 238
Russell, Donald A., 18, 257n4
Russell, Donald A. and M. Winterbottom, 18
Ruthven, K.K., 18

Sandnes, Karl Olav, 40 n82
Sasson, Jack M., 82, 83
Satlow, Michael, 95, 95n60, 96
Schaberg, Jane, 68n41, 68n42, 80n12, 85, 85n31, 99n66, 101, 102
Schellenberg, Ryan, 166n8
Schiler, Heinrich, 99–100
Schmidt, K. L., 168
Sim, David C., 168
Smit, Peter-Ben, 80n12
Smith, Morton, 13
Smith, Dennis E. and Joseph B., Tyson, 181n1, 207n48
Smyth, Herbert W., 54n11, 64n34, 166, 169, 169n16, 171, 175n42, 238n138, 284

Soards, Marion, 234n134
Stauffer, Ethelbert, 68n42
Strecker, Georg, 164, 165
Sumney, Jerry L., 164n1
Swete, Henry Barclay, 67

Taşlialan, Mehmet, 233
Tatum, W. Barnes, 88n45
Taussig, Hal E., 242n151
Thomas, Rosalind, 76n3
Trebelico, Paul, R., 231
Trobisch, David, 182n2, 252n4
Tyson, Joseph B., 9, 156n63, 156, 157, 158, 159, 182n2, 290–294

Vegge, Tor, 54n12
Vermes, Geza, 66n36, 68

Walker, Jeffrey, 18 n.6, 253
Walker, William O., 166n7, 182n2, 228n110, 283, 287n12
Wall, Robert W., 222, 224
Warner, David, 179
Watson Duane, 1
Watson, Francis, 122
Wellborn, L. L., 173n36
Weren, W. J. C., 80n12, 85n31, 86n36
Wildberger, Hans, 106
Williams, R.D., 25, 33
Wilson, Robert, 76
Wineland, John D., 232
Winn, Adam, 38–39
Witherington, Ben, 1, 2

Yarbro-Collins, Adela, 53n2, 53n5, 54n11, 56, 57n25, 66, 68, 68n41
Yosef, Uri 109, 110, 111
Young, George, W., 45

Ancient Document Index

Old Testament (Septuagint; if Hebrew Bible, HB)

Genesis

11:30	127
15:1	104
15:8	128
16:11	105
17	125
17:9–11	159
17:12	135, 135n35, 146
17:19	105
18:11	127
18:14	131
21:17–18	104
24:43	109, 113, 116 HB
25:21	127n22
25:22	131
25:24	134, 141
26:24	104
28:13	105n83
29:31	127
29:32	133
30:13	133
30:23	128
34:2–3	113 HB
Ch. 38	80
46:3	105n83
46.12	79

Exodus

2:8	109–10 HB
9:3	135
11:6	131n29
12:6	128n25
12:30	131n29
16:10	141
40:34–35	131

Leviticus

4:7	128
12	125
12:3	135

Numbers

1:11	127
1.7	79
10:4	127n22
14:1	141
21:34	105

Deuteronomy

3:2	105n83
10:1	133
17:2–7	98
22–24	130
22:20	98
22:22	98
22:13–21	100
22:22	100
22:23–24	100
22:28–29	100
24:1–4	102
28:4	132

Joshua

Ch. 2	79, 81–82
Ch. 6	79
10:8	105
24:1	127n23

Judges

5:24	132
6:23	105n83
13:3	127n22
13:5B	105, 130
13:24	136

Ruth

1:1	79
1:8	79
3:2–9	82–84
4:18–22	76

1 Kings (1 Samuel)

1:1	126–27
1:1–2	125
1:1–20	126
1:2–11	125
1:3–8	125
1:11	133
1:19	125, 127
1:20	125
1:22–24	147
2:1	133
2:7–8	134
2:20	148
2:26	125, 148
4:19	110 HB
12:15	135

2 Kings (2 Samuel)

2:23	170n21
6:10, 12, 16	141n47
7:13	128n25
11:1—12:19	84–85
15:30	107
16:9	107
22:3	135

3 Kingdoms (1 Kings)

2:35; 5:16; 12:24	141n47

3 Kingdoms (4 Kings)

15:30; 16:19	107

1 Chronicles

1:27—2:15	76
Chpts. 2–3	80
2:9	79
3:11–20	79
11:7; 13:6; 13:13	141n47
24:1	127n23
29:16	128n25

2 Chronicles

31:18	128n25

Ezra

3:23; 29:11	128n25

Micah

5:1	139
7:20	134, 136

Habakkuk

3:13	133

Job

12:19	134

Psalms

7:17	110 HB

17:3	135	7:14	107–111 HB
30:7	133	9:2	136
34:9	133	23:4	112 HB
41:14	135	37:22	112 HB
71:18	135, 136	39:2	141
88:10	134	40:3	136
90:4	131n28	40:5	147
97:3	134	47:1	112 HB
102:17	133	52:9	147
104:8	136	53:7–8	192
105:10	135, 136	58:8	136
105:48	135, 136	66:13	147
106:9	134		
110:9	133, 135		
117:15	134		

Jeremiah

3:25	127n23

117:26	170
139:7	131n28

Daniel

Proverbs

10:12	105
10:13, 21; 12:1	158n71

30:19	108 HB

Song

Jonah

1:3	108 HB
6:8	108 HB

1:10	141
4:1	141

Isaiah

Malachi

7:13–16	107 HB
7:14	106, 130, 139–40

3:1	136

Apocrypha

Tobit

1 Maccabees

3:16	128n26

1:33; 7:32	141n47
6:58	289n17
9:63	128n25
10:8	141
11:50, 62, 66	289n17
13:45, 50	289n17

Sirach

10:14	134

Susanna

28, 41, 42, 44	101n72

2 Maccabees

4:35	289n17
11:26, 30	289n17
12:11, 12	289n17
14:19	289n17

3 Maccabees

	128n25

1 Esdras

9:6, 10, 28, 41, 47	128n25

Pseudepigrapha

1 Enoch 9:1, 40		158n71

Life of Adam and Eve

277, 260	170

New Testament

Matthew

1–2	74–119
1:1	120
1:1–16	77–87, 149–54
1:16	120
1:16–17	76–94
1:18–25	125, 129–30
1:18—2:23	88
1:20–21	120
1:18—2:12	142–44
1:18	120
1:21	106
2:1–12	126, 137–38
2:1	120
2:6	139–40
3:13	288
4:1–11	97
5:17–19	167
9:3	97
9:18–26	58
10:1–4	58
11:25	58
12:15	58n29
12:22–32	55n14, 58, 59, 60
13:1–23	58
13:53–58	65–67
13:55	92
14:9	97
14:30	97
16:17–18	166
17:1–13	288
21:9	170n21
21:18	97
21:45–46	97
26:1–16	58n28
26:20–35	58n28
26:36–46	97, 288
26:57–75	58n28

Mark

1:19	288
3:20–35	51–64
5:21	288
6:1–6	64–71
6:3	92–93
9:2–13	288
11:9	170n22
14:1–11	58n28
14:17–31	58n28
14:32–42	288
14:53–72	58n28

Luke

1–2	120–160
1:5–25	125
1:5—2:52	158
1:5	120
1:8–35	127–28
1:13–15	127

1:26–38	125, 128	**John**	
1:26—2:20	142–44		
1:27	34, 35, 120	1:45	92
1:23–30	120	6:42	92
1:31	120, 158	12:13	170n22
1:32	120		
1:34	120	**Acts**	
1:35	120		
1:39–45	158	1:1—7:57	186
1:41, 44	158	1:18	293
1:39–55	128	1:19	293
1:57–79	128	1:21–22	185
1:68–79	135–6	2:41	185
1:29–80	125	3:1–11	293
2:1–20	125, 137–38	4:5–22	293
2:4–7	120	4:32	186
2:4	120	4:36–37	186
2:5	120	6:1	186, 204
2:11	120	6:6	196
2:12, 16	158	7:38	183, 186
2:22–40	146–47	7:52	189
2:27	93n58	7:53	183
2:27, 40	158	7:58—8:3	187, 188
2:22—2:39	147–48	7:58—15:30	174, 163–80, 186, 187
2:32, 38	159	8:1—15:2	183
2:33	93n58	8:3	192
2:5–39	88	8:4–40	187, 191–92, 240
2:39	120	8:14–25	293
2:41–50	91	8:41	288
2:43	93n58, 158	9:1	194
2:48	93n58	9:1–19a	192
2:51	120	9:3	194
2:52	158–59	9:4–5	187
3:23–37	149–54	9:3–4	193
3:23–24	157	9:3–19	186, 191
4:16–22	65–67	9:4	188
4:22	92	9:4–5	189
5:1–11	288	9:10	196
6:45	170n22	9:15	194, 195
8:19–21	62–64	9:15–21	182
8:27	199	9:17	196
8:49–56	288	9:19	200
9:28–36	288	9:19–20	197
11:14–23	55n14, 60–62	9:19b–20	197–98
13:35	170n22	9:19b–28	202–3
19:38	170n22	9:19, 22, 27	193
22:39–46	288		

Acts (continued)

9:20	195
9:20–25	187
9:21	183, 188
9:23	199
9:23–25	200
9:26–30	182, 187, 202
9:31—11:25	187, 205–15, 240
9:32–35	240
9:43	199
10–11	240
10:15	240
10:31	128
10:48	196
11:2, 3	183
11:25—12:24a	188, 216–20
11:29–30	182, 219–20
11:30	183
11:30–12:25	182, 221–29
12:2	288
12:24b—14:23	188, 230–39
12:25	176n45, 183, 220–21, 288
13:1—14:23	196, 240
13:2	183
13:5	195, 288
13:13	288
13:14–43	195
14:1	195
14:27–15:3	188
15:1–30	182, 183, 241–44
15:1–35 compared to Galatians 2	242–44
15:2	128n25
15:3	141
15:4–35	188
15:10	183
15:23	183
15:24–49	182
15:41	183
15:37	176n45
15:38	177n45
16:12	196
17:1	195
17:10	195
17:17	195
18:4–17	195
18:9–26	195
18:18	199
20:9	199
21:17–40	182
21:20	183
21:37	204
22:3	183, 187, 191
22:4	188, 189–90
22:7–8	186, 189
25:24	128n25
26:1, 14, 15	186, 189–90
28:8	196

Romans

1:1	168
5:3–32	290
16:17	290

1 Corinthians

1–4	165
1:1	168
1:10–13	165
1:12	165n7, 287
3:22	165n7, 287
9:1–6	168
9:5	165n7, 287
9:6	204
15:5	165n7, 287

2 Corinthians

1:1	168
10–13	169–74
11:2–5	169
11:7–9	174
11:10	176n43
11:13—15	171
11:22—12:1a	172
11:16—12:10	201
11:31	176n43
11:32	197, 200
11:32–33	193, 201
11:33	187
12:6	176n43
12:12–13	174

13:8	176n43	3:19	183
15:9	189	3:28–29	167
		4:10–11	167, 174
		4:16–17	174

Galatians

		5:1	183
		5:2–4	167, 174
1–2	240	5:4–12	174
1:1—2:14	174–80		
1:6–9	175–76		
1:1	168		

Philippians

3:6	189

1:11–13a	196
1:13	183, 194
1:13b	187, 188
1:13–23	176–77

Philemon

24	288

1:13—2:14	183
1:14	183, 190, 191
1:15	183, 194
1:15–16	187

Colossians

2:15	100
4:10	288

1:15–17	192–93
1:16	182
1:16–17	197–198
1:17	194
1:18	198

1 Timothy

3:15	288

1:18–20	182, 186, 202–3
1:22–23	188
1:21	183

2 Timothy

4:11	288

2 compared to Acts 15	242–44
2:1	182–83, 220–21
2:1–2	176–77

Titus

1:5	239

2:1–10	186, 216–20
2:1–14	182
2:2	182
2:3	178
2:6–10	179, 219–20, 283–94

1 Peter

5:3	288

2:7	183
2:7–9	166n7, 174, 283–94

2 Peter

3:15–16	292

2:10	183, 240–41
2:11	230
2:11–12	176
2:11–14	186, 240
2:12	183
2:14	180
2:15–16	167
3:1	174
3:10–11	167

Greco-Roman Writings

Ad Herennium 5

4.1.1	258n6
4.1.2	258n7
4.2.3	258
4.3.5	20–21, 258
4.4.1	258n6
4.4.7	259
4.5.7	259

Celsus 68–69

Cicero 5, 258n7

Brut.
§6	25
§76	260

De Fin. 1.3   260–61

De Inv.
2.1.4	20n13, 259

De or.
1.151–55	23, 261
2.89–90	21–22, 261
3.125	260

'Demetrius' 5

Eloc. §112–113   21, 24, 25, 257–58

Demosthenes

In Tim. 128.2   93n57

Dionysius of Halicarnassus 5, 21

Comp.
§1	262

Dem. 345   286

Din.
§5	266
§6–7	22–23, 266, 267n46

Isoc.
§4	20n15, 263

Lys.
§1	262
§9–10	20n15, 263

Pomp.
§3	20n15, 264
§4–6	266

Thucyd.
§8–35	20n15
§1	263
§8–55	263–64

Homer 5

Table comparing *Aeneid* to *Iliad* and *Odyssey*   27–28

Odyssey
5.293–99	29–30
9.96–10	31
9.136–41	31
10.158–203	31
11.206–7	28
12.208–12	31
12.309–10	31–32
13.96–110	31

Herodotus 265

"Longinus" on,   269

Hippocrates (corpus)

De articulis 14.91   199

Horace 5, 19

Ars.
§128–135	24, 268
§268–269	20; 267

Ep 1.3. §14–20	25, 268	*Hypoth* 7.1	102

Isocrates 5, 19

Soph.
1.17–18 19–20, 255–56

Paneg.
§16 21, 256

Panath.
§16 256–57

Josephus

Antiq. 10.7.114 54
Ag. Ap. 1.83 286

'Longinus' 5

on Plato 269

Subl.
§13 19–23, 269–70

Lucian 5, 19

Rhet praec.
§1–14 20n18, 280–81

How to Write History
§7–15, 31 20n18, 22, 25, 281–82
§39, 42, 43 281n102

Lysias

85.195.10 (frag) 93n57

Martial

Epigrams 1.52–53 25, 277

Philo

*De Spec.*1.31.2 93n57

Plato

"Longinus" on 269
Phaedo 66a7 93n57
Apology 145 179

Pliny the Younger

Ep. 9 "To Fuscus" 24, 276–77

Quintilian 5, 19

Inst.
1.1.5 272
2.4.12 272

Sections from Book 10 20, 23, 24, 32, 272–76

Seneca the Elder 5

Cont.
1.6 20, 268

Suas.
3.7 22, 268

Seneca the Younger 5

Ep. 79 21, 271
Ep. 84 22, 24, 25, 32, 270–71

Theon 5, 19

(From) *Progymnasmata*
5—7 23–24, 279
13 279
68 279
70 279–80

Thucydides 265

Vergil

Aeneid 4, 72
as imitation of Homer 26–32
1.60–310 29–32
1.180–90 31
1.215–22 31
6.700–3 28

Xenophon

Mem. 54

Early Christian Writings

1 Clement
4:24 239
5:2 289

Irenaeus

Ag. Her.
3:3 292
3.21 115, 117
90 164

Justin Martyr

Dial. 43, 71 115, 117

Kerygmata Petrou

"Homily 17" 164–65

www.ingramcontent.com/pod-product-compliance
Lightning Source LLC
Chambersburg PA
CBHW052146300426
44115CB00011B/1540